HINDI

Rupert Snell
Simon Weightman

TEACH YOURSELF BOOKS
Hodder and Stoughton

First published 1989

British Library Cataloguing in Publication Data

Snell, Rupert
Hindi.—(Teach Yourself books)
1. Hindi language
I. Title II. Weightman, Simon
491'. 4383421

ISBN 0 340 42464 8

*Printed in Great Britain for
Hodder and Stoughton Educational,
a division of Hodder and Stoughton Ltd,
Mill Road, Dunton Green, Sevenoaks, Kent,
by Richard Clay Ltd, Bungay, Suffolk
Typeset by Thomson Press (India) Ltd*

Contents

Introduction 1

The Hindi Script and Sound System 5

1 Dialogue 1A *I am Ram* 20
1 Personal pronouns and 'am', 'is', 'are' 2 Questions and answers
Dialogue 1B *Is this house large?*
3 Nouns 4 Adjectives 5 The simple sentence

2 Dialogue 2A *Who is that man?* 29
6 Interrogative words 7 Agreement of adjectives with two nouns or pronouns
Dialogue 2B *Hello, how are you?*
8 Some conversational features 9 The agreement of adjectives

3 Dialogue 3A *What is the new house like?* 38
10 Simple postpositions 11 Nouns with postpositions
Dialogue 3B *Are there any large rooms in this hotel?*
12 Adjectives in the oblique case

4 Dialogue 4A *Is the new house better than the old one?* 47
13 'Was' and 'were' 14 Comparison of adjectives
Dialogue 4B *Do you know where Ramdas is?*
15 Pronouns with simple postpositions 16 Some constructions with को **ko**

5 Dialogue 5A *Mr Varma comes to tea* 56
17 The simple verb 18 The imperatives 19 को **ko** as postposition of the indirect and direct object 20 The vocative case
Dialogue 5B *At the cloth-merchant's shop*
21 The possessive particle का **kā** 22 Alternative forms of the oblique pronouns with को **ko**

6 Dialogue 6A *Where does Sunil's elder brother live?* 66
23 The imperfective present 24 Agreement between the verb and its subject
Dialogue 6B *Hotels in the hill station*
25 The possessive pronouns 26 The possessive adjective अपना *one's own* 27 Compound postpositions

7 Dialogue 7A *Hari's grandparents* 76
28 The past imperfective 29 कुछ and कोई 30 Further uses of को
Dialogue 7B *The days of the week and the months of the year*
31 The ordinal numbers 32 Conjunct verbs

8 Dialogue 8A *An unexpected meeting* 86
33 The continuous tenses 34 Expressions for 'to have'
Dialogue 8B *How do you go to work?*
35 Some adverbial usages 36 Dates 37 Word order

9 Dialogue 9A *Holiday plans* 97
38 The future tense 39 The emphatic particle ही 40 Some expressions of quantity
Dialogue 9B *Come to the cinema*
41 The infinitive as a verbal noun

10 Dialogue 10A *I must speak to Dharmendra!* 109
42 The subjunctive 43 The verb चाहना
Dialogue 10B *Dharmendra returns the phone call*
44 Introduction to conditional sentences 45 The particle तो 46 The suffix -वाला

11 Dialogue 11A *Sushila arrives in Delhi* 121
47 Past perfective tenses
Dialogue 11B *Ravi has been shopping*
48 The conjunctive particle -कर, -के 49 Times of day 50 The vocabulary of Hindi

12 Dialogue 12A *Talking about homework* 137
51 सकना and चुकना 52 Compound verbs 53 Verbs in combination

Dialogue 12B *Missing luggage on a train journey*
54 The relative pronoun and adjective जो
13 Dialogue 13A *Plans for the day* 151
55 'Should' and 'ought' 56 'Must' and 'have to'
57 The verb मिलना
Dialogue 13B *Maya's new home, and her husband's job*
58 The verb लगना 59 Relative-correlative constructions for time 60 Indirect speech
14 Dialogue 14A *Learning languages* 166
61 The passive 62 The oblique infinitive with लगना *to begin to* 63 The oblique infinitive with देना *to allow to*
Dialogue 14B *Hindi as the national language*
64 Relative-correlative constructions of quantity
65 Purpose clauses 66 Aggregatives
15 Dialogue 15A *A proposed trip to India* 178
67 The imperfective participle with रहना and जाना
68 The invariable masculine singular perfective with करना 69 Relative-correlatives of kind and manner
Dialogue 15B *Setting up business in England*
70 जैसा as postposition and adverb 71 The postposition से 72 Inverted postpositions 73 Reflexive pronouns
16 Dialogue 16A *Problems with the car* 190
74 Conjunct verbs 75 Conjunct verbs with याद
Dialogue 16B *Looking for a job*
76 Relative-correlative adverbs of place 77 Other adverbs of place 78 कहीं 79 Repetition of words
80 या तो...या न...न चाहे...चाहे/या 81 'Echo-words' and word pairings
17 Dialogue 17A *Talking about Holi* 201
82 Conditional sentences
Dialogue 17B *Why Arun is late*
83 Concessive sentences 84 Further compound verbs
18 Dialogue 18A *Some family photographs, and an invitation* 210

85 Participial constructions
Dialogue 18B *An introduction*
Dialogue 18C *Waiting to see the minister*
86 The particle -सा 87 Conversational etiquette

Appendix A	Numbers, money and the calendar	222
Appendix B	Terms of relationship	225
Appendix C	Parts of the body, and health	227
Appendix D	Letter-writing	229
Appendix E	Intransitive, transitive and causative verbs	231
Appendix F	The Hindi verb: summary of tenses and constructions	233
Key to Exercises		235
Hindi-English Vocabulary		251
Index		303

Acknowledgements

The authors wish to thank Dr A.S. Kalsi, Mr M. D. Mundhra and Dr R. D. Gupta for their invaluable comments and suggestions on the Hindi text.

Introduction

This course is designed to enable those with no previous knowledge of Hindi to reach the point where they can communicate effectively in Hindi and can read, write and converse on a range of topics. It is also intended for speakers of other Indian languages who may or may not know some Hindi already, but who wish to be able to speak and write India's national language accurately and with increasing fluency. The course has also proved effective as teaching material for both class and individual tuition.

The Hindi presented in this course is primarily colloquial and practical, and here some explanation of the position of Hindi may be helpful. Hindi is the national language of India; but, as the language map (Fig. 1) shows, it is one of several languages used in different parts of the sub-continent. 'National', then, has to be understood as meaning the 'official' or 'link' language. Although the map shows the homeland of Hindi to be in the North, it is studied, taught, spoken and understood widely throughout the sub-continent, whether as mother tongue or as a second or a third language.

Hindi has a special relationship with Urdu: their grammar is virtually identical, and they have a substantial vocabulary in common. The two languages, however, quickly part company, because Urdu is written from right to left in a modified form of the Arabic script and has drawn the bulk of its vocabulary from Persian and Arabic, while Hindi is written in the Devanagari script and, in common with other Indian languages, has drawn much of its vocabulary from Sanskrit. Like all languages, Hindi has many different styles and speech registers, appropriate in different contexts. At the most colloquial level it reflects more the common ground with Urdu, while in formal and official contexts a more Sanskritized style is found. The language of this course is that which is used unselfconsciously by Hindi speakers and writers in the various, mainly informal, situations which are introduced. The more formal Sanskritized Hindi is best learnt *after* acquiring the basic communicative competence which is the primary aim of this course. We have chosen not to include here many of the English

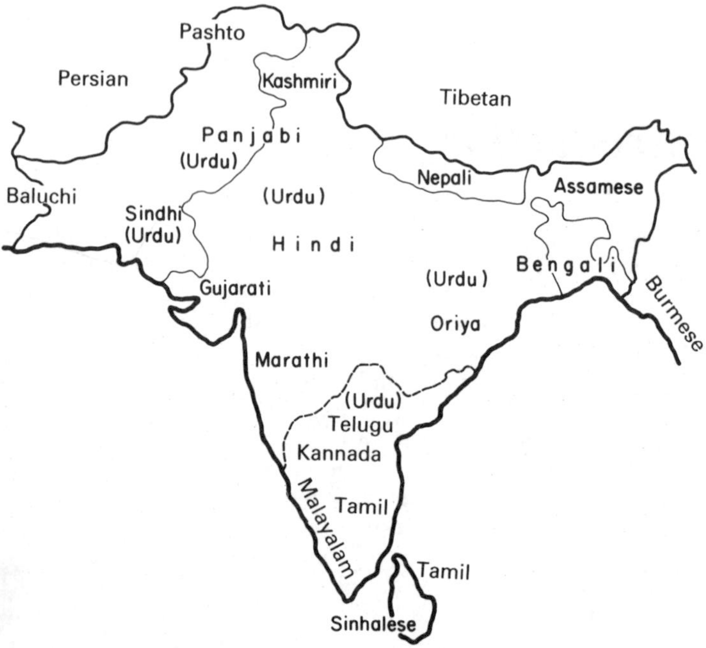

Fig. 1: The principal languages of South Asia

words which some Hindi speakers use freely in their conversations.

Hindi is a most enjoyable language, and is not difficult to learn. By the time you finish this course, you should be able to handle a wide range of the topics and subjects that occur in everyday situations. A good command of Hindi is an entry into a fascinating and richly diversified culture, and well worth the effort needed to acquire it.

How to use the course

The course is divided into 18 units. Each unit contains two Hindi dialogues with deliberately close and literal English translations, two sections of grammatical explanation with examples, exercises on the new material introduced by the unit (usually including a reading passage), and in Units 1–15, a vocabulary of new words. There are also six Appendices, containing material for reference.

There is a key to all the exercises, and a complete end vocabulary of all the words in the course.

You should begin by working carefully through the section on pronunciation and learning the characters of the Devanagari script. Roman transliteration is given for all the Devanagari text up to Unit 5, by which time you should have mastered the script completely; as a guide to pronunciation we have also included Roman transliteration throughout the end vocabulary. (Transliteration has been dropped from the exercises after Unit 3.) Although the book can be used entirely on its own, we do urge you if possible to use the cassette and/or to enlist the help of a native speaker when working on the pronunciation, since the sound system of Hindi is different from that of European languages and it is important to develop accurate pronunciation at the initial stage. We have tried to describe the sounds as clearly as possible, but you should be aware that this can only be an approximate guide.

There are two ways in which you can approach each unit. Either you can learn the dialogue and its meaning (ideally by hearing and repeating it) and then work through the grammar section to understand exactly how it comes to mean what it does; or you can work through the grammar section first and then turn back to the dialogue. It is very important not to move on before you have done two things: mastered the dialogue, and fully digested all the grammar section and its examples. New words are introduced in the dialogues, in the examples to the grammar sections, and in the reading passages. Not all the points given in the grammar sections are illustrated in the dialogues, so you must learn both thoroughly. When you have completed the two dialogues and the grammar sections of a unit, then work on the exercises, checking with the key at the back. Finally, use the vocabulary given in the unit to test yourself on all the words in that unit. We strongly recommend that as you progress, you continually revise the previous units also.

In our grammatical explanations we have aimed to be as clear and untechnical as possible, so the lack of a linguistic background need not be a cause for concern. Although we do not claim to have covered every conceivable feature of Hindi, in practice you have very nearly the complete grammatical structure of the language. The vocabulary has had to be limited to about 2000 words, and we are very conscious of the many commonly used words and expressions for which space could not be found; your vocabulary will, however, increase quickly as you converse and read more. It is a good idea to learn as much as possible by heart, especially the dialogues. What is needed in learning to speak a language is not a towering intellect, but the powers of mimicry and memory. If you apply yourself to this course as we suggest, we are sure that you will go a long way towards an initial mastery of one of the world's most widely-spoken languages.

The Hindi Script and Sound System

Hindi is written in the Devanagari or 'Nagari' script, which is both elegant and easy to learn. The script is phonetic, so that Hindi, unlike English, is pronounced as it is written (with a few exceptions, noted below): it is therefore possible to learn the characters of the script and the sounds of the language at the same time. In Figure 2, the consonants are set out in a table based on the place and manner of their articulation in the mouth, in accordance with the traditional Indian classification; the vowels are set out in a row at the bottom of the table. Each Devanagari character is followed by its Roman transliteration. The transliteration shows each consonant to end in 'a': this is because, in the absence of any other vowel sign, the Devanagari consonant is followed by an inherent 'a' sound (pronounced like the 'a' in '**ma**jority'), *unless* it occurs at the end of the word, when it is not pronounced, or is otherwise silenced. Thus each Devanagari character represents a syllable, and the totality is strictly speaking a 'syllabary' rather than an 'alphabet'. Note that Devanagari has no capital letters.

The syllabary in Figure 2 gives an overall view of the Hindi sound system. Before taking each character and sound individually, there are two features that require special attention, being important contrasts in Hindi which do not occur in English. The first is the contrast between aspirated and non-aspirated consonants, and the second is that between dental and retroflex consonants.

Aspirated consonants are those produced with an audible expulsion of breath, non-aspirated consonants are those produced with minimal breath. Hindi for example distinguishes unaspirated **ka** and **ta** from aspirated **kha** and **tha**.

The English 'k' and 't' sounds are usually half-aspirated, and in words like 'kill' and 'ten' they are quite close to the Hindi aspirates (although Hindi would require a more audible expulsion of breath than is normally given to the English sounds). It is the *non*-aspirated consonants which cause the greatest difficulty to the English speaker. To hear the full differentiation between non-aspirated and aspirated sounds, try saying the words 'kill' and 'ten' while holding the breath, and then saying them again as the breath is suddenly released. The aspiration and the plosion of the **kha** sound occur as a single operation, and the same is true for the **tha**; the fact that the second letter of the transliteration of the Devanagari aspirates is ‘h’ indicates solely that there is a simultaneous release of breath over the sound as it is produced, *not* that there are two separate sounds.

The second contrast is between dental and retroflex consonants: the syllabary shows, for example, that Hindi differentiates dental **ta** and **da** from retroflex **ṭa** and **ḍa**. In dental consonants the tongue touches the upper front teeth, whereas with the retroflex consonants the tip of the tongue is curled upwards against the palate, and when the tongue is released from this position it gives the Indian retroflex sound. The English ‘t’ and ‘d’ are pronounced with the tongue halfway between these two positions, and are equivalent to neither dental *nor* retroflex sounds in Hindi. (To the Indian ear, the English ‘t’ and ‘d’ are considered non-dental, and therefore nearer to the Indian retroflex sounds, so that when English words are used in Hindi the ‘t’ and ‘d’ are written and pronounced as retroflex **ṭa** and **ḍa**.) The nearest approximations in English to these distinctions are the dental-like ‘t’ which is sometimes heard in the pronunciation of the word ‘eighth’, and the retroflex-like ‘t’ in ‘true’, and the dental-like ‘d’ in ‘breadth’ and the retroflex-like ‘d’ in ‘drum’. The learner usually has to work harder to produce the dental consonants than the retroflex ones.

Lined paper is best for practising the Devanagari characters. The horizontal headstroke is written *on* the line, and the character hangs *from* the line. The character should occupy approximately the upper two thirds of the space between the lines. As a general rule, you should start from the left of the character and work towards the right: then put in the downstroke if there is one, and finally complete the character with the headstroke (remembering that the headstroke is broken in some characters). Copy each character carefully, maintaining the overall proportions and not allowing the character to become too long or straggly.

The characters are introduced below in groups, following the classes of the syllabary. A few of the characters have alternative forms, given here in brackets. Use of the cassette, or the assistance of a native speaker, will be very helpful as you set out to master each sound.

Fig. 2: The Hindi Syllabary

Consonants			1 *Velar*	2 *Palatal*	3 *Retroflex*	4 *Dental*	5 *Labial*
Plosives	*Voiceless*	*Unaspirated*	क ka	च ca	ट ṭa	त ta	प pa
		Aspirated	ख kha	छ cha	ठ ṭha	थ tha	फ pha
	Voiced	*Unaspirated*	ग ga	ज ja	ड ḍa	द da	ब ba
		Aspirated	घ gha	झ jha	ढ ḍha	ध dha	भ bha
Nasals			ङ ṅa	ञ ña	ण ṇa	न na	म ma
Fricatives		*Voiceless*	ख़ <u>kh</u>a	श śa	ष ṣa	स sa	फ़ fa
		Voiced	ग़ <u>g</u>a	—	—	ज़ za	—
Flapped and tapped sounds					*Unaspirated* ड़ ṛa *Aspirated* ढ़ ṛha	र ra	
Uvular plosive			क़ qa				
Aspirate, semi-vowels and liquid			ह ha	य ya		ल la	व va

Vowels						
	अ a	आ ā	इ i	ई ī	उ u	ऊ ū
	ऋ ṛ	ए e	ऐ ai	ओ o	औ au	

The Hindi Syllabary

(*Note:* The suffix -कार **-kār** is often added to the Devanagari characters when referring to them by name: e.g. क-कार **ka-kār** *the letter 'ka'*.)

Consonants

The plosives

क	**ka**	The 'k' sound in '**sk**it', but with less release of breath.
ख	**kha**	The aspirate counterpart of the above: as 'k' in '**k**it', but with stronger release of breath.
ग	**ga**	As 'g' in '**g**immick', but with less release of breath.
घ	**gha**	The aspirate counterpart of the above: as 'gh' in 'do**g-h**ouse' spoken quickly.
च	**ca**	Like the 'ch' in '**ch**eese', but with less release of breath and with the tongue against the lower teeth; also close to the 'ty' sound in '**tu**be'.
छ	**cha**	Strongly aspirated form of the 'ch' in '**ch**urch'.
ज	**ja**	Like the 'j' in '**j**eer', but with less release of breath and with the tongue against the lower teeth; also close to the 'dy' sound in '**du**ty'.
झ (भ्क)	**jha**	Strongly aspirated form of the 'j' in '**j**ar'.
ट	**ṭa**	The first of the retroflex sounds already described. Rather like the 't' in '**t**rain', but with the tongue further back, and with less release of breath.
ठ	**ṭha**	Strongly aspirated form of the above.
ड	**ḍa**	Rather like the retroflex 'd' sound in 'drum', but with the tongue further back, and with less release of breath.
ढ	**ḍha**	Strongly aspirated form of the above.
त	**ta**	The first of the dental sounds already discussed. Produced with the relaxed tip of the tongue against the back of the upper front teeth, and with minimal release of breath.
थ	**tha**	Strongly aspirated form of the above.
द	**da**	The dental 'd' sound in 'brea**d**th', with less release of breath.

ध **dha** Strongly aspirated form of the above.

प **pa** As 'p' in 's**p**in', but with less release of breath.

फ **pha** Rather like 'p' in '**p**in', but with stronger release of breath.

ब **ba** As 'b' in '**b**in', but with less release of breath.

भ **bha** Strongly aspirated form of the above: as 'bh' in 'clu**b-h**ouse' spoken quickly.

The nasals

Although Hindi has five nasal consonants, they present little difficulty as they are all broadly accommodated by various forms of the English 'n' and 'm' sounds. As the syllabary shows, the nasal consonants are classified after the five classes of consonants to which they respectively belong.

ङ **ṅa** As 'n' in 'i**n**k'.

ञ **ña** As 'n' in 'i**n**jury'.

ण (रगा) **ṇa** The retroflex nasal, produced with the tongue high on the palate as with retroflex consonants.

न **na** Like 'n' in '**n**ice', but with the tongue flatter against the front teeth.

म **ma** As 'm' in '**m**other'.

The fricatives

ख़ **k͟ha** Like the 'ch' in Scottish 'loch', but strictly pronounced further back with a slight scrape.

ग़ **g͟a** A 'g' sound pronounced as far back as possible, with a scrape as in **k͟ha** (of which this is the voiced counterpart). Many speakers do not distinguish it from **ga.** Both this and **k͟ha** occur only in loan words from Arabic and Persian.

श **śa** As 'sh' in '**sh**ip'.

ष **ṣa** Strictly speaking a retroflex, but in practice rarely distinguished from the preceding in pronunciation.

स **sa** As 's' in '**s**ip'.

ज़ **za** As 'z' in '**z**ip'.

फ़ **fa** As 'f' in '**f**ind'.

Flapped and tapped sounds

ड़ **ṛa** This is the retroflex **ḍa** when it is between two vowels, flapped to produced a kind of 'r' sound somewhat similar to the 'rr' in 'wo**rr**y'.

ढ़ **ṛha** The aspirated counterpart of the above.

र **ra** An 'r' which is trilled or tapped, not unlike the Scottish rolled 'r' but shorter. It is never lost like the 'r' in 'more'.

The uvular plosive

क़ **qa** A sound like 'k', but produced as far back in the throat as possible. Many speakers do not distinguish it from **ka**. It occurs only in Arabic and Persian loan words.

Aspirate, semi-vowels and liquid

ह **ha** This 'h' sound is always fully voiced, as in 'a**h**ead'.

य **ya** Close to the 'y' sound in '**y**et', but less tense.

व **va** This sound lies between the English sounds 'v' and 'w'. Unlike the English 'v', the lower lip hardly touches the upper teeth; but unlike the English 'w', there is no lip-rounding.

ल **la** A clear 'l' sound, as in '**l**ife' but with the tongue positioned as for dental **ta**, etc.

Vowels

There are eleven vowels in Hindi. In the script, each has two forms: the first, its full form, is used when it begins a word or syllable, while the second is used when following a consonant. The consonant क **ka** will be used here to demonstrate the second form.

अ (ग्र)	**a**	क	**ka**	As in '**a**rrive'.
आ	**ā**	का	**kā**	As in 'p**ar**t'.
इ	**i**	कि	**ki**	As in 'h**i**t'.

ई	**ī**	की	**kī**	As in '**hea**t'.
उ	**u**	कु	**ku**	As in '**foo**t'. (**ru** is written रु)
ऊ	**ū**	कू	**kū**	As in '**foo**l'. (**rū** is written रू)
ऋ	**ṛ**	कृ	**kṛ**	As in '**ri**pple'. Only occurs in Sanskrit loan words (**hṛ** is written हृ, **śṛ** शृ).
ए	**e**	के	**ke**	As in the *first part* of the vowel sound in '**ca**ble': a pure vowel sound and not a diphthong like the English.
ऐ	**ai**	कै	**kai**	As in '**he**n'.
ओ	**o**	को	**ko**	As in the *first part* of the vowel sound in '**ho**tel'; a pure vowel sound and not a diphthong like the English.
औ	**au**	कौ	**kau**	As in 'off'

Before ह **ha**, the अ **a** vowel is often pronounced (but never written) as if it were the ऐ **ai** vowel: that is, to rhyme with 'pen'. The exception to this is in the pronoun वह **vah** *he, she, it, that,* which is normally pronounced as though it were **vo**.

It should be noted that a consonant can support only *one* vowel at a time. To write **huā** you must first write **hu** and then **ā** in its full form: हुआ **huā.** Likewise जाओ **jāo**, लिए **lie**, etc. Notice also the difference between की **kī** and कई **kaī.**

Nasalization

Each of the vowels above, except ऋ **ṛ**, may occur with nasalization. Nasalization of a vowel is produced by directing a substantial part of the breath towards the nasal cavity as the vowel is being uttered. To indicate that a vowel is nasalized, the sign ँ *candrabindu* is used: in transliteration, nasalization is shown by a tilde sign over the transliterated vowel, as in **ã**. *Candrabindu* is written either over the headstroke of the vowel itself, e.g. हाँ **hā̃**, or over the headstroke of the consonant to which the vowel is attached, e.g. हूँ **hū̃**. If any part of the vowel is written above the headstroke, then the dot alone is used instead of the full *candrabindu*: e.g. गईं **gaī̃**, में **mẽ**, हैं **haĩ**, थीं **thī̃**. In some books, only the dot is used, even when the full *candrabindu* should technically be written, but it is better not to follow this practice.

Visarga

Visarga is a sign looking like a colon (but with the dots more widely spaced) that occurs without a headstroke in the middle or at the end of a word. It is pronounced as ह **ha**, and is transliterated **ḥ**–thus दुःख **duḥkh**, छः **chaḥ**. It occurs only rarely in Hindi.

PRACTICE DRILL 1 Write out the following in Devanagari, and then check what you have written against the key on p. 18.

ab sab āp kām in din īd bhī udhar tum
ūn dūr ṛtu kṛpayā ek ye aisā hai oṛho bulāo
aur paudhā mahā̃gī pā̃c thī̃ pahū̃cā ū̃cā mẽ maĩ
auratõ khāie <u>kh</u>uśī gā̃v <u>g</u>alat ghar cīzẽ chai jagahẽ
zarūr jhūṭh ṭā̃g ṭhīk ḍāk ḍhāī taraf thoṛā dūdh
dhokhā naī pīche foṭo bāqī bhāī mū̃h yahā̃ ruci
lāṭhī vahī̃ śābāś saṛak hālā̃ki kāraṇ bhāṣā duḥkh

Conjunct characters

Many Hindi words require consonants to be written in a conjunct form, thereby showing that there is no inherent **a** vowel between them. The list below contains most of the conjuncts that are likely to be needed, and is intended for gradual assimilation and reference–not for immediate memorisation! You will see that although the way in which any two consonants combine depends upon their respective shapes, most are in fact very straightforward: indeed 60 per cent simply drop the down-stroke of the first member and join the remainder to the full form of the second member. The characters क़ **qa**, ख़ **<u>kh</u>a**, ग़ **<u>g</u>a**, ज़ **za**, and फ़ **fa** are not shown because they behave exactly like क **ka,** ख **kha,** ग **ga,** ज **ja,** and फ **pha,** of which they are modifications. The sign ्, used on the first of the two component characters, is called *halant* or *virām,* and indicates that the consonant has its inherent vowel silenced. Alternative forms of the conjuncts are shown in brackets.

क्	+	क	=	क्क	क्	+	य	=	क्य
क्	+	ख	=	क्ख	क्	+	र	=	क्र
क्	+	ट	=	क्ट	क्	+	ल	=	क्ल
क्	+	त	=	क्त (क्त)	क्	+	व	=	क्व
क्	+	म	=	क्म	क्	+	श	=	क्श

क्	+	ष	=	क्ष (क्ष)
क्ष्	+	म	=	क्ष्म
क्	+	स	=	क्स
ख्	+	य	=	ख्य
ग्	+	द	=	ग्द
ग्	+	ध	=	ग्ध
ग्	+	न	=	ग्न
ग्	+	म	=	ग्म
ग्	+	य	=	ग्य
ग्	+	र	=	ग्र
ग्	+	ल	=	ग्ल
ग्	+	व	=	ग्व
घ्	+	न	=	घ्न
घ्	+	य	=	घ्य
घ्	+	र	=	घ्र
ङ्	+	क	=	ङ्क
च्	+	च	=	च्च
च्	+	छ	=	च्छ
च्	+	य	=	च्य
ज्	+	ज	=	ज्ज
ज्	+	ञ	=	ज्ञ
ज्	+	य	=	ज्य
ज्	+	र	=	ज्र
ज्	+	व	=	ज्व
ञ्	+	च	=	ञ्च
ट्	+	ट	=	ट्ट
ट्	+	ठ	=	ट्ठ
ट्	+	य	=	ट्य
ट्	+	र	=	ट्र
ड्	+	ड	=	ड्ड
ड्	+	ढ	=	ड्ढ
ड्	+	य	=	ड्य
ड्	+	र	=	ड्र
ढ्	+	य	=	ढ्य
ण्	+	ट	=	ण्ट
ण्	+	ठ	=	ण्ठ
ण्	+	ड	=	ण्ड
ण्	+	य	=	ण्य
त्	+	क	=	त्क
त्	+	त	=	त्त
त् + त्	+	व	=	त्त्व
त्	+	थ	=	त्थ
त्	+	न	=	त्न
त्	+	प	=	त्प
त्	+	म	=	त्म
त्	+	य	=	त्य
त्	+	र	=	त्र
त्	+	व	=	त्व
त्	+	स	=	त्स
त् + स्	+	य	=	त्स्य
थ्	+	य	=	थ्य
द्	+	ग	=	द्ग
द्	+	द	=	द्द
द्	+	ध	=	द्ध
द्	+	भ	=	द्भ
द्	+	म	=	द्म
द्	+	य	=	द्य
द्	+	र	=	द्र

द्	+	व			=	द्व
ध्	+	य			=	ध्य
ध्	+	व			=	ध्व
न्	+	त			=	न्त
न्	+	द्	+	र	=	न्द्र
न्	+	ध			=	न्ध
न्	+	न			=	न्न (न्न)
न्	+	म			=	न्म
न्	+	य			=	न्य
न्	+	व			=	न्व
न्	+	ह			=	न्ह
प्	+	त			=	प्त
प्	+	न			=	प्न
प्	+	प			=	प्प
प्	+	य			=	प्य
प्	+	र			=	प्र
प्	+	ल			=	प्ल
प्	+	स			=	प्स
ब्	+	ज			=	ब्ज
ब्	+	द			=	ब्द
ब्	+	ध			=	ब्ध
ब्	+	ब			=	ब्ब
ब्	+	य			=	ब्य
ब्	+	र			=	ब्र
भ्	+	य			=	भ्य
भ्	+	र			=	भ्र
म्	+	न			=	म्न
म्	+	प			=	म्प
म्	+	ब			=	म्ब
म्	+	भ			=	म्भ
म्	+	म			=	म्म
म्	+	य			=	म्य
म्	+	र			=	म्र
म्	+	ल			=	म्ल
म्	+	ह			=	म्ह
य्	+	य			=	य्य
र	+	थ			=	र्थ
ल्	+	क			=	ल्क
ल्	+	द			=	ल्द
ल्	+	प			=	ल्प
ल्	+	म			=	ल्म
ल्	+	य			=	ल्य
व्	+	य			=	व्य
व्	+	र			=	व्र
व्	+	व			=	व्व
श्	+	क			=	श्क
श्	+	च			=	श्च
श्	+	य			=	श्य
श्	+	र			=	श्र
श्	+	ल			=	श्ल
श्	+	व			=	श्व
ष्	+	क			=	ष्क
ष्	+	ट			=	ष्ट
ष्	+	ट्	+	र	=	ष्ट्र
ष्	+	ठ			=	ष्ठ
ष्	+	ण			=	ष्ण
ष्	+	प			=	ष्प
ष्	+	म			=	ष्म

ष् + य = ष्य	स् + फ = स्फ
ष् + व = ष्व	स् + म = स्म
स् + क = स्क	स् + य = स्य
स् + ख = स्ख	स् + र = स्र
स् + ज = स्ज	स् + व = स्व
स् + ट = स्ट	स् + स = स्स
स् + त = स्त	ह् + न = ह्न
स् + त् + र = स्त्र	ह् + म = ह्म
स् + थ = स्थ	ह् + य = ह्य
स् + थ् + य = स्थ्य	ह् + र = ह्र
स् + न = स्न	ह् + ल = ह्ल
स् + प = स्प	ह् + व = ह्व

Most of the conjuncts, then, present little difficulty, but there are a few that require special attention. Two in particular are regarded as characters in their own right: क्ष **kṣa**, pronounced as in English 'bu**cksh**ot', and ज्ञ **jña**, which in Hindi is pronounced as '**gya**'.

Conjuncts involving र **ra** also need care. When र **ra** is the first member of a conjunct, it is represented by the sign ॅ above the headstroke at the very end of the *syllable* which it precedes: thus **urdū** is written उर्दू, **śarmā** is written शर्मा. When र **ra** is the second member of a conjunct, its characteristic sign is ्र, but precisely where it comes in the conjunct depends upon the shape of the first member: thus प्र **pra**, त्र **tra**, ह्र **hra**, while with ट **ṭa** and ड **ḍa** it needs a little supporting line: ट्र **ṭra**, ड्र **ḍra**.

Anusvāra

Anusvāra is a convenient and commonly used device which stands for any of the five nasal consonants of the syllabary when they occur as the first member of a conjunct. It is a dot written above the headstroke at the right-hand end of the preceding character. In the list below, both spellings are correct and equivalent, although in the case of the first two the use of *anusvāra* is to be preferred.

रंग	=	रङ्ग	raṅg
पंजाबी	=	पञ्जाबी	pañjābī

अंडा	=	अण्डा	aṇḍā
हिंदी	=	हिन्दी	hindī
लंबा	=	लम्बा	lambā

Notice where the *anusvāra* comes when the preceding vowel has its own vowel sign: फ्रांसीसी **frānsīsī**, आंदोलन **āndolan**. No special symbol is used for *anusvāra* in the transliteration, the appropriate nasal consonant being written to avoid confusion in pronunciation. Thus both लंबा and लम्बा are transliterated as **lambā**.

PRACTICE DRILL **2** To gain familiarity with the use of conjunct characters, write out the following in Devanagari, and then check what you have written against the key on pp. 18–19.

pakkā makkhan ḍākṭar vaqt kyā zikr klās kṣaṇ
baksā khyāl ṛgved gyārah ãgrez raṅg śīghr kaccā
acchā lajjā ājñā rājy pañjābī chuṭṭī ciṭṭhī ṭren
haḍḍī ḍrāivar ghaṇṭā pattā mahattv patnī khatm sāhity
patr utsav svāsthy buddh yadyapi pandrah dvārā dhyān
ant sundar rājendr andhā prasann janm unyāsī hinsā
unhẽ saptāh cappal pyār prakṛti flaiṭ frāns sabzī
śabd ḍibbā byorā brek lambā ammā̃ tumhẽ garm
vidyārthī kharrāṭā balki jaldī film dillī vyakti
muśkil niścay riśtedār avaśy śrī viśvās rāṣṭr viṣṇu
īrṣyā skūl sṭeśan vyast sthiti snān aspatāl ism
samasyā sahasr svīkār hissā brāhmaṇ

Pronunciation

It is of course hoped that you will either use the cassette or the assistance of a native speaker to help you perfect your pronunciation of Hindi, but certain general points need to be noted:

1 When a consonant is doubled, either in a conjunct as in पक्का **pakkā**, or when one word ends and the next begins with the same consonant as in उस से **us se**, it is important that the consonant should be lengthened to reflect this. The difference between a single and a double consonant can be felt in the contrast between English 'nigh**t** rain' and 'nigh**t t**rain'.

2 The inherent **a** vowel is not pronounced at the end of a word. When, however, a word ends in a conjunct of two (or even three) consonants, then an 'echo' of the **a** vowel may be heard at the end of the consonant cluster: thus योग्य **yogy(a)**, राष्ट्र **rāṣṭr(a).**

3 There are times when an inherent **a** vowel is not pronounced in the *middle* of a word, even though the spelling is not with a conjunct. The general rule is that when a word has three or more script syllables, and ends in a vowel *other than* the inherent **a**, the penultimate inherent vowel is not pronounced. Thus समझ **samajh**, but समझा **samjhā**; रहन **rahan**, but रहना **rahnā**. For a number of reasons this general rule does not always hold, so it is important to refer to the transliteration, or to the cassette, in order to be sure whether a medial inherent **a** vowel is pronounced. (Although the transliteration does not extend beyond Unit 5, the end vocabulary gives the transliteration of all vocabulary items.)

4 Finally, when you hear Hindi spoken you will find the stress much more even than in English, and the pronounced emphasis often given to a word in an English sentence is more likely to be conveyed in Hindi by the word order or by the content of the sentence itself.

Punctuation and other signs

Hindi uses the same punctuation as English, except that a full stop is normally represented by the sign । (called **daṇḍ** or **khaṛī pāī**).

For abbreviations, Hindi uses a small circle (॰) after the first syllable of the word abbreviated: thus रु॰ stands for रुपया **rupayā**, पं॰ for पंडित **paṇḍit**. With the initials of proper names, a Devanagari transliteration of the English form may also be used: thus both उ॰ प्र॰ and यू॰पी॰ stand for 'Uttar Pradeś', and Vinod Kumar Mehra may sign his name either as वि॰ कु॰ मेहरा or as वी॰ के॰ मेहरा.

The sign ॅ is sometimes written over the vowel आ **ā** to represent the English sound 'o' in words like जॉन 'John' and चॉक्लेट **cākleṭ** (chocolate).

Alternative spellings

A few words and verb endings have alternative spellings. The ending ए **e** following an आ **ā** vowel can take a number of forms: thus जाए **jāe** can be found as जाये **jāye**, as जाय **jāy**, and even as जावे **jāve**. The imperative ending -इए **-ie** is sometimes found with a -य- **-ya-**, as when जाइए **jāie** is written जाइये **jāiye**, etc. Such forms will be readily recognised.

Some Persian loan words with a र **ra** are often spelt in two ways, so that गर्म **garm** is also found as गरम **garm**, कुर्सी **kursī** as कुरसी **kursī**, and सर्दी **sardī** as सरदी **sardī**. The second of these forms is used throughout this book.

Numerals

The Hindi numerals are as follows:

१(१)	२	३	४	५(५)	६(६)	७	८(८)	९(९)	०
1	2	3	4	5	6	7	8	9	0

Dictionary order

The dictionary order of the Devanagari script is as shown below, working vertically down the columns. Syllables with *candrabindu* or *anusvara* precede those without: thus गाँव **gā̃v** precedes गाड़ी **gāṛī**. Conjunct forms of a consonant come after all its non-conjunct forms: thus ट्रेन **ṭren** comes after टोपी **ṭopī**.

अ **a**	क/क़ **ka/qa**	ठ **ṭha**	ब **ba**
आ **ā**	ख/ख़ **kha/<u>kh</u>a**	ड/ड़ **ḍa/ṛa**	भ **bha**
इ **i**	ग/ग़ **ga/<u>g</u>a**	ढ/ढ़ **ḍha/ṛha**	म **ma**
ई **ī**	घ **gha**	ण **ṇa**	य **ya**
उ **u**	ङ **ṅa**	त **ta**	र **ra**
ऊ **ū**	च **ca**	थ **tha**	ल **la**
ऋ **ṛ**	छ **cha**	द **da**	व **va**
ए **e**	ज/ज़ **ja/za**	ध **dha**	श **śa**
ऐ **ai**	झ **jha**	न **na**	ष **ṣa**
ओ **o**	ञ **ña**	प **pa**	स **sa**
औ **au**	ट **ṭa**	फ/फ़ **pha/fa**	ह **ha**

Key to practice drills

1 अब सब आप काम इन दिन ईद भी उधर तुम
ऊन दूर ऋतु कृपया एक ये ऐसा है ओढ़ो बुलाओ
और पौधा महँगी पाँच थीं पहुँचा ऊँचा में मैं
औरतों खाइए ख़ुशी गाँव ग़लत घर चीज़ें छै जगहें
ज़रूर झूठ टाँग ठीक डाक ढाई तरफ़ थोड़ा दूध
धोखा नई पीछे फ़ोटो बाक़ी भाई मुँह यहाँ रुचि
लाठी वहीं शाबाश सड़क हालाँकि कारण भाषा दुःख

2 पक्का मक्खन डाक्टर वक़्त क्या ज़िक्र क्लास क्षण
बक्सा ख़्याल ऋग्वेद ग्यारह अँग्रेज़ रंग शीघ्र कच्चा
अच्छा लज्जा आज्ञा राज्य पंजाबी छुट्टी चिट्ठी ट्रेन
हड्डी ड्राइवर घंटा पत्ता महत्त्व पत्नी ख़त्म साहित्य
पत्र उत्सव स्वास्थ्य बुद्ध यद्यपि पन्द्रह द्वारा ध्यान
अंत सुंदर राजेन्द्र अन्धा प्रसन्न जन्म उन्यासी हिंसा
उन्हें सप्ताह चप्पल प्यार प्रकृति फ़्लैट फ़्रांस सब्ज़ी
शब्द डिब्बा ब्योरा ब्रेक लंबा अम्माँ तुम्हें गर्म
विद्यार्थी खर्राटा बल्कि जल्दी फ़िल्म दिल्ली व्यक्ति
मुश्किल निश्चय रिश्तेदार अवश्य श्री विश्वास राष्ट्र विष्णु
ईर्ष्या स्कूल स्टेशन व्यस्त स्थिति स्नान अस्पताल इस्म
समस्या सहस्र स्वीकार हिस्सा ब्राह्मण

Unit One

Dialogue 1A *I am Ram*

राम	नमस्ते। मैं राम हूँ। क्या आप उमा हैं ?
Rām	namaste. maĩ Rām hū̃, kyā āp Umā haĩ?
उमा	जी हाँ, मैं उमा हूँ, और यह लड़की सुशीला है। हम दोनों हिन्दुस्तानी हैं।
Umā	jī hā̃, maĩ Umā hū̃, aur yah laṛkī Suśīlā hai. ham donō hindustānī haĩ.
राम	नमस्ते सुशीला। क्या तुम पंजाबी हो ?
Rām	namaste Suśīlā. kyā tum pañjābī ho?
सुशीला	जी नहीं, मैं पंजाबी नहीं हूँ। मैं गुजराती हूँ।
Suśīlā	jī nahī̃, maĩ pañjābī nahī̃ hū̃. maĩ gujarātī hū̃.
राम	क्या वे लोग अँग्रेज़ हैं ?
Rām	kyā ve log ãgrez haĩ?
सुशीला	जी नहीं, वे अँग्रेज़ नहीं हैं, वे पाकिस्तानी हैं।
Suśīlā	jī nahī̃, ve ãgrez nahī̃ haĩ, ve pākistānī haĩ.

Ram	Hello. I am Ram. Are you Uma?
Uma	Yes, I am Uma, and this girl is Sushila. We are both Indian.
Ram	Hello Sushila. Are you Panjabi?
Sushila	No, I'm not Panjabi. I am Gujarati.
Ram	Are those people English?
Sushila	No, they're not English, they're Pakistani.

1 Personal pronouns and 'am', 'is', 'are'

The personal pronouns with their appropriate verb forms are as follows:

Singular

मैं हूँ	maĩ hū̃	*I am*
तू है	tū hai	*you are* (intimate)

यह है	yah hai	*this, he, she, it is*
वह है	vah hai	*that, he, she, it is*
Plural		
हम हैं	ham haĩ	*we are*
तुम हो	tum ho	*you are* (familiar)
आप हैं	āp haĩ	*you are* (formal)
ये हैं	ye haĩ	*these, they are*
वे हैं	ve haĩ	*those, they are*

While मैं **maĩ** is the usual word for 'I', speakers in some areas, and especially women, use हम **ham** *we* for 'I'. This practice should not be followed.

The grammatically singular pronoun तू **tū** *you* is used in situations of intimacy on the one hand and contempt on the other. It is not likely that the learner will need to use it.

The two pronouns that require the greatest sensitivity in usage are आप **āp** and तुम **tum**, both grammatically plural pronouns meaning 'you'. तुम **tum** is the familiar pronoun, used between close friends and by various members of the family, one to another. (It is also used in speaking to people of clearly lower status, such as servants.) आप **āp** is the formal, polite (honorific) pronoun used to equals and to people entitled to respect on account of age, seniority or social standing. Unless it is apparent that तुम **tum** is expected or would be preferred, it is safest to use आप **āp.**

यह **yah** *this* and ये **ye** *these* are used for 'he', 'she', 'it', and 'they' when the persons or things referred to are present or near the speaker; otherwise वह **vah** and वे **ve** are used. ये **ye** and वे **ve** should also be used for 'he' and 'she' when speaking of someone whom one addresses as आप **āp.**

मैं अँग्रेज़ हूँ।	maĩ ãgrez hũ.	*I am English.*
वह जर्मन है।	vah jarman hai.	*He is German.*
यह गुजराती है।	yah gujarātī hai.	*He is Gujarati.*
हम पंजाबी हैं।	ham pañjābī haĩ.	*We are Panjabis.*
तुम धोबी हो?	tum dhobī ho?	*You are the washerman?*
आप हिन्दुस्तानी हैं?	āp hindustānī haĩ?	*You are Indian?*
वे भारतीय हैं।	ve bhāratīy haĩ.	*They are Indian.* [1]
वे हिन्दू हैं।	ve hindū haĩ.	*They are Hindus.* [1]

[1] 'He' or 'she', if plural is honorific.

2 Questions and answers

The sentence तुम धोबी हो? **tum dhobī ho?** *You are the washerman?* is a question in English and in Hindi because of the stress and intonation with which it is pronounced. This way of asking questions by means of voice inflexion is as common in Hindi as it is in English. More common in English would be to change the word order to 'Are you the washerman?'. Hindi does not form questions in this way, but does so by putting the word क्या **kyā** at the beginning of the sentence, thus indicating that what follows is a question:

क्या तुम धोबी हो?	kyā tum dhobī ho?	*Are you the washerman?*
क्या आप जर्मन हैं?	kyā āp jarman haĩ?	*Are you German?*
क्या यह साफ़ है?	kyā yah sāf hai?	*Is this clean?*

Answers to such questions tend to be fuller in Hindi than they are in English, and often repeat part of the question after the words जी हाँ **jī hā̃** *Yes* or जी नहीं **jī nahī̃** *No*.

Dialogue 1B *Is this house large?*

राम क्या यह मकान बड़ा है?
Rām kyā yah makān baṛā hai?
उमा जी हाँ, यह मकान बड़ा है, लेकिन वे मकान छोटे हैं।
Umā jī hā̃, yah makān baṛā hai, lekin ve makān choṭe haĩ.
राम क्या यह कमरा बड़ा है?
Rām kyā yah kamrā baṛā hai?
उमा जी नहीं, यह कमरा छोटा है, लेकिन वे दो कमरे बड़े हैं। यहाँ सिर्फ़ एक मेज़ और एक कुरसी है, लेकिन वहाँ दो मेज़ें और चार कुरसियाँ हैं।
Umā jī nahī̃, yah kamrā choṭā hai, lekin ve do kamre baṛe haĩ. yahā̃ sirf ek mez aur ek kursī hai, lekin vahā̃ do mezẽ aur cār kursiyā̃ haĩ.
राम अच्छा। क्या यह छोटा कमरा साफ़ है?
Rām acchā. kyā yah choṭā kamrā sāf hai?
उमा जी हाँ, यह कमरा साफ़ है, लेकिन वे बड़े कमरे साफ़ नहीं हैं, गंदे हैं।
Umā jī hā̃, yah kamrā sāf hai, lekin ve baṛe kamre sāf nahī̃ haĩ, gande haĩ.

राम	क्या यह मेज़ साफ़ है?
Rām	kyā yah mez sāf hai?
उमा	जी नहीं, यह गंदी है, लेकिन वे बड़ी मेज़ें साफ़ हैं।
Umā	jī nahī̃, yah gandī hai, lekin ve baṛī mezẽ sāf haĩ.

Ram	Is this house large?
Uma	Yes, this house is large, but those houses are small.
Ram	Is this room large?
Uma	No, this room is small, but those two rooms are large. Here, there is only one table and one chair, but there, there are two tables and four chairs.
Ram	Good. Is this small room clean?
Uma	Yes, this room is clean, but those big rooms aren't clean, they're dirty.
Ram	Is this table clean?
Uma	No, it's dirty, but those big tables are clean.

3 Nouns

Hindi nouns are either masculine or feminine. The grammatical gender of each new noun must therefore be learnt. There is no definite article *the* in Hindi; एक **ek** *one* is sometimes used as the indefinite article *a*.

Masculine nouns are of two types: those ending in a final -आ **-ā** in the singular which changes to -ए **-e** in the plural, and all others, which are the same in both singular and plural:

Type 1

लड़का	laṛkā	*boy*	लड़के	laṛke	*boys*
कमरा	kamrā	*room*	कमरे	kamre	*rooms*

Type 2

मकान	makān	*house*	मकान	makān	*houses*
आदमी	ādmī	*man*	आदमी	ādmī	*men*

Not all Hindi nouns ending in -आ **-ā** are masculine, nor do all masculine nouns ending in -आ **-ā** follow लड़का **laṛkā**. A few masculine nouns, such as पिता **pitā** *father*, राजा **rājā** *king*, चाचा **cācā** *paternal uncle*, follow the pattern of मकान **makān**. These are mainly nouns of relationship.

Feminine nouns are also of two types: those ending in -ई **-ī**, -इ **-i** or -इया **-iyā** in the singular which form their plural in -इयाँ **-iyā̃**, and all others, which add -एँ **-ẽ** in the plural.

Type 1

लड़की	laṛkī	*girl*	लड़कियाँ	laṛkiyā̃	*girls*
बेटी	beṭī	*daughter*	बेटियाँ	beṭiyā̃	*daughters*
शक्ति	śakti	*power*	शक्तियाँ	śaktiyā̃	*powers*
बुढ़िया	buṛhiyā	*old woman*	बुढ़ियाँ	buṛhiyā̃	*old women*[1]

Type 2

मेज़	mez	*table*	मेज़ें	mezẽ	*tables*
क़मीज़	qamīz	*shirt*	क़मीज़ें	qamīzẽ	*shirts*
माता	mātā	*mother*	माताएँ	mātāẽ	*mothers*

Feminine nouns ending in -ऊ **-ū** follow the pattern of मेज़ **mez**, but shorten the final vowel before the feminine ending:

बहू	bahū	*bride, wife, daughter-in-law*	बहुएँ	bahuẽ	*brides*, etc.

4 Adjectives

Adjectives agree with the nouns they qualify. Hindi adjectives are of two types: those that inflect (change their endings), and those that are invariable. Those which inflect, such as बड़ा **baṛā** *big*, and छोटा **choṭā** *small*, end in -आ **-ā** in the masculine singular, -ए **-e** in the masculine plural and -ई **-ī** in the feminine singular and plural. The invariable adjectives, like साफ़ **sāf** *clean*, never change. Any adjectives ending in -आ **-ā** that are invariable are marked (inv.) in the end vocabulary.

Type 1: Inflecting

बड़ा लड़का	baṛā laṛkā	*big boy*
बड़े लड़के	baṛe laṛke	*big boys*
बड़ी लड़की	baṛī laṛkī	*big girl*
बड़ी लड़कियाँ	baṛī laṛkiyā̃	*big girls*
छोटा मकान	choṭā makān	*small house*
छोटे मकान	choṭe makān	*small houses*
छोटी मेज़	choṭī mez	*small table*
छोटी मेज़ें	choṭī mezẽ	*small tables*

[1] An alternative plural form of बुढ़िया **buṛhiyā** is बुढ़ियाएँ **buṛhiyāẽ**, on the model of माता **mātā** - माताएँ **mātāẽ**

Type 2: Invariable

साफ़ कमरा	sāf kamrā	*clean room*
साफ़ कमरे	sāf kamre	*clean rooms*
साफ़ कुरसी	sāf kursī	*clean chair*
साफ़ कुरसियाँ	sāf kursiyā̃	*clean chairs*
सफ़ेद मकान	safed makān	*white house* or *white houses*
सफ़ेद मेज़	safed mez	*white table*
सफ़ेद मेज़ें	safed mezẽ	*white tables*

5 The simple sentence

As can be seen, the subject usually comes at the beginning of the sentence (though क्या **kyā** precedes it), and the verb comes at the end. The negative नहीं **nahī̃** comes just before the verb. Notice the important distinction between the following two sentences:

यह कमरा बड़ा है।	yah kamrā baṛā hai.	*This room is large.*
यह बड़ा कमरा है।	yah baṛā kamrā hai.	*This is a large room.*

EXERCISE **1.1** Put the following into the plural:

साफ़ क़मीज़ sāf qamīz	बड़ा आदमी baṛā ādmī	हिन्दुस्तानी धोबी hindustānī dhobī
अँग्रेज़ लड़की ā̃grez laṛkī	माता mātā	हिन्दू राजा hindū rājā
सफ़ेद मेज़ safed mez	छोटी शक्ति choṭī śakti	छोटा लड़का choṭā laṛkā
सफ़ेद कुरसी safed kursī	गुजराती बहू gujarātī bahū	वह मकान vah makān
यह बड़ा कमरा yah baṛā kamrā	वह छोटी बेटी vah choṭī beṭī	यह बुढ़िया yah buṛhiyā

EXERCISE **1.2** Translate into English:

१	यह कमरा बड़ा है, वे कमरे छोटे हैं।	yah kamrā baṛā hai, ve kamre choṭe haĩ.
२	वे मेज़ें छोटी नहीं हैं।	ve mezẽ choṭī nahī̃ haĩ.
३	क्या यह लड़की छोटी है?	kyā yah laṛkī choṭī hai?
४	वे लड़कियाँ गुजराती हैं।	ve laṛkiyā̃ gujarātī haĩ.

५	यह छोटी मेज़ है।	yah choṭī mez hai.
६	ये छोटी मेज़ें साफ़ नहीं हैं, गंदी हैं।	ye choṭī mezẽ sāf nahī̃ haĩ, gandī haĩ.
७	वे आदमी भारतीय हैं?	ve ādmī bhāratīy haĩ?
८	वे बुढ़ियाँ हिन्दू हैं।	ve buṛhiyā̃ hindū haĩ.
९	ये बड़े मकान हैं, लेकिन वह बड़ा नहीं है।	ye baṛe makān haĩ, lekin vah baṛā nahī̃ hai.
१०	क्या वह मकान बड़ा है?	kyā vah makān baṛā hai?
११	सफ़ेद क़मीज़ें साफ़ नहीं हैं।	safed qamīzẽ sāf nahī haĩ.
१२	क्या तुम धोबी नहीं हो?	kyā tum dhobī nahī̃ ho?
१३	क्या वे लोग पाकिस्तानी हैं?	kyā ve log pākistānī haĩ?
१४	यहाँ सिर्फ़ दो मेज़ें हैं।	yahā̃ sirf do mezẽ haĩ.

EXERCISE 1.3 Translate into Hindi:

1 Are those people Gujarati?
2 Those white chairs are not big, they are small.
3 You are a little girl.
4 These are clean shirts.
5 Those shirts are not clean.
6 This table is big, but those tables are small.
7 Is this house big? No, but those houses are big.
8 Hello. I am English. Are you Indian?
9 Are those four men kings?
10 Uncle is here. He is not a Hindu.

Vocabulary

अँग्रेज़	āgrez	*Englishman/-woman* (m./f.)
अच्छा	acchā	*good*
आदमी	ādmī	*man, person* (m.)
आप	āp	*you* (formal/polite)
एक	ek	*one; a*
और	aur	*and; more*
कमरा	kamrā	*room* (m.)
क़मीज़	qamīz	*shirt* (f.)
कुरसी	kursī	*chair* (f.)

क्या	kyā	[interrogative word: makes a following statement into a question]
गंदा	gandā	*dirty*
गुजराती	gujarātī	*Gujarati* (m./f./adj.)
चाचा	cācā	*paternal uncle* (m.)
चार	cār	*four*
छोटा	choṭā	*small*
जर्मन	jarman	*German* (m./f./adj.)
जी नहीं	jī nahī̃	*no*
जी हाँ	jī hā̃	*yes*
तुम	tum	*you* (familiar)
तू	tū	*you* (intimate)
दो	do	*two*
दोनों	donõ	*both, the two*
धोबी	dhobī	*washerman* (m.)
नमस्ते	namaste	*greetings, goodbye* (f.)
नहीं	nahī̃	*not*
पंजाबी	pañjābī	*Panjabi* (m./f./adj.)
पाकिस्तानी	pākistānī	*Pakistani* (m./f./adj.)
पिता	pitā	*father* (m.)
बड़ा	baṛā	*big*
बहू	bahū	*daughter-in-law, wife* (f.)
बुढ़िया	buṛhiyā	*old woman* (f.)
बेटी	beṭī	*girl, daughter* (f.)
भारतीय	bhāratīy	*Indian* (m./f./adj.)
मकान	makān	*house* (m.)
माता	mātā	*mother* (f.)
मेज़	mez	*table* (f.)
मैं	maĩ	*I*
यह	yah	*this, he, she, it*
यहाँ	yahā̃	*here*
ये	ye	*these, they; he, she* (honorific)
राजा	rājā	*king, rajah* (m.)
लड़का	laṛkā	*boy* (m.)
लड़की	laṛkī	*girl* (f.)
लेकिन	lekin	*but*
लोग	log	*people* (m.)
वह	vah	*that, he, she, it*
वहाँ	vahā̃	*there*
वे	ve	*those, they; he, she* (honorific)
शक्ति	śakti	*power* (f.)

सफ़ेद	safed	*white*
साफ़	sāf	*clean, clear*
सिर्फ़	sirf	*only*
हम	ham	*we*
हिन्दुस्तानी	hindustānī	*Indian* (m./f./adj.)
हिन्दू	hindū	*Hindu* (m./f./adj.)
हूँ	hū̃	*am*
हैं	haĩ	*are*
है	hai	*is; are* (with **tū**)
हो	ho	*are* (with **tum**)

Unit Two

Dialogue 2A *Who is that man?*

प्रमोद	वह आदमी कौन है?
Pramod	vah ādmī kaun hai?
उषा	वह राजू है। राजू विद्यार्थी है।
Uṣā	vah Rājū hai. Rājū vidyārthī hai.
प्रमोद	अच्छा। वे औरतें कौन हैं?
Pramod	acchā. ve auratẽ kaun haĩ?
उषा	वे माताजी और उमा हैं। लंबी महिला माताजी हैं।
Uṣā	ve mātājī aur Umā haĩ. lambī mahilā mātājī haĩ.
प्रमोद	यह क्या है? क्या यह किताब है?
Pramod	yah kyā hai? kyā yah kitāb hai?
उषा	जी नहीं, यह किताब नहीं, अख़बार है।
Uṣā	jī nahī̃, yah kitāb nahī̃, akhbār hai.
प्रमोद	यहाँ कितने अख़बार और किताबें हैं?
Pramod	yahā̃ kitne akhḅār aur kitābẽ haĩ?
उषा	यहाँ नौ अख़बार और सात किताबें हैं।
Uṣā	yahā̃ nau akhbār aur sāt kitābẽ haĩ.
प्रमोद	किताबें कैसी हैं? क्या वे बड़ी हैं?
Pramod	kitābẽ kaisī haĩ? kya ve baṛī haĩ?
उषा	जी हाँ, बड़ी हैं। वह क़लम कैसा है?
Uṣā	jī hā̃, baṛī haĩ. vah qalam kaisā hai?
प्रमोद	यह लाल क़लम है। ये दोनों क़लम लाल हैं।
Pramod	yah lāl qalam hai. ye donõ qalam lāl haĩ.
उषा	यहाँ कितनी पेंसिलें और क़लम हैं?
Uṣā	yahā̃ kitnī pensilẽ aur qalam haĩ?

प्रमोद यहाँ सिर्फ़ दो क़लम और दो पेंसिलें हैं, बस।
Pramod yahā̃ sirf do qalam aur do pensilẽ haĩ, bas.

Pramod Who is that man?
Usha He is Raju. Raju is a student.
Pramod I see. Who are those women?
Usha They are Mother and Uma. The tall lady is Mother.
Pramod What is this? Is it a book?
Usha No, it's not a book, it's a newspaper.
Pramod How many newspapers and books are there here?
Usha Here there are nine newspapers and seven books.
Pramod What are the books like? Are they big?
Usha Yes, they are big. What is that pen like?
Pramod This is a red pen. Both these pens are red.
Usha How many pencils and pens are there here?
Pramod Here there are only two pens and two pencils, that's all.

6 Interrogative words

Many questions contain interrogative words, such as 'who?', 'what?', 'why?', etc. In Hindi, such interrogative words begin with the letter क् **k**. They do not usually appear at the beginning of the sentence. Dialogue 2A introduces the interrogative pronouns क्या **kyā** *what?* and कौन **kaun** *who?*, both of which are both singular and plural, and the interrogative adjectives कैसा **kaisā** *of what kind?* and कितना **kitnā** *how much/many?*, which inflect like बड़ा **baṛā**.

7 Agreement of adjectives with two nouns or pronouns

An adjective can be used to qualify two or more nouns or pronouns. When the nouns or pronouns refer to things (inanimate objects), then usually the adjective will agree with the one nearest to it in the sentence. If the nouns or pronouns refer to animals or people, then the adjective will be masculine if all are males, feminine if all are female, and masculine if both sexes are represented:

वे हिन्दी अख़बार और किताबें महँगी हैं।

ve hindī akhbār aur kitābẽ mahãgī haĩ. — *Those Hindi newspapers and books are expensive.*

ये चप्पलें और जूते काले नहीं, नीले हैं।
ye cappalẽ aur jūte kāle nahī̃, nīle haĩ. *These sandals and shoes aren't black, they're blue.*

ये क़लम और पेंसिलें सस्ती हैं।
ye qalam aur pensilẽ sastī haĩ. *These pens and pencils are cheap.*

ये पेंसिलें और क़लम महँगे हैं।
ye pensilẽ aur qalam mahãge haĩ. *These pencils and pens are expensive.*

राधा और सीता लंबी हैं।
Rādhā aur Sītā lambī haĩ. *Radha and Sita are tall.* (Both female)

राम और रमेश मोटे हैं।
Ram aur Rameś moṭe haĩ. *Ram and Ramesh are fat.* (Both male)

राम और राधा छोटे हैं।
Rām aur Rādhā choṭe haĩ. *Ram and Radha are small.*

Note that the adjective दोनों **donõ**, *both, the two* does not always imply as much emphasis as its English equivalents, and may be left unexpressed in the English version of a Hindi sentence:

राधा और सीता दोनों लंबी हैं।
Rādhā aur Sītā donõ lambī haĩ. *Radha and Sita are (both) tall.*

हम दोनों अँग्रेज़ हैं।
ham donõ ãgrez haĩ. *We (two) are English.*

Dialogue 2B *Hello, how are you?*

प्रमोद नमस्ते राम जी।
Pramod namaste Rām jī.
राम नमस्ते प्रमोद भाई! क्या हाल है?
Rām namaste Pramod bhāī! kyā hāl hai?
प्रमोद मेहरबानी है, सब ठीक है। आप कैसे हैं?
Pramod meharbānī hai, sab ṭhīk hai. āp kaise haĩ?

राम	मैं भी ठीक हूँ, शुक्रिया। अच्छा प्रमोद, आज अहमद साहब यहाँ नहीं हैं?
Rām	maĩ bhī ṭhīk hū̃, śukriyā. acchā Pramod, āj Ahmad sāhab yahā̃ nahī̃ haĩ?
प्रमोद	नहीं, अहमद साहब और वर्मा जी दोनों बीमार हैं।
Pramod	nahī̃, Ahmad sāhab aur Varmā jī donõ bīmār haĩ.
राम	अफ़सोस है। आजकल कितने बुज़ुर्ग लोग बीमार हैं!
Rām	afsos hai. ājkal kitne buzurg log bīmār haĩ!
प्रमोद	हाँ, यह मौसम बहुत ख़राब है। यह लड़का कौन है, भाई साहब?
Pramod	hā̃, yah mausam bahut kharāb hai. yah laṛkā kaun hai, bhāī sāhab?
राम	यह रवि है। रवि, ये श्री कुमार हैं।
Rām	yah Ravi hai. Ravi, ye śrī Kumār haĩ.
रवि	नमस्ते जी।
Ravi	namaste jī.
प्रमोद	हलो रवि। तुम कैसे हो?
Pramod	halo Ravi. tum kaise ho?
रवि	मैं ठीक हूँ, धन्यवाद।
Ravi	maĩ ṭhīk hū̃, dhanyavād.
प्रमोद	तुम अच्छे बच्चो हो। माता-पिता कैसे हैं?
Pramod	tum acche bacce ho. mātā-pitā kaise haĩ?
रवि	माताजी अच्छी हैं, लेकिन पिताजी अच्छे नहीं हैं। वे बीमार हैं।
Ravi	mātājī acchī haĩ, lekin pitājī acche nahī̃ haĩ. ve bīmār haĩ.

Pramod	Hello Ram.
Ram	Hello Pramod, my friend! How are thing?
Pramod	Thank you, everything's fine. How are you?
Ram	I'm all right too, thanks. Now Pramod, isn't Mr Ahmad here today?
Pramod	No. Mr Ahmad and Mr Varma are both ill.
Ram	That's a pity. How many elderly people are ill these days!
Pramod	Yes this weather's very bad. Who is this boy (my friend)?
Ram	This is Ravi. Ravi, this is Mr Kumar.
Ravi	Hello (sir).
Pramod	Hello Ravi. How are you?
Ravi	I'm well, thank you.
Pramod	You're a good lad. How are your parents?
Ravi	Mother is well, but Father isn't well, he's ill.

8 Some conversational features

The customary Hindu greetings are नमस्ते **namaste** or नमस्कार

namaskār, often said with the hands folded in front of the chest. These are all-purpose greetings, covering the English 'Hello', 'Good morning', 'Goodbye', etc.

The word जी **jī** can always be added to a man's surname, where it approximates to 'Mr'–though its tone is rather more cordial; साहब **sāhab** has similar usage, more commonly with Muslim names (e.g. 'Ahmad sāhab' in the dialogue) or non-Indian names. जी **jī** can also be used after the first or given names of both men and women in situations of greater familiarity; it should always be added to terms of relationship referring to one's elders, as in माताजी **mātājī** *mother,* पिताजी **pitājī** *father,* both when addressing them directly or when speaking about them (or about somebody else's relatives). जी **jī** and साहब **sāhab** can also be used alone, approximating in sense to 'sir' though जी **jī** is considerably less formal.

भाई **bhāī,** literally 'brother', is commonly used between males of roughly equal status; भाई साहब **bhāī sāhab** is less familiar and can be used with more distant acquaintances and also with strangers–useful, for example, when approaching somebody in the street for directions. The same pattern of use applies with बहिन **bahin** *sister* among females. Use of these terms *between* the sexes is rather more restricted.

The expression क्या हाल है? **kyā hāl hai?** means literally 'What is [your] condition?', and is used in the sense 'How are things generally?'; it is a useful idiomatic expression, very common in conversation. मेहरबानी है **meharbānī hai** means 'It is [your] kindness', i.e. 'Thank you'. श्री **śrī** approximates to 'Mr'; the feminine form is श्रीमती **śrīmatī** *Mrs.* As in English, कुमारी **kumārī** *Miss* tends to be used in formal contexts only. Note the rhetorical use of कितना **kitnā** in the sentence आजकल कितने बुज़ुर्ग लोग बीमार हैं! **ājkal kitne buzurg log bīmār haĩ**! *What a lot of* [lit. *how many*] *elderly people are ill these days!*

There are two words in Hindi which translate 'Thank you': शुक्रिया **śukriyā** and धन्यवाद **dhanyavād.** These terms tend to be reserved for occasions of real obligation, when there is truly something to be grateful for: but increasingly they are being used along the lines of English 'Thank you', and learners should follow suit as this may well be what is expected of them.

The adjective अच्छा **acchā** *good* is used in speech with a wide range of meanings depending on the tone and stress with which it is pronounced. Its range covers 'Good!', 'Right then!', 'Ah, I see', 'Really', and so on.

Finally, note this very common usage:

आप कैसे हैं?	āp kaise haĩ?	*How are you?*	(male)
आप कैसी हैं?	āp kaisī haĩ?	*How are you?*	(female)

9 The agreement of adjectives

आप **āp** and तुम **tum** are grammatically plural pronouns even when they refer to just one person. Adjectives agreeing with them must therefore also be in the plural. This was seen in the last two examples, although it was not apparent in the feminine, where singular and plural adjectives are the same. When people whom one would address as आप **āp** are referred to in the third person, adjectives used of them must also be in the plural.

तुम अच्छे आदमी हो।	tum acche ādmī ho.	*You are a good man.*
आप बहुत लंबे हैं।	āp bahut lambe haĩ.	*You are very tall.*
राजा बहुत बड़े आदमी हैं।	rājā bahut baṛe ādmī haĩ.	*The king is a very important man.*
तुम छोटे नहीं हो।	tum choṭe nahī̃ ho.	*You are not small.*
वे बूढ़ी हैं।	ve būṛhī haĩ.	*She is old.*

These could all refer either to one or to several persons, but the context will usually make it clear which applies. To indicate that several people are referred to, the word लोग **log** *people* is sometimes added to the pronouns, giving आप लोग **āp log** and तुम लोग **tum log** *you (people)*; हम लोग **ham log** *we (people)*, and वे लोग **ve log** *those (people)* also occur. The same usage may apply with nouns: हिन्दू लोग **hindū log,** *Hindus.*

आप लोग मुसलमान हैं।	āp log musalmān haĩ.	*You are Muslims.*
तुम लोग बहुत ख़ुश हो।	tum log bahut k͟huś ho.	*You are very happy.*
हम लोग अँग्रेज़ हैं।	ham log ãgrez haĩ.	*We are English.*
वे लोग गुजराती हैं।	ve log gujarātī haĩ.	*They are Gujaratis.*

When a masculine noun which changes to -ए **-e** in the plural occurs with आप **āp** or तुम **tum,** then it must show the plural form even when only one person is being referred to. Feminine nouns, however, only show a plural ending when more than one person is involved.

तुम अच्छे बेटे हो।	tum acche beṭe ho.	*You are a good son.*
तुम बुरे बच्चे हो।	tum bure bacce ho.	*You are a bad child.*

आप अच्छी बेटी हैं।	āp acchī beṭī haĩ.	*You are a good daughter.*
आप लोग अच्छी बेटियाँ हैं।	āp log acchī beṭiyā̃ haĩ.	*You are good daughters.*

EXERCISE 2.1 Translate into English:

१	ये हिन्दी किताबें बहुत महँगी नहीं हैं।	ye hindī kitābẽ bahut mahãgī nahī̃ haĩ.
२	हम सब लोग बहुत ख़ुश हैं।	ham sab log bahut khuś haĩ.
३	तुम मोटे हो, लेकिन बहिन मोटी नहीं है।	tum moṭe ho, lekin bahin moṭī nahī̃ hai.
४	भाई साहब, आप कैसे हैं?	bhāī sāhab, āp kaise haĩ?
५	आज गोपाल और श्रीमती वर्मा यहाँ नहीं हैं।	āj Gopāl aur śrīmatī Varmā yahā̃ nahī̃ haĩ.
६	आज बच्चे भी बीमार हैं। अफ़सोस है।	āj bacce bhī bīmār haĩ. afsos hai.
७	वे जूते और चप्पलें बहुत सस्ती हैं।	ve jūte aur cappalẽ bahut sastī haĩ.
८	वह लंबा लड़का कौन है? क्या वह विद्यार्थी है?	vah lambā laṛkā kaun hai? kyā vah vidyārthī hai?
९	रवि और उमा दोनों अच्छे हैं लेकिन माताजी अच्छी नहीं हैं।	Ravi aur Umā donõ acche haĩ lekin mātājī acchī nahī̃ haĩ.
१०	क्या अहमद साहब और वर्मा जी दोनों मुसलमान हैं?	kyā Ahmad sāhab aur Varmā jī donõ musalmān haĩ?

EXERCISE 2.2 Translate into Hindi:

1 Who are those old men? Are they Indians?
2 No, they're not Indians, they are English.
3 Is Mr. Varma an important [big] man? Yes, he is a very important man.
4 How is Father? Thank you, he's fine.
5 Ram and Radha are both very tall. Yes, and Ram is fat [also].
6 What are those? They are expensive pens and pencils.
7 You are not a bad child. You are a good son.
8 What kind of table is it? It is long and black.
9 What is that big book like? It is very good.
10 Are you all Hindus? No, we are Hindus, but those people are Muslims.

Vocabulary

अख़बार	akhbār	*newspaper* (m.)
अफ़सोस	afsos	*regret, pity* (m.)
आज	āj	*today* (m.)
आजकल	ājkal	*nowadays*
औरत	aurat	*woman* (f.)
क़लम	qalam	*pen* (m./f.)
काला	kālā	*black*
कितना	kitnā	*how much/many?*
किताब	kitāb	*book* (f.)
कुमारी	kumārī	*unmarried girl; miss* (f.)
कैसा	kaisā	*of what kind?*
कौन	kaun	*who?*
क्या	kyā	*what?*
ख़राब	kharāb	*bad*
ख़ुश	khuś	*happy*
चप्पल	cappal	*sandal* (f.)
जूता	jūtā	*shoe* (m.)
ठीक	ṭhīk	*all right, correct, fine, O.K.*
तीन	tīn	*three*
धन्यवाद	dhanyavād	*thanks; thank you* (m.)
नमस्कार	namaskār	*greetings* (m.)
नीला	nīlā	*blue*
नौ	nau	*nine*
पेंसिल	pensil	*pencil* (f.)
बच्चा	baccā	*child* (m.)
बस	bas	*that's all*
बहिन (बहन)	bahin (bahan)	*sister* (f.)
बहुत	bahut	*very; much, many*
बीमार	bīmār	*ill*
बुज़ुर्ग	buzurg	*elderly*
बुरा	burā	*bad*
बूढ़ा	būṛhā	*old* (of people)
बेटा	beṭā	*son* (m.)
भाई	bhāī	*brother* (m.)
भी	bhī	*also, too; even*
महँगा	mahãgā	*expensive*
महिला	mahilā	*lady* (f.)
माता-पिता	mātā-pitā	*parents* (m.)
मुसलमान	musalmān	*Muslim* (m./f./adj.)
मेहरबानी	meharbānī	*kindness* (f.)

मोटा	moṭā	*fat, coarse*
मौसम	mausam	*weather* (m.)
लंबा	lambā	*tall* (of people, trees); *long*
लाल	lāl	*red*
विद्यार्थी	vidyārthī	*student* (m.)
शुक्रिया	śukriyā	*thanks; thank you* (m.)
श्री	śrī	*Mr.*
श्रीमती	śrīmatī	*Mrs.*
सब	sab	*all*
सस्ता	sastā	*cheap*
सात	sāt	*seven*
साहब	sāhab	*sir, master* (m.)
हलो	halo	*hello*
हाल	hāl	*condition, state* (m.)
हिन्दी	hindī	*Hindi* (f.)

Unit Three

Dialogue 3A *What is the new house like?*

मोहन	राम जी, नया मकान कैसा है?
Mohan	Rām jī, nayā makān kaisā hai?
राम	काफ़ी सुंदर है, और यहाँ से दूर भी नहीं है। मकान में पाँच कमरे हैं।
Rām	kāfī sundar hai, aur yahā̃ se dūr bhī nahī̃ hai. makān mẽ pā̃c kamre haĩ.
	हर कमरे में नया सामान है। दो कमरों में पलंग हैं। पलंगों पर नए कंबल और चादरें हैं।
	har kamre mẽ nayā sāmān hai. do kamrõ mẽ palaṅg haĩ. palaṅgõ par nae kambal aur cādarẽ haĩ.
	एक कमरे में बड़ी मेज़ और कई आराम कुरसियाँ हैं। मेज़ पर पंखा है।
	ek kamre mẽ baṛī mez aur kaī ārām kursiyā̃ haĩ. mez par paṅkhā hai.
मोहन	क्या खिड़कियों पर परदे हैं?
Mohan	kyā khiṛkiyõ par parde haĩ?
राम	चार कमरों में परदे हैं। सिर्फ़ रसोईघर में परदे नहीं हैं।
Rām	cār kamrõ mẽ parde haĩ. sirf rasoīghar mẽ parde nahī̃ haĩ.
मोहन	अच्छा। क्या घर में अलमारियाँ हैं?
Mohan	acchā. kyā ghar mẽ almāriyā̃ haĩ?
राम	हाँ, दो कमरों में पुरानी अलमारियाँ हैं, लेकिन एक कमरे में अलमारियाँ नई हैं।
Rām	hā̃, do kamrõ mẽ purānī almāriyā̃ haĩ, lekin ek kamre mẽ almāriyā̃ naī haĩ.
	एक दीवार पर, खिड़की से दरवाज़े तक बड़ी अलमारियाँ हैं।
	ek dīvār par, khiṛkī se darvāze tak baṛī almāriyā̃ haĩ.
	वह कमरा सचमुच बहुत सुंदर है। खिड़कियाँ काफ़ी बड़ी हैं, और दीवारों पर कई तस्वीरें हैं।

	vah kamrā sacmuc bahut sundar hai. khiṛkiyā̃ kāfī baṛī haĩ, aur dīvārõ par kaī tasvīrẽ haĩ.
मोहन	ठीक है—लेकिन किराया कितना है भाई?
Mohan	ṭhīk hai—lekin kirāyā kitnā hai bhāī?
राम	किराया भी बहुत नहीं, सिर्फ़ नौ सौ रुपये।
Rām	kirāyā bhī bahut nahī̃, sirf nau sau rupaye.
मोहन	बस! काफ़ी सस्ता है। मकान बहुत अच्छा है।
Mohan	bas! kāfī sastā hai. makān bahut acchā hai.

Mohan	Ram, what is the new house like?
Ram	It's pretty nice, and it's not far from here either. There are five rooms in the house. In every room there is new furniture. In two rooms there are beds. On the beds there are new blankets and sheets. In one room there's a big table and several armchairs. On the table there is a fan.
Mohan	Are there curtains on the windows?
Ram	There are curtains in four rooms. Only in the kitchen are there no curtains.
Mohan	I see. Are there cupboards in the house?
Ram	Yes, in two rooms there are old cupboards, but in one room the cupboards are new. On one wall there are big cupboards from the window to the door. That room really is very beautiful. The windows are quite big, and there are several pictures on the walls.
Ram	Fine–but how much is the rent (brother)?
Mohan	The rent's not much either, only nine hundred rupees [per month].
Ram	Is that all! It's quite cheap. The house is very good indeed.

10 Simple postpositions

In English, prepositions such as 'in', 'from', etc. precede the words to which they relate. In Hindi, such words are called postpositions, because they *follow* the words they govern. In Hindi there are five simple postpositions, so named because they consist of only one word. These are: में **mẽ** *in*; पर **par** *on*; तक **tak** *up to, as far as, until*; से **se** *from, with, by*; and को **ko** which, like से **se,** is used in a variety of senses:

दिल्ली में	dillī mẽ	*in Delhi*
मेज़ पर	mez par	*on the table*
बम्बई से	bambaī se	*from Bombay*

बस से	bas se	*by bus*
क़लम से	qalam se	*by/with pen*
आज तक	āj tak	*until today*
लन्दन तक	landan tak	*up to London*
रात को	rāt ko	*at night*
राम को	Rām ko	*to Ram*

11 Nouns with postpositions

The Hindi noun has two grammatical cases[1]: the direct and the oblique. So far in this course, all nouns have been in the direct case. The oblique case is the case that all nouns *must* take before postpositions. In the examples above, the nouns are all in the oblique case because they are governed by postpositions, although their case is not apparent from their forms.

Masculine nouns form the oblique before postpositions as follows:

Type 1

Singular					
कमरा	kamrā	*room*	कमरे में	kamre mẽ	*in the room*
लड़का	laṛkā	*boy*	लड़के से	laṛke se	*from the boy*
Plural					
कमरे	kamre	*rooms*	कमरों में	kamrõ mẽ	*in the rooms*
लड़के	laṛke	*boys*	लड़कों से	laṛkõ se	*from the boys*

Type 2

Singular					
मकान	makān	*house*	मकान में	makān mẽ	*in the house*
आदमी	ādmī	*man*	आदमी से	ādmī se	*from the man*
हिन्दू	hindū	*Hindu*	हिन्दू से	hindū se	*from the Hindu*
Plural					
मकान	makān	*houses*	मकानों में	makānõ mẽ	*in the houses*
आदमी	ādmī	*men*	आदमियों से	ādmiyõ se	*from the men*
हिन्दू	hindū	*Hindus*	हिन्दुओं से	hinduõ se	*from the Hindus*

1 There is also a vocative, which will be introduced in Unit 5.

Feminine nouns form the oblique before postpositions as follows:

Type 1

Singular

लड़की	laṛkī	*girl*	लड़की से	laṛkī se	*from the girl*
शक्ति	śakti	*power*	शक्ति से	śakti se	*with power*
बुढ़िया	buṛhiyā	*old woman*	बुढ़िया से	buṛhiyā se	*from the old woman*

Plural

लड़कियाँ	laṛkiyā̃	*girls*	लड़कियों से	laṛkiyõ se	*from the girls*
शक्तियाँ	śaktiyā̃	*powers*	शक्तियों से	śaktiyõ se	*with the powers*
बुढ़ियाँ	buṛhiyā̃	*old women*	बुढ़ियों से	buṛhiyõ se	*from the old women*

Type 2

Singular

मेज़	mez	*table*	मेज़ पर	mez par	*on the table*
क़मीज़	qamīz	*shirt*	क़मीज़ में	qamīz mẽ	*in the shirt*
माता	mātā	*mother*	माता से	mātā se	*from the mother*

Plural

मेज़ें	mezẽ	*tables*	मेज़ों पर	mezõ par	*on the tables*
क़मीज़ें	qamīzẽ	*shirts*	क़मीज़ों में	qamīzõ mẽ	*in shirts*
माताएँ	mātāẽ	*mothers*	माताओं से	mātāõ se	*from the mothers*

Thus only Type 1 masculine nouns change at all in the oblique singular; and all nouns end in -ओं **-õ** in the oblique plural. Notice how nouns ending in -ऊ **-ū** shorten it before the oblique plural ending: हिन्दू **hindū**, हिन्दुओं **hinduõ**; and similarly how nouns ending in -ई **-ī** both shorten the vowel *and* insert a य् **y:** आदमी **ādmī**, आदमियों **ādmiyõ**:

मकान में सात कमरे हैं।

makān mẽ sāt kamre haĩ. — *In the house there are seven rooms.*

एक कमरे में दो दरवाज़े हैं।

ek kamre mẽ do darvāze haĩ. — *In one room there are two doors.*

खिड़कियों पर चार हरे परदे हैं।

khiṛkiyõ par cār hare parde haĩ. — *On the windows there are four green curtains.*

दीवारों पर नौ सुन्दर तस्वीरें हैं।

dīvārõ par nau sundar tasvīrẽ haĩ. — *On the walls there are nine beautiful pictures.*

कमरे में तीन मेज़ें भी हैं।
kamre mẽ tīn mezẽ bhī haĩ. — *In the room there are also three tables.*

एक मेज़ पर छह किताबें हैं।
ek mez par chah kitābẽ haĩ. — *On one table there are six books.*

आठ और किताबें अलमारी में हैं।
āṭh aur kitābẽ almārī mẽ haĩ. — *Eight more books are in the cupboard.*

Note that to express the sense 'There is…', 'There are …', Hindi inverts the word order:

क़लम मेज़ पर हैं।	qalam mez par haĩ.	*The pens are on the table.*
मेज़ पर क़लम हैं।	mez par qalam haĩ.	*There are pens on the table.*
कोट कुरसी पर है।	koṭ kursī par hai.	*The coat is on the chair.*
कुरसी पर कोट है।	kursī par koṭ hai.	*There is a coat on the chair.*

Dialogue 3B *Are there any large rooms in this hotel?*

श्री पटेल उन छोटे होटलों में सब कमरे बहुत छोटे हैं। क्या इस होटल में कुछ बड़े कमरे हैं?

śrī Paṭel un choṭe hoṭalõ mẽ sab kamre bahut choṭe haĩ. kyā is hoṭal mẽ kuch baṛe kamre haĩ?

मुजीब साहब जी हाँ, हैं। इन कमरों में से तीन काफ़ी बड़े हैं और पाँच छोटे।

Mujīb sāhab jī hā̃, haĩ. in kamrõ mẽ se tīn kāfī baṛe haĩ aur pā̃c choṭe.

श्री पटेल क्या उस हरे कमरे में दो पलंग हैं? वह कैसा कमरा है?

śrī Paṭel kyā us hare kamre mẽ do palaṅg haĩ? vah kaisā kamrā hai?

मुजीब साहब	यह बड़ा कमरा है। इस कमरे में दो पलंग और दो अलमारियाँ हैं।
Mujīb sāhab	yah baṛā kamrā hai. is kamre mẽ do palaṅg aur do almāriyā̃ haĩ.
	दूसरे कमरों में अलमारियाँ नहीं हैं।
	dūsre kamrõ mẽ almāriyā̃ nahī̃ haĩ.
श्री पटेल	अच्छा, ठीक है। उन अलमारियों में क्या है?
śrī Paṭel	acchā, ṭhīk hai. un almāriyõ mẽ kyā hai?
मुजीब साहब	इस बड़ी अलमारी में कुछ साफ़ चादरें हैं, और दूसरी अलमारी में कुछ भारी कंबल। यहाँ रात को काफ़ी...
Mujīb sāhab	is baṛī almārī mẽ kuch sāf cādarẽ haĩ, aur dūsrī almārī mẽ kuch bhārī kambal. yahā̃ rāt ko kāfī...
श्री पटेल	हाँ, हाँ, ठीक है। क्या उस पलंग पर साफ़ चादरें हैं?
śrī Paṭel	hā̃, hā̃, ṭhīk hai. kyā us palaṅg par sāf cādarẽ haĩ?
मुजीब साहब	अभी तक नहीं। पटेल जी, आप कहाँ से हैं? दिल्ली से?
Mujīb sāhab	abhī tak nahī̃. Paṭel jī, āp kahā̃ se haĩ? dillī se?
श्री पटेल	जी नहीं, दिल्ली से नहीं, बंबई से हूँ। मैं अभी यहाँ सोमवार तक हूँ।
śrī Paṭel	jī nahī̃, dillī se nahī̃, bambaī se hū̃. maĩ abhī yahā̃ somvār tak hū̃.

Mr Patel	In those small hotels all the rooms are very small. Are there some big rooms in this hotel?
Mujib Sahib	Yes, there are. Out of these rooms, three are quite big and five are small.
Mr Patel	Are there two beds in that green room? What kind of room is it?
Mujib Sahib	This is a big room. In this room there are two beds and two cupboards. There aren't cupboards in the other rooms.
Mr Patel	All right, that's fine. What is in those cupboards?
Mujib Sahib	In this big cupboard there are some clean sheets, and in the other cupboard some heavy blankets. In the night here it's quite ...
Mr Patel	Yes, yes, that's fine. Are there clean sheets on that bed?
Mujib Sahib	Not yet. Mr Patel, where are you from? Delhi?
Mr Patel	No, I'm not from Delhi, I'm from Bombay. Just now I'm here until Monday.

12 Adjectives in the oblique case

Adjectives must agree with the nouns they qualify: if a noun is in the oblique case because it is followed by a postposition, then any adjective qualifying that noun must also be in the oblique. Inflecting adjectives like बड़ा **baṛā** *big* form both the masculine singular oblique and the masculine plural oblique in -ए **-e,** giving बड़े **baṛe**; and both the feminine singular and the feminine plural in -ई **-ī**, giving बड़ी **baṛī**. Invariable adjectives such as साफ़ **sāf** *clean* never change.

बड़े कमरे में	baṛe kamre mẽ	*in the large room*
बड़े कमरों में	baṛe kamrõ mẽ	*in the large rooms*
छोटे मकान में	choṭe makān mẽ	*in the small house*
छोटे मकानों में	choṭe makānõ mẽ	*in the small houses*
बड़ी अलमारी में	baṛī almārī mẽ	*in the large cupboard*
बड़ी अलमारियों में	baṛī almāriyõ mẽ	*in the large cupboards*
छोटी मेज़ पर	choṭī mez par	*on the small table*
छोटी मेज़ों पर	choṭī mezõ par	*on the small tables*
लाल दरवाज़े पर	lāl darvāze par	*on the red door*
सफ़ेद दीवारों पर	safed dīvārõ par	*on the white walls*

The oblique forms of यह **yah,** वह **vah** ये **ye** and वे **ve** are shown below:

यह कमरा	yah kamrā	*this room*	इस कमरे में	is kamre mẽ	*in this room*
वह मेज	vah mez	*that table*	उस मेज़ पर	us mez par	*on that table*
ये कमरे	ye kamre	*these rooms*	इन कमरों में	in kamrõ mẽ	*in these rooms*
वे मेज़ें	ve mezẽ	*those tables*	उन मेज़ों पर	un mezõ par	*on those tables*

EXERCISE 3.1 Put the following into the oblique followed by the postposition में **mẽ** in column one, पर **par** in column two, and से **se** in column three:

बड़े कमरे	साफ़ मेजें	मोटे आदमी
baṛe kamre	sāf mezẽ	moṭe ādmī
छोटे मकान	यह नया पलंग	नीली पेंसिल
choṭe makān	yah nayā palaṅg	nīlī pensil
हरी किताब	लाल कुरसी	लंबी लड़कियाँ
harī kitāb	lāl kursī	lambī laṛkiyā̃
सस्ता होटल	दूसरी खिड़कियाँ	वह क़लम
sastā hoṭal	dūsrī khiṛkiyā̃	vah qalam
पुरानी अलमारियाँ	ये परदे	वे बसें
purānī almāriyā̃	ye parde	ve basẽ

EXERCISE 3.2 Translate into English:

यह एक नया मकान है। इस मकान में सात कमरे हैं। इन कमरों में से एक बहुत बड़ा कमरा है, दूसरे कमरे छोटे हैं। बड़े कमरे में दीवारें सफ़ेद हैं, और बहुत साफ़। एक दीवार में दो खिड़कियाँ हैं और उन पर हरे परदे हैं। एक दूसरी दीवार पर तीन सुन्दर तस्वीरें हैं। कमरे में तीन मेज़ें हैं, एक बड़ी और दो छोटी। दो अलमारियाँ और कई कुरसियाँ भी हैं। बड़ी मेज़ पर एक काला क़लम और दो पेंसिलें हैं। छोटे कमरों में भी कुछ मेज़ें और कुरसियाँ हैं, लेकिन अभी तक खिड़कियों पर परदे नहीं हैं। नए परदे कहाँ हैं? अभी यहाँ इस बड़ी अलमारी में हैं।

yah ek nayā makān hai. is makān mẽ sāt kamre haĩ. in kamrõ mẽ se ek bahut baṛā kamrā hai, dūsre kamre choṭe haĩ. baṛe kamre mẽ dīvārẽ safed haĩ, aur bahut sāf. ek dīvār mẽ do khiṛkiyā̃ haĩ aur un par hare parde haĩ. ek dūsrī dīvār par tīn sundar tasvīrẽ haĩ. kamre mẽ tīn mezẽ haĩ, ek baṛī aur do choṭī. do almāriyā̃ aur kaī kursiyā̃ bhī haĩ. baṛī mez par ek kālā qalam aur do pensilẽ haĩ. choṭe kamrõ mẽ bhī kuch mezẽ aur kursiyā̃ haĩ, lekin abhī tak khiṛkiyõ par parde nahī̃ haĩ. nae parde kahā̃ haĩ? abhī yahā̃ is baṛī almārī mẽ haĩ.

EXERCISE 3.3 Translate into Hindi:

1 On those beds there are clean sheets and heavy blankets.
2 In these large cupboards there are several old books.
3 In those small hotels all the rooms are cheap.
4 On the other walls there are several beautiful pictures.
5 In that room there are not curtains on the windows.
6 What kind of fan is there on that table?
7 How many people are there in this house?
8 Delhi is really quite far from Bombay.
9 How many chairs are there in the kitchen?
10 There are some new newspapers and books on the long table.

Vocabulary

अभी	abhī	*right now*
अभी तक	abhī tak	*yet, up to now*
अलमारी	almārī	*cupboard* (f.)
आठ	āṭh	*eight*
आराम	ārām	*rest, comfort* (m.)
आराम-कुरसी	ārām-kursī	*armchair* (f.)
कंबल	kambal	*blanket* (m.)
कई	kaī	*several*
कहाँ	kahā̃	*where?*
काफ़ी	kāfī	*quite, quite a few; enough; very*
किराया	kirāyā	*rent, fare* (m.)

कुछ	kuch	*some*
को	ko	*to* (etc.)
कोट	koṭ	*coat* (m.)
खिड़की	khiṛkī	*window* (f.)
घर	ghar	*house, home* (m.)
चादर	cādar	*sheet* (f.)
छह	chah	*six*
तक	tak	*up to, as far as, unitl*
तस्वीर	tasvīr	*picture* (f.)
दरवाज़ा	darvāzā	*door* (m.)
दिल्ली	dillī	*Delhi* (f.)
दीवार	dīvār	*wall* (f.)
दूर	dūr	*far, distant; distance* (f.)
दूसरा	dūsrā	*second, other*
नया	nayā	*new*
पंखा	paṅkhā	*fan* (m.)
पर	par	*on; at* (etc.)
परदा	pardā	*curtain, purdah* (m.)
पलंग	palaṅg	*bed* (m.)
पाँच	pā̃c	*five*
पुराना	purānā	*old* (not of people)
बंबई	bambaī	*Bombay* (f.)
बस	bas	*bus* (f.)
भारी	bhārī	*heavy*
में	mẽ	*in*
में से	mẽ se	*from amongst, out of*
रसोईघर	rasoīghar	*kitchen* (m.)
रात	rāt	*night* (f.)
रुपया	rupayā	*rupee* (m.)
लन्दन	landan	*London* (m.)
सचमुच	sacmuc	*really, truly*
सामान	sāmān	*furniture, luggage, goods* (m.)
सुंदर	sundar	*beautiful, nice*
से	se	*from* (etc.)
सोमवार	somvār	*Monday* (m.)
सौ	sau	*hundred*
हर	har	*every, each*
हरा	harā	*green*
होटल	hoṭal	*hoṭel, café* (m.)

Unit Four

Dialogue 4A *Is the new house better than the old one?*

विनोद क्या नया मकान पुराने मकान से अच्छा है? नया बग़ीचा कैसा है?
Vinod kyā nayā makān purāne makān se acchā hai? nayā bagīcā kaisā hai?

राम नया मकान यहाँ शहर में है और पुराना मकान गाँव में था। गाँव में बड़ा बाग़ था।
Rām nayā makān yahā̃ śahar mẽ hai aur purānā makān gā̃v mẽ thā. gā̃v mẽ baṛā bāg thā.

वहाँ पौधे, सुंदर फूल और फल थे! पर नया बग़ीचा और छोटा है।
vahā̃ paudhe, sundar phūl aur phal the! par nayā bagīcā aur choṭā hai.

विनोद क्या वह गाँव इस शहर से सचमुच अच्छा था?
Vinod kyā vah gā̃v is śahar se sacmuc acchā thā?

राम हाँ, गाँव ज़्यादा अच्छा था क्योंकि वहाँ लोग कम थे और गाड़ियाँ भी बहुत कम थीं।
Rām hā̃, gā̃v zyādā acchā thā kyõki vahā̃ log kam the aur gāṛiyā̃ bhī bahut kam thī̃.

हरी घास थी, लंबे पेड़ थे, बड़े खेत थे। शहर में क्या है—गाड़ियाँ, मकान, लोग और बड़ी सड़कें!
harī ghās thī, lambe peṛ the, baṛe khet the. śahar mẽ kyā hai —gāṛiyā̃, makān, log aur baṛī saṛakẽ!

विनोद पर गाँव में दुकानें अच्छी नहीं थीं! शहर में दुकानें और अच्छी हैं।
Vinod par gā̃v mẽ dukānẽ acchī nahī̃ thī̃! śahar mẽ dukānẽ aur acchī haĩ.

राम हाँ ज़रूर, पर दूध था, घी था, मक्खन था, सब्ज़ियाँ और कपड़े भी थे।

Rām hã̄ zarūr, par dūdh thā, ghī thā, makkhan thā, sabziyā̃ aur kapṛe bhī the.
गाँव में ज़िंदगी और सरल थी, और आसान थी। वहाँ मुश्किलें बहुत कम थीं।
gā̃v mẽ zindagī aur saral thī̃, aur āsān thī. vahā̃ muśkilẽ bahut kam thī̃.

विनोद अरे भाई, शहर में ज़िंदगी मुश्किल ज़रूर है, पर ज़्यादा दिलचस्प भी है।
Vinod are bhāī, śahar mẽ zindagī muśkil zarūr hai, par zyādā dilcasp bhī hai.

राम नहीं, गाँव ज़्यादा दिलचस्प है और वे दिन सबसे अच्छे दिन थे!
Rām nahī̃, gā̃v zyādā dilcasp hai aur ve din sabse acche din the!

Vinod Is the new house better than the old house? What is the new garden like?

Ram The new house is here in the town and the old house was in the village. In the village there was a big garden. There were plants, lovely flowers and fruits! But the new garden is smaller.

Vinod Was that village really better than this town?

Ram Yes, the village was better because the people were fewer there and the cars too were far fewer. There was green grass, there were tall trees, there were big fields. What is there in the town–cars, houses, people and big roads!

Vinod But in the village the shops were not good! In the town the shops are better.

Ram Yes of course, but there was milk, there was ghee, there was butter, there were vegetables and clothes too. In the village, life was simpler, easier. There the difficulties were very few.

Vinod Oh (brother), in the town life is difficult of course, but it is also more interesting.

Ram No, the village is more interesting, and those days were the best days!

13 'Was' and 'were'

In Hindi, 'was' and 'were' have both masculine and feminine forms: the verb must agree with its subject in both number and gender. If the subject is a pronoun, the gender will be that of the noun to which the pronoun refers. The verbal forms and their pronouns are given below:

		Masculine		Feminine		
मैं	maĩ	था	thā	थी	thī	*I was*
तू	tū	था	thā	थी	thī	*you were*
यह	yah	था	thā	थी	thī	*this, he, she, it was*
वह	vah	था	thā	थी	thī	*that, he, she, it was*
हम	ham	थे	the	थीं	thī̃	*we were*
तुम	tum	थे	the	थीं	thī̃	*you were*
आप	āp	थे	the	थीं	thī̃	*you were*
ये	ye	थे	the	थीं	thī̃	*they, those, were*
वे	ve	थे	the	थीं	thī̃	*they, those, were*

The negative particles used with this tense are नहीं **nahī̃,** for ordinary neutral statements, and न **na** which carries an emphasis of some kind:

पिता जी वहाँ नहीं थे।	pitā jī vahā̃ nahī̃ the.	*Father was not there.*
मैं कल घर पर था।	maĩ kal ghar par thā.	*I was at home yesterday.*
राधा घर में नहीं थी।	Rādhā ghar mẽ nahī̃ thī.	*Radha was not in the house.*
किताबें मेज़ पर थीं।	kitābẽ mez par thī̃.	*The books were on the table.*
बहू मोटी नहीं थी।	bahū moṭī nahī̃ thī.	*The bride was not fat.*

Notice how घर **ghar** means 'a house' or 'a home'; घर पर **ghar par** means 'at home', but घर में **ghar mẽ** means 'in the house'. कल **kal** is an adverb meaning 'one day away from today', so that it means 'yesterday' or 'tomorrow' depending on context.

14 Comparison of adjectives

There are no special forms of the Hindi adjective corresponding to the English series 'good – better – best'. When two things or people are compared, the postposition से **se** is used.

राम राधा से लंबा है।	Rām Rādhā se lambā hai.	*Ram is taller than Radha.*
राधा राम से लंबी है।	Rādhā Rām se lambī hai.	*Radha is taller than Ram.*

If the comparative degree is required without the object of comparison being expressed ('he is taller', without 'than....'), then the words और **aur** *more*, or और भी **aur bhī** *more, even more* are placed before the adjective: और लंबा **aur lambā** *taller*, और भी लंबा **aur bhī lambā** *taller, even taller*. For the superlative, the words सब से **sab se** are placed before the adjective: सब से लंबा **sab se lambā** *tallest (of all)*, सब से अच्छा **sab se acchā** *best (of all)*.

The words ज़्यादा **zyādā** *more, much, too much* and कम **kam** *little, less* are also used in comparisons: ज़्यादा अच्छा **zyādā acchā** *better*; कम अच्छा **kam acchā** *less good*.

राम रमेश से लंबा है।	Rām Rameś se lambā hai.	*Ram is taller than Ramesh.*
राधा और भी लंबी है, लेकिन मैं सब से लंबा हूँ।	Rādhā aur bhī lambī hai, lekin maĩ sab se lambā hū̃.	*Radha is even taller, but I am the tallest.*
यह किताब उस किताब से अच्छी है।	yah kitāb us kitāb se acchī hai.	*This book is better than that book.*
इन किताबों में से यह सब से अच्छी है।	in kitābõ mẽ se yah sab se acchī hai.	*From amongst these books this one is the best.*
यह कपड़ा ज़्यादा मोटा है।	yah kapṛā zyādā moṭā hai.	*This cloth is thicker.*
ये चीज़ें कम महँगी हैं।	ye cīzẽ kam mahãgī haĩ.	*These things are less dear.*
दस आठ से ज़्यादा है।	das āṭh se zyādā hai.	*Ten is more than eight.*
छह आठ से कम है।	chah āṭh se kam hai.	*Six is less than eight.*

Dialogue 4B *Do you know where Ramdas is?*

विमल	क्या आपको मालूम है कि रामदास कहाँ है?
Vimal	kyā āpko mālūm hai ki Rāmdās kahā̃ hai?
आनन्द	जी हाँ, वह घर पर है। उसको ज़ुकाम है।
Ānand	jī hā̃, vah ghar par hai. usko zukām hai.
विमल	वह कल भी घर पर था! विनोद कहाँ है?
Vimal	vah kal bhī ghar par thā! Vinod kahā̃ hai?
आनन्द	वह भी आज यहाँ नहीं है।
Ānand	vah bhī āj yahā̃ nahī̃ hai.

विमल	क्यों? क्या बात है?
Vimal	kyõ? kyā bāt hai?
आनन्द	उसको बुख़ार है, वह बहुत बीमार है।
Ānand	usko bukhār hai, vah bahut bīmār hai.
विमल	मुझको अफ़सोस है कि वे दोनों बीमार हैं क्योंकि आज काफ़ी काम है।
Vimal	mujhko afsos hai ki ve donõ bīmār haĩ kyõki āj kāfī kām hai.
आनन्द	क्या नया दरवाज़ा आपको पसंद है?
Ānand	kyā nayā darvāzā āpko pasand hai?
विमल	जी नहीं, क्योंकि मुझको वह पीला रंग नहीं पसंद है।
Vimal	jī nahī̃, kyõki mujhko vah pīlā raṅg nahī̃ pasand hai.
आनन्द	आपको कौनसा रंग पसंद है?
Ānand	āpko kaunsā raṅg pasand hai?
विमल	घर पर सभी दरवाज़े हरे हैं; मुझको हलका हरा रंग सबसे ज़्यादा पसंद है।
Vimal	ghar par sabhī darvāze hare haĩ; mujhko halkā harā raṅg sabse zyādā pasand hai.
आनन्द	अच्छा। मुझको मालूम नहीं था कि आपको पीला रंग पसंद नहीं।
Ānand	acchā. mujhko mālūm nahī̃ thā ki āpko pīlā raṅg pasand nahī̃.
	पर मुझको ख़ुशी है कि वह दरवाज़ा अब काला नहीं है।
	par mujhko khuśī hai ki vah darvāzā ab kālā nahī̃ hai.

Vimal	Do you know where Ramdas is?
Anand	Yes, he's at home. He's got a cold.
Vimal	He was at home yesterday too! Where's Vinod?
Anand	He's not here today either.
Vimal	Why? What's the matter?
Anand	He's got a temperature, he's very sick.
Vimal	I'm sorry that they're both ill because there's a lot of work today.
Anand	Do you like the new door?
Vimal	No, because I don't like that yellow colour.
Anand	Which colour do you like?
Vimal	At home all the doors are green; I like light green best.
Anand	All right. I didn't know that you didn't like yellow. But I'm glad that that door's not black now.

15 Pronouns with simple postpositions

The oblique forms of the pronouns used before postpositions are set out below with the direct forms already given:

Singular				**Plural**			
मैं	maĩ	मुझ	mujh	हम	ham	हम	ham
तू	tū	तुझ	tujh	तुम	tum	तुम	tum
यह	yah	इस	is	आप	āp	आप	āp
वह	vah	उस	us	ये	ye	इन	in
कौन	kaun	किस	kis	वे	ve	उन	un
क्या	kyā	किस	kis	कौन	kaun	किन	kin
				क्या	kyā	किन	kin

आप मुझ से लंबे हैं।	āp mujh se lambe haĩ.	*You are taller than me.*
मैं तुम से बड़ा हूँ।	maĩ tum se baṛā hũ.	*I am bigger than you.*
वे हम से बड़े हैं।	ve ham se baṛe haĩ.	*They are older than us.*
ये उन से सस्ते हैं।	ye un se saste haĩ.	*These are cheaper than those.*

Postpositions following pronouns may be written separately or as one word: मुझ से **mujh se**, मुझसे **mujhse**.

16 Some constructions with को *ko*

Many different constructions use the postposition को **ko.** In the following usages, को **ko** roughly translates as 'to' with regard to the person or pronoun it governs. Four nouns are introduced here with this construction:

जुकाम	zukām (m.)	*a cold*
बुख़ार	bukhār (m.)	*fever*
अफ़सोस	afsos (m.)	*regret*
ख़ुशी	khuśī (f.)	*happiness*

The construction translates literally (in the first example below) as 'to you a cold is' with the noun as the grammatical subject of the verb. The last two examples are similar in construction, but introduce two adjectives:

पसंद	pasand	*pleasing*
मालूम	mālūm	*known*

तुमको जुकाम है।	tumko zukām hai.	*You have a cold.*
राम को बुख़ार है।	rām ko bukhār hai.	*Ram has a fever.*
लन्दन हमको पसंद है।	landan hamko pasand hai.	*We like London.*
उनको ख़ुशी है।	unko khuśī hai.	*They are glad.*
मुझको अफ़सोस है।	mujhko afsos hai.	*I am sorry.*
मुझको मालूम है।	mujhko mālūm hai.	*I know.*
हमको मालूम नहीं।	hamko mālūm nahī̃.	*We don't know.*

The construction of the last four examples can be extended to express the sense 'I am glad *that*...', 'I am sorry *that*...', 'Do you know...'. This is done by adding the particle कि ki, here equivalent to 'that' in the English sentence, followed by the statement in the usual word order:

मुझको अफ़सोस है कि तुम ठीक नहीं हो। *I am sorry that you are not all right.*
mujhko afsos hai ki tum ṭhīk nahī̃ ho.

हमको बड़ी ख़ुशी है कि आप सब लोग यहाँ हैं। *We are very glad that all of you are here.*
hamko baṛī khuśī hai ki āp sab log yahā̃ haĩ.

क्या आपको मालूम है कि राम कहाँ है? *Do you know where Ram is?*
kyā āpko mālūm hai ki Rām kahā̃ hai?

मुझको नहीं मालूम कि राम कहाँ है। *I don't know where Ram is.*
mujhko nahī̃ mālūm ki Rām kahā̃ hai?

क्या तुमको मालूम है कि उस कमरे में कितने लोग हैं? *Do you know how many people are in that room?*
kyā tumko mālūm hai ki us kamre mẽ kitne log haĩ?

EXERCISE 4.1 Translate into English:

ये नए मकान मुझको बहुत पसंद हैं। इस सड़क पर चार नए मकान हैं, और इन में से यह लाल मकान सबसे छोटा है। यह लाल रंग बहुत सुंदर है, और बच्चों को बहुत पसंद है। लाल रंग किसको पसंद नहीं? मुझको मालूम नहीं कि दूसरे मकानों में कितने कमरे हैं, पर इस में छह हैं। ये सब काफ़ी बड़े हैं। एक सुंदर बग़ीचा भी है। पुराना मकान इस मकान से बहुत बड़ा था, पर मुझको पसंद नहीं था क्योंकि उसमें सभी कमरे बहुत छोटे थे। दूसरे नए मकानों में कितने लोग हैं, यह मुझको मालूम नहीं। इस मकान में हम चार लोग हैं; हम लोग बहुत ख़ुश हैं।

EXERCISE 4.2 Translate into Hindi:

1. Do you know where Father was yesterday?
2. He was sorry that I had a cold and a temperature.
3. We are happy that you like London.
4. Ram is taller than Vinod but Vimal is tallest.
5. Is the new house bigger than the old house? Yes, but the old house was more beautiful.
6. Which of these books do you like best?
7. Who knows where Bombay is?
8. The children liked the new garden less.
9. Did they know that there weren't shops in the village?
10. In Delhi life was difficult but more interesting.

Vocabulary

अरे	are	*Oh! Hey! Come off it!*
आसान	āsān	*easy*
कपड़ा	kapṛā	*cloth; garment* (usually pl.) (m.)
कम	kam	*little, less*
कल	kal	*yesterday; tomorrow* (m.)
काम	kām	*work* (m.)
कि	ki	*that* (conj.)
कौनसा	kaunsā	*which?*
क्यों	kyõ	*why?*
क्योंकि	kyõki	*because*
ख़ुशी	khuśī	*happiness, pleasure* (f.)
खेत	khet	*field, farming land* (m.)
गाँव	gā̃v	*village* (m.)
गाड़ी	gāṛī	*car; train* (f.)
घर पर	ghar par	*at home*
घास	ghās	*grass* (f.)
घी	ghī	*clarified butter, ghee* (m.)
चीज़	cīz	*thing* (f.)
ज़रूर	zarūr	*of course, certainly*
ज़िन्दगी	zindagī	*life* (f.)
ज़ुकाम	zukām	*a cold, catarrh* (m.)
ज़्यादा	zyādā	*more, much, too much*
था	thā	*was; were* (with **tū**)
थीं	thī̃	*were*
थी	thī	*was; were* (with **tū**)
थे	the	*were*
दस	das	*ten*
दिन	din	*day* (m.)
दिलचस्प	dilcasp	*interesting*
दुकान	dukān	*shop* (f.)
दूध	dūdh	*milk* (m.)
न	na	*not*
पर	par	*but*
पसंद	pasand	*pleasing, favourite; liking* (f.)
पीला	pīlā	*yellow*
पेड़	peṛ	*tree* (m.)
पौधा	paudhā	*plant* (m.)
फल	phal	*fruit* (m.)
फूल	phūl	*flower* (m.)
बग़ीचा	bag̠īcā	*garden* (m.)

बाग़	bāg	*garden, large garden* (m.)
बात	bāt	*thing, matter, idea, thing said* (f.)
बुख़ार	bukhār	*temperature, fever* (m.)
मक्खन	makkhan	*butter* (m.)
मालूम	mālūm	*known*
मुश्किल	muśkil	*difficult; difficulty* (f.)
रंग	raṅg	*colour* (m.)
शहर	śahar	*town, city* (m.)
सड़क	saṛak	*road* (f.)
सब्ज़ी	sabzī	*vegetable* (f.)
सभी	sabhī	*all* (emphatic)
सरल	saral	*simple, easy*
हलका	halkā	*light* (of weight, colour, etc.)

Unit Five

Dialogue 5A *Mr Varma comes to tea*

कमला नमस्ते वर्मा जी। कहिए, तबियत कैसी है?
Kamlā namaste Varmā jī. kahie, tabiyat kaisī hai?
वर्मा जी नमस्कार कमला जी। शुक्रिया, मैं अच्छा हूँ। आप बताइए, क्या हाल है?
Varmā jī namaskār Kamlā jī. śukriyā, maĩ acchā hū̃. āp batāie, kyā hāl hai?
कमला बस, ठीक है। आइए, बैठिए, चाय तैयार है। बेटे, कुरसियाँ लाओ और दूसरे बच्चों को बुलाओ। उनसे कहो कि चाय तैयार है।
Kamlā bas, ṭhīk hai. āie, baiṭhie, cāy taiyār hai. beṭe, kursiyā̃ lāo aur dūsre baccõ ko bulāo. unse kaho ki cāy taiyār hai.
रवि वे लोग अभी यहाँ नहीं हैं, अम्माँ, वे अभी स्कूल में हैं।
Ravi ve log abhī yahā̃ nahī̃ haĩ, ammā̃, ve abhī skūl mẽ haĩ.
कमला अच्छा, तुम बैठो। उधर मत बैठो, इधर बैठो। वर्मा जी को यह प्याला दो।
Kamlā acchā, tum baiṭho. udhar mat baiṭho, idhar baiṭho. Varmā jī ko yah pyālā do.
रवि यह लीजिए वर्मा जी। अम्माँ, मुझको भी चाय दो।
Ravi yah lījie Varmā jī. ammā̃, mujhko bhī cāy do.
कमला तुम चाय मत पियो, दूध पियो। और सुनो बेटे, वर्मा जी को चीनी भी दो।
Kamlā tum cāy mat piyo, dūdh piyo. aur suno beṭe, Varmā jī ko cīnī bhī do.
वर्मा जी देखो रवि, यह चम्मच बड़ा है। इसको लो और मुझको छोटा चम्मच दो।
Varmā jī dekho Ravi, yah cammac baṛā hai. isko lo aur mujhko choṭā cammac do.
कमला वर्मा जी, कुछ और चीनी लीजिएगा, यह बहुत कम है!
Kamlā Varmā jī, kuch aur cīnī lījiegā, yah bahut kam hai!
वर्मा जी बस, बस! यह ठीक है। मुझको ज़्यादा मीठी चाय पसंद नहीं, धन्यवाद।
Varmā jī bas, bas! yah ṭhīk hai. mujhko zyādā mīṭhī cāy pasand nahī̃, dhanyavād.

Kamala Hello Mr Varma. (Say,)[1] how are you?
Mr Varma Hello Kamala jī. Thank you, I'm well. (You tell,) how are things?
Kamala Well,[2] things are OK. Come, sit down, tea's ready. Son, bring the chairs and call the other children. Tell them that tea's ready.
Ravi They're not here yet, Mummy, they're still in school.
Kamala All right, you sit down. Don't sit over there, sit over here. Give this cup to Mr Varma.
Ravi Please take this, Varma jī. Mummy, give me tea too!
Kamala Don't drink tea, drink milk. And listen son, give Mr Varma the sugar too.
Mr Varma Look Ravi, this spoon is big. Take it and give me a small spoon.
Kamala Varma jī, please do take some more sugar, this is very little!
Mr Varma Enough, enough! This is fine. I don't like very sweet tea, thank you.

17 The simple verb

The Hindi verb is usually quoted in the infinitive form, e.g. बोलना **bolnā** *'to speak, say'*. This form consists of the stem बोल- **bol-** plus the infinitive ending -ना **-nā.**[3] Some of the most common verbs are given below:

आना	ānā	*to come*	पूछना	pūchnā	*to ask*
करना	karnā	*to do*	बताना	batānā	*to tell*
कहना	kahnā	*to say*	बुलाना	bulānā	*to call, invite*
खाना	khānā	*to eat*	बैठना	baiṭhnā	*to sit*
चलना	calnā	*to move, go*	मारना	mārnā	*to beat, kill*
जाना	jānā	*to go*	लाना	lānā	*to bring*
देखना	dekhnā	*to see, look*	लिखना	likhnā	*to write*
देना	denā	*to give*	लेना	lenā	*to take*

1 Some imperative verbs such as कहिए **kahie** *'Say'*, बताइए **batāie** *'Tell [me]'* are used conversationally, typically as part of a greeting; these often have no real translation equivalent in English usage.

2 Note the use of the expression बस **bas** *'that's all'* at the beginning of the third line of the dialogue: this common usage has the sense *'Well, that's about all there is to say about it'*, *'Can't complain'*.

3 Note that while no inherent vowel is pronounced at the end of a verb stem ending in a consonant (e.g. बोल- **bol-**), this consonant never forms a conjunct with a following consonant (e.g. as in बोलना **bolnā**).

पढ़ना	paṛhnā	*to read, study*	सुनना	sunnā	*to listen, hear*
पीना	pīnā	*to drink, smoke*	होना	honā	*to be, become*

18 The imperatives

Imperatives are the verbal forms used to express orders or requests. As in English, the extent to which they represent an order or a request is largely determined by the tone of voice and the context. An आप **āp** imperative is intrinsically polite. The different Hindi imperatives are as follows:

1 The तू **tū** imperative. This is used in तू **tū** contexts–that is, in situations of intimacy or contempt–and will not usually be used by the learner. It consists of the verb stem itself, and is made negative most commonly by the particle मत **mat.** E.g. पानी ला **pānī lā** *'Bring the water'*; वहाँ मत जा **vahā̃ mat jā** *'Don't go there'*.

2 The तुम **tum** imperative. This imperative, used to people addressed as तुम **tum,** is formed by adding -ओ **-o** to the verb stem, and is made negative by either न **na** or मत **mat.** The latter, which may either precede or follow the verb, is considered to be sharper in tone. Examples: वहाँ देखो **vahā̃ dekho** *Look there*; वहाँ मत जाओ **vahā̃ mat jāo** *Don't go there*; एक कुरसी लाओ **ek kursī lāo** *Bring a chair.*

In forming this imperative, verbs whose stems end in -ऊ **-ū** shorten this stem before the -ओ **-o** ending. Thus छूना **chūnā** *to touch* gives छुओ **chuo** *Touch.* Verbs whose stems end in -ई **-ī** change to -इय- **-iy-** or -इ- **-i-** before the -ओ- **-o-** ending. Thus पीना **pīnā** *to drink* gives पियो **piyo** or पिओ **pio,** *Drink*. The verbs लेना **lenā** *to take* and देना **denā** *to give* have the irregular forms लो **lo** *Take* and दो **do** *Give.*

3 The आप **āp** imperative. This imperative, used to people one would address as आप **āp**, is formed by adding -इए **-ie** or -इये **-iye** to the verb stem; it is made negative by न **na,** नहीं **nahī̃**, or, less commonly, by मत **mat.** Examples: उस कुरसी पर बैठिए **us kursī par baiṭhie** *Sit on that chair;* यह किताब पढ़िए **yah kitāb paṛhie** *Read this book;* वहाँ न जाइए **vahā̃ na jāie** *Don't go there.*

Verb stems in -ऊ **-ū** shorten to -उ **-u** before the ending, e.g. छुइए **chuie** *Touch.*

Four verbs have irregular आप **āp** imperatives:

करना	karnā	कीजिए	kījie
लेना	lenā	लीजिए	lījie

देना	denā	दीजिए	dījie
पीना	pīnā	पीजिए	pījie

4 A further imperative is formed by adding -गा **-gā** to the आप **āp** imperative, giving the ending -इएगा **-iegā**. This is a formal, polite usage in which the element of command is muted as in the English request 'Would you be so kind as to...'. Examples: नाम लिखिएगा **nām likhiegā** *Be so kind as to write your name;* वह किताब दीजिएगा **vah kitāb dījiegā** *Would you mind passing that book?*

5 The infinitive is also used as an imperative, mainly in तुम **tum** contexts, conveying both specific commands (usually relating to an event at some distance in the future) and general directives. Negative commands usually take न **na.**

जल्दी आना	**jaldī ānā**	*Come (back) soon*
सच बोलना	**sac bolnā**	*Speak the truth*
सिगरेट न पीना।	**sigreṭ na pīnā**	*Don't smoke.*

The adverb ज़रा **zarā** *just, a little* softens the tone of a request:

ज़रा यहाँ ठहरो।	**zarā yahā̃ ṭhaharo.**	*Just wait here.*
ज़रा पानी लाइए।	**zarā pānī lāie.**	*Kindly bring some water.*

More formal equivalents of the English 'please' include the expression कृपया **kṛpayā:**

कृपया सिगरेट न पीजिए। **kṛpayā sigreṭ na pījie.** *Please do not smoke.*

Much more commonly, however, the sense of English 'please' is implied by the tone of voice and by the use of appropriate imperative forms, making any specific equivalent of 'please' unnecessary.

19 को *ko* as postposition of the indirect and direct object

को **ko** is used as the postposition of the indirect, and sometimes the direct, object of the verb. As a postposition, it requires the noun or pronoun preceding it to be in the oblique case. When acting as the postposition of the indirect object it corresponds to the English 'to':

राम को पानी न दीजिए। Rām ko pānī na dījie. *Don't give water to Ram.*

मुझको पत्र लिखिए।	mujhko patr likhie.	*Write me a letter (Write a letter to me).*
बच्चे को दूध दीजिए।	bacce ko dūdh dījie.	*Give the child milk.*
लड़कों को कुरसियाँ देना।	laṛkõ ko kursiyā̃ denā.	*Give the boys chairs.*

को **ko** is used with the direct object when it is a specific person (whether noun, name or pronoun), sometimes with animals, but only with things when there is a need to individualize them. If there is no need to particularize, the direct object remains in the direct case without को **ko**.

बच्चे को मत छुओ।	bacce ko mat chuo.	*Don't touch the child.*
मोहन को बुलाइए।	Mohan ko bulāie.	*Call (invite) Mohan.*
घोड़े को मारो मत!	ghoṛe ko māro mat!	*Don't beat the horse!*
इस किताब को पढ़िए।	is kitāb ko paṛhie.	*Read this book.*
but:		
एक पत्र लिखिए।	ek patr likhie.	*Write a letter.*
कमरा साफ़ करना।	kamrā sāf karnā.	*Clean the room.*
दरवाज़ा बन्द करो।	darvāzā band karo.	*Close the door.*

The verbs कहना **kahnā** and पूछना **pūchnā** take the postposition से **se**: उससे कहो **usse kaho** *Tell him*; उनसे पूछो **unse pūcho** *Ask them.*

20 The vocative case

The vocative (the case used when addressing somebody) is the same as the oblique, except that in the plural the -ओ **-o** ending is not nasalized:

बेटे	beṭe!	*Son!*
बच्चो	bacco!	*Children!*
भाइयो-बहिनो	bhāiyo-bahino!	*Brothers and sisters!*

Dialogue 5B *At the cloth-merchant's shop*

विनोद अरे विमल! कपड़े की दुकान पर चलो।
Vinod are Vimal! kapṛe kī dukān par calo.

विमल	अच्छा भाई। देखो, दलाल जी की नई दुकान उधर है।
Vimal	acchā bhāī. dekho, Dalāl jī kī naī dukān udhar hai.
दलाल	आइए, दुकान में आइए! अरे लड़के, दुकान का दरवाज़ा बन्द कर। गरम चाय ला। साहब लोगों के कोट ले।
Dalāl	āie, dukān mẽ āie! are laṛke, dukān kā darvāzā band kar. garam cāy lā. sāhab logõ ke koṭ le.
विनोद	ज़रा ठहरिए, कोट की जेब में घर की चाबियाँ हैं। उन्हें मुझको देना।
Vinod	zarā ṭhaharie, koṭ kī jeb mẽ ghar kī cābiyā̃ haĩ. unhẽ mujhko denā.
दलाल	बेटे, साहब के कोट में चाबियाँ हैं। उन्हें जल्दी ला।
Dalāl	beṭe, sāhab ke koṭ mẽ cābiyā̃ haĩ. unhẽ jaldī lā.
विनोद	अच्छा। अब मुझे कुछ बढ़िया कपड़ा दिखाइए-कोट का भारी कपड़ा।
Vinod	acchā. ab mujhe kuch baṛhiyā kapṛā dikhāie–koṭ kā bhārī kapṛā.
दलाल	जी, ज़रूर। इधर बैठिएगा, यह कपड़ा देखिए। एक प्याला चाय भी पीजिए। आपको कैसी चाय पसंद है?
Dalāl	jī, zarūr. idhar baiṭhiegā, yah kapṛā dekhie. ek pyālā cāy bhī pījie. āpko kaisī cāy pasand hai?
विमल	हमें मीठी चाय पसंद है। हाँ, दो चम्मच चीनी देना। बस, ठीक है।
Vimal	hamẽ mīṭhī cāy pasand hai. hā̃, do cammac cīnī denā. bas, ṭhīk hai.
दलाल	यह अहमदाबाद का कपड़ा लीजिए, यह उस कपड़े से और भी अच्छा है।
Dalāl	yah Ahmadābād kā kapṛā lījie, yah us kapṛe se aur bhī acchā hai.
विनोद	नहीं, हमें वह हरा कपड़ा दिखाना, वह इससे भारी है।
Vinod	nahī̃, hamẽ vah harā kapṛā dikhānā, vah isse bhārī hai.
दलाल	वह कोट का कपड़ा नहीं है साहब, वह बच्चे का कंबल है!
Dalāl	vah koṭ kā kapṛā nahī̃ hai sāhab, vah bacce kā kambal hai!

Vinod	Hey Vimal! Come[1] to[2] the cloth shop.
Vimal	All right (brother). Look, Dalal jī's new shop is over there.

[1] चलना **calnā** commonly has the sense 'to come along, accompany'.
[2] पर **par** is the postposition used with दुकान **dukān** and some other nouns in the context 'to, towards'.

Dalal	Come, come into the shop! Hey boy, close[1] the shop door. Bring hot tea. Take the sahibs' coats.
Vinod	Just wait a minute, the house keys are in the coat pocket. Give them to me.
Dalal	Son, there are keys in the sahib's coat. Bring them quickly.
Vinod	Good. Now show me some good quality cloth–heavy cloth for a coat.
Dalal	Yes, of course. Please sit over here, take this cloth. Have a cup of tea too. How do you like your tea?
Vimal	We like sweet tea. Yes, give two spoons of sugar. That's it, that's fine.
Dalal	Take this Ahmedabad cloth,[2] this is even better than that cloth.
Vinod	No, show us that green cloth, it's heavier than this.
Dalal	That's not coat cloth, Sahib, that's a child's blanket!

21 The possessive particle का *kā*

Possession is expressed by the particle का **kā**; this acts on the one hand as a postposition, requiring the possessor to be in the oblique case, and on the other hand as an adjective with the forms का **kā**, की **kī**, के **ke** agreeing with the thing possessed:

लड़के का कमरा	laṛke kā kamrā	*the boy's room*
लड़के की कुरसी	laṛke kī kursī	*the boy's chair*
लड़कों का कमरा	larkõ kā kamrā	*the boys' room*
लड़कों के कमरे	laṛkõ ke kamre	*the boys' rooms*
लड़कों की कुरसियाँ	laṛkõ kī kursiyā̃	*the boys' chairs*

When the thing possessed is in the oblique, then the appropriate form of the particle का **kā** must show the usual adjectival agreement with the noun it qualifies:

लड़के के कमरे में	laṛke ke kamre mẽ	*in the boy's room*
लड़के की कुरसी पर	laṛke kī kursī par	*on the boy's chair*
लड़कों के कमरे में	laṛkõ ke kamre mẽ	*in the boys' room*
लड़कों के कमरों में	laṛkõ ke kamrõ mẽ	*in the boys' rooms*
लड़कों की कुरसियों पर	laṛkõ kī kursiyõ par	*on the boys' chairs*

1 Note how the shopkeeper addresses his boy with the intimate तू **tū** form.

2 यह **yah** qualifies कपड़ा **kapṛā**, not अहमदाबाद **Ahmadābād**, and is therefore in the direct case and not the oblique.

It can be seen that the particle का **kā** behaves, both in grammatical function and in terms of word order, like the English apostrophe 's':

बच्चों का खाना तैयार है।	*The children's food is ready.*
baccõ kā khānā taiyār hai.	
उस आदमी का बेटा विद्यार्थी है।	*That man's son is a student.*
us ādmī kā beṭā vidyārthī hai.	
रामदास की बहिनें शहर में थीं।	*Rāmdās's sisters were in the town.*
Rāmdās kī bahinẽ śahar mẽ thī̃.	
उन लोगों के कपड़े बहुत गंदे हैं।	*Those people's clothes are very*
un logõ ke kapṛe bahut gande haĩ.	*dirty.*
उस मकान के बाग़ में दस पेड़ हैं।	*In the garden of that house there*
us makān ke bāg mẽ das peṛ haĩ.	*are ten trees.*
सीता के भाई की गाड़ी नई है।	*Sita's brother's car is new.*
Sītā ke bhāī kī gāṛī naī hai.	

22 Alternative forms of the oblique pronouns with को *ko*

It is not considered good style for को **ko** to occur twice in the same clause or simple sentence, for example with both the direct and the indirect object. In such contexts the indirect object will take को **ko**, and the direct object will remain in the direct case.

The pronouns have alternative oblique forms which correspond in all respects to the pronouns plus को **ko**; these alternative forms are especially common in the spoken language.

		alternative form:	
मुझको	mujhko	मुझे	mujhe
तुझको	tujhko	तुझे	tujhe
इसको	isko	इसे	ise
उसको	usko	उसे	use
हमको	hamko	हमें	hamẽ
तुमको	tumko	तुम्हें	tumhẽ
आपको	āpko	(no alternative form)	
इनको	inko	इन्हें	inhẽ

उनको	unko	उन्हें	unhē
किसको	kisko	किसे	kise
किनको	kinko	किन्हें	kinhē

These terms are completely interchangeable, although those in the right-hand column will be preferred if there is another को **ko** nearby in the sentence:

मुझको ख़ुशी है।	mujh ko <u>kh</u>uśī hai.	*I am glad.*
or मुझे ख़ुशी है।	mujhe <u>kh</u>uśī hai.	
हमको मालूम है।	hamko mālūm hai.	*We know.*
or हमें मालूम है।	hamẽ mālūm hai.	

But:

उस किताब को मुझे दीजिए।	us kitāb ko mujhe dījie.	*Give that book to me.*
इस प्याले को उसे दो।	is pyāle ko use do.	*Give this cup to him.*

The individualizing emphasis given by को **ko** in the last two examples distinguishes *that book* and *this cup* from anything else possible in the context. If such emphasis were not needed, को **ko** would not be used: मुझे (or मुझको) किताब दीजिए **mujhe** (or **mujh ko**) **kitāb dījie**, etc.

EXERCISE 5.1 Give the आप **āp** and तुम **tum** imperatives of all the verbs listed in para. 17, **except** होना **honā**.

EXERCISE 5.2 Translate into English:

१ राम के भाई को यह पत्र दीजिए।
२ संजय की किताब में न लिखना।
३ इन कमरों को साफ़ कर।
४ लड़कों के कमरे में न जाइए।
५ मुझे उस आदमी का नाम बताओ।
६ हमें ख़ुशी है कि आप यहाँ हैं।
७ राम की चाबियाँ उस बड़ी मेज़ पर हैं।
८ लड़की की जेब में क्या है?
९ कृपया सिगरेट न पीजिए।
१० इस अख़बार को पढ़ो लेकिन इसे अम्माँ को न दिखाओ।

EXERCISE 5.3 Translate into Hindi:

1 Don't touch that, give it to me.
2 Please call Vinod, and bring Vimal too.
3 Just sit here.
4 Tell me where Father is.
5 Look, this cup is not clean, take it and give me another one.
6 I do not know who is in Ram's room just now.
7 This man's shirt is on that chair.
8 Ram's father has a cold.
9 Say hello to Father.
10 Hey son, shut that door!

Vocabulary

अब	ab	*now*
अम्माँ	ammā̃	*mother, mummy* (f.)
अहमदाबाद	Ahmadābād	*Ahmedabad* (m.)
आना	ānā	*to come*
इधर	idhar	*here, over here*
उधर	udhar	*there, over there*
करना	karnā	*to do*
कहना	kahnā	*to say*
कुछ और	kuch aur	*some more*
कृपया	kr̥payā	*please*
खाना[1]	khānā	*food* (m.)
खाना[2]	khānā	*to eat*
गरम	garam	*warm, hot*
घोड़ा	ghoṛā	*horse* (m.)
चम्मच	cammac	*spoon* (m.)
चलना	calnā	*to move, go*
चाबी	cābī	*key* (f.)
चाय	cāy	*tea* (f.)
चीनी	cīnī	*sugar* (f.)
छूना	chūnā	*to touch*
ज़रा	zarā	*just, a little*
जल्दी	jaldī	*quickly, early; hurry* (f.)
जाना	jānā	*to go*
जेब	jeb	*pocket* (f.)
ठहरना	ṭhaharnā	*to stop, stay, wait*
तबियत	tabiyat	*health, disposition* (f.)
तैयार	taiyār	*ready, prepared*

दिखाना	dikhānā	*to show*
देखना	dekhnā	*to see, look*
देना	denā	*to give*
नाम	nām	*name* (m.)
पढ़ना	paṛhnā	*to read, study*
पत्र	patr	*letter, paper* (m.)
पानी	pānī	*water* (m.)
पीना	pīnā	*to drink*
पूछना	pūchnā	*to ask*
प्याला	pyālā	*cup* (m.)
बढ़िया	baṛhiyā	*fine, excellent, of good quality* (inv.)
बताना	batānā	*to tell*
बन्द	band	*closed*
बन्द करना	band karnā	*to close*
बुलाना	bulānā	*to call, invite*
बैठना	baiṭhnā	*to sit*
बोलना	bolnā	*to speak, say*
मत	mat	*do not* (with imperative)
मारना	mārnā	*to beat, kill*
मीठा	mīṭhā	*sweet*
लाना	lānā	*to bring*
लिखना	likhnā	*to write*
लेना	lenā	*to take*
सच	sac	*true; truth* (m.)
साफ़ करना	sāf karnā	*to clean*
सिगरेट	sigreṭ	*cigarette* (f.)
सुनना	sunnā	*to listen, hear*
स्कूल	skūl	*school* (m.)
होना	honā	*to be, become*

Unit Six

Dialogue 6A *Where does Sunil's elder brother live?*

प्रमोद	सुनो रमेश, सुनील के बड़े भाई कहाँ रहते हैं?
रमेश	वे अब नई दिल्ली में रहते हैं। वहाँ एक दफ़्तर में काम करते हैं।
प्रमोद	अच्छा! कहते हैं कि वहाँ मकान बहुत महँगे होते हैं–वे कैसे इलाक़े में रहते हैं?
रमेश	मालूम होता है कि काफ़ी अच्छा इलाक़ा है, और सारे पड़ोसी बहुत मिलनसार हैं।
प्रमोद	और क्या सुनील की बहिन भी वहाँ रहती है?
रमेश	हाँ, वह वहाँ के एक बड़े स्कूल में उर्दू और पंजाबी पढ़ाती है।
प्रमोद	अच्छा, भाई और बहिन दोनों काम करते हैं–पर घर का काम कौन करता है?
रमेश	वे दोनों घर को साफ़ करते हैं, और दोनों खाना भी बनाते हैं। मैं भी कभी कभी वहाँ जाता हूँ और खाना बनाता हूँ।
प्रमोद	उमा कहती है कि तुम लोग गोश्त नहीं खाते–क्या तुम कभी शराब पीते हो?
रमेश	माता जी गोश्त कभी नहीं खातीं, लेकिन वे अब इंग्लैंड में रहती हैं, इसलिए हम गोश्त भी खाते हैं और शराब भी पीते हैं!

Pramod	Hey Ramesh, where does Sunil's elder brother live?
Ramesh	He lives in New Delhi now. He works in an office there.
Pramod	Oh! They say houses are very expensive there–what kind of area does he live in?
Ramesh	It seems it's quite a good area, and all the neighbours are very friendly.
Pramod	And does Sunil's sister live there too?
Ramesh	Yes, she teaches Urdu and Panjabi in a big school there.
Pramod	I see, brother and sister both work–but who does the housework?
Ramesh	They both clean the house, and they both cook (the food) as well. I go there sometimes too, and cook.
Pramod	Uma says that you (people) don't eat meat–do you ever drink?
Ramesh	Mother never eats meat, but she lives in England now, so we eat meat and we drink!

23 The imperfective present

The Hindi verb distinguishes not only tense–past, present and future–but also different kinds of action: those that are completed *(perfective)*, those that are habitual *(imperfective)*, and those that are going on (*continuous*). The imperfective tenses are used for habitual actions or states or general statements of permanent validity. Thus the statement 'We speak Hindi' would be in the imperfective present, while the statement 'We are speaking Hindi' would be in the continuous present.

The imperfective present tense of बोलना *to speak* is formed as follows:

Masculine	**Feminine**	
Singular		
मैं बोलता हूँ	मैं बोलती हूँ	*I speak*
तू बोलता है	तू बोलती है	*you speak*
यह, वह बोलता है	यह, वह बोलती है	*he, she, it speaks*
Plural		
हम बोलते हैं	हम बोलती हैं	*we speak*
तुम बोलते हो	तुम बोलती हो	*you speak*
आप बोलते हैं	आप बोलती हैं	*you speak*
ये, वे बोलते हैं	ये, वे बोलती हैं	*they speak*

This tense consists of the imperfective participle बोलता, formed by adding -ता, -ती, -ते to the verb stem, followed by हूँ, है, हो or हैं. The verb is made negative by adding नहीं just before the participle. In the negative it is usual to drop the forms हूँ, है, हो and हैं; when this happens with a feminine plural verb, the participle becomes nasalized: वे बोलती हैं, *but* वे नहीं बोलतीं.

मैं अँग्रेज़ी बोलता हूँ।	*I speak English.*
वह हिंदी नहीं बोलता।	*He does not speak Hindi.*
आप पंजाबी बोलते हैं?	*You speak Panjabi?*
तुम क्या काम करते हो?	*What work do you do?*
आप कहाँ रहते हैं?	*Where do you live?*
सिख लोग सिगरेट नहीं पीते।	*Sikhs do not smoke.*
अम्माँ गोश्त नहीं खातीं।	*Mother doesn't eat meat.*

Notice also the following construction, which provides a useful way of acquiring new vocabulary:

इंडिया को हिंदी में क्या कहते हैं?	*What is India called in Hindi?*
इंडिया को हिंदी में भारत या भारतवर्ष कहते हैं।	*India is called 'Bhārat' or 'Bhārat-varṣ' in Hindi.*

(A literal translation of the first example would be 'What do they call India in Hindi?'.)

The imperfective present of the verb होना *to be, become* (होता है etc.) is used for general statements of lasting validity; for specific statements relating to particular occurrences, है or हैं are used alone. Compare the following pairs of sentences–the first of each pair demonstrates a general statement, and hence uses the होता form, while the second of each pair is a specific statement and uses the है form.

हफ़्ते में सात दिन होते हैं।	*There are seven days in a week.*
इस महीने में तीस दिन हैं।	*There are 30 days in this month.*
कश्मीरी सेब मीठे होते हैं।	*Kashmiri apples are sweet.*
यह फल ताज़ा नहीं है!	*This fruit isn't fresh!*
छह और पाँच ग्यारह होते हैं।	*Six and five are eleven.*
बाग़ में बारह लंबे पेड़ हैं।	*In the garden are twelve tall trees.*

Notice also the similar distinction between the expressions मालूम होता है and मालूम है in the following:

मालूम होता है कि वह यहाँ नहीं है।	*It seems that he is not here.*
मुझे मालूम है कि वह यहाँ नहीं है।	*I know that he is not here.*

24 Agreement between the verb and its subject

As has been seen, the verb agrees with its subject in gender and in number. When the verb has two subjects which are people of the same sex, then naturally the verb also has that gender; if the two people are of different sexes, then the verb will be in the masculine plural. When the two subjects are inanimate objects or things, then again the verb will agree with a shared gender; if the two subjects are of different genders, the verb will normally agree with the subject nearest to it in sentence order.

राधा और सीता संस्कृत पढ़ती हैं। *Radha and Sita study Sanskrit.*
राधा और कृष्ण बाग़ में खेलते हैं। *Radha and Krishna play in the garden.*
क़लम और पेंसिलें महँगी होती हैं। *Pens and pencils are expensive.*

Dialogue 6B *Hotels in the hill station*

राजू कहिए जी, आपकी तबियत कैसी है? सब ठीक है?

सलीम आपकी मेहरबानी है। हमारे लिए पहाड़ का यह मौसम सबसे अच्छा मौसम होता है। आपका होटल कैसा है?

राजू बहुत अच्छा है। मेरे कमरे की खिड़कियों के बाहर ऊँचे पहाड़ हैं, और मालूम होता है पहाड़ों के ऊपर बर्फ़ हमेशा रहती है। सारा शहर हमारे नीचे है। होटल के अंदर सारे कमरे बहुत सुंदर हैं। उसके आगे चौड़ा बरामदा है, और होटल के पीछे बहुत बड़ा बाग़। कभी कभी हम लोग होटल के दूसरे मेहमानों के साथ खाना खाते हैं, कभी कभी हम अपने कमरे में अकेले खाते हैं। आप अपने होटल के बारे में बताइए।

सलीम हमारा होटल स्टेशन के पास है। कमरे ठीक हैं, पर वहाँ का खाना हमें पसंद नहीं। और होटल की चाय और काफ़ी के बारे में न पूछिए!

राजू क्या आप अपने लिए खाना बनाते हैं?

सलीम नहीं, सिर्फ़ बच्चों के लिए। उनके लिए बनाते हैं, अपने लिए नहीं। दिन में हम ताज़ा फल खाते हैं, और रात का खाना हम एक दोस्त के यहाँ खाते हैं।

राजू सुनिए भाई, कल रात को आप हमारे होटल में खाना खाइए, उसके बाद हमारे साथ सिनेमा चलिए। और हाँ, अपने दोस्तों को भी अपने साथ लाइए। ठीक है?

सलीम बहुत शुक्रिया राजू जी, यह आपकी बड़ी मेहरबानी है।

Raju (Tell me), how are you? Is everything OK?

Salim Thank you, yes. This hill weather is the best weather for us! What's your hotel like?

Raju It's very good. There are tall hills outside my window, and it seems snow stays on the hills all the time. The whole city is below us. Inside the hotel all the rooms are very nice. In front of it there is a wide verandah, and behind the hotel a very big garden. Sometimes we eat with the other guests in the hotel, and sometimes we eat alone in our room. You tell (me) about your hotel.

Salim Our hotel is near the station. The rooms are all right, but we don't like the food there. And don't ask about the hotel tea and coffee!

Raju Do you make food for yourselves?

Salim No, only for the children. We make it for them, not for ourselves. In the day we eat fresh fruit, and the evening meal we eat at a friend's.

Raju Listen (brother), tomorrow night eat at our hotel, after that come to the cinema with us. And yes–bring your friends with you. All right?

Salim Thank you very much Raju ji, that's very kind of you.

25 The possessive pronouns

The pronouns have their own adjectival forms to express possession, like the English 'my', 'your', etc. These decline like adjectives and agree with whatever they qualify. They are as follows:

मैं	*I*	मेरा	*my, mine*
तू	*you*	तेरा	*your, yours*
यह	*he, she, it*	इसका	*his, her, its*
वह	*he, she, it*	उसका	*his, her, its*
हम	*we*	हमारा	*our, ours*
तुम	*you*	तुम्हारा	*your, yours*
आप	*you*	आपका	*your, yours*
ये	*they*	इनका	*their, theirs*
वे	*they*	उनका	*their, theirs*
कौन	*who?*	किसका	*whose?* (singular)
		किनका	*whose?* (plural)

वे कपड़े किसके हैं?	*Whose are those clothes?*
वे कपड़े मेरे हैं।	*Those clothes are mine.*
यह उसका घर है।	*This is his house.*
वह हमारी गाड़ी है।	*That is our car.*
तुम्हारा भाई यहाँ है।	*Your brother is here.*
आपके हाथ में क्या है?	*What is in your hand?*
उनकी किताबें इस कमरे में नहीं हैं।	*Their books are not in this room.*

Those possessive pronouns which are composed of the oblique pronoun plus का may also be written as two words: इसका or इस का etc.

26 The possessive adjective अपना one's own

The possessive adjective अपना *one's own* must be used when the thing which is possessed belongs to the subject of the verb in the same clause. Compare the following:

वह अपने कमरे में था।	*He was in his (own) room.*
वह उसके कमरे में था।	*He was in his (someone else's) room.*

How अपना is translated will depend on who it refers to:

मैं उसको अपना पैसा देता हूँ।	*I give him my money.*
वह मुझे अपना पैसा देता है।	*He gives me his money.*

In the first of these sentences, अपना refers to मैं and hence translates as 'my'; in the second, अपना refers to वह and translates as 'his'.

वह अपने भाई के मकान में रहता है।	*He lives in his brother's house.*
अपना काम करो।	*Do your work.*
हम अपने दोस्तों को ख़त लिखते हैं।	*We write letters to our friends.*
राधा और उसका भाई अपनी किताबें लाते हैं।	*Radha and her brother bring their (own) books.*

Notice that in the sentence अपना काम करो, अपना is required even though the subject, तुम, is not expressed. The subject of an imperative verb is necessarily 'you'.

27 Compound postpositions

Five postpositions have already been introduced (para. **10**). These are called 'simple postpositions' because they consist of only one word. Postpositions consisting of more than one word are called 'compound postpositions'. These behave in exactly the same way as the simple postpositions in that they follow the words they govern and require them to be in the oblique case. Some of the most common are listed below:

के अंदर	*inside*	के पीछे	*behind*
के आगे	*in front of*	के बाद	*after*
के ऊपर	*on top of*	के बारे में	*concerning, about*
की ओर	*towards*	के बाहर	*outside*
की तरफ़	*towards*	के लिए	*for*
के नीचे	*below*	के यहाँ	*at the place of*
के पहले	*before*	के साथ	*with*
के पास	*near*	के सामने	*facing, opposite*

मोहन के यहाँ	*at Mohan's house/place*
मकान के बाहर	*outside the house*

लड़कियों के साथ	*with the girls*
कुएँ के पास[1]	*near the well*
आज के बाद	*after today*
इस के पहले	*before this*
दूसरों के लिए	*for others*

The first word in the compound postposition is the oblique of the possessive particle, के or की. When the compound postpositions are used with the pronouns मैं, तू, हम, तुम, and अपना, the के or की is dropped and the appropriate form of मेरा, तेरा, हमारा, तुम्हारा or अपना is used instead.

मेरे पास आओ।	*Come to me.*
उसे हमारे बारे में बताओ।	*Tell him about us.*
वह मेरे लिए चाय लाता है।	*He brings tea for me.*
आप भी हमारे साथ आइए।	*You come with us too.*
नया मकान तेरे सामने है।	*The new house is in front of you.*
बड़ी कुरसी तुम्हारे पीछे है।	*The big chair is behind you.*
अपने लिए खाना लीजिए।	*Take food for yourself.*

EXERCISE 6.1 Translate into English:

यह मेरा घर है। मैं यहाँ अपने कुछ दोस्तों के साथ रहता हूँ। मेरे घर के सामने मेरे छोटे भाई का मकान है। मेरी माता जी अब हमारे साथ नहीं रहतीं, वे एक दूसरे मकान में रहतीं हैं। उनका नया मकान इस मकान से बहुत छोटा है। आजकल मकान बहुत महँगे होते हैं, इसलिए ज़्यादा लोग छोटे मकानों में रहते हैं। मेरी माता जी की तबियत अच्छी नहीं है, इसलिए उनके पड़ोसी उनके लिए खाना बनाते हैं और दुकानों से चीज़ें लाते हैं। वे अपने लिए सिर्फ़ चाय बनाती हैं। कभी कभी मेरे बड़े भाई के ख़त लन्दन से आते हैं, और माता जी मुझसे इंग्लैंड के बारे में पूछती हैं। माता जी अँग्रेज़ी नहीं बोलतीं, सिर्फ़ उर्दू और हिंदी बोलती हैं।

EXERCISE 6.2 Translate into Hindi:

1 Those women don't live here; it seems that their house is over there.
2 Their room is beneath our room, opposite the kitchen.
3 He brings a book for himself, but he brings nothing for his friend.
4 We always go there with the girls, but the boys stay at home.

[1] कुआँ is a masculine noun that inflects like कमरा, but with all its endings nasalized.

5 I do not know what Raju does–where does he live?
6 I am glad that you too go to school.
7 We don't say anything about ourselves. Do they say anything about us?
8 She doesn't live in her (own) house, she lives in her sister's house.
9 Come to our place tomorrow, and bring your children too.
10 Does he not know that there are only seven days in a week?

Vocabulary

अँग्रेज़ी	*the English language* (f.)
अकेला	*alone*
अपना	*one's own*
इंग्लैंड	*England* (m.)
इंडिया	*India* (m.)
इलाक़ा	*area, district, locality* (m.)
इसलिए	*so, therefore, because of this*
उर्दू	*Urdu* (f.)
ऊँचा	*high, tall* (not of trees or people: see लंबा)
कभी	*sometime, ever*
कभी कभी	*sometimes*
कभी नहीं	*never*
कश्मीरी	*Kashmiri* (m./f./adj.)
काफ़ी	*coffee* (f.)
की ओर	*towards*
की तरफ़	*towards*
कुआँ	*well* (m.)
के अंदर	*inside, within*
के आगे	*in front of, before*
के ऊपर	*on top of, on*
के नीचे	*beneath, below*
के पहले	*before*
के पास	*near*
के पीछे	*behind*
के बाद	*after*
के बारे में	*about, concerning*
के बाहर	*outside*
के यहाँ	*at the place of*
के लिए	*for*
के साथ	*with*
के सामने	*opposite*

ख़त	*letter* (correspondence) (m.)
खेलना	*to play*
गोश्त	*meat* (m.)
ग्यारह	*eleven*
चौड़ा	*wide, broad*
ताज़ा	*fresh*
तीस	*thirty*
तुम्हारा	*your, yours*
तेरा	*your, yours*
दफ़्तर	*office* (m.)
दोस्त	*friend* (m.)
पंजाबी	*the Panjabi language* (f.)
पड़ोसी	*neighbour* (m.)
पढ़ाना	*to teach*
पहाड़	*mountain, hill* (m.)
पैसा	*money; hundredth of a rupee* (m.)
बनाना	*to make*
बरामदा	*verandah* (m.)
बर्फ़	*snow, ice* (f.)
बारह	*twelve*
भारत	*India* (m.)
भारतवर्ष	*India* (m.)
भी ... भी	*both ... and*
महीना	*month* (m.)
मिलनसार	*friendly, sociable*
मेरा	*my, mine*
मेहमान	*guest* (m.)
रहना	*to stay, remain, reside, live*
शराब	*alcoholic drink* (f.)
संस्कृत	*Sanskrit* (f.)
सारा	*entire, whole, all*
सिख	*Sikh* (m./f./adj.)
सिनेमा	*cinema* (m.)
सेब	*apple* (m.)
स्टेशन	*station* (m.)
हफ़्ता	*week* (m.)
हमारा	*our, ours*
हमेशा	*always*
हाथ	*hand* (m.)

Unit Seven

Dialogue 7A *Hari's grandparents*

हरि सुनाओ, रवि, क्या हाल है? कोई नई बात?

रवि कोई ख़ास बात नहीं। वह तुम्हारे हाथ में क्या है?

हरि ये मेरे परिवार की कुछ पुरानी तस्वीरें हैं। देखो, इस तस्वीर में मेरे दादाजी अपने मकान के आगे खड़े हैं। स्कूल की छुट्टियों में हम लोग उनके यहाँ ठहरते थे।

रवि वे कहाँ रहते थे? यह दिल्ली का मकान नहीं मालूम होता।

हरि नहीं, वे कलकत्ते के पास रहते थे, छोटे गाँव में। दादीजी कलकत्ते के किसी स्कूल में पढ़ाती थीं, क्योंकि गाँव में कोई स्कूल नहीं था।

रवि क्या तुम्हारे दादा-दादी हिन्दी बोलते थे?

हरि दादीजी कोई पाँच भाषाएँ जानती थीं, पर उन्हें हिन्दी नहीं आती थी। मैं उनसे बंगला में बात करता था। दादाजी कुछ हिन्दी समझते थे, पर बोलते न थे।

रवि दिल्ली से तुम अपने दादाजी के यहाँ कैसे जाते थे? ट्रेन से या बस से?

हरि हम अक्सर रेलगाड़ी से कलकत्ते तक जाते थे, फिर उसके बाद बस से गाँव पहुँचते थे। रेलगाड़ी का सफ़र बहुत दिलचस्प होता था। हम ट्रेन में खाते थे और सोते थे और दूसरे मुसाफ़िरों से बात करते थे।

Hari Tell me, Ravi, how are things? Anything new?

Ravi Nothing special. What is that in your hand?

Hari These are some old pictures of my family. Look, in this picture my grandfather is standing in front of his house. We used to stay with him in the school holidays.

Ravi Where did he live? This doesn't seem to be a Delhi house.

Hari No, he lived near Calcutta, in a small village. My grandmother used to teach in some school in Calcutta because there was no school in the village.

Ravi Did your grandparents speak Hindi?

Hari Grandmother knew about five languages, but she didn't know Hindi. I used to speak to her in Bengali. Grandfather understood some Hindi, but didn't speak it.

Ravi How did you go to your grandfather's place from Delhi? By train or by bus?

Hari We usually went as far as Calcutta by train, then after that reached the village by bus. The train journey was very interesting. We used to eat, sleep, and talk to the other passengers in the train.

28 The past imperfective

This tense, which gives the sense 'used to...', is formed as below (remember that imperfective tenses are used for habitual actions or states):

Masculine	**Feminine**	
Singular		
मैं बोलता था	बोलती थी	*I used to speak*
तू बोलता था	बोलती थी	*you used to speak*
यह, वह बोलता था	बोलती थी	*he, she, it used to speak*
Plural		
हम बोलते थे	बोलती थीं	*we used to speak*
तुम बोलते थे	बोलती थीं	*you used to speak*
आप बोलते थे	बोलती थीं	*you used to speak*
ये, वे बोलते थे	बोलती थीं	*they used to speak*

The verb is made negative by the particle नहीं, placed just before the participle.

पुराने ज़माने में ज़्यादा लोग गाँव में रहते थे।	*In the old days more people lived in the village.*
मैं उसके ख़त पढ़ता था।	*I used to read his letters.*
पुस्तकें सस्ती होती थीं।	*Books used to be cheap.*
वह तमिल नहीं बोलती थी।	*She used not to speak Tamil.*
आप कभी नहीं आते थे।	*You never used to come.*
क्या तुम अँग्रेज़ी पढ़ते थे?	*Used you to study English?*
वे कहाँ खेलते थे?	*Where used they to play?*

29 कुछ and कोई

कुछ meaning 'some' has already occurred. It also covers the sense of 'something', 'somewhat', and in questions, 'anything'. कुछ नहीं means 'nothing'; कुछ न कुछ means 'something or other'.

मेज़ पर कुछ पड़ा था।	*Something was lying on the table.*
उसके प्याले में कुछ चाय नहीं थी।	*There was no tea in his cup.*
पेड़ पर कुछ कच्चे संतरे हैं।	*There are some unripe oranges on the tree.*
मंदिर के बारे में कुछ बताइए।	*Tell [me, us, etc.] something about the temple.*
उसके बारे में वे कुछ नहीं जानते थे।	*They knew nothing about it.*
क्या वह कुछ लाती थी?	*Used she to bring anything?*
साधु के सिर पर कुछ न कुछ था।	*There was something or other on the sadhu's head.*
मेरी तबियत कुछ ख़राब है।	*I am not feeling very well. ('My health is somewhat bad.')*

The various uses of कोई ('someone, anyone, some, any') are illustrated in the following examples:

1 as a pronoun:

कमरे में कोई था।	*There was somebody in the room.*
कमरे में कोई नहीं था।	*There was nobody in the room.*
कमरे में कोई है?	*Is there anybody in the room?*
वहाँ कोई न कोई था।	*Somebody or other was there.*
यहाँ कोई अँग्रेज़ी नहीं बोलता।	*Nobody here speaks English.*

2 as an adjective:

इस शहर में कोई सिनेमा नहीं है।	*There is no (not any) cinema in this town.*
कोई आदमी बाहर खड़ा है।	*Some man is standing outside.*
कोई बीस लोग पेड़ के नीचे खड़े थे।	*Some twenty people were standing under the tree.*
कोई बात नहीं।	*No matter; it doesn't matter; never mind; don't mention it.*

When कोई is used alone as a pronoun, it generally refers to humans: 'someone'. The equivalent pronoun for inanimate objects, as already shown, is कुछ:

मकान में कोई था।	*There was somebody in the house.*
मकान में कुछ था।	*There was something in the house.*

कोई न कोई	*somebody or other*
कुछ न कुछ	*something or other*
और कोई	*someone else*
और कुछ	*something else*

कोई has the singular oblique form किसी. When used as a pronoun, this too will normally refer to humans only. कुछ does not change in the oblique.

किसी को चाय पसंद है, किसी को काफ़ी।	*Someone likes tea, someone likes coffee.*
किसी को यह पैसा दीजिए।	*Give this money to someone.*
किसी देश में एक बड़ा राजा रहता था।	*A great king lived in a certain country.*
किसी काग़ज़ पर अपना नाम लिखिए।	*Write your name on some piece of paper.*

30 Further uses of को

1 One very common construction using को is with the word चाहिए (*is*) *wanted, needed*. In this construction the English subject takes को, and the thing wanted becomes the Hindi subject: मुझको सिगरेट चाहिए *I want a cigarette*. Agreement with the Hindi subject is apparent in past tense sentences, where था, थी, थे or थीं are used: मुझको सिगरेट चाहिए थी *I wanted a cigarette*. Some Hindi speakers show plural agreement in the present tense also by using the nasalized form चाहिएँ in agreement with plural subjects: उसे दो नई कमीज़ें चाहिएँ *He needs two new shirts*.

मुझे नया चश्मा चाहिए।	*I need new glasses.*
हमें एक नई गाड़ी चाहिए।	*We need a new car.*
तुम्हें क्या चाहिए?	*What do you want?*
उन्हें कुछ हिंदी की किताबें चाहिएँ।	*They need some Hindi books.*
मुझको पाँच कमीज़ें चाहिए थीं।	*I needed five shirts.*
मुझे तीन किलो पक्के आम चाहिए।	*I need three kilos of ripe mangoes.*

2 A very useful construction with को involves the verb आना:

क्या आप को उड़िया आती है?	*Do you know Oriya?*
जी नहीं, मुझे सिर्फ़ हिंदी आती है।	*No, I only know Hindi.*
मुझे हिन्दुस्तानी खाना बनाना नहीं आता।	*I don't know how to make Indian food.*

3 को is used to particularize times of day, days of the week, dates, etc.:

शनिवार को	*on Saturday*
शाम को	*in the evening*
कल रात को	*yesterday night; tomorrow night*
मंगलवार की सुबह को	*on Tuesday morning*
इतवार को कोई काम नहीं करता।	*Nobody works on Sundays.*
बुधवार की रात को आना।	*Come on Wednesday night.*
विद्यार्थी शाम को हमारे यहाँ आते हैं।	*The students come to our place in the evening.*

Expressions with सुबह often omit को:

कल सुबह आइए।	*Come tomorrow morning.*

Dialogue 7B *Days of the week and months of the year*

अध्यापक रमेश, हफ़्ते के दिनों के नाम बताओ।

विद्यार्थी हफ़्ते में सात दिन होते हैं। उनके नाम हैं, रविवार या इतवार, सोमवार, मंगलवार, बुधवार, गुरुवार या बृहस्पतिवार, शुक्रवार और शनिवार। पहले और पाँचवें दिनों के दो दो नाम हैं, लेकिन दूसरे, तीसरे, चौथे, छठे और सातवें दिनों का सिर्फ़ एक एक नाम है।

अध्यापक शाबाश। आज कौनसा दिन है?

विद्यार्थी आज बुधवार है और कल मंगलवार था।

अध्यापक और परसों कौनसा दिन था?

विद्यार्थी परसों सोमवार था।

अध्यापक क्या तुम्हें मालूम है कि स्कूल की छुट्टियाँ कब शुरू होती हैं?

विद्यार्थी जी हाँ, छुट्टियाँ जुलाई के पहले या दूसरे हफ़्ते में शुरू होती हैं और अक्सर सितंबर के तीसरे या चौथे हफ़्ते में ख़त्म होती हैं।

अध्यापक छुट्टियों में तुम क्या करते हो?

विद्यार्थी छुट्टियों के दूसरे हफ़्ते से मैं हमेशा पिताजी की दुकान में काम शुरू करता हूँ, और अगस्त के आख़िर में मैं काम ख़त्म करता हूँ। फिर कोई तेरह चौदह दिन के लिए अपने दोस्त के यहाँ जाता हूँ।

Teacher Ramesh, tell me the names of the days of the week.

Student There are seven days in a week. Their names are, Sunday (or

Sunday), Monday, Tuesday, Wednesday, Thursday (or Thursday), Friday and Saturday. The first and fifth days have two names each,[1] but the second, third, fourth, sixth and seventh days have only one name each.

Teacher Well done. What day is today?
Student Today is Wednesday and yesterday was Tuesday.
Teacher And what was the day before yesterday?
Student The day before yesterday was Monday.
Teacher Do you know when the school holidays begin?
Student Yes, the holidays begin in the first or second week of July and usually end in the third or fourth week of September.
Teacher What do you do in the holidays?
Student From the second week of the holidays I always begin work in father's shop, and at the end of August I finish work. Then I go to a friend's for thirteen or fourteen[2] days[3].

31 The ordinal numbers

पहला	*first*	पाँचवाँ	*fifth*
दूसरा	*second*	छठा	*sixth*
तीसरा	*third*	सातवाँ	*seventh*
चौथा	*fourth*	आठवाँ	*eighth*

From 'seventh' onwards, the ordinals are formed, like पाँचवाँ, by adding -वाँ to the number.

As in English, the Hindi ordinals are adjectives; they inflect like बड़ा and those ending in -वाँ have all their endings nasalized. Examples: पाँचवीं सड़क *the fifth road;* दसवें मकान में *in the tenth house.*

32 Conjunct verbs

Many verbs are formed by combining करना *to do* with a noun or adjective:

शुरू करना	*to begin*	ख़त्म करना	*to finish*
बन्द करना	*to shut*	साफ़ करना	*to clean.*

1 Repeating the word दो gives a sense of distribution: 'two names **each**'. The same applies with एक एक 'one name **each**'.
2 No word for 'or' is included in expressions such as तेरह चौदह *thirteen or fourteen,* दो तीन *three or four,* etc.
3 Since the period of time is seen as an aggregate whole, दिन is used in the singular. A further example is दो साल के बाद *after two years.*

These are called transitive verbs because they take a direct object:

दरवाज़ा बन्द करो। *Shut the door.* काम शुरू कीजिए। *Start work.*

Many of these verbs have intransitive counterparts (not taking an object), in which होना is used in place of करना:

काम सुबह को शुरू होता है। *Work begins in the morning.*
रात को दरवाज़े बन्द होते हैं। *The doors close at night.*

Numerous such pairs of transitive and intransitive verbs will be met with.

छुट्टियाँ हमेशा गुरुवार को शुरू होती हैं। *The holidays always start on Thursday.*
दुकानें शाम तक कभी बन्द नहीं होतीं। *The shops never close until evening.*
हम रात तक काम ख़त्म नहीं करते थे। *We used not to finish work until night time.*

EXERCISE 7.1 Translate into English:

फल की दुकान पर

1 आइए साहब, आपको कौनसा फल चाहिए?
2 मुझे कुछ आम चाहिए—कुछ पक्के आम हैं?
3 जी हाँ, ज़रूर। ये आम बंबई के हैं–देखिए, बड़े भी हैं और मीठे भी!
4 अच्छा, दो किलो दो। दस ताज़े संतरे भी दो।
5 और कुछ चाहिए? आपको सेब पसंद हैं?
6 हाँ, कुछ सेब भी चाहिए। सबसे अच्छे कौनसे होते हैं?
7 ये कश्मीरी सेब बहुत बढ़िया हैं, आप इनको लीजिए।
8 ठीक है। पर देखो, वह सेब कच्चा है। कोई दूसरा दो।

EXERCISE 7.2 Translate into English:

1 कुछ लोग बंगला पढ़ते थे और कुछ लोग उड़िया पढ़ते थे।
2 बुधवार की शाम को कई महिलाएँ यहाँ आती थीं।
3 सुबह को पिताजी कुछ नहीं खाते थे।
4 कमरे में कोई न था, पर बाग़ में कोई खड़ा था।
5 किसी की चाबियाँ मेज़ के ऊपर पड़ी थीं।
6 इस बात के बारे में किसी से कुछ मत कहना!
7 क्या तेरे भाई को अँग्रेज़ी आती है?
8 मैं अपना काम शाम को ख़त्म करता था।
9 किसी को मालूम नहीं था कि पुराना मंदिर कहाँ था।
10 मालूम होता है कि वह हमेशा बस से आता था।

EXERCISE 7.3 Translate into Hindi:

1 We used to live in India with our father.
2 Someone or other used to bring food from the market.
3 We needed some ripe oranges.
4 How many languages do you know ?
5 She often came here on Thursday morning.
6 Nobody knew where he used to sleep.
7 The holidays begin in the third week of August.
8 I used to close the door at night.
9 I need about seven new books.
10 The first and fifth days of the week have two names each.

Vocabulary

अक्सर	*often, usually*
अगस्त	*August* (m.)
अध्यापक	*teacher* (m.)
आख़िर	*end* (m.)
आठवाँ	*eighth*
आम	*mango* (m.)
इतवार	*Sunday* (m.)
उड़िया	*the Oriya language* (f.)
और कुछ	*something else*
और कोई	*someone else, some other*
कच्चा	*unripe, raw, uncooked; crude, rough*
कब	*when?*
कलकत्ता	*Calcutta* (m.)
काग़ज़	*paper, piece of paper* (m.)
किलो	*kilo (-gram)* (m.)
कुछ न कुछ	*something or other*
कुछ नहीं	*nothing*
कैसे	*how?*
कोई	*some, any; someone, anyone;* (with number) *about*
कोई न कोई	*someone or other*
कोई नहीं	*nobody*
खड़ा होना	*to stand* (intr.)
ख़त्म करना	*to finish* (tr.)
ख़त्म होना	*to end* (intr.)
ख़ास	*special*
गुरुवार	*Thursday* (m.)
चश्मा	*glasses, spectacles* (m.)

चाहिए	*wanted, needed*
चौथा	*fourth*
चौदह	*fourteen*
छठा	*sixth*
छुट्टी	*holiday, leave, release from work* (f.)
ज़माना	*period, time* (m.)
जानना	*to know*
जुलाई	*July* (f.)
ट्रेन	*train* (f.)
तमिल	*the Tamil language* (f.)
तीसरा	*third*
तेरह	*thirteen*
दादा	*paternal grandfather* (m.)
दादा-दादी	*paternal grandparents* (m.)
दादी	*paternal grandmother* (f.)
देश	*country, region* (m.)
पक्का	*ripe, cooked; well-made*
पड़ा	*lying*
परसों	*the day before yesterday; the day after tomorrow*
परिवार	*family* (m.)
पहला	*first*
पहुँचना	*to reach, arrive at*
पाँचवाँ	*fifth*
पुस्तक	*book* (f.)
फिर	*then, again*
बंगला	*the Bengali language* (f.)
बंद होना	*to close* (intr.)
बाज़ार	*bazaar, shopping area, market* (m.)
बात करना	*to talk, converse* (with से)
बाहर	*outside*
बीस	*twenty*
बुधवार	*Wednesday* (m.)
बृहस्पतिवार	*Thursday* (m.)
भाषा	*language* (f.)
मंगलवार	*Tuesday* (m.)
मंदिर	*temple* (m.)
मुसाफ़िर	*traveller* (m.)
या	*or*
रविवार	*Sunday* (m.)
रेलगाड़ी	*train* (f.)
शनिवार	*Saturday* (m.)

शाबाश	*well done! bravo!*
शाम	*evening, dusk* (f.)
शुक्रवार	*Friday* (m.)
शुरू	*beginning* (m.)
शुरू करना	*to begin* (tr.)
शुरू होना	*to begin* (intr.)
संतरा	*orange* (m.)
सफ़र	*journey, travel* (m.)
समझना	*to understand, think, consider*
सातवाँ	*seventh*
साधु	*Hindu holy man, sadhu* (m.)
साल	*year* (m.)
सितंबर	*September* (m.)
सिर	*head* (m.)
सुनाना	*to tell, relate*
सुबह	*morning* (f.)
सोना	*to sleep*

Unit Eight

Dialogue 8A *An unexpected meeting*

हरि रवि, तुम यहाँ क्या कर रहे हो? तुम लोग आजकल दिल्ली में रहते हो क्या?

रवि मैं अभी दिल्ली में काम कर रहा हूँ, इसलिए हम लोग घर बदल रहे हैं। पहले हम पुरानी दिल्ली में नया मकान ढूँढ़ रहे थे, आजकल हम नई दिल्ली में ढूँढ़ रहे हैं।

हरि बहुत दिनों के बाद तुमसे बातें हो रही हैं। अब तुम्हारे कितने बच्चे हैं?

रवि हमारे तीन बच्चे हैं, एक लड़की, दो लड़के। अभी वे सब सिनेमा देख रहे हैं। तुम सुनाओ, तुम्हारे दो बच्चे हैं, न? उन की उम्र क्या है?

हरि लड़का पंद्रह साल का है, और लड़की सोलह साल की। वे अभी यहाँ आ रहे हैं, मेरी पत्नी के साथ। कल तक वे किसी मित्र के यहाँ ठहरे रहे थे, पर आज वे हमारे साथ हैं। अभी वे उषा के साथ कुछ कपड़े ख़रीद रहे हैं।

रवि सुनो हरि, मुझे देर हो रही है। फ़िल्म के बाद मैं बच्चों को होटल पहुँचा रहा हूँ। उनके पास पैसे नहीं हैं।

हरि पर सुनो, मेरे पास गाड़ी है। हम लोग सिनेमा की तरफ़ जा रहे हैं – तुम हमारे साथ चलो। ठीक है?

रवि लेकिन मैं तुम्हें तकलीफ़ दे रहा हूँ – सिनेमा तुम्हारे घर के पास भी नहीं है।

हरि कोई बात नहीं, हमारे पास बहुत समय है। तुम हमारे साथ ज़रूर चलो।

Hari Ravi, what are you doing here? Do you (people) live in Delhi now?[1]

Ravi I'm working in Delhi just now, so we're moving (lit. changing) house. Previously we were looking for a new house in Old Delhi, nowadays we're looking in New Delhi.

Hari We haven't had a chat for a long time. How many children do you have now?

Ravi We've got three children – one girl, two boys. They're watching a film at the moment. You tell me, you've got two children, haven't you[2]? How old are they?

Hari The boy is fifteen years old[3], and the girl is sixteen. They're just coming here with my wife. They were staying at some friend's place until yesterday, but today they're with us. Right now they are buying some clothes with Usha.

Ravi Listen Hari, I'm getting late.[4] After the film I'm taking the children to the hotel. They don't have (any) money.

Hari But listen, I've got the car. We're going in the direction of the cinema–you come with us. All right?

Ravi But I'm putting you to trouble–the cinema isn't even near your house.

Hari It doesn't matter, we've got lots of time. Certainly come with us.

33 The continuous tenses

Whereas the imperfective tenses are used for habitual actions or states, the continuous tenses are used for what is actually going on at a particular time. They are formed as follows:

Present

Masculine	Feminine	
मैं बोल रहा हूँ	रही हूँ	*I am speaking*
तू बोल रहा है	रही है	*you are speaking*
यह, वह बोल रहा है	रही है	*he, she, it is speaking*
हम बोल रहे हैं	रही हैं	*we are speaking*
तुम बोल रहे हो	रही हो	*you are speaking*
आप बोल रहे हैं	रही हैं	*you are speaking*
ये, वे बोल रहे हैं	रही हैं	*they are speaking*

Past

मैं बोल रहा था	रही थी	*I was speaking*
तू बोल रहा था	रही थी	*you were speaking*
यह, वह बोल रहा था	रही थी	*he, she, it was speaking*
हम बोल रहे थे	रही थीं	*we were speaking*
तुम बोल रहे थे	रही थीं	*you were speaking*
आप बोल रहे थे	रही थीं	*you were speaking*
ये, वे बोल रहे थे	रही थीं	*they were speaking*

1 क्या usually comes at the beginning of a sentence when indicating that the sentence is a question, but colloquially it may come at the end.

2 न at the end of a sentence asks for confirmation that something is true –*isn't that right?*.

3 Lit. *of fifteen years.*

4 देर means 'period of time', as in थोड़ी देर में *in a little while;* it also means 'lateness', as here in मुझे देर हो रही है *I'm getting late.*

When the continuous tenses need to be made negative, नहीं is inserted before the verb.

हम लोग हिंदी सीख रहे हैं।	*We are learning Hindi.*
वह अपने भाई के बारे में पूछ रही थी।	*She was asking about her brother.*
तुम कौनसी कहानी पढ़ रही हो?	*Which story are you reading?*
गाड़ी मकान की तरफ़ चल रही थी।	*The car was moving towards the house.*
आप क्या लिख रहे हैं?	*What are you writing?*
मैं घर नहीं जा रहा हूँ।	*I am not going home.*
ड्राइवर नई गाड़ी चला रहा था।	*The driver was driving the new car.*
सोमवार को मैं लन्दन जा रहा हूँ।	*On Monday I am going to London.*
घर के भीतर कोई बोल रहा था।	*Inside the house somebody was talking.*

34 Expressions for 'to have'

There is no Hindi verb 'to have', and possession is expressed in a variety of ways. One such way has already been seen in मुझको जुकाम है *I have a cold.* Broadly, the main distinction made in Hindi is between having things that are movable and those that involve a more permanent relationship.

With movable objects, chattels, things that can be sold, etc., it is usual to use the postposition के पास:

राम के पास एक नई गाड़ी है।	*Ram has a new car.*
मेरे पास कुछ पैसा नहीं है।	*I don't have any money.*
हमारी चाबियाँ किस के पास हैं?	*Who has got our keys?*

With immovable objects (e.g. houses), relatives, and parts of the body it is usual to use the possessive particles का, की, के:

दुकानदार की दो दुकानें हैं।	*The shopkeeper has two shops.*
उसका एक बहुत सुन्दर मकान है।	*He has a very beautiful house.*
आपके कितने बच्चे हैं?	*How many children do you have?*
मेरे दो छोटे बेटे हैं।	*I have two small sons.*
मूर्ति के तीन सिर हैं।	*The statue has three heads.*
बुढ़िया की सिर्फ़ एक आँख है।	*The old woman has only one eye.*

Some speakers, however, when referring to relatives simply use के, irrespective of number or gender:

रमेश के आठ लड़कियाँ हैं।	*Ramesh has eight daughters.*
मेरे एक बेटा है।	*I have a son.*

This is thought to be a contraction of the postposition के यहाँ *at the place of, at the house of*. This postposition is also used in its full form to express possession:

उनके यहाँ नल का पानी नहीं है।	*They do not have tap water at their house.*
हमारे यहाँ चार नौकर हैं।	*We have four servants.*

Some other usages are:

मेरे सिर में दर्द है।	*I have a headache.*
उसके हाथ में ज़ोर नहीं है।	*He has no strength in his hand.*
इस मेज़ के चार पाँव हैं।	*This table has four legs.*
इस कमरे में पाँच खिड़कियाँ हैं।	*This room has five windows.*
हमारे मकान में सात कमरे हैं।	*Our house has seven rooms.*

Dialogue 8B *How do you go to work?*

सरोज क्या तुम आज दफ़्तर बस से जा रही हो?

अनीता नहीं, मैं रेलगाड़ी से जा रही हूँ, क्योंकि बस हमेशा देर से पहुँचती है। ट्रेन अक्सर ठीक समय पर छूटती है। तुम कैसे जा रही हो?

सरोज मैं भी ट्रेन से जा रही हूँ। पिछले साल मैं अपनी गाड़ी से जाती थी, पर इन दिनों रास्तों पर बहुत भीड़ होती है सो मैं आम तौर पर ट्रेन से दफ़्तर जाती हूँ।

अनीता तुम किस समय जा रही हो – अभी?

सरोज नहीं, मैं पहले एअर इंडिया के दफ़्तर जा रही हूँ। मुझे वहाँ कुछ ज़रूरी काम है। क्या तुम्हें मालूम है कि वह किधर है?

अनीता हाँ, यहाँ से दूर नहीं है। तुम स्टेशन से सीधे चलना, और दूसरे मोड़ पर बायें मुड़ना। थोड़ी दूर फिर सीधे चलो – सामने गणेश जी का मंदिर है और दाहिने हाथ पर एअर इंडिया का दफ़्तर। क़रीब दस मिनट का रास्ता है, बस।

सरोज शुक्रिया। सुशीला भी उस मुहल्ले में रहती है न?

अनीता नहीं, कुछ साल पहले वह वहाँ रहती थी अपने माँ-बाप के साथ, पर अब उसका अपना मकान है। काफ़ी अमीर लोग हैं। यह बताओ, तुम लन्दन कब जा रही हो?

सरोज तेईस मई को जा रही हूँ। बाईस तारीख़ को मेरा भाई यहाँ आ रहा है, और तेईस को हम साथ-साथ लन्दन जा रहे हैं।

Saroj	Are you going to the office by bus today?
Anita	No, I'm going by train, because the bus always arrives late. The train usually leaves on time. How are you going?
Saroj	I'm going by train too. Last year I used to go in my own car, but these days the roads are very crowded so I usually go to the office by train.
Anita	What time are you going–right now?
Saroj	No, first I'm going to the Air India office. I've got some urgent business there. Do you know which way it is?
Anita	Yes, it's not far from here. From the station go straight on, and at the second turning turn left. Go straight a little way[1] again–ahead is the Ganesh temple and on the right hand the Air India office. It's about ten minutes' walk, that's all.
Saroj	Thanks. Sushila lives in that district too, doesn't she?
Anita	No, some years ago she used to live there with her parents, but now she's got her own house. They're pretty wealthy people. Tell me (this), when are you going to London?
Saroj	I'm going on the twenty-third of May. On the twenty-second my brother is coming here, and on the twenty-third we're going to London together.

35 Some adverbial usages

को has already been seen in adverbial expressions such as सोमवार को, रात को, etc. There are many adverbial usages in which को is dropped and only the oblique case remains to indicate the adverbial force. Some such expressions are:

अगले महीने	*next month*	बायें हाथ	*to the left hand*
इस तरफ़	*in this direction*	तीसरे पहर	*in the afternoon*
दाहिने हाथ	*to the right hand*	दूसरे दिन	*the next day*
सवेरे	*in the early morning*	उन दिनों	*in those days*
पिछले साल	*last year*	सारे दिन	*all day*
उस दिन	*that day*	किस समय	*at what time?*

[1] थोड़ी दूर notice the feminine agreement in this adverbial expression; it derives from दूर, a feminine noun meaning 'distance', and can also be seen in कितनी दूर *how far*?

Motion towards a place can be expressed by को with the oblique, but this को is often dropped, leaving just the oblique case without a postposition:

कलकत्ते को जाना/ कलकत्ते जाना *to go to Calcutta*

से is another postposition used to form adverbial expressions; as with को, it too may sometimes be dropped:

बस से	*by bus*
देर (से)	*late*
अच्छी तरह (से)	*well*
ख़ुशी से	*happily, gladly*
हाथ से	*by hand*
जल्दी (से)	*quickly*
ठीक तरह (से)	*properly*
ठीक से	*properly*
ज़ोर (से)	*forcefully, loudly*
किस तरह (से)	*how? in what way?*
ध्यान से	*attentively*

पर is another postposition used to form adverbial expressions:

ठीक समय पर *punctually* आम तौर पर *usually* ख़ास तौर पर *specially*

The second element of certain compound postpositions can also be used adverbially:

बाहर बैठो।	*Sit outside.*
आगे चलो।	*Move ahead.*
अंदर आओ।	*Come in.*
भीतर मत जा।	*Don't go in.*
उस तरफ़ देखो।	*Look in that direction.*
तुम भी साथ चलो।	*You come along too.*
तुम पीछे चलो।	*You follow behind.*
पीछे मुड़ो।	*Turn back.*
पहले हम भी वहाँ जाते थे।	*Previously we used to go there too.*
वह नीचे/ऊपर रहती है।	*She lives downstairs/upstairs.*
कोई आदमी पास खड़ा था।	*Some man was standing nearby.*
दस साल पहले वह कारख़ाने में नौकरी करता था।	*Ten years ago he used to work in a factory.*
दस साल बाद	*ten years later*

Finally, there are some adjectives which are used in the oblique as adverbs:

कैसे	*how?*	दाहिने	*to the right*
सीधे	*straight*	बायें	*to the left*
धीरे-धीरे	*slowly*		

36 Dates

The traditional Hindu calendar will be introduced in Appendix A; the most commonly used calendar, however, is that derived from English:

जनवरी	*January* (f.)	जुलाई	*July* (f.)
फ़रवरी	*February* (f.)	अगस्त	*August* (m.)
मार्च	*March* (m.)	सितंबर	*September* (m.)
अप्रैल	*April* (m.)	अक्तूबर	*October* (m.)
मई	*May* (f.)	नवंबर	*November* (m.)
जून	*June* (m.)	दिसंबर	*December* (m.)

Dates are expressed as follows:

सत्रह अगस्त	*the seventeenth of August*
अठारह दिसंबर	*the eighteenth of December*

The only exception to this is with the first and second of the month:

पहली मई	*the first of May*
दूसरी जून	*the second of June*

Feminine agreement in पहली and दूसरी is with the implied word तारीख़ (f.) *date*. This word appears in such expressions as

जून की दस तारीख़	*the tenth of June*
अप्रैल की पहली तारीख़	*the first of April*
आज क्या तारीख़ है?	*What is the date today?*

The postposition को expresses 'on':

मार्च की उन्नीस तारीख़ को	*on the nineteenth of March*
इक्कीस सितंबर को	*on September the twenty-first*

37 Word order

With regard to the order of adverbs or adverbial phrases relative to each other, the standard order (that which gives no special emphasis to any part of the sentence) is: first, adverbs of time (रात को, कल, etc.); second, adverbs of place (वहाँ, बाहर, etc.); and third, adverbs of manner (ज़ोर से, सीधे, etc.).

In a sentence as a whole, the standard order is: first, the subject; second, the adverbs in the order given above; third, the indirect object; fourth, the direct object; and finally the verb. If there is an interrogative word or phrase, such as कब *when*? कहाँ *where*? कैसे *how*? or किस समय *at what time*?, then this will come immediately before the verb.

मैं हमेशा वहाँ बस से जाती हूँ।	*I always go there by bus.*
उमा अपने भाई को किस समय ला रही है?	*What time is Uma bringing her brother?*
शिव शाम को यहाँ कुछ छात्रों को पढ़ाता है।	*Shiv teaches some students here in the evening.*
आप कल मुझे पैसा दीजिए।	*You give me the money tomorrow.*

This standard order will be changed to give a special emphasis:

कल मुझे पैसा आप दीजिए।	*Tomorrow* **you** *give me the money.*
आप मुझे पैसा कल दीजिए।	*You give me the money* **tomorrow**.
आप कल पैसा मुझे दीजिए।	*Tomorrow you give* **me** *the money.*

EXERCISE **8.1** Translate into English:

मेरा नाम गणेश है, और मैं अपने भाई महेश के साथ एक छोटे गाँव में रहता हूँ। गाँव में कोई बड़ी दुकान नहीं है, इसलिए हर हफ़्ते हम शहर जाते हैं और बाज़ार से कुछ ज़रूरी चीज़ें ख़रीदते हैं। हमारे पास गाड़ी नहीं है, और शहर गाँव से काफ़ी दूर है, इसलिए आम तौर पर हम शहर बस से जाते हैं। मैं गाँव के पास एक बड़े कारख़ाने में काम करता हूँ, और मेरा छोटा भाई भी वहाँ काम करता है। उसके तीन बच्चे हैं। वे सब स्कूल जाते हैं और इस साल वे हिन्दी पढ़ रहे हैं। कल महेश कह रहा था कि बच्चों को स्कूल बहुत पसंद है, और वहाँ उनके कई दोस्त हैं। पिछले साल वे सिर्फ़ सुबह के समय स्कूल में पढ़ते थे, और स्कूल के बाद बग़ीचे में खेलते थे, लेकिन अब वे सारे दिन स्कूल में रहते हैं और बहुत ध्यान से पढ़ते हैं।

आज शनिवार है। शनिवार को कोई काम नहीं करता और बच्चे स्कूल नहीं जाते, इसलिए हम सब शहर जा रहे हैं। हमारे साथ हमारे कुछ मित्र भी आ रहे हैं। उनके पास गाड़ी है, सो आज हम बस से नहीं जा रहे हैं। कभी कभी बस देर से आती है; ड्राइवर की सिर्फ़ एक आँख है और वह बस को अच्छी तरह से नहीं चलाता, इसलिए अच्छी बात है कि हमारे मित्र अपनी गाड़ी ला रहे हैं! वे लोग काफ़ी

अमीर मालूम होते हैं। उनके दो मकान हैं—एक यहाँ, हमारे घर के सामने, और दूसरा बंबई के किसी अच्छे मुहल्ले में। उनका अपना एक कारख़ाना भी है ! पहले वे बंबई में रहते थे पर अब उनको गाँव की ज़िन्दगी ज़्यादा पसंद है। उनका लड़का बंबई में फ़िल्मों में नौकरी करता था; अब वह अख़बारों के लिए बच्चों की कहानियाँ लिखता है। अगले साल वह अपनी पत्नी के साथ लन्दन जा रहा है।

EXERCISE **8.2** Translate into Hindi:

1 Tomorrow evening we are going to the town by car.
2 Previously he used to have a big house in London.
3 My brother has four children, and the biggest goes to school with my son.
4 Last month I was studying Urdu, but this month I am studying Hindi.
5 What time are your friends coming?
6 The train moves slowly and arrives late.
7 I was saying that I don't like this food.
8 How many languages do you speak well?
9 My sisters do not usually go by bus, they go by train.
10 I have a headache and my mother has a cold, so we're not going to the market today.

Vocabulary

अंदर	*inside*
अक्तूबर	*October* (m.)
अगला	*next*
अच्छी तरह (से)	*well*
अठारह	*eighteen*
अप्रैल	*April* (m.)
अमीर	*rich, wealthy*
आँख	*eye* (f.)
आगे	*forward, ahead; hereafter*
आम	*general, usual; public*
आम तौर पर	*generally, usually*
इक्कीस	*twenty-one*
उन्नीस	*nineteen*
उम्र	*age* (f.)
ऊपर	*above, up*
एअर इंडिया	*Air India* (m.)
क़रीब	*near* (adj.); *about, near, almost, nearly*
कहानी	*story* (f.)
कारख़ाना	*factory, workshop* (m.)
किधर	*which way? where?*
किस तरह (से)	*how? in what manner?*

किस समय	*at what time?*
के भीतर	*inside, within*
ख़रीदना	*to buy*
ख़ास तौर पर	*specially, particularly*
ख़ुशी से	*happily, gladly*
गणेश	*Ganesh, elephant-headed god of wisdom, remover of obstacles* (m.)
चलाना	*to drive*
छात्र	*pupil, student* (m.)
छूटना	*to leave, be left*
जनवरी	*January* (m.)
ज़रूरी	*important, necessary, urgent*
जल्दी से	*quickly*
जून	*June* (m.)
ज़ोर	*force, strength* (m.)
ज़ोर से	*forcefully, loudly*
ठीक तरह (से)	*properly*
ठीक समय (पर)	*punctually, at the right time*
ठीक से	*properly*
ड्राइवर	*driver* (m.)
ढूँढ़ना	*to look for, search, trace*
तकलीफ़	*trouble* (f.)
तकलीफ़ देना	*to trouble, to bother*
तरफ़	*direction, side* (f.)
तरह	*manner, kind* (f.)
तारीख़	*date* (f.)
तीसरे पहर	*in the afternoon*
तेईस	*twenty-three*
तौर	*manner* (m.)
थोड़ा	*little, few*
दर्द	*pain* (m.)
दाहिना	*right* (of direction)
दिसंबर	*December* (m.)
दुकानदार	*shopkeeper* (m.)
देर	*delay, lateness, period of time* (f.)
देर से	*late*
देर होना	*to get late*
धीरे-धीरे	*slowly*
ध्यान	*attention* (m.)
ध्यान से	*attentively*
नल	*pipe, tap* (m.)
नवंबर	*November* (m.)
नीचे	*under, below, beneath*

नौकर	*servant* (m.)
नौकरी	*service, job* (f.)
नौकरी करना	*to serve, do a job*
पंद्रह	*fifteen*
पत्नी	*wife* (f.)
पहर	*8th part of a day, three-hour period* (m.)
पहले	*previously, ago,* (*at*) *first*
पहुँचाना	*to convey, cause to reach, deliver*
पाँव	*foot, leg* (m.)
पास	*nearby*
पिछला	*previous, last*
पीछे	*behind, after*
फ़रवरी	*February* (f.)
फ़िल्म	*film* (f.)
बदलना	*to change*
बाईस	*twenty-two*
बातें होना	*a conversation to take place*
बाद	*later*
बायाँ	*left* (inflects like पाँचवाँ)
भीड़	*crowd* (f.)
भीतर	*inside, within*
मई	*May* (f.)
माँ-बाप	*parents* (m.)
मार्च	*March* (m.)
मित्र	*friend* (m.)
मिनट	*minute* (m.)
मुड़ना	*to turn* (intr.)
मुहल्ला	*quarter of town, locality* (m.)
मूर्ति	*idol, image, statue* (f.)
मोड़	*bend, turning, fold* (m.)
रास्ता	*road, way, route* (m.)
सत्रह	*seventeen*
समय	*time* (m.)
सवेरा	*early morning, daybreak, dawn* (m.)
सवेरे	*in the early morning*
साथ-साथ	*together*
सामने	*opposite, facing*
सिनेमा देखना	*to see a film*
सीखना	*to learn*
सीधा	*straight, straightforward*
सीधे	*straight*
सो	*so*
सोलह	*sixteen*

Unit Nine

Dialogue 9A *Holiday plans*

चंपा कहिए गोपाल, आप दिल्ली कब जाएँगे? इसी महीने?

गोपाल इसी महीने नहीं, चौबीस जुलाई को जाऊँगा। जुलाई में मौसम कैसा होगा?

चंपा जुलाई में बहुत ज़्यादा गरमी होगी। आप दिल्ली में ही रहेंगे क्या?

गोपाल मैं दिल्ली में कम से कम दो हफ़्ते रहूँगा और उसके बाद अल्मोड़ा जाऊँगा। आपको मालूम होगा कि वहाँ मेरे कुछ रिश्तेदार रहते हैं।

चंपा हाँ, पर मुझे आशा है कि आप अपना सारा समय अल्मोड़ा में ही नहीं बिताएँगे। पहाड़ों में बहुत-सी दिलचस्प जगहें हैं। कश्मीर में भी घूमेंगे न?

गोपाल हाँ ज़रूर। कहते हैं कि वहाँ गरमियों में भी ठंडी हवा चलती है, इसलिए गरमी कम पड़ती है। लेकिन आपको कश्मीर की अच्छी जानकारी होगी?

चंपा जी हाँ, मेरे नाना-नानी वहाँ रहते हैं, श्रीनगर के पास। श्रीनगर कश्मीर की राजधानी है। मैं अपने छोटे भाई के साथ वहाँ नवंबर में जाऊँगी।

गोपाल क्या आप जाड़े की छुट्टियाँ वहीं बिताएँगी?

चंपा हाँ हाँ, छुट्टियाँ मनाने के लिए ही कश्मीर जा रही हूँ। पर मेरा भाई क़रीब पहली दिसंबर तक यहाँ लौटेगा क्योंकि उसे ठंडा मौसम पसंद नहीं है। जाड़ों में वह हमेशा यहीं बंबई में ही रहता है।

Champa Well Gopal, when will you go to Delhi? **This** month?

Gopal Not this month, I'll go on the twenty-fourth of July. What will the weather be like in July?

Champa It'll be very hot in July. Will you stay just in Delhi?

Gopal I'll stay at least two weeks in Delhi and after that I'll go to Almora. You must know that some relatives of mine live there.

Champa Yes, but I hope that you won't spend all your time just in Almora. There are lots of interesting places in the hills. You'll tour in Kashmir too, won't you?

Gopal Yes of course. They say that even in the summer[1] a cool wind

1 Note the use of the plural form गरमियाँ *the heats* to mean 'summer'; and see also the plural जाड़े *winter*.

blows there, so it doesn't get so hot. But you must know Kashmir well?

Champa Yes, my grandparents live there, near Srinagar. Srinagar is the capital of Kashmir. I shall go there with my younger brother in November.

Gopal Will you spend the winter holidays there?

Champa Yes of course, it's in order to pass the holidays that I'm going to Kashmir. But my brother will come back here by about the first of December because he doesn't like the cold weather. In the winter he always stays right here in Bombay.

38 The future tense

The future is formed as follows:

Masculine	**Feminine**	
मैं बोलूँगा	बोलूँगी	*I will speak*
तू बोलेगा	बोलेगी	*you will speak*
यह, वह बोलेगा	बोलेगी	*he / she will speak*
हम बोलेंगे	बोलेंगी	*we will speak*
तुम बोलोगे	बोलोगी	*you will speak*
आप बोलेंगे	बोलेंगी	*you will speak*
ये, वे बोलेंगे	बोलेंगी	*they will speak*

होना *to be, become,* लेना *to take* and देना *to give* form their future tenses as follows:

Masculine	**Feminine**	**Masculine**	**Feminine**	**Masculine**	**Feminine**
मैं हूँगा	हूँगी	लूँगा	लूँगी	दूँगा	दूँगी
तू होगा	होगी	लेगा	लेगी	देगा	देगी
यह, वह होगा	होगी	लेगा	लेगी	देगा	देगी
हम होंगे	होंगी	लेंगे	लेंगी	देंगे	देंगी
तुम होगे	होगी	लोगे	लोगी	दोगे	दोगी
आप होंगे	होंगी	लेंगे	लेंगी	देंगे	देंगी
ये, वे होंगे	होंगी	लेंगे	लेंगी	देंगे	देंगी

Verbs whose stem ends in -ई or -ऊ shorten this long vowel before the future endings: thus पीना *to drink* gives पिऊँगा *I will drink*. The future is made negative by either नहीं or न.

क्या आप उसे तार देंगे? — *Will you send him a telegram?*

हम फ़िल्म परसों देखेंगे। — *We shall see the film the day after tomorrow.*

मैं कल दिल्ली हवाई जहाज़ से जाऊँगा। *I shall fly to Delhi tomorrow.*
वह आज शाम को गाना गाएगी। *She will sing this evening.*

As in English, the future in Hindi is used both to refer to future events, e.g. 'He will come tomorrow', and to make assumptions about the present, e.g. 'Those people will be your new neighbours', when we mean 'I assume' or 'I suppose that those people must be your new neighbours'.

वे लोग आपके नए पड़ोसी होंगे। *Those people will be your new neighbours.*
आजकल मकान का किराया बहुत ज़्यादा होगा। *Nowadays the house rent will be very high.*
वह लंबी महिला उसकी सहेली होगी। *That tall lady will be her friend.*
आपको मालूम होगा कि मेरी पढ़ाई अच्छी तरह नहीं चल रही है। *You will be aware that my studies aren't going well.*

In this 'presumptive' usage, the future of होना can also be used with the imperfective and continuous tenses of other verbs, होगा etc. simply replacing present tense है etc. Compare the following:

आप उसे जानते हैं। *You know him.*
आप उसे जानते होंगे। *You will (must presumably) know him.*
वह किसी बड़े मकान में रहता होगा। *He probably lives (will be living) in some big house.*
आप मेरा नाम जानते होंगे? *You will know my name?*
सारा गाँव उसे पहचानता होगा। *The whole village will know him.*
वह अभी आती होगी। *She will be on her way now.*
वे अकेले आ रहे होंगे। *They will be coming alone.*

39 The emphatic particle ही

ही is a particle that emphasises the word or words which precede it; it is not a postposition, and does not require them to change their form or case. In some contexts it translates as 'only'.

कुछ ही लोग कालेज रोज़ जाते हैं। *Only some (a few) people go to college every day.*
इस बड़े मकान में दो ही आदमी रहते हैं। *Only two men live in this big house.*
यह इमारत बहुत ही पुरानी है। *This building is very old indeed.*

यहाँ से दूर न था, पास ही था।	*It wasn't far from here, it was just nearby.*
हम खेलते ही नहीं, काम भी करते हैं।	*We don't just play, we also work.*
मैं ही नहीं, सारा गाँव जानता है।	*Not just me, the whole village knows.*
यह जगह शान्त है ही।	*This place is certainly quiet.*

Certain of the forms of the pronouns coalesce with ही to give special forms:

मुझ	+	ही	=	मुझी				उस	+	ही	=	उसी
तुझ	+	ही	=	तुझी				हम	+	ही	=	हमीं
यह	+	ही	=	यही				तुम	+	ही	=	तुम्हीं
वह	+	ही	=	वही				इन	+	ही	=	इन्हीं
इस	+	ही	=	इसी				उन	+	ही	=	उन्हीं

(Nasality in the final vowel is frequently dropped.)

The other pronouns have simply ही following their usual forms: मैं ही *'I alone'*, मुझे ही *'to me alone'*, मेरा ही ***'my'*** (emphatic), etc.

Notice also the following forms, in which ही coalesces with adverbs:[1]

यहाँ	+	ही	=	यहीं	*in this very place, right here*
वहाँ	+	ही	=	वहीं	*in that very place, right there*
अब	+	ही	=	अभी	*at this very moment; yet*
सब	+	ही	=	सभी	***all*** (emphatic)

असली हिन्दी हमीं बोलते हैं।	*It is we who speak the real Hindi.*
वह मुझी को पत्र लिखती थी।	*She used to write only to me.*
पंडित जी उसी कमरे में बैठे हैं।	*Pandit ji is sitting in that very (that same) room.*
उन्हीं को पैसा चाहिए।	*It is they who need money.*
मैं यह पुस्तक आप को ही दे रहा हूँ।	*I am giving this book to* ***you.***
मेरी ही गाड़ी लाल है।	***My*** *car is red.*

1 When the sense 'only' is intended, ही remains separate from the adverb: अब ही *only now,* यहाँ ही *only here, etc.*

बच्चे यहीं खेल रहे थे।	*The children were playing right here.*
अभी आइयेगा।	*Please come at once.*
यह बात सभी लोग मानते हैं।	*Everybody accepts this.*

40 Some expressions of quantity

As has already been seen, बहुत acts both as an adjective (बहुत लोग *many people*) and as an adverb (बहुत बड़ा *very big*). When it is necessary to specify an adjectival sense, the adjective बहुत-सा *much, many* may be used:

बहुत अच्छी किताबें	*very good books*
but बहुत-सी अच्छी किताबें	*many good books*

बहुत-सा is not restricted to these contexts, but may also be used more generally:

बहुत (-से) भारतीय लोग शाकाहारी होते हैं।	*Many Indians are vegetarians.*
उसके पास बहुत-सा पैसा होगा।	*He must have quite a lot of money.*

Similarly, the adjective थोड़ा-सा *a little* is used alongside थोड़ा. *Both* parts of थोड़ा-सा inflect:

थोड़ी और चाय लीजिए।	*Have a little more tea.*
हाँ, थोड़ी-सी दीजिए।	*Yes, please give me a little.*

ज़्यादा and अधिक *much, many, more,* act both as adverbs and as adjectives. They may in certain contexts give the sense 'too much, too many'; this sense is made more explicit by adding बहुत:

गरमियों में ज़्यादा लोग यहाँ आते हैं।	*Many people come here in the summer.*
मेज़ पर अधिक किताबें न रखो।	*Don't put (too) many books on the table.*
दाल में नमक बहुत ज़्यादा है।	*There's too much salt in the lentils.*
इस दुकान में सब कुछ बहुत ज़्यादा महँगा है।	*Everything in this shop is too expensive.*

कम *few, less, little* may similarly be emphasised by adding बहुत:

इस साल कम लोग मकान ख़रीदेंगे।	*Few (fewer) people will buy houses this year.*

उस क्लास में बहुत कम विद्यार्थी थे।	*There were very few (too few) students in that class.*

Notice also the following expressions:

कम से कम	*at least*
ज़्यादा से ज़्यादा	*at the most*
अधिक से अधिक	*at the most*
थोड़ा-बहुत	*a certain amount, a little*

काफ़ी *enough, very,* often has the sense 'quite a fair amount', etc.: काफ़ी पैसा *enough money*; काफ़ी पुराना *pretty old*; काफ़ी दूर *quite far away*.

हमें कम से कम दस रुपये चाहिए।	*We need at least ten rupees.*
आप थोड़ी-बहुत उर्दू समझते होंगे?	*You must understand a certain amount of Urdu?*
दाम बहुत ही ज़्यादा है। कुछ कम करो।	*The price is far too high. Reduce it a bit.*
इस मुहल्ले में बहुत-से ग़रीब लोग रहते हैं।	*Many poor people live in this district.*
हवाई अड्डा यहाँ से काफ़ी दूर होगा?	*The airport will be quite a way from here?*
मई के महीने में अधिक पानी नहीं पड़ता।	*Not much rain falls in (the month of) May.*
आप काफ़ी अच्छी हिन्दी बोलते हैं!	*You speak pretty good Hindi!*

Dialogue 9B *Come to the cinema*

सोनी कहो राजू, क्या तुम कल हमारे साथ नई फ़िल्म देखने जाओगे?

राजू मैं नहीं जाऊँगा। तुम्हारे ख़्याल में वह देखने लायक़ होगी?

सोनी हाँ ज़रूर। हर कोई जा रहा होगा – तुम भी साथ चलो!

राजू नहीं यार, मुझे ऐसी फ़िल्में पसंद नहीं। हमेशा वही गाना, लड़ना और रोना-धोना होता है, और कुछ नहीं!

सोनी तुम्हारी बात बिलकुल ग़लत है। मालूम होता है, तुम फ़िल्मों के बारे में कुछ नहीं जानते।

राजू जानने को क्या है? और वहाँ टिकटों का दाम भी बहुत ज़्यादा होगा।

सोनी तुमसे कुछ कहने में क्या फ़ायदा है, तुम मेरी बात सुनते ही नहीं।

राजू ऐसे बोलने की कोई ज़रूरत नहीं भाई, तुम गुस्से हो रहे हो!

सोनी सुनो, मैं बस यह कह रहा हूँ कि यह नई फ़िल्म देखने लायक है। मैं ही नहीं, हर कोई कहता है। फ़िल्म का संगीत भी बहुत अच्छा है।

राजू अच्छा ही होगा, पर मुझे गरमियों में सिनेमा में बैठना पसंद नहीं। सरदियों में किसी दिन तुम्हारे साथ जाऊँगा।

सोनी ठीक है। अच्छा, हम कल काम पर मिलेंगे। और सुनो, मेरी बात का तुम बुरा न मानो।

राजू अरे भाई, कोई बात नहीं!

Soni Tell me Raju, will you go with us to see the new film tomorrow?

Raju I shan't go. Will it be worth seeing in your opinion?

Soni Yes of course. Everyone will be going – you come along too!

Raju No (friend), I don't like such films. There's always that same singing, fighting, and weeping and wailing, nothing else!

Soni What you say is quite wrong. It seems you don't know anything about films.

Raju What is there to know? And the tickets will be very expensive there as well.

Soni What's the point in saying anything to you, you just don't listen to what I say.

Raju There's no need to talk like that (brother), you're getting angry!

Soni Listen, all I'm saying is that this new film is worth seeing. Everybody says (so), not just me. The film's music is also very good.

Raju No doubt[1], but I don't like sitting in the cinema in the summer. I'll go with you some day in the winter.[2]

Soni All right. OK, we'll meet at work tomorrow.[3] And listen, don't take offence at what I said.

Raju (Oh brother), it's nothing.

41 The infinitive as a verbal noun

The infinitive is used as a verbal noun which is masculine and inflects like कमरा. The negative, 'not to do something', is expressed by न plus the infinitive.

1 The future tense is here used to give a presumptive sense: 'No doubt it will be good', 'It's sure to be good'.

2 Note that the plural of सरदी (f.) *cold* is used in the same way as the plurals of जाड़ा *cold* and गरमी *heat* (see Dialogue 9A, Note 1).

3 कल मिलेंगे *See you tomorrow*, a very common way of 'signing off' at the end of a conversation. Also फिर मिलेंगे *See you again*.

आदित्य

१०३

Examples in the direct case

पढ़ना आसान है, लिखना मुश्किल।	*To read is easy, to write difficult.*
माँस खाना उचित नहीं होता।	*Eating meat is not right.*
उनके लिए शराब पीना मना है।	*For them to drink alcohol is forbidden.*
तेरा यहाँ न रहना अफ़सोस की बात है।	*Your not staying here is a pity.*
उसका वहाँ जाना बिलकुल ज़रूरी होगा।	*His going there will be absolutely necessary.*
ऐसा करना अच्छा नहीं होता।	*It is not good to do this.*

When followed by the possessive particle or any other postposition, the infinitive inflects like any other masculine noun: पीने का पानी *drinking water;* सोने का कमरा *bedroom;* हँसने की बात *a laughing matter.*

Examples with postpositions

मेरे जाने के बाद आप क्या करेंगे?	*What will you do after I have gone?*
उस के आने के पहले तू अपना कमरा साफ़ कर।	*Clean your room before he comes.*
वहाँ पहुँचने पर हमें फ़ोन कीजिए।	*Phone us on arriving there.*
आपके वहाँ जाने में क्या फ़ायदा है?	*What is the point in your going there?*
वह शायद बाहर जाने को थी।	*She was perhaps about to go out.*
मैं बाहर जाने को तैयार हूँ।	*I am ready to go out.*
भारत लौटने के पहले हमारे यहाँ ठहरिए।	*Stay with us before returning to India.*
ऐसा करने से आप ज़्यादा सीखेंगे।	*You will learn more by doing this.*
अपनी माँ के कहने पर ही वह कुछ खाएगा।	*He will only eat something if his mother tells him.*
तुझे इसके बारे में कुछ जानने की ज़रूरत नहीं है।	*You don't need (have any need) to know about this.*
क्या आपको वहाँ जाने की आवश्यकता होगी?	*Will you need to go there?*

To express purpose, the oblique infinitive is usually used alone; it may also be used with को or के लिए:

वह कल फ़िल्म देखने जाएगी।	*She will go to see the film tomorrow.*
मुझे उम्मीद है कि आप हमसे मिलने आएँगे।	*I hope that you will come to visit us.*
किसीको मेरी गाड़ी ठीक करने के लिए भेजो।	*Send someone to fix my car.*

मैं आप का ही गाना सुनने को आऊँगा! — *I will come to hear just your singing!*

The adjectives योग्य and लायक़ *worth…, suitable for…,* usually take the oblique infinitive alone, but may take the oblique infinitive with के:

यह पुस्तक पढ़ने (के) योग्य है। — *This book is worth reading.*
यह नई फ़िल्म देखने (के) लायक़ है। — *This new film is worth seeing.*

There are many more uses of the infinitive in Hindi; here it may be noted that the direct infinitive is used before the verbs जानना, सीखना and शुरू करना to mean 'to know how to', 'to learn to' and 'to begin to'; and 'to tell someone to do something' involves the use of the oblique infinitive with को.

मैं गाड़ी चलाना नहीं जानता। — *I don't know how to drive a car.*
मेरी सहेली सितार बजाना सीख रही है। — *My friend is learning to play the sitar.*
अगले महीने वह नया मकान बनाना शुरू करेगा। — *Next month he will begin to build the new house.*
उससे यहाँ आने को कहो। — *Tell him to come here.*

EXERCISE **9.1** Translate into English:

मैं परसों हिन्दी सीखने के लिए दिल्ली जा रही हूँ। मैं वहाँ कम से कम दो महीने रहूँगी और मुझे आशा है कि बहुत ध्यान से पढ़ने के बाद मैं हिन्दी काफ़ी अच्छी तरह से सीखूँगी। मेरी एक सहेली की बहिन दिल्ली में ही नौकरी करती है और मैं उसी के साथ रहूँगी। उसका मकान कालेज से काफ़ी दूर है लेकिन स्टेशन पास ही है, इसलिए मैं रोज़ रेलगाड़ी से कालेज जाऊँगी। मालूम होता है कि उस मुहल्ले में बहुत-से विद्यार्थी रहते हैं। वे भी इसी तरह रेलगाड़ी से कालेज जाते होंगे और मैं भी उनके साथ जाऊँगी क्योंकि पिताजी कहते हैं कि मेरा अकेले जाना ठीक न होगा। मैं उनकी बात मानती नहीं पर उनसे कुछ कहती नहीं क्योंकि बड़ों के सामने ऐसा कहना उचित नहीं होगा। मेरी सहेली कहती है कि आजकल भारत में, ख़ास तौर पर बड़े शहरों में, चीज़ों के दाम बहुत ज़्यादा होते हैं और मुझे काफ़ी पैसे की ज़रूरत होगी।

हवाई जहाज़ यहाँ से सवेरे जाता है और दिल्ली रात तक पहुँचेगा। मेरी सहेली की बहिन मुझसे मिलने हवाई अड्डे आएगी। मैं उसे नहीं जानती सो मुझे मालून नहीं कि मैं उसे कैसे पहचानूँगी। शायद वह मुझको पहचानेगी क्योंकि उसके पास मेरी एक पुरानी तस्वीर है। उसके दो लड़के हैं, और वे भी उसके साथ हवाई अड्डे पर आ रहे होंगे। बड़ा लड़का किसी कारख़ाने में नौकरी करता है। छोटा लड़का अभी स्कूल में है, पर अपनी पढ़ाई ख़त्म करने पर वह भी उसी कारख़ाने में काम करना शुरू करेगा। मेरी सहेली का कहना है कि किसी छोटे गाँव में उन लोगों का एक दूसरा मकान भी है। रविवार को और

स्कूल की छुट्टियों में वे लोग वहाँ घूमने जाते हैं, और मैं भी उनके साथ वहाँ जाऊँगी। यह बड़ी अच्छी बात होगी क्योंकि मुझे गाँव की ज़िन्दगी बहुत पसंद है, और दूसरी बात यह है कि गाँव के लोग हिन्दी ही जानते होंगे इसलिए उनसे बात करने में मुझे बहुत फ़ायदा होगा।

EXERCISE 9.2 Translate into Hindi:

Tomorrow we shall go to Delhi to meet our friends. We do not have a car, so we shall go by train. Perhaps our friends will come to meet us at the station, because they live very near; after meeting them we shall go to eat in some hotel, and then we shall go to their house in the afternoon. I don't like eating in hotels, but the children like it very much. Our friends have two boys, and our children will play happily with them till evening. Their house is very beautiful indeed, and just nearby there is a very big garden. It is a very peaceful place and the children like to wander around there. In the summer a lot of people go there, but in the winter nobody does. We won't need our coats tomorrow, because they say that it won't rain; we hope that what they say won't be wrong!

Vocabulary

अकेले	*alone* (adv.)
अधिक	*much*
अधिक से अधिक	*at the most*
अल्मोड़ा	*Almora* (m.)
असली	*real, genuine*
आवश्यकता	*necessity, need* (f.)
आशा	*hope* (f.)
इमारत	*building* (f.)
इसी लिए	*that's why, for this very reason*
उचित	*fitting, proper, right*
उम्मीद	*hope* (f.)
ऐसा	*such, of this kind* (adj.); *thus, so* (adv.)
ऐसे	*thus, in this way, so* (adv.)
कम करना	*to reduce*
कम से कम	*at least*
कश्मीर	*Kashmir* (m.)
कालेज	*college* (m.)
के योग्य	*worthy of, worth*
के लायक़	*worthy of, worth*
क्लास	*class* (f./m.)
ख़्याल	*opinion, thought* (m.)
गरमी	*heat* (f.); *summer* (pl.)

गरमी पड़ना	*to get hot* (of weather)
ग़रीब	*poor*
ग़लत	*wrong, mistaken*
गाना[1]	*to sing*
गाना[2]	*song* (m.)
गुस्सा	*anger* (m.)
गुस्सा/गुस्से होना	*to get angry* (*with*, पर)
घूमना	*to tour, visit, wander about, turn* (intr.)
चौबीस	*twenty-four*
जगह	*place* (f.)
ज़रूरत	*need, necessity* (f.)
जाड़ा	*cold* (m.); *winter* (pl.)
जानकारी	*knowledge, information* (f.)
ज़्यादा से ज़्यादा	*at the most*
टिकट	*ticket; stamp* (m.)
ठंडा	*cold* (adj.)
ठीक करना	*to fix, put right*
तार	*telegram, cable* (m.)
तार देना	*to send a telegram*
थोड़ा-बहुत	*a certain amount*
थोड़ा-सा	*a few, a little* (adj.)
दाम	*price* (m.)
दाल	*pulse, lentil* (f.)
नमक	*salt* (m.)
नाना	*maternal grandfather* (m.)
नाना-नानी	*maternal grandparents* (m.)
नानी	*matenal grandmother* (f.)
पंडित	*learned man, pandit* (m.)
पड़ना	*to fall, lie*
पढ़ाई	*study, studies* (f.)
पहचानना	*to recognise, identify*
पानी पड़ना	*to rain*
फ़ायदा	*advantage, profit, gain* (m.)
फ़ोन करना	*to telephone*
बजाना	*to play* (musical instrument)
बहुत-सा	*many, much, quite a few* (adj.)
बिताना	*to spend, pass* (time)
बिल्कुल	*absolutely*
बुरा मानना	*to take amiss, take offence (at)*
बैठा	*sitting, seated*
भेजना	*to send*
मना	*forbidden, prohibited* (inv.)
मनाना	*to celebrate* (festival, holiday, etc.)

माँ	*mother* (f.)
माँस	*meat* (m.)
मानना	*to accept, agree, believe*
मिलना	*to meet* (*with*, से)
यहीं	*right here, at this very place*
यार	*friend, mate* (m./f.)
योग्य	*capable, worth, suitable, worthy*
रखना	*to put, place, keep, hold*
राजधानी	*capital city* (f.)
रिश्तेदार	*relative* (m.)
रोज़	*daily, everyday; day* (m.)
रोना	*to cry, weep*
रोना-धोना	*to weep and wail*
लड़ना	*to fight*
लायक़	*capable, worth, suitable, worthy*
लौटना	*to return* (intr.)
वहीं	*right there, in that very place*
शाकाहारी	*vegetarian* (m./adj.)
शान्त	*peaceful, quiet*
शायद	*perhaps*
श्रीनगर	*Srinagar* (m.)
संगीत	*music* (m.)
सब कुछ	*everything*
सरदी	*cold* (f.); *winter* (pl.)
सहेली	(girl's) *female friend* (f.)
सितार	*sitar* (f.)
हँसना	*to laugh*
हर कोई	*everyone*
हवा	*air, wind, breeze* (f.)
हवाई अड्डा	*airport* (m.)
हवाई जहाज़	*aeroplane* (m.)
ही	*only* (etc.) (emphatic particle)

Unit Ten

Dialogue 10A *'I must speak to Dharmendra'*

कमल हलो, मैं कमल किशोर बोल रहा हूँ। क्या धर्मेन्द्र जी हैं ?

सीता नमस्कार कमल जी, मैं सीता बोल रही हूँ। धर्मेन्द्र जी अभी यहाँ नहीं हैं — शायद अपने नए दफ़्तर पर हों। आप उन्हें शाम को फ़ोन करें।

कमल बहुत ज़रूरी है कि मैं उनसे अभी बात करूँ — कल ही मैं बाहर जा रहा हूँ और मंगलवार तक नहीं लौटूँगा। क्या करें ?

सीता आप चाहते हैं कि मैं आपको उनका दफ़्तर का नंबर दूँ ? मेरे पास है। या मैं ही उन्हें फ़ोन करूँ ? आपकी मरज़ी।

कमल मैं आपको कष्ट देना नहीं चाहता — पर काफ़ी व्यस्त तो हूँ। आप ही उन्हें फ़ोन करें और उनसे कहें कि मैं उनसे मंगल को मिलना चाहता हूँ। उनसे पूछें कि क्या मंगल की सुबह को उन्हें फ़ुरसत है।

सीता अच्छी बात। आप मुझे अपना नंबर भी दें, शायद धर्मेन्द्र आपको आज ही फ़ोन करना चाहें।

कमल नंबर देने की ज़रूरत नहीं, उनके पास होगा। सुनिए, मैं चाहता हूँ कि मेरे लौटने के बाद आप और धर्मेन्द्र जी दोनों किसी दिन हमारे यहाँ भोजन करने आएँ। आएँगे, न ?

सीता जी हाँ ज़रूर, क्यों नहीं आएँगे ? बड़ा अच्छा रहेगा। और हाँ, सुनीता से मेरी नमस्ते कहना न भूलें। अच्छा जी नमस्कार, फ़ोन करने के लिए धन्यवाद।

कमल नमस्ते जी, अगले महीने मिलेंगे।

Kamal Hello, this is Kamal Kishor speaking.[1] Is Dharmendra jī in?[2]

Sita Hello Kamal jī, this is Sita here. Dharmendra jī is not here just at the moment – he may perhaps be at his new office. Would you phone him in the evening?

Kamal It's very important that I speak to him right away – I'm going

1 Notice that the Hindi equivalent of 'This is x speaking' uses the first person – literally, 'I x am speaking'.

2 In expressions like 'Is x in?', 'Is x there?', the Hindi sentence needs no adverb.

	away[1] actually tomorrow, and I shan't be back until Tuesday. What should we do?
Sita	Would you like me to give you his office number?[2] I have it. Or should I phone him myself? It's up to you.
Kamal	I don't want to cause you inconvenience–but I am pretty busy! Would *you* phone him and say to him that I want to meet him on Tuesday.[3] Would you ask him whether he's free on Tuesday morning.
Sita	Very well. Would you give me your number too–perhaps Dharmendra may want to phone you today.
Kamal	There's no need (for me) to give the number–he's sure to have it. Listen, I want you and Dharmendra jī both to come and have a meal with us some day after I get back. You will come, won't you?
Sita	Yes of course, why wouldn't we come[4]? That will be very nice.[5,6] And yes, please don't forget to give my greetings to Sunita. All right, goodbye then, and thanks for phoning.
Kamal	Goodbye, see you next month.

42 The subjunctive

The subjunctive is formed in exactly the same way as the future, but without the -गा/-गे/-गी ending (and therefore not distinguishing gender):

मैं बोलूँ	हम बोलें
तू बोले	तुम बोलो
यह, वह बोले	आप बोलें
	ये वे बोलें

Because this results in मैं हूँ being used for both present 'I am' and subjunctive 'I may be', an alternative form मैं होऊँ is sometimes used for the subjunctive.

1 मैं बाहर जा रहा हूँ, lit. *I am going out,* but बाहर here has the sense 'away from home', 'out of town', etc.
2 उनका दफ़्तर का नंबर: उनका here refers to the number, and not to the office–and therefore stays in the direct case.
3 मंगल: a commonly used short form of मंगलवार. The forms बुध, बृहस्पति and शुक्र also occur. (वार means 'day'.)
4 Rhetorical questions of this kind are much more common in Hindi than in English; in English they may sound abrupt or impolite, but in Hindi they form a natural part of the conversation.
5 Notice the adverbial use of बड़ा in बड़ा अच्छा *very nice* (=बहुत अच्छा)
6 रहना often takes the place of होना in future contexts of this kind.

The range of meanings that the subjunctive can express is best understood from examples. Compare the following sentences:

Future

क्या वह भी आएगा?	*Will he come too?*
वह कहाँ जाएगी?	*Where will she go?*
मैं कुछ बोलूँगा।	*I shall say something.*
हम क्या करेंगे?	*What shall we do?*

Subjunctive

क्या वह भी आए?	*May/should he come too?*
वह कहाँ जाए?	*Where might/should she go?*
मैं कुछ बोलूँ?	*May I/should I say something?*
हम क्या करें?	*What should we do?*

The subjunctive is also commonly used in making suggestions, polite requests and for expressing wishes; the negative particle used with the subjunctive is न, not नहीं.

हम बाहर चलें।	*Let's go out.*
आप अन्दर आएँ।	*Would you come in?*
हमारी माँगें पूरी हों!	*May our demands be fulfilled!* (Demonstrators' slogan)
आप भी 'भारत माता की जय' कहें!	*You too should say, 'Victory to Mother India'!*
मुझे उम्मीद है कि वह न आए।	*I hope that he might not come.*
ऐसा न हो कि पैसा कम हो।	*May it not happen that the money be too little.*

The subjunctive is also used in expressions of possibility. Notice also how it is used with imperfective (बोलता) and continuous (बोल रहा) forms, giving imperfective and continuous subjunctives:

शायद वह बाहर खड़ा हो।	*Perhaps he is standing outside.*
संभव है कि वे न आएँ।	*It is possible that they may not come.*
बच्चे बग़ीचे में खेल रहे हों।	*The children may be playing in the garden.*
वे अँग्रेज़ी सीखते हों।	*They might be learning English.*
संभव नहीं है कि कोई आदमी अपने बच्चे को मारे।	*It is not possible that a man beat his child.*

Further uses of the subjunctive will be introduced later; here it should be noted that it is commonly used in expressions of rightness, necessity or obligation:

उचित है कि माँ-बाप अपने बच्चों को प्यार करें।[1]	*It is right that parents should love their children.*
आवश्यक है कि तुम खाना खाने के पहले हाथ धोओ।	*It is necessary that you should wash your hands before meals.*
बहुत ज़रूरी है कि हम सुबह की गाड़ी पकड़ें।	*It is vital that we catch the morning train.*
उनको यह चाहिए था कि वे कारख़ाने में नौकरी करें।	*They had to take employment in the factory.*
उससे कहिए कि वह चुप रहे!	*Tell him to keep quiet!*

43 The verb चाहना

चाहना means 'to want, wish'. In a sentence of the type 'I want to go', in which the desired action ('to go') is to be performed by the subject ('I'), then चाहना is used with an infinitive: मैं जाना चाहता हूँ. If the action is to be performed by somebody other than the subject, then a subjunctive clause is used, introduced by कि: मैं चाहता हूँ कि वह जाए *I want him to go.*

मैं उस दुकान से कुछ फल खरीदना चाहता हूँ।	*I want to buy some fruit from that shop.*
वह चाहती है कि मैं उसके साथ चलूँ।	*She wants me to go with her.*
हम अभी लौटना नहीं चाहते।	*We don't want to go back just yet.*
तुम चाहते हो कि मैं उर्दू पढ़ूँ?	*You want me to study Urdu?*

It is important to understand the difference between the use of the verb चाहना and the use of the चाहिए construction introduced in paragraph 30.

Dialogue 10B *Dharmendra returns the phone call*

धर्मेन्द्र हलो कमल, मैं धर्मेन्द्र बोल रहा हूँ। सीता कह रही थी कि आप मुझसे बात करना चाहते हैं। कोई ख़ास बात है क्या?

[1] The distinction between प्यार करना with को and with से is similar to that between 'to love' and 'to be in love with' in English.

कमल	नमस्कार धर्मेन्द्र। सुनिए, बहुत ज़रूरी है कि हम जल्दी मिलें। अगर आपको फ़ुरसत हो तो आज ही मेरे दफ़्तर आएँ। आज का क्या प्रोग्राम है आपका?
धर्मेन्द्र	मैं तो अभी बाहर जानेवाला था – पर अगर आप चाहें तो हम शाम को मिलें।
कमल	अच्छी बात। अगर आपको असुविधा न हो तो हम आपके यहाँ मिलें क्योंकि शाम को सुनीता की कुछ सहेलियाँ हमारे यहाँ आ रही हैं।
धर्मेन्द्र	हाँ ज़रूर, आप हमारे यहाँ अवश्य आएँ। पर बात क्या है भई? इतनी जल्दी क्यों है मिलने के लिए? घर में सब ठीक तो है?
कमल	अरे, घर में तो सब ठीक है, पर नौकरी-वाला मामला है। आपको याद है न कि मैं नई नौकरी ढूँढ़ रहा हूँ? इसी मामले में तो आपकी सलाह लेना चाहता था।
धर्मेन्द्र	मेरा ख़्याल तो यह है कि अगर आपको अच्छी नौकरी चाहिए तो आप किसी सरकारी दफ़्तर में अर्ज़ी दें। सरकार तो अच्छी तनख़ाह देती होगी। आप आने वाले हफ़्ते का समाचार पत्र पढ़ें, तो कम से कम तीन चार सरकारी विज्ञापन पाएँगे।
कमल	वैसे मैं ऐसी नौकरी के लिए अर्ज़ी देने ही वाला था, पर सुनीता यह नहीं चाहती कि मैं सरकार में काम करूँ। सच पूछिए तो मैं किसी व्यापार करनेवाली कंपनी में नौकरी करना चाहता हूँ, शायद विदेश में ही। आप तो विदेशी कंपनियों की गति-विधियों के बारे में बहुत जानते हैं, इस लिए आप की सलाह लेना बहुत ज़रूरी समझता हूँ।
धर्मेन्द्र	अच्छा जी, तो शाम को ही हम बात करेंगे इस मामले में।

Dharm-endra	Hello Kamal, it's Dharmendra speaking. Sita was saying that you want to talk to me. Is it anything special?
Kamal	Hello Dharmendra. Listen, it's very important that we meet soon. If you're free would you come to my office *today*? What have you got to do today?[1]
Dharm-endra	I was just about to go out–but if you like we could meet in the evening.
Kamal	Very good. If it's not inconvenient to you, let's meet at your place, because in the evening some friends of Sunita's are coming here.
Dharm-endra	Yes of course, do certainly come here. But what's up? Why so much hurry about meeting? Everything's all right at home I hope?
Kamal	Oh, everything's all right at home, but it's to do with work. You remember, don't you, that I'm looking for a new job? It's in this connection that I wanted to take your advice.
Dharm-endra	What I think is that if you want a good job you should apply to some government office. The government must be paying a good salary. If you read the coming week's newspaper, you'll find at least three or four government advertisements.

1 Lit. *What's your programme for today?* A colloquial word order relocates आपका at the end of the sentence.

Kamal	Actually I *was* about to apply for such a job, but Sunita doesn't want me to work in the government. As a matter of fact[1] I want to serve in some trading company, perhaps abroad. You know a lot about the workings of foreign companies, so I consider it essential to take your advice.
Dharm-endra	All right, so we'll talk about this matter in the evening.

44 Introduction to conditional sentences

Conditional sentences comprise an 'if' clause followed by a 'then' clause: 'If it rains, then I won't go out'. In Hindi, the 'if' clause begins with अगर or यदि, and the 'then' clause with तो. (अगर/यदि may sometimes be dropped, but तो may not.)

In conditional sentences referring to the future, either the future tense or the subjunctive will occur in the 'if' clause (use of the subjunctive indicates that the event is seen as being less likely or definite); the future tense, the subjunctive, or an imperative may be found in the 'then' clause.

अगर वह आएगी तो मैं उसे पुस्तक दूँगा।	*If she comes I'll give her the book.*
अगर वह आए तो मैं उसे पुस्तक दूँगा।	*Should she come I'll give her the book.*
अगर आप चाहें तो हम साथ साथ जाएँगे।	*If you wish we will go together.*
यदि वे हिंदी बोलेंगे तो आप समझेंगे?	*If they speak Hindi, will you understand?*
मौसम अच्छा न हो तो हम घर में ही रहें?	*If the weather's not good should we stay indoors?*
सीढ़ियाँ ज़्यादा ऊँची होंगी तो मैं नीचेवाले कमरे में सोऊँगा।	*If the stairs are very high I'll sleep in the downstairs room.*

It is possible for a subjunctive to appear in the 'then' clause, usually giving the sense 'should' or 'might'; imperatives also may appear in the 'then' clause.

यदि वह आए तो पूरे दिन रहे।	*If he comes he might stay all day.*
अगर भारत जाएँ तो आप हिंदी ही बोलें।	*If you go to India you should speak only Hindi.*

1 सच पूछिए *Ask the truth*, i.e. 'If you want to know the truth', 'To tell you the truth'.

अगर वह पत्र माँगे तो उसे दिखाना।	*If he asks for the letter, show it to him.*
अगर फ़ुरसत हो तो मेरे साथ चलो।	*Come with me if you've got the time.*
अगर उसे केला पसंद नहीं तो उसे अंगूर खिलाइए।	*If he doesn't like bananas give him grapes to eat.*
अगर वह नहा रहा हो तो मैं उसे बाद में फ़ोन करूँ?	*If he's bathing should I phone him later?*
यदि लड़कों के बीच में झगड़ा हो तो अध्यापक को बुलाना।	*If there's a quarrel between the boys, call the teacher.*

45 The particle तो

तो has just been encountered introducing the 'then' clause of conditional sentences. तो means 'then' in the sense of 'as a result', rather than in the sense of 'at that time'; it is often used in other contexts also with this same sense of 'then', or with the sense 'so':

अच्छा, तो मैं चलूँगा।	*Right, then I'll be off.*
तो आप यहाँ कितने दिन रहेंगे?	*So how long will you stay here?*
तो बेटे, परीक्षा कब दोगे?	*Well then son, when will you sit the exam?*

When तो occurs in the middle of a sentence or clause, it gives to the preceding words or phrase an emphasis which would be expressed in English by phrases such as 'as for', 'admittedly', 'of course', 'actually'. The emphatic stress of तो is often 'adversitive', that is it contrasts one statement or fact with a second; the function of तो here is to anticipate a contrasting statement, as in the sentence मैं तो नहीं जानता, मेरा भाई जानता होगा *'I don't know, my brother must know'*. Very often the anticipated contrast is implied rather than actually stated: मैं तो नहीं जानता *'I don't know [but perhaps someone else does]'*. In a spoken English sentence, the emphasis equivalent to that given by तो is often carried by stress alone.

राम तो यहाँ नहीं रहता; उसका भाई ही यहाँ रहता है।	***Ram**, of course, doesn't live here; only his brother lives here.*
राम यहाँ तो नहीं रहता; उसका मकान किसी और गाँव में है।	*Ram doesn't live actually **here**; his house is in some other village.*
राम यहाँ रहता तो नहीं, लेकिन रोज यहाँ आता है।	*Ram doesn't actually **live** here, but he comes here every day.*

सच तो यह है कि वह ज़्यादा खाना खाता है।	*Actually the truth is that he over-eats.*
बात तो यह है कि गणेश बहुत ही ग़रीब है।	*The thing is that Ganesh is very poor.*
हम लोग तो पैदल चलेंगे।	*As for us, we shall go on foot.*
पत्र जल्दी लिखो, नहीं तो मैं घबराऊँगा।	*Write a letter soon, otherwise I shall get worried.*

This last example illustrates the common use of नहीं तो as 'otherwise'. Certain other set uses of तो may also be learned:

आप अच्छे तो हैं?	*You are well, I hope?*
आप बीमार तो नहीं हैं?	*You're not ill, I hope?*
माँस तो क्या, वह अंडे भी नहीं खाती!	*She doesn't even eat eggs, let alone meat!*
संस्कृत तो दूर, मैं तो हिंदी ही अच्छी तरह से नहीं समझता!	*As for me, I don't even understand Hindi properly, never mind Sanskrit!*

46 The suffix -वाला

-वाला is a suffix added mainly to nouns, adverbs and the oblique infinitive to produce a range of meanings. It is declinable like an adjective. Examples of -वाला with nouns are दूधवाला *milkman,* मिठाईवाला *sweetseller,* पगड़ीवाला *one wearing a turban,* गाँववाला *villager,* मद्रासवाला *one from Madras.* Examples with adverbs are the adjectives ऊपरवाला *upstairs,* नीचेवाला *downstairs,* पासवाला *nearby.*

Examples with the oblique infinitive are हिंदी बोलनेवाला *Hindi-speaking,* देखनेवाला *spectator,* रहनेवाला *inhabitant,* आनेवाला हफ़्ता *the coming week.*

The oblique infinitive with -वाला can also express the sense 'on the point of doing': thus मैं बाहर जानेवाला था *I was on the point of going out.*

कुछ पैसेवाले तो बड़े कंजूस होते हैं।	*Some wealthy people are very mean.*
आप कहाँ के रहनेवाले हैं?	*Where are you from?*
इन तस्वीरों में से बीचवाली मुझे पसंद है।	*Out of these pictures I prefer the middle one.*
वह साड़ीवाली औरत उसकी माँ है।	*That woman wearing a sari is his mother.*

टैक्सीवाले से कहो कि वह दस मिनट में लौटे। *Tell the taxi driver to come back in ten minutes.*

किसी पासवाली दुकान से अख़बार ख़रीदें। *Let's buy a paper from some nearby shop.*

ऊपरवाले कमरों में बिजली नहीं है। *There's no electricity in the upstairs rooms.*

मैं आप को पत्र लिखनेवाला था। *I was about to write you a letter!*

मैं ज़मीनवाले मामले के बारे में परेशान था। *I was worried about the land question.*

EXERCISE 10.1 Translate the following letter into English:

कानपुर
१२ अगस्त १९८७

प्रिय सुनील जी,

मुझे बहुत ख़ुशी है कि आप यहाँ दीवाली मनाने आ रहे हैं। अगर आपको घर लौटने की जल्दी न हो तो आप हमारे यहाँ कम से कम दस दिन ठहरें। हम लोग तो अभी दीवाली की तैयारियाँ पूरी करने में काफ़ी व्यस्त हैं। मेरा बड़ा भाई रवि तो दीवाली के दिन यहाँ नहीं होगा, वह अभी कुछ दिनों के लिए लंदन जानेवाला है। अगर उसके लिए संभव होगा, तो वह हमें लंदन से ही दीवाली की बधाइयाँ देने के लिए फ़ोन करेगा। आपको मालूम न हो कि रवि की शादी की बातचीत चल रही है। लड़कीवाले तो बड़े पैसेवाले हैं – अगर बातचीत पक्की होगी तो बड़ी ख़ुशी की बात होगी। वैसे लड़की को तो रवि कई सालों से जानता है, वह उसके एक साथी की बहिन है। नानी जी का कहना है कि पुराने ज़माने में बिरादरी के बड़े-बूढ़े ही कन्या को पसंद करते थे, और गाँवों में तो अभी भी यह रिवाज चल रहा है; पर शहरवाले परिवारों की गति-विधियाँ तो कुछ भिन्न होती हैं। यदि कोई रवि से कहे कि कन्या को पसंद करने का अधिकार बड़े-बूढ़ों को ही है, तो उसे बहुत आश्चर्य होगा!

अगर संभव हो तो आप बाल-बच्चों को भी दीवाली मनाने के लिए साथ लाएँ। घर में काफ़ी जगह है, और माता जी कहती हैं कि उन्हें तो आपके आने से किसी तरह की असुविधा नहीं होगी। दिल्ली से आप वाराणसी-वाली गाड़ी पकड़ें तो कानपुर कुछ ही घंटों में पहुँचेंगे। स्टेशन पहुँचने पर आप मुझे फ़ोन करें, तो मैं आप से तुरंत मिलने आऊँगा। अगर दीवाली के समय मौसम भी अच्छा होगा तो हम एकाध दिन कहीं सैर करने चलें। वैसे शहर तो इतना दिलचस्प नहीं है, पर उसके आस-पास बहुत-सी जगहें देखने लायक़ हैं। अच्छा, मैं इस पत्र को समाप्त करता हूँ। अपने माता-पिता से मेरा नमस्कार कहें। और बच्चों को प्यार। पत्र का जवाब जल्दी दें!

आपका
रमेश

EXERCISE 10.2 Translate into Hindi:

1 If you don't study attentively, how will you take the exam?
2 I want her to stay here, but she wants to go home.

3 Perhaps he may know about this.
4 It is possible that he might phone, so you should not go out yet.
5 If I have the time I'll read this book as well.
6 If it is not inconvenient, let's meet in the hotel opposite.
7 If you look you will find advertisements in all the newspapers.
8 You should phone him immediately, otherwise he might go to the market with the others.
9 If you wish you could take my parents' advice on the marriage matter.
10 As for me, I shall stay in the downstairs room tonight.

Vocabulary

अंगूर	*grape* (m.)
अंडा	*egg* (m.)
अगर	*if*
अधिकार	*right, authority* (m.)
अरज़ी	*application* (f.)
अरज़ी देना	*to apply* (tr.)
अवश्य	*certainly*
असुविधा	*inconvenience* (f.)
आवश्यक	*necessary*
आश्चर्य	*surprise* (m.)
(किसी को) आश्चर्य होना	*(someone) to be surprised*
इतना	*so much/many, this much/many*
एकाध	*a few, one or two*
कंजूस	*miserly, mean*
कंपनी	*firm, company* (f.)
कन्या	*girl, daughter, virgin* (f.)
कष्ट	*trouble* (m.)
कष्ट देना	*to trouble*
कहीं	*somewhere*
कानपुर	*Kanpur* (m.) (previously 'Cawnpore')
के आस-पास	*around, in the vicinity of*
के बीच (में)	*between, amidst, among*
केला	*banana* (m.)
खिलाना	*to give to eat, feed*
गति-विधि	*working(s), activities, behaviour* (f.)
गाँववाला	*villager* (m.)
घंटा	*hour* (m.)
घबराना	*to worry, be nervous, panic*
चाहना	*to wish, to want*

चुप	*quiet, silent*
चुप रहना	*to be quiet, stay quiet*
ज़मीन	*land, earth, ground* (f.)
जय	*victory* (f.)
जवाब	*answer* (m.)
जवाब देना	*to answer*
झगड़ा	*quarrel* (m.)
टैक्सी	*taxi* (f.)
तनख़ाह	*pay, salary* (f.)
तुरत (तुरंत)	*immediately*
तैयारी	*preparation* (f.)
तो	*then; so; at any rate*
दीवाली	*Diwali, festival of lamps* (f.)
धोना	*to wash* (clothes etc.)
नंबर	*number* (m.)
नहाना	*to bathe, wash oneself*
नहीं तो	*otherwise*
पकड़ना	*to catch, grab, hold*
पगड़ी	*turban* (f.)
परीक्षा	*examination* (f.)
परीक्षा देना	*to sit an examination*
परेशान	*worried, anxious*
पसंद करना	*to choose, prefer, like*
पाना	*to find, obtain*
पूरा	*full, complete, whole*
पूरा करना	*to complete, finish*
पूरा होना	*to be complete*
पैदल	*on foot*
प्यार	*love* (m.)
प्यार करना	*to love* (with से)
प्रिय	*dear, favourite*
प्रोग्राम	*programme* (m.)
फ़ुरसत	*leisure, spare time, free time* (f.)
बड़े-बूढ़े	*elders* (m.pl.)
बधाई	*congratulations, felicitations* (f.)
बातचीत	*conversation, dialogue, negotiations* (f.)
बाद में	*afterwards, later*
बाल-बच्चे	*children, family* (m.pl.)
बिजली	*electricity, lightning* (f.)
बिरादरी	*community, fraternity* (f.)
बीच	*middle* (m.)
बुध	*Wednesday* (m.)

बृहस्पति	*Thursday* (m.)
भई	*eh, well* (etc.)
भिन्न	*different*
भूलना	*to forget*
भोजन	*food* (m.)
भोजन करना	*to eat, dine*
मंगल	*Tuesday* (m.)
मद्रास	*Madras* (m.)
मरज़ी	*wish, preference* (f.)
माँग	*demand* (f.)
माँगना	*to ask for, demand*
मामला	*matter, affair* (m.)
मिठाई	*sweet, sweetmeat* (f.)
यदि	*if*
याद	*memory, recollection* (f.)
रहनेवाला	*inhabitant* (m.)
रिवाज	*practice, custom, usage* (m.)
वाराणसी	*Varanasi, Benares* (f.)
-वाला	(see para. 46)
विज्ञापन	*advertisement* (m.)
विदेश	*foreign country* (m.); *abroad*
विदेशी	*foreigner* (m.); *foreign* (adj.)
वैसे	*actually*
व्यस्त	*busy*
व्यापार	*trade* (m.)
व्यापार करना	*to trade*
शादी	*wedding, marriage* (f.)
शुक्र	*Friday* (m.)
संभव	*possible, probable*
समाचार पत्र	*newspaper* (m.)
समाप्त	*finished, concluded*
समाप्त करना	*to finish, conclude*
सरकार	*government* (f.)
सरकारी	*governmental*
सलाह	*advice* (f.)
सलाह लेना	*to take advice*
साड़ी	*sari* (f.)
साथी	*companion, friend* (m.)
सीढ़ी	*step, stair* (f.)
सैर	*walk, trip* (f.)
सैर करना	*to take a walk, go for a trip*

Unit Eleven

Dialogue 11A *Sushila arrives in Delhi*

राधा	कहो सुशीला, तुम दिल्ली कब पहुँचीं?
सुशीला	मैं कल ही आई। पर सीधे लन्दन से नहीं आई, पहले बंबई गई थी।
राधा	अच्छा। बंबई क्यों गई थीं? वहाँ तुमने क्या किया?
सुशीला	चाचाजी ने मुझे बुलाया था, इसलिए मैं पन्द्रह दिन उनके यहाँ ठहरी।
राधा	मैंने तो सुना था कि आपके चाचाजी लखनऊ जानेवाले थे। वे नहीं गए क्या?
सुशीला	अभी तो वे नहीं गए हैं, इसी महीने के अंत में जानेवाले होंगे।
राधा	अब मैं समझी। तो बंबई में तुमने क्या देखा? तुमने बहुत-सी जगहें देखी होंगी?
सुशीला	देखी तो थीं, पर असल में मुझे दिल्ली ज़्यादा पसंद है। बंबई में तो गरमी बहुत ज़्यादा पड़ती है।
राधा	दिल्ली के बारे में तुमने थोड़ा-बहुत सुना होगा?
सुशीला	जी हाँ, मेरे यहाँ आने से पहले अंबिका ने मुझे बहुत-कुछ बताया था। वह हर महीने मुझे पत्र लिखती थी। और लन्दन में ही मैंने दिल्ली के बारे में एक किताब भी पढ़ी थी।
राधा	तो तुम भारत में कितने महीने रहोगी?
सुशीला	मैं कम से कम दो तीन महीने रहना चाहती हूँ। अंबिका चाहती है कि मैं मार्च तक रहूँ। मैंने सुना है कि मार्च तक मौसम काफ़ी सुहावना होता है।

Radha	Well Sushila, when did you arrive in Delhi?
Sushila	I came just yesterday. But I didn't come straight from London, I went to Bombay first.
Radha	I see. Why did you go to Bombay? What did you do there?
Sushila	Uncle had invited me, so I stayed at his place for a fortnight.[1]
Radha	I had heard that your uncle was about to go to Lucknow. Didn't he go?
Sushila	He hasn't gone yet, he'll be going at the end of *this* month.
Radha	Now I understand.[2] So what did you see in Bombay? You will have seen lots of places?

1 Lit. *fifteen days,* but equivalent to 'a fortnight' in colloquial usage.
2 Lit. *Now I [have] understood.*

Sushila	I did indeed, but actually I prefer Delhi. It's terribly hot in Bombay.
Radha	You must have heard a certain amount about Delhi?
Sushila	Yes, before my coming here[1] Ambika told me quite a lot. She used to write me a letter every month. And while still in London I'd read a book about Delhi too.
Radha	So how many months will you stay in India?
Sushila	I want to stay at least two or three months. Ambika wants me to stay until March. I've heard that the weather's pretty nice up till March.

47 Past perfective tenses

So far, only continuous and imperfective past tenses have been introduced – मैं जा रहा था, *I was going*, and मैं जाता था *I used to go*. This section is devoted to perfective tenses – those which refer to an action which has been completed: *'I went'*, *'I have gone'*, or *'I had gone'*. The simple past perfective of बोलना *to speak* is formed as follows:

Masculine	**Feminine**	
मैं बोला	बोली	*I spoke*
तू बोला	बोली	*you spoke*
यह, वह बोला	बोली	*he, she, it spoke*
हम बोले	बोलीं	*we spoke*
तुम बोले	बोलीं	*you spoke*
ये, वे बोले	बोलीं	*they spoke*
आप बोले	बोलीं	*you spoke*

There are two further perfective tenses: the perfect 'I have spoken', and a more remote past 'I spoke' or 'I had spoken'. These are formed as follows:

Masculine	**Feminine**	
मैं बोला हूँ	बोली हूँ	*I have spoken*
तू बोला है	बोली है	*you have spoken*
यह, वह बोला है	बोली है	*he, she has spoken*
हम बोले हैं	बोली हैं	*we have spoken*
तुम बोले हो	बोली हो	*you have spoken*
ये, वे बोले हैं	बोली हैं	*they have spoken*
आप बोले हैं	बोली हैं	*you have spoken*

1 मेरे goes with आने, not यहाँ.

Masculine	**Feminine**	
मैं बोला था	बोली थी	*I spoke, had spoken*
तू बोला था	बोली थी	*you spoke, had spoken*
यह, वह बोला था	बोली थी	*he, she spoke, had spoken*
हम बोले थे	बोली थीं	*we spoke, had spoken*
तुम बोले थे	बोली थीं	*you spoke, had spoken*
ये, वे बोले थे	बोली थीं	*they spoke, had spoken*
आप बोले थे	बोली थीं	*you spoke, had spoken*

Both negative particles, न and नहीं, are used with perfective tenses.

In forming the perfective, verbs whose stems end in -आ, -ओ, -ए or -ई usually insert य before the masculine singular -आ ending; and verbs whose stem ends in -ऊ or -ई shorten this vowel before all perfective endings. The following examples are from the verbs आना *to come,* रोना *to cry* and छूना *to touch* respectively:

Masc. sing.	**Fem. sing.**	**Masc. plur.**	**Fem plur.**	
आया	आई	आए	आईं	*came*
रोया	रोई	रोए	रोईं	*cried*
छुआ	छुई	छुए	छुईं	*touched*

The verbs जाना *to go,* करना *to do,* लेना *to take,* देना *to give,* पीना *to drink* and होना *to be, become* have the following perfective forms:

Masc. sing.	**Fem. sing.**	**Masc. plur.**	**Fem. plur.**	
गया	गई	गए	गईं	*went*
किया	की	किए	कीं	*did*
लिया	ली	लिए	लीं	*took*
दिया	दी	दिए	दीं	*gave*
पिया	पी	पिए	पीं	*drank*
हुआ	हुई	हुए	हुईं	*became, happened*

In past perfective tenses, Hindi verbs fall into two categories. In the first are those verbs, nearly all intransitive, which agree grammatically with the subject of the sentence; in the second are those verbs, nearly all transitive, which use a construction involving the postposition ने.

In the first category are, for the most part, those verbs which do not take a direct object, the intransitives–'to go', 'to come', 'to arrive', etc. Also included in this category are some verbs which might normally be considered transitive; of these, लाना *to bring*, बोलना *to speak, say*, भूलना *to forget*, and समझना *to understand* are among the most common. The following examples illustrate these verbs in the three past perfective tenses–the simple past, the perfect and the remote past:

क्या हुआ?	*What happened?*
वह कल रात को मेरे यहाँ आया।	*He came to my place last night.*
लड़की ऊपरवाले कमरे में सोई।	*The girl slept in the upstairs room.*
हम पिछले हफ़्ते सिनेमा गए।	*We went to the cinema last week.*
कुछ देर के बाद औरतें पहुँचीं।	*After some time the women arrived.*
मैं कई बार दिल्ली गया हूँ।	*I have been to Delhi several times.*
क्या तुम बाक़ी कपड़े लाए हो?	*Have you brought the rest of the clothes?*
वे वहाँ कभी नहीं रही हैं।	*They have never stayed there.*
क्या उषा लौटी है?	*Has Usha returned?*
मैं एक घंटे के लिए ठहरी थी।	*I stayed for one hour.*
वे दस साल के बाद लौटे थे।	*They came back after ten years.*

With certain verbs such as बैठना *to sit*, the perfect tense may describe a situation existing in the present: thus मैं बैठा हूँ, literally 'I have sat', has the sense 'I am sitting'. Further examples are:

दीवार पर गांधी जी की तस्वीर टँगी है।	*A picture of Gandhi jī is hanging on the wall.*
दुकान में दस औरतें बैठी थीं।	*Ten women were sitting in the shop.*

Verbs belonging to the second category are mainly those which take a direct object–the transitives, such as 'to make', 'to give', 'to take'. Also included in this category are certain verbs which might not always seem to be transitive: कहना *to say*, सुनना *to hear, listen to*, पूछना *to ask*, सोचना *to think* and बताना *to tell* are among the most common, while verbs concerned with bodily functions, such as खाँसना *to cough*, छींकना *to sneeze*, थूकना *to spit* are also of this kind. Even when no direct object is expressed, verbs in this category always take a construction involving the use of an 'agentive' postposition ने, in the perfective tenses. In this construction, the English subject is in the oblique case followed by the postposition ने, and the verb agrees grammatically with the English **direct object**. If no direct object is expressed, or if the direct object has the postposition को, then the verb is always in the masculine singular form.

राम ने एक किताब पढ़ी।	*Ram read a book.*
राम ने दो किताबें पढ़ीं।	*Ram read two books.*
राम ने पढ़ा।	*Ram read.*
राम ने इस किताब को पढ़ा।	*Ram read this book.*
राम ने इन किताबों को पढ़ा।	*Ram read these books.*

The forms of the pronouns before ने are as follows:

मैं	मैंने	हम	हमने	कौन	किसने	(singular)
तू	तूने	तुम	तुमने		किन्होंने	(plural)
यह	इसने	ये	इन्होंने	कोई	किसीने	
वह	उसने	वे	उन्होंने			
		आप	आपने			

किसने यह तस्वीर खींची?	*Who drew this picture?*
उन्होंने बहुत काम किया।	*They did a lot of work.*
राजा ने दो सुन्दर महल बनाए।	*The king built two fine palaces.*
मैंने एक अच्छी फ़िल्म देखी।	*I saw a good film.*
धोबी ने हमारी क़मीज़ें धोईं।	*The washerman washed our shirts.*
मैंने राम को शहर में देखा।	*I saw Ram in town.*
मैंने राधा को शहर में देखा।	*I saw Radha in town.*
श्याम ने अपना खाना खाया है।	*Shyam has eaten his meal.*
हमने सुना है कि आप बीमार हैं।	*We have heard that you are ill.*
किसी ने मेरी बात सुनी थी।	*Somebody had heard what I had said.*
उन्होंने दस अंडे खाए थे।	*They had eaten ten eggs.*
अध्यापक ने उन्हें भारत के बारे में कुछ बताया था।	*The teacher had told them something about India.*
मैंने परसों कहा था कि मौसम सुहावना होगा।	*I (had) said two days ago that the weather would be pleasant.*
उन्होंने बहुत-सी पुस्तकें पढ़ी थीं।	*They (had) read a lot of books.*
मेरा क़लम किसने लिया? किसी लड़के ने।	*Who took my pen? Some boy.*

There are a number of verbs which can be in either category. समझना *to understand* is usually in the first category, but if an object is expressed it may be used with the ने construction. The same applies with हारना *to lose* and जीतना *to win*: only if an object (such as a game or battle) is expressed will the ने construction be used. पढ़ना, when meaning 'to read', takes the ने construction, but does not when meaning 'to study'. भरना *to fill* takes the ने construction when it is transitive, and does not when it is intransitive; the same applies with बदलना *to change*.

क्या आप समझे?	*Do you understand?* (Lit. '*Did you understand?*')
उसने मेरी बात ख़ूब समझी।	*He understood very well what I said.*
उसने बाज़ी जीती, मैंने बाज़ी हारी।	*He won the game, I lost the game.*
मैं जीता, वह हारा।	*I won, he lost.*
प्याले में किसने पानी भरा था?	*Who filled the cup with water?*
कुआँ पानी से भरा था।	*The well had filled with water.*

The perfective can also be used with the subjunctive and the future of होना:

आपने मेरे पति का नाम सुना होगा।	*You will have heard my husband's name.*
उसने कुछ फ़ोटो खींचे हों।	*He may have taken some photographs.*
नई किताब १९८९ तक निकली होगी।	*The new book will have come out by* 1989.
उन्होंने उससे पूछा होगा कि उसका नाम क्या है।	*They will have asked him what his name is.*
संभव है कि वह उत्तर भारत न गया हो।	*It is possible that he didn't go to Northern India.*
शायद मेला न हुआ हो।	*Perhaps the fair didn't take place.*
वह बचपन में फ़्रांसीसी पढ़ा होगा।	*He must have studied French in his childhood.*

Dialogue 11B *Ravi has been shopping*

सुनीता सुनो बेटे, आज तुम लोगों ने बाज़ार जाकर क्या ख़रीदा? क्या तुम मेरे लिए भी कुछ लाए हो? या सिर्फ़ घूम रहे थे?

रवि मैंने तो कुछ नहीं ख़रीदा, पर गोपाल ने अपने लिए कुछ सूती कुरते ख़रीदे, और सरोज ने एक रेडियो भी ख़रीद लिया है।

सुनीता अरे, वह नया रेडियो लेके क्या करेगी ? घर में तो तीन चार रेडियो पड़े होंगे। क्या वह मेरी दवा और गोलियाँ नहीं लाई है ? दवा न होने से मुझे बहुत तकलीफ़ होती है। मैंने उससे कहा था कि वह दवाख़ाने से होकर बाज़ार जाए।

रवि क्यों, वह आपका सारा सामान लाई है। वह बाज़ार से लौटकर दवाख़ाने गई थी। आपकी दवा के अलावा उसने साबुन वग़ैरह भी ख़रीदा। और रेडियो तो अपने लिए नहीं ख़रीदा है, वह एक सहेली के जन्मदिन के लिए भेंट है।

सुनीता अच्छा। तो क्या तुमने कुछ खाया है ? तुम कितने बजे घर लौटे थे ? अभी कितने बजे हैं ?

रवि मैं तो क़रीब ढाई बजे आया—पर मेरी घड़ी पीछे है, सो शायद पौने तीन बजे थे। बाज़ार जाकर मैंने कुछ मूँगफलियाँ और समोसे खाए, और लस्सी भी पी। इनके अलावा तो मैंने कुछ नहीं खाया है। दूसरे लोगों ने भी कुछ नहीं खाया है, वे घर लौटकर ही खाना खाएँगे। अभी तो पाँच बजकर दस मिनट हुए हैं।

सुनीता तो क्या वे लोग अभी नहीं लौटे हैं ? कितने बजे तक आएँगे वे ? मैंने सोचा था कि वे पौने चार तक ज़रूर आएँगे। मैंने उनके लिए तरकारी और चावल तैयार करके रखा है।

रवि मेरे ख़्याल से तो वे आठ बजे से पहले नहीं लौटेंगे। उन्होंने मुझसे कहा कि वे किसी ढाबे में चाय पीकर कोई फ़िल्म या तमाशा देखने जाएँगे। पर आज इतनी गरमी पड़ रही है, मैं तो भूलकर भी सिनेमा नहीं देखूँगा।

Sunita Listen son, what did you all buy when you went to the market today? Have you brought anything for me too? Or were you just wandering about?

Ravi I actually didn't buy anything, but Gopal bought some cotton kurtas for himself, and Saroj has bought a radio too.

Sunita Oh, what will she do with a new radio?[1] There must be three or four radios lying around in the house. Hasn't she brought my medicine and tablets? I get a lot of discomfort through not having my medicine. I had told her to go to the market via the pharmacy.

Ravi Why, she has brought all your things. She went to the pharmacy after coming back from the market. She bought soap and so on as well as your medicine. And she didn't buy the radio for herself, it's a present for a friend's birthday.

Sunita I see. So have you eaten anything? What time did you get back home? What's the time now?

Ravi I got back at about half past two–but my watch is slow, so maybe it was a quarter to three. When I went to the shops I ate some peanuts and samosas, and had some lassi to drink too. Apart from these I haven't eaten anything. The others haven't eaten anything either, they'll eat only when they get back. Right now it's ten past five.

1 *What will she do taking* (i.e. '*having*') *a new radio?*

Sunita So haven't they got back yet? By what time will they come?[1] I'd thought they would surely get back by quarter to four. I've made vegetable curry and rice for them and put it aside.[2]

Ravi I think they won't be back before eight o' clock. They told me that they'd have tea at some stall and then go and see some film or show. But it's so hot today, I wouldn't dream of going to the cinema.[3]

48 The conjunctive particle -कर/-के.

The conjunctive particle is formed by adding -कर or -के to the stem of the verb. -कर is preferred in formal or written Hindi, giving जाकर, मारकर etc., but -के is often used in colloquial speech, giving जाके, मारके etc. -के is always used with करना, giving करके.

Where in an English sentence two verbs with the same subject are joined by the conjunction 'and', Hindi commonly uses the conjunctive particle with the first of the two verbs: 'He opened the door and came into the room', दरवाज़ा खोलकर वह कमरे में आया. Thus the conjunctive particle often translates literally as 'having done' or 'doing'—in this example, 'having opened' or 'opening'. The conjunctive participle is made negative by न.

उसने पत्र लिखकर डाक से भेजा।	*He wrote a letter and sent it by post.*
उसने हाथ मुँह धोकर खाना खाया।	*He washed his face and hands, and ate his meal.*
दुकान जाकर कुछ अंडे लाना।	*Go to the shop and bring some eggs.*
दुकान न जाकर डाकघर जाओ।	*Go to the post office, not the shop.*
वह अपना कमरा झाड़कर ही बाहर गया।	*He went out only after sweeping his room.*
काम ख़त्म करके उसने किताब खोली।	*After finishing work he opened a book.*
राम को बुलाकर मेरे पास लाइए।	*Call Ram and bring him to me.*

[1] Locating the pronoun at the end of the sentence suggests a kind of irritation with the people concerned: *By what time will they come, that lot?*

[2] Lit. *I have prepared and placed.*

[3] Lit. *I wouldn't go…even by mistake.*

Some conjunctive particles may be used adverbially:

हँसकर	*laughingly*	(from हँसना *to laugh*)
मुस्कराकर	*with a smile*	(from मुस्कराना *to smile*)
सोचकर	*thoughtfully*	(from सोचना *to think*)
दौड़कर	*running, at a run*	(from दौड़ना *to run*)
कृपा करके	*kindly*	(from कृपा *kindness* + करना)
जान-बूझकर	*knowingly, deliberately*	(from जानना *to know* + बूझना *to understand*)
भूलकर भी	(*even*) *by mistake*	(from भूलना *to forget, err*)
आगे चलकर	*in future, from now on*	(from आगे *ahead* + चलना *to move*)

Other idiomatic usages are:

को छोड़कर	*apart from*	(from छोड़ना *to leave*)
से बढ़कर	*superior to*	(from बढ़ना *to increase*)
(से) होकर	*via*	(from होना *to be*)

उसने मेरी तरफ़ मुस्कराकर देखा।	*He looked at me* [lit. *in my direction*] *with a smile.*
उसने हँसकर कहा कि तुम पागल हो।	*He said laughingly, 'You're mad'.*
तुमने मेरी किताब जान-बूझकर ली!	*You took my book on purpose!*
वहाँ भूलकर भी न जाना।	*Don't go there under any circumstances.* [Lit. *'Don't go there even by mistake.*]
राम को छोड़कर कोई नहीं आया।	*Apart from Ram, nobody came.*
इससे बढ़कर मकान आप नहीं देखेंगे।	*You won't see a better house than this.*
हम लोग बंबई से होकर दिल्ली पहुँचे।	*We reached Delhi via Bombay.*

49 Times of the day

The time of day is expressed by using forms of the verb बजना *to chime, resound*: एक बजा *one o' clock*; एक बजे *at one o' clock*; दो बजे हैं *It is two o' clock*, etc. The quarter- and half-hours before and after one and two o'clock are expressed as follows:

पौन बजा	*a quarter to one*	(पौना is $\frac{3}{4}$ or 'less a quarter')

सवा बजा	*a quarter past one*	(सवा is $1\frac{1}{4}$, or 'plus a quarter')
डेढ़ बजा	*half past one*	(डेढ़ is $1\frac{1}{2}$, grammatically singular)
पौने दो बजे	*a quarter to two*	(पौने is $\frac{3}{4}$, or 'less a quarter')
सवा दो बजे	*a quarter past two*	
ढाई बजे	*half past two*	(ढाई is $2\frac{1}{2}$)

From 2.45 the pattern is regular:

पौने तीन बजे	*a quarter to three*
सवा तीन बजे	*a quarter past three*
साढ़े तीन बजे	*half past three*

Minutes before and after the hour are expressed by बजने में and बजकर respectively:

चार बजने में पच्चीस मिनट (बाक़ी) हैं।	*It's twenty-five minutes to four.*
चार बजकर छब्बीस मिनट (हुए) हैं।	*It's twenty-six minutes past four.*

When it is necessary to distinguish between am and pm the words सुबह *morning* (dawn to about 11 am), दिन *day* (to about 4 pm) शाम *evening* (about 4 to 8 pm) and रात *night* may be used as follows:

दस बजे सुबह को	or	सुबह के दस बजे	*10 am*
पाँच बजे शाम को	or	शाम के पाँच बजे	*5 pm*

The expressions दोपहर *noon,* तीसरे पहर *in the early afternoon,* and आठों पहर *all day long, constantly* derive from the traditional division of the 24-hour period into eight पहर or 'watches' of three hours each; the cycle starts at about 6 am (dawn).

Further usages are included in the following examples:

क्या बजा है? or कितने बजे हैं?	*What is the time?*
आप कितने बजे आएँगे?	*What time will you come?*
पाँच बजकर दस मिनट पर।	*At ten past five.*
सात बजनेवाले हैं।	*It is nearly seven o'clock.*
सात बज रहे हैं।	*It is just seven o'clock. (Seven is striking.)*
आठ बजने पर प्रोग्राम शुरू हुआ।	*The programme began on the stroke of eight.*
आपकी घड़ी में कितने बजे हैं?	*What is the time by your watch?*

मेरी घड़ी दस मिनट आगे/पीछे है।	*My watch is ten minutes fast/slow.*
दस चालीस। ग्यारह दस।	*10.40. 11.10.* (Following English usage.)
ठीक ग्यारह बजे आना!	*Come at eleven o'clock on the dot!*
क़रीब डेढ़ बजे पिताजी पहुँचे।	*At about half past one, father arrived.*

50 The vocabulary of Hindi

By now you will have noticed that a single English word often has two Hindi equivalents: for example किताब and पुस्तक, *book;* अगर and यदि, *if;* ख़त्म करना and समाप्त करना, *to finish.* As was explained in the introduction, the vocabulary of Hindi derives from two main sources–Sanskrit and Persian (including loans into Persian from Arabic). In the following list of pairs of words already encountered, the words from Persian are on the left and those from Sanskrit are on the right. No matter what their origin, these words are all commonly used in Hindi. In general terms, the ones on the left are more frequent in colloquial Hindi, while those on the right are preferred in more formal Hindi, though many speakers will treat them as interchangeable in a wide variety of contexts.

किताब (f.)	पुस्तक (f.)	*book*
दोस्त (m.)	मित्र (m.)	*friend*
ख़त्म	समाप्त	*finished*
गोश्त (m.)	माँस (m.)	*meat*
अगर	यदि	*if*
ज़्यादा	अधिक	*more, much, too much*
उम्मीद (f.)	आशा (f.)	*hope*
ज़रूर	अवश्य	*certainly, of course*
ज़रूरत (f.)	आवश्यकता (f.)	*need*
आख़िर (m.)	अंत (m.)	*end*
लायक़	योग्य	*capable, worth, suitable*
तक़लीफ़ (f.)	कष्ट (m.)	*trouble*
अख़बार (m.)	समाचार पत्र (m.)	*newspaper*
शुक्रिया (m.)	धन्यवाद (m.)	*thanks; thankyou*
ख़त (m.)	पत्र (m.)	*letter*
ज़ोर (f.)	शक्ति (f.)	*force, strength*

Further pairs, of which only one member has so far been encountered, are listed below; these should be learnt as they are all in common use:

मुबारक (*'blessed'*)	शुभकामना(एँ) (f.)	*good wish(es)*
अफ़सोस (m.)	खेद (m.)	*regret*
मुश्किल	कठिन	*difficult*
हफ़्ता (m.)	सप्ताह (m.)	*week*
ख़बर (f.)	समाचार (m.)	*news*
वक़्त (m.)	समय (m.)	*time*
ख़ास	विशेष	*special, particular*
आम	साधारण	*ordinary*
तनख़ाह (f.)	वेतन (m.)	*wage, salary, pay*
फ़ायदा (m.)	लाभ (m.)	*profit, advantage*
फ़ुरसत (f.)	अवकाश (m.)	*leisure, spare time*
ज़बान (f.)	भाषा (f.)	*language*
महीना (m.)	मास (m.)	*month*
साल (m.)	वर्ष (m.)	*year*
मुसाफ़िर (m.)	यात्री (m.)	*traveller*
सफ़र (m.)	यात्रा (f.)	*journey, travel*
लेकिन	परंतु	*but*
इश्तहार (m.)	विज्ञापन (m.)	*advertisement*
शहर (m.)	नगर (m.)	*town, city*
मुमकिन	संभव	*possible*
सिर्फ़	केवल	*only*
ख़ूबसूरत	सुंदर	*beautiful*
शादी (f.)	विवाह (m.)	*wedding, marriage*
जवाब (m.)	उत्तर (m.)	*reply, answer*
शुरू (m.)	आरंभ (m.)	*beginning*

EXERCISE 11.1 Translate the following letter into English:

प्रिय रफ़ीक़, १५ दिसंबर १९८७

आशा है कि आप लोग अच्छे होंगे। आपने तो पिछले वर्ष से कोई पत्र नहीं लिखा है, और मैं भी यह पत्र बड़ी देर के बाद ही लिख रहा हूँ। पहले आपको उर्दू ज़बान ही आती थी, पर पिताजी ने मुझसे कहा कि अब तक आपने हिन्दी भी सीखी होगी, इस लिए मैं यह पत्र हिन्दी में ही लिख रहा हूँ।

यहाँ समाचार यह है कि मैंने जुलाई में अपनी पुरानी नौकरी को छोड़ा था। अब मैंने नगर के एक समाचार पत्र के दफ़्तर में काम करना शुरू किया है। आरंभ में तो मैं केवल इश्तहार वगैरह तैयार करता था, पर पिछले मास मैंने समाचार लिखना भी आरंभ किया और आगे चलकर मैं और भी दिलचस्प काम करूँगा। वेतन तो अभी इतना अच्छा नहीं है, परंतु मेरे विचार में यहाँ काम करने में मुझे बहुत लाभ

होगा। मेरे बचपन के दिनों में मेरे दादाजी मुझसे हमेशा कहते थे कि अगर तुम बड़े होकर जीवन के बारे में कुछ सीखना चाहते तो जाकर किसी समाचार पत्र में नौकरी करो। अब मुझे पता चला है कि दादाजी की बात बिलकुल ठीक निकली है। हर सप्ताह कोई न कोई विशेष समाचार आता है। वैसे साधारण समाचार भी किसी न किसी पढ़नेवाले के लिए विशेष ही होता है –अगर किसी के विवाह की बातचीत चल रही हो तो उसे शादी-विवाह वाले मामलों के बारे में पढ़ना पसंद होगा; यात्रियों को तो यात्रा की कहानियाँ ही दिलचस्प होती हैं; और विद्यार्थी लोग अपने इम्तहानों की तैयारियों के बारे में कुछ सुझाव पढ़ना चाहेंगे। इसलिए अख़बार का काम बहुत दिलचस्प होता है, और यहाँ काम करने में मुझे बहुत खुशी है।

यहाँ जगह भी बहुत खूबसूरत है। सुबह के साढ़े आठ बजे से रात के सवा छह बजे तक कठिन काम करके मुझे बाग़ में सैर करना पसंद है। सरदियों में भी इतनी ठंड नहीं पड़ती। जनवरी के मास में अगर आपको अवकाश हो तो आप भी बाल-बच्चे लेकर यहाँ तीन चार दिन के लिए आएँ। मुझे खेद है कि आनेवाली छुट्टियों में, मेरा आपसे मिलना मुमकिन नहीं होगा, क्योंकि उस वक्त मैं दफ़्तर में काम कर रहा हूँगा। पत्र का उत्तर जल्दी दें!

शुभकामनाओं के साथ,
आपका मित्र,

अशोक

EXERCISE 11.2 Translate the following letter into Hindi:

Dear Ravi,

I hope you are well. You will have returned home from your holidays, and must be making preparations for your new job. I am writing this letter from Madras. I arrived here last night after staying in Delhi for some days. Father had written to me from London, to tell me that some friends of ours would be[1] in Delhi at that time: that's why I came to Madras via Delhi. The train arrived at six in the morning, and I reached the hotel by half past six. After having something to eat I went out to see the city, and I saw that at that time lots of people were going to work or were eating and drinking in the cafés. I bought some things for the children, took some photographs and then, having had a stroll in the market, came back to the hotel. Now I'll sleep until about two o'clock or half past two, and then I'll go to a friend's house because he has just phoned me and invited me to have a meal.

I'll write another letter after a few days.

Yours,
Ram

[1] Use future.

Vocabulary

अंत	*end* (m.)
अवकाश	*leisure, leave, free time* (m.)
असल में	*in fact, actually*
आगे चलकर	*in future, from now on*
आठों पहर	*all day long, constantly*
आरंभ	*beginning* (m.)
आरंभ करना	*to begin, commence* (tr.)
इम्तहान	*examination* (m.)
इश्तहार	*advertisement* (m.)
उत्तर[1]	*north* (m.); *northern* (adj.)
उत्तर[2]	*reply, answer* (m.)
कठिन	*difficult, hard*
कुरता	*kurta, loose-cut shirt* (m.)
कृपा	*kindness* (f.)
कृपा करके	*kindly*
के अलावा	*besides, apart from, as well as*
के बिना	*without*
केवल	*only*
खाँसना	*to cough*
खींचना	*to pull, drag, draw*
ख़ूब	*good, abundant* (adj.); *very, very much, very well* (adv.)
ख़ूबसूरत	*beautiful*
खेद	*regret* (m.)
खोलना	*to open* (tr.)
गोली	*tablet, pill* (f.)
घड़ी	*clock, watch* (f.)
चालीस	*forty*
चावल	*rice* (m.)
छब्बीस	*twenty-six*
छींकना	*to sneeze*
छोड़ना	*to leave, abandon, give up*
को छोड़कर	*apart from*
जन्मदिन	*birthday* (m.)
ज़बान	*language, tongue* (f.)
जान-बूझकर	*deliberately*
जीतना	*to win, defeat*
जीवन	*life* (m.)
झाड़ना	*to sweep, dust*
टँगना	*to hang, be suspended*

डाक	*post* (f.)
डाकघर	*post office* (m.)
डेढ़	*one and a half*
ढाई	*two and a half*
ढाबा	*small café, food stall* (m.)
तमाशा	*show, spectacle* (m.)
तरकारी	*vegetable dish* (f.)
तैयार करना	*to prepare*
थूकना	*to spit*
दवा	*medicine* (f.)
दवाख़ाना	*pharmacy, dispensary* (m.)
दोपहर	*noon, midday* (m.)
दौड़ना	*to run*
नगर	*city, town* (m.)
निकलना	*to emerge, come/go out*
पच्चीस	*twenty-five*
पता चलना	*to become aware of, learn of*
पति	*husband* (m.)
परंतु	*but*
पागल	*mad, crazy; madman* (m.)
पौन	*three-quarters*
पौना	*three-quarters*
पौने	*less a quarter; a quarter to (the hour)*
फ़ोटो	*photograph* (m.)
फ़ोटो खींचना	*to take a photograph*
फ्रांसीसी	*French* (adj.); *the French language* (f.)
बचपन	*childhood* (m.)
बजना	*to resound, ring, chime*
बढ़ना	*to increase, advance* (intr.)
से बढ़कर	*better than, superior to*
बाकी	*remaining, left over; remainder* (f.)
बाज़ी	*turn (in game), play, bet* (f.)
बार	*time, occasion* (f.)
बूझना	*to understand* (*in* जान बूझकर)
भरना	*to fill; to be filled*
भूलकर भी	*even by mistake*
भेंट	*gift; meeting* (f.)
महल	*palace* (m.)
मास	*month* (m.)
मुँह	*mouth, face* (m.)
मुबारक	*blessed*
मुमकिन	*possible*

मुस्कराना	*to smile*
मूँगफली	*peanut* (f.)
मेला	*fair* (m.)
यात्रा	*journey, travel* (f.)
यात्री	*traveller* (m.)
रेडियो	*radio* (m.)
लखनऊ	*Lucknow, capital of U.P.* (m.)
लस्सी	*lassi* (f.) (a yoghourt drink)
लाभ	*profit, advantage* (m.)
वक़्त	*time* (m.)
वगैरह	*etc., and so on*
वर्ष	*year* (m.)
विचार	*thought, idea, opinion* (m.)
विवाह	*wedding, marriage* (m.)
विशेष	*special, particular*
वेतन	*wage, salary, pay* (m.)
शुभकामनाएँ	*good wishes* (f. pl.)
सप्ताह	*week* (m.)
समाचार	*news* (m.)
समोसा	*samosa* (m.) (fried triangular pie)
सवा	*one and a quarter; a quarter past* (*the hour*)
साढ़े	*plus a half; half past* (*the hour*)
साधारण	*ordinary*
साबुन	*soap* (m.)
सुझाव	*suggestion* (m.)
सुहावना	*pleasant, lovely*
सूती	*made of cotton*
सोचना	*to think*
हारना	*to be defeated, lose*
(से) होकर	*via*

Unit Twelve

Dialogue 12A *Talking about homework*

ख़ालिद	सुनो मोहन, क्या तुम आज का पाठ पूरा कर चुके हो?
मोहन	आज का तो मैंने पूरा कर लिया है, पर कलवाला पाठ मैं पूरा नहीं कर सका। बहुत ही कठिन था वह!
ख़ालिद	क्यों? उसमें कोई ख़ास मुश्किल तो नहीं थी? पहला हिस्सा तो ख़ासकर काफ़ी आसान था।
मोहन	पर मैं तो दूसरे भाग की बात कर रहा था। उसमें तो हरेक वाक्य में कठिनाई ही कठिनाई दीखती है। मेरी समझ में नहीं आता कि मैं इतने लंबे-चौड़े शब्दों को कैसे सीख लूँगा।
ख़ालिद	तो यह नई किताब ले लो। इसे पढ़ जाओ, तो तुम पूरा पाठ आसानी से समझ जाओगे। तुम इसे कल तक रख सकते हो, मैं इसे पढ़ चुका हूँ। कल सुबह इसे स्कूल ले आना और क्लास से पहले मुझे वापस कर देना।
मोहन	बस यही समझ लो भैया, तुमने मेरी जान बचाई है! मैंने अध्यापक से कह दिया था कि मैं पाठ को कल सुबह तक पूरा करके उन्हें दे दूँगा। अगर मैं उन्हें ठीक समय पर पाठ न दूँ तो वे शायद मुझे क्लास में से निकाल ही देंगे!
ख़ालिद	फ़िक्र मत करो, अध्यापक इतने सख़्त तो नहीं हैं! सुनो, क्या तुम खाना खा चुके हो? अगर तुम चाहो तो मेरे यहाँ चलकर कुछ खाना खा लो।
मोहन	अभी तो मैं तुम्हारे साथ नहीं जा सकता। मैं तुम्हारी पुस्तक पढ़कर जल्दी ही सो जाऊँगा। फिर कल सवेरे उठकर अपना वह काम पूरा कर लूँगा।

Khalid	Listen Mohan, have you already completed today's lesson?
Mohan	I've completed today's, but I couldn't complete yesterday's lesson. It was very hard!
Khalid	Why? There wasn't any special difficulty in it? The first part in particular was pretty easy.
Mohan	But I was talking about the second part. I see[1] nothing but

[1] Lit. *Nothing but difficulty appears:* कठिनाई is the subject of दीखती है. Note this emphatic use, कठिनाई ही कठिनाई, equivalent to 'difficulty and nothing but difficulty'.

	difficulty in every sentence in it. I don't understand[1] how I'll learn so many great long words.
Khalid	Then take this new book. Read it through, then you'll easily grasp the whole lesson. You can keep it until tomorrow, I've read it already. Bring it to school tomorrow morning and return it to me before class.
Mohan	Honestly[2] brother, you've saved my life! I'd told the teacher that I'd complete the lesson by tomorrow morning and give it to him. If I don't give the lesson to him on time then maybe he might throw me out of the class![3]
Khalid	Don't worry, the teacher isn't so strict! Listen, have you eaten yet? If you like, come to my place and have something to eat.
Mohan	I can't go with you just now. I'll read your book and go to bed very early. Then I'll get up early tomorrow morning and complete that work of mine.

51 सकना and चुकना

A verb stem followed by सकना means 'to be able to do':

मैं हिन्दी बोल सकता हूँ।	*I am able to speak (can speak) Hindi.*
मैं कल जा सकूँगा।	*I will be able to come tomorrow.*

सकना never occurs on its own: the reply to क्या आप जा सकते हैं? *Can you go?* will be जी हाँ, जा सकता हूँ *Yes, I can (go)*, in which the stem जा must be retained.

A verb stem followed by चुकना means 'to have finished doing', or 'to have already done':

मैं चाय पी चुका हूँ।	*I have already had tea.*
वह घर जा चुकी थी।	*She had already gone home.*

Like सकना, चुकना can never occur on its own. In perfective tenses, सकना and चुकना do not use the ने construction:

1 Lit. *It doesn't come into my understanding:* समझ is a feminine noun.
2 Lit. *Just realise this.*
3 निकाल ही देंगे: notice that emphatic ही can come between the stem of the main verb and the intensive verb.

मैंने वह काम नहीं किया।	*I did not do that work.*
but मैं वह काम नहीं कर सका।	*I could not do that work.*
मैंने अख़बार पढ़ा है।	*I have read the paper.*
but मैं अख़बार पढ़ चुका हूँ।	*I have already read (finished reading) the paper.*
मैं उसकी बात नहीं समझ सका।	*I couldn't understand what he said.*
वे अँग्रेज़ी नहीं बोल सकतीं।	*They cannot speak English.*
अगर राम आ सके तो आए।	*If Ram is able to come, he may come.*
वह दरवाज़ा नहीं खोल सकी।	*She could not open the door.*
वह नाश्ता कर चुका है।	*He has already had breakfast.*
हम इस काम को कल तक कर चुकेंगे।	*We will finish this work by tomorrow.*
धोबी शायद कपड़े धो चुका हो।	*Perhaps the washerman might have finished washing the clothes.*
एक बज चुका है।	*It's gone one o'clock.*

52 Compound verbs

Compound verbs operate in a construction similar to that using सकना and चुकना. The verb stem is followed by an auxiliary verb (sometimes called an 'intensive'), which loses its own meaning and adds a force or emphasis to the sense of the main verb. The emphasis that an auxiliary verb gives is less easily defined than that of सकना and चुकना, since it depends upon both the meaning of the main verb and the context of the sentence.

The ने construction is used with compound verbs only when it is required by both the main verb *and* the auxiliary.

Three auxiliary verbs are introduced in this section: जाना, लेना and देना. जाना is by far the most common auxiliary with intransitive verbs; it also occurs with certain transitive verbs. जाना as auxiliary conveys a sense of completeness, finality, or change of state:

बैठना	*to sit*	बैठ जाना	*to sit down*
सोना	*to sleep*	सो जाना	*to go to sleep*
समझना	*to understand*	समझ जाना	*to grasp fully, realise*
आना	*to come*	आ जाना	*to arrive, turn up*
खाना	*to eat*	खा जाना	*to eat up*

पीना	*to drink*	पी जाना	*to drink up*
पढ़ना	*to read*	पढ़ जाना	*to read through* (*to the end*)
सुनना	*to listen*	सुन जाना	*to listen right through*

With certain verbs such as भरना *to fill,* बदलना *to change* and खोना *to lose, be lost,* which are both transitive and intransitive, use of auxiliary जाना specifies intransitive usage. With होना, auxiliary जाना gives the specific sense 'become':

इस महीने रातें गरम होती हैं।	*The nights are hot this month.*
इस महीने रातें गरम हो जाती हैं।	*The nights become hot this month.*

लेना and देना are by far the most common auxiliaries with transitive verbs. लेना is used to refer the action *to* the performer of the action, typically indicating that it is done for the performer's benefit; देना refers the action *away from* the performer:

वह अपनी किताब पढ़ लेता है।	*He reads his book* (*to himself*).
वह अपनी किताब पढ़ देता है।	*He reads out his book.*
यह थैला अपने पास रख लो।	*Keep this bag with you.*
यह थैला मेज़ पर रख दो।	*Put this bag on the table.*

लेना and देना may add a sense of finality or completeness to an action, as well as indicating the direction of the benefit of the action. लेना can also convey a sense that the action was completed or achieved only with some effort: पाँच बजे तक मैंने सारे काम कर लिये थे *By five o'clock I had done* (*completed*) *all the jobs*. देना occurs rarely with intransitive main verbs, but चल देना *to set off,* रो देना *to begin to cry* and हँस देना *to begin to laugh* are common.

Use of an auxiliary verb focuses attention on the actual *performance* of a specific action. For this reason, compound verbs rarely occur in the negative (when, by definition, nothing happened); thus a negative reply to the question क्या आपने चाय पी ली है? *Have you had tea*? would *not* involve लेना: जी नहीं, मैंने चाय अभी नहीं पी है *No, I haven't had tea yet.*

Similarly, compound verbs are rarely used in the continuous tenses. Further compound verbs will be introduced in Unit 17.

हमारा नंबर बदल गया है।	*Our number has changed.*
वह सारी कहानी सुन गई।	*She listened to the whole story.*

बदमाश आधी बोतल से ज़्यादा पी गया था।	*The rogue had drunk up more than half a bottle.*
मेरा पता लिख लेना, और फिर अपना पता लिख देना।	*Take down my address, then write out your address.*
दस बजने पर पुलिस यहाँ आ गई।	*The police got here at ten o'clock exactly.*
सारी दुकानें साढ़े सात बजे बन्द हो जाती हैं।	*All the shops close at half past seven.*
मैं थोड़ी-बहुत उर्दू बोल लेता हूँ।	*I speak a certain amount of Urdu.*
इस पत्र को पढ़ लो, फिर इसे राम को दे दो।	*Read this letter, then give it to Ram.*
कुली ने सारा सामान फ़र्श पर रख दिया।	*The porter put all the luggage on the floor.*
आप समझ गए होंगे कि वह दिक़्क़त में पड़ गया है।	*You must have realised that he's fallen into a difficulty.*
बस ठीक समय पर चल दी।	*The bus set off at the right time.*
इस बात को सुनकर राम तो रो दिया पर सीता हँस दी।	*Hearing this, Ram began to cry but Sita began to laugh.*
बुढ़िया फ़र्श पर बैठ गई और कुछ मिनट बाद सो भी गई।	*The old woman sat down on the floor and a few minutes later she went to sleep.*
चोर की उँगली चाकू से बुरी तरह कट गई थी।	*The thief's finger had been badly cut by the knife.*
दराज़ में से बीड़ियों का पैकेट निकालकर युवक ने उन्हें अपने साथियों में बाँट दिया।	*Taking a packet of biris out of the drawer, the youth distributed them among his companions.*
बाढ़ के कारण तरह तरह की बीमारियाँ गाँव में फैल गईं।	*Because of the flood, all sorts of illnesses spread through the village.*
मैंने डिब्बे में से बक्सा उतार लिया और उसे रिक्शे पर लाद दिया।	*I took the box down out of the compartment and loaded it onto the rickshaw.*
उसकी टाँग टूट गई, मगर जान तो बच गई थी।	*His leg did break, but his life had been saved.*
सूरज पहाड़ों के पीछे डूब गया।	*The sun sank down behind the mountains.*

53 Verbs in combination

Certain verbs, mainly intransitives, combine together to produce a single verbal expression to which each of the two verbs adds its own meaning. आना and जाना are the verbs most commonly appearing as the second member of the pair:

लौट आना	*to come back*	लौट जाना	*to go back*
ले आना	*to bring*	ले जाना	*to take away*
उतर आना	*to come down*	उतर जाना	*to go down*
निकल आना	*to come out*	निकल जाना	*to go out*
चढ़ आना	*to come up*	चढ़ जाना	*to go up*

Slightly different from these verbs are चला जाना *to set off, leave* and चला आना *to come up to;* here चला is not the stem but the perfective form of the verb चलना, and must agree grammatically with the subject: सीता चली गई *Sita left.*

None of the verbs in combination takes the ने construction.

थोड़ी देर में बच्चे स्कूल से निकल आएँगे।	*In a little while the children will come out of school.*
कुछ साल बाद वह अपने देश को लौट गया।	*Some years later he went back to his own country.*
इस किताब को ले जाओ और दूसरी ले आओ।	*Take this book away and bring another.*
दस औरतें रेलगाड़ी से उतर आईं।	*Ten women got out of the train.*
वह कल उसे यहाँ ले आई और आज ले गई।	*She brought him here yesterday and took him away today.*
चाय पीकर वह चला गया।	*After drinking tea he went away.*
हमें दूर से देखकर वह चला आया।	*Seeing us from a distance, he came up to us.*
उषा कुछ ही दिन पहले ससुराल चली गई थी।	*Usha had gone off to her in-laws' just a few days earlier.*
चाँद आकाश में चढ़ आया।	*The moon climbed up into the sky.*

Dialogue 12B *Missing luggage on a train journey*

यात्री सुनिए, सरदार जी! मेरा सामान खो गया है! यहीं रैक पर जो बक्सा मैंने रख दिया था, वह ग़ायब हो गया है। आप कुछ कर सकते हैं?

गार्ड चोरी तो नहीं हो गई? आजकल चोरी बहुत होती है, ख़ासकर रात को। जो आदमी आपके सामने बैठा था, वह कहाँ गया है?

यात्री वह चश्मा-वाला लड़का जो बीड़ी पी रहा था? वह तो पिछले स्टेशन पर उतर गया था।

गार्ड तो वह आपका बक्सा भी ले गया होगा। मुझे अपना नाम और पता दे दें, तो मैं सवेरे पुलिस को बता दूँगा। वह थैला किसका है, जो फ़र्श पर पड़ा है?

यात्री वह भी मेरा है – वह तो बच गया। मेरे पास पैसे वग़ैरह और जो क़ीमती चीज़ें होती हैं, मैं उन्हें इसी थैले में रख लेता हूँ।

गार्ड उसमें भी देख लेना, शायद उसमें से भी चोर ने कुछ ग़ायब कर दिया हो।

यात्री नहीं जी, इसमें मैं देख चुका हूँ। इसमें तो सब कुछ सुरक्षित है। जिस समय चोर ने रैक पर से बक्सा उतारा होगा, उस समय मैं सो तो रहा था मगर थैला मैंने इस कंबल के नीचे रख लिया था। इतना बुद्धू तो नहीं हूँ!

गार्ड अच्छा, तो जो चीज़ें ग़ायब हैं, उनके ब्योरे इस कागज़ पर लिख देना। फिर जिस किसी ने चोर को देखा होगा, उससे मैं पूछ-ताछ करूँगा। मगर वह किसका बक्सा है, जिस पर आपका बेटा बैठा है?

यात्री अरे हाँ! यह वही बक्सा है जिसे मैं ढूँढ़ रहा था। मैं भूल गया था कि मैंने उसे कुछ चीज़ें निकालने के लिए उतार लिया था! माफ़ कीजिएगा सरदार जी, मैंने आपको बहुत तकलीफ़ दी है।

Passenger Excuse me, Sardar jī! My luggage has gone missing! The box which I'd put on this rack has disappeared. Can you do something?

Guard There hasn't been a theft, has there? There's a lot of theft these days, especially at night. Where's that man gone who was sitting opposite you?

Passenger That boy wearing glasses, who was smoking a biri? He got off at the previous station.

Guard Then he must have taken your box too. If you give me your name and address, than I'll tell the police in the morning. Whose is that bag, which is lying on the floor?

Passenger That's mine too – that at least escaped. What valuable things and money etc. that I have with me, I keep in this bag.

Guard Have a look in that too, the thief might have made off with something from there as well.

Passenger No, I've looked in this already. In this at least, everything is safe. At the time when the thief must have taken the box from off[1] the rack I was sleeping[2] but I'd kept the bag[3] under this blanket. I'm not such a fool!

Guard All right, so write down on this piece of paper the details of the things which are missing. Then I'll make enquiries with anyone who would have seen the thief. But whose is that box that your son's sitting on?

Passenger Oh yes! It's the very box that I was looking for! I'd forgotten that I'd taken it down to get some things out of it! I'm very sorry Sardar jī, I've put you to a lot of trouble.

54 The relative pronoun and adjective जो

In English, relative clauses follow the pattern 'The man who came today lives in London'. In Hindi, the preferred pattern is ***Which*** *man came today,* ***he*** *lives in London.* Another example is *Read the book which is on the table,* which in the Hindi construction would be, ***which*** *book is on the table, read* ***that one***. In these examples, *which* is the relative pronoun, and *he* and *that one* are known as the correlative, which must be expressed.

The relative pronoun and adjective जो *that which, which, he who,* etc. is both singular and plural. In the singular it has the oblique form जिस (giving जिसको or जिसे, जिसका, जिसने); in the plural it has the oblique form जिन (giving जिनको or जिन्हें, जिनका, जिन्होंने): these forms are exactly parallel to the oblique forms किस, etc. from क्या and कौन. The correlative is usually वह or वे, or an appropriate form of one of these (e.g. उस, उसे, उन्होंने, etc.).

Relative clause	Main clause	
जो जानता है	**वह** नहीं बोलता।	*He who knows does not speak.*
Who knows,	**he** does not speak.	

जिसके लिए मैं काम करता हूँ **वह** बहुत अमीर है। *The person for whom I work is very rich.*
For **whom** I work, **he** is very rich.

[1] Notice the double postposition: रैक पर से *from on the rack.*
[2] Emphatic तो here comes between the stem सो and रहा था. The effect of this is to emphasize the fact that 'Although it's true I was sleeping, I had taken proper steps to safeguard my property'.
[3] थैला precedes मैंने: the effect of this is to emphasize 'the bag': *as for the bag, I'd kept it under this blanket.*

जिसे ज़ुकाम हो To **whom** there is ('may be') a cold	**वह** बाहर न जाए। **he** should not go out.	*A person who has a cold should not go out.*
जिसने यह पत्र लिखा था **Who** wrote this letter, call **him.**	**उसे** बुलाओ।	*Call the person who wrote this letter.*

Examples:

जो बोलता है वह नहीं जानता।	*He who speaks does not know.*
जो आदमी आज यहाँ आया वह दिल्ली का रहने-वाला है।	*The man who came here today lives in Delhi.*
जो पुस्तक मेज़ पर पड़ी है उसे पढ़ लेना।	*Read the book which is lying on the table.*
जिस लड़के ने प्याला तोड़ दिया उसे बुलाओ।	*Call the boy who broke the cup.*
जिस चीज़ के बारे में हम कल बात कर रहे थे, उसको मत भूलो।	*Do not forget the matter we were talking about yesterday.*
जिस तरह वह लिखता है उसी तरह वह बोलता भी है।	*He speaks just as he writes.*
जिन लोगों को हमने कल देखा था वे तो नहीं आ सकते।	*The people we saw yesterday cannot come.*
जिन्होंने यह फ़िल्म बनाई है वे पागल होंगे।	*Those who made this film must be mad.*
कल शाम को मैंने जो तमाशा देखा था, उसे आप ज़रूर देखें।	*You should certainly see the show I saw last evening.*

(Notice in the last example that it is not necessary for the relative word actually to *begin* the relative clause).

Although this pattern, with the relative clause coming first, is a standard order, it is not uncommon for the relative clause to come *after* the main clause:

उस लड़के को बुलाओ जिसने यह प्याला तोड़ दिया।	*Call the boy who broke this cup.*
वह बात न भूलो जिसके बारे में हम बात कर रहे थे।	*Don't forget the matter we were talking about.*
यह वही किताब है जिसे मैंने कल पढ़ लिया था।	*This is the very book that I read yesterday.*

In addition to the relative जो on its own, notice also the following:

जो कोई (oblique जिस किसी) *whoever* जो कुछ *whatever*
जो भी *whoever, whichever*

All of these forms correlate with वह, etc. जो भी is rather more emphatic than जो कोई/कुछ, and gives a sense 'no matter who / what':

आपके पास जो कुछ हो, वह दे देना।	*Give whatever you may have.*
साधु जो कुछ बोलता है उसको उसके शिष्य लिख लेते हैं।	*Whatever the holy man utters, his disciples write it down.*
जो भी यहाँ आए उसे बताना कि हम को फ़ुरसत नहीं है।	*No matter who comes, tell him that we don't have any time.*
जो भी हिन्दी जानता हो उससे कहो कि वह यहाँ आए।	*Tell anyone at all who may know Hindi that he should come here.*
जो कोई समझता है कि हिन्दी आसान है उसका विचार ग़लत है।	*Whoever thinks that Hindi is easy, (his idea) is mistaken.*
जिस किसी को पैसे की ज़रूरत हो, वह मुझसे ले ले।	*Whoever needs money may take it from me.*

There are further relative-correlative constructions in Hindi, which will be introduced in Units 13–16. It is a feature of the relative words in Hindi that they begin with ज्, just as the interrogative words begin with क्. English speakers need to be aware of when a pronoun is interrogative (as *who*? कौन) and when it is relative (as *who* जो).

EXERCISE **12.1** Translate into English:

गार्ड की कहानी

कल हमारी गाड़ी में एक मुसाफ़िर ने जो किया था, उसे सुनकर आपको आश्चर्य होगा। दिल्लीवाली गाड़ी थी, जो रात के साढ़े सात बजे कलकत्ते से छूटती है और दिल्ली सवेरे पहुँचती है। काफ़ी लंबा सफ़र है, पर हवाई जहाज़ से यात्रा करना इतना महँगा हो गया है कि ज़्यादातर लोग ट्रेन से ही यात्रा करना पसंद करते हैं। सिर्फ़ वे लोग हवाई जहाज़ से जा सकते हैं जिनके पास बहुत पैसा है, या जिनकी कंपनी उन्हें सफ़र ख़र्च दे देती है। ख़ैर, कल तो हमेशा की तरह गाड़ी में बहुत भीड़ थी। जो लोग जल्दी आ गए थे, वे अपना सामान वग़ैरह गाड़ी में लादकर आराम से बैठ चुके थे और स्टेशन का दृश्य देख रहे थे। जिनके साथ बाल-बच्चे भी थे, वे उन्हें सीटों पर या बक्सों पर या फ़र्श पर भी बिठा रहे थे। कुछ यात्री सो भी गए थे। ज़्यादातर लोग अपने लिए खाना भी ले आए थे। जिन्होंने खाना खा लिया था, वे सो गए थे या सोने की तैयारियाँ कर रहे थे।

क़रीब सात बजे मैंने देखा कि एक डिब्बे में एक ऐसा आदमी चढ़कर बैठ गया जिसे मैं शायद दो तीन बार इसी ट्रेन पर देख चुका हूँ। वह उन व्यापारियों में से होगा जो हर महीने दिल्ली या बंबई जाते हैं। पर अब की बार तो उसके बाल-बच्चे भी साथ थे। क़रीब आधी रात को इस आदमी ने मुझे पुकारकर कहा कि उसका एक बक्सा खो गया है, जिसे उसने रैक पर रख दिया था। वैसे मैं मुसाफ़िरों से हमेशा कह देता हूँ कि जिस समय वे सोते हैं, उस समय वे अपनी क़ीमती चीज़ें रैक पर न छोड़ें, पर वे तो इतने

लापरवाह होते हैं कि पूछो मत। कभी-कभी तो वे यह भी भूल जाते हैं कि सामान भी है उनके पास-गाड़ी से उतरकर बड़ी ख़ुशी से घर का रास्ता पकड़ लेते हैं या चाय पीने चले जाते हैं, और सारा सामान वहीं डिब्बे में छूट जाता है। ख़ैर, जो बक्सा इस आदमी ने रैक पर रख दिया था, वह ग़ायब हो गया था इस लिए वह काफ़ी परेशान हो गया था। मैं उससे बातें कर रहा था, तो अचानक उसे पता चला कि जिस बक्से को वह ढूँढ़ रहा था, वह वहीं उसके बिलकुल सामने पड़ा था! उसका बेटा बक्से के ऊपर बैठा था। तो मैं अच्छी तरह समझ गया कि इस दुनिया में कैसे बुद्धू होते हैं। जिसने मेरी तरह रेलवे में नौकरी की हो, वही समझ सकता है कि गार्ड की ज़िंदगी कितनी मुश्किल होती है।

EXERCISE 12.2 Translate into Hindi:

Somebody has made off with my watch. The watch wasn't very valuable, and my father, who is usually very strict about such matters, says that I should not worry about it. But I want the person who took it to return it right now. I have made enquiries with the people who work here, but they don't know anything. Usually I keep the watch with me, but yesterday I had put it on the table, thinking that nothing would happen to it for a few hours. But the little table I had put it on is just near the window; the man who took it must have climbed on top of something and broken the window. There is no point in calling the police[1] now, because they cannot do anything at all.

Vocabulary

अचानक	*suddenly*
अब की बार	*this time*
आकाश	*sky* (m.)
आधा	*half*
आधीरात	*midnight* (f.)
आराम से	*comfortably, easily*
आसानी	*ease* (f.)
आसानी से	*easily*
उँगली	*finger* (f.)
उठना	*to rise, get up*
उतरना	*to get down, come down, descend, alight*
उतारना	*to take down; to take off* (clothes)
कटना	*to be cut*
कठिनाई	*difficulty* (f.)
की तरह	*like*

[1] Use singular noun (feminine).

क़ीमती	*valuable, costly*
कुली	*porter* (m.)
के कारण	*because of*
ख़र्च	*expenditure, expenses* (m.)
ख़ासकर	*specially*
ख़ैर	*well, anyway* (interjection)
खोना	*to lose; to be lost*
ग़ायब	*disappeared, missing*
ग़ायब करना	*to make off with*
ग़ायब होना	*to disappear, go missing*
गार्ड	*railway guard* (m.)
चढ़ना	*to climb, rise, mount, board*
चला आना	*to come along*
चला जाना	*to go along, set off*
चाँद	*moon* (m.)
चाक़ू	*knife* (m.)
चुकना	*to be finished* (see para. **51**)
चोर	*thief* (m.)
चोरी	*theft* (f.)
जान	*life* (f.)
जो	*that which, which, who, the one who*
जो कुछ	*whatever*
जो कोई	*whoever*
जो भी	*whoever; whatever*
ज़्यादातर	*mostly; most*
टाँग	*leg* (f.)
टूटना	*to break* (intr.)
डिब्बा	*train compartment* (m.)
डूबना	*to sink* (intr.)
तरह तरह का	*of various kinds*
तोड़ना	*to break* (tr.)
थैला	*bag* (m.)
दराज़	*drawer* (f.)
दिक़्क़त	*difficulty, trouble* (f.)
दीखना	*to be seen, appear*
दुनिया	*world* (f.)
दृश्य	*view* (m.)
नाश्ता	*breakfast* (m.)
नाश्ता करना	*to have breakfast*
निकालना	*to take out, extract, turn out, bring out*
पता	*address* (m.)
पर से	*from on*

पाठ	*lesson; reading* (m.)
पुकारना	*to call, call out*
पुलिस	*the police* (f.)
पूछ-ताछ	*enquiry, investigation* (f.)
पूछ-ताछ करना	*to enquire, make enquiries*(with से)
पैकेट	*packet* (m.)
फ़र्श	*floor* (m.)
फ़िक्र	*anxiety, worry, concern* (f.)
फ़िक्र करना	*to worry, be anxious*
फैलना	*to spread* (intr.)
बक्सा	*box* (m.)
बचना	*to be saved, escape, survive*
बचाना	*to save*
बदमाश	*rogue, villain* (m.)
बाँटना	*to distribute, share out*
बाढ़	*flood* (f.)
बिठाना	*to make sit*
बीड़ी	*small cigarette rolled in leaf* (f.)
बीमारी	*illness* (f.)
बुद्धू	*foolish; fool* (m.)
बुरी तरह (से)	*badly*
बोतल	*bottle* (f.)
ब्योरा	*details, particulars* (m.)
भाग	*part, portion* (m.)
भैया	*brother* (m.)
मगर	*but*
माफ़ करना	*to pardon, forgive*
मुश्किल	*difficulty* (f.)
युवक	*youth, young man* (m.)
रिक्शा	*rickshaw* (m.)
रेलवे	*railway* (f.)
रैक	*rack* (m.)
लंबा-चौड़ा	*huge, vast, 'great big'*
लादना	*to load*
लापरवाह	*careless*
वाक्य	*sentence* (m.)
वापस करना	*to return, give back*
व्यक्ति	*person, individual* (m.)
शब्द	*word* (m.)
शिष्य	*disciple* (m.)
सकना	*to be able to* (see para. **51**)
सख़्त	*hard, severe, harsh, strict*

सफ़र ख़र्च	*travel expenses* (m.)
समझ	*understanding* (f.)
समझ में आना	*to understand*
सरदार	(lit. '*chief*'; used as title of respect for Sikh men)
सवेरे	*early in the morning*
ससुराल	*father-in-law's house* (f.)
सीट	*seat* (f.)
सुरक्षित	*safe*
सूरज	*sun* (m.)
हरेक	*each, every*
हिस्सा	*part, portion* (m.)

Unit Thirteen

Dialogue 13A *Plans for the day*

राजू	सुनो हसन, आज तुम्हें क्या करना है?
हसन	अभी तो मुझे कुछ ज़रूरी ख़त लिखने हैं, फिर मुझे बाज़ार से कुछ चीज़ें लानी हैं। तुम्हें याद है न, सनीचर को मुझे हमेशा बाज़ार जाना पड़ता है।
राजू	पर उन ख़तों को तुम्हें कल ही लिख देना चाहिए था – तुम्हें हर काम ठीक समय पर करना चाहिए, नहीं तो दिक़्क़त में पड़ जाओगे।
हसन	हाँ बेशक, पर कल मेरी बीवी की तबियत ख़राब हो गई थी, सो मुझे बच्चों की देखभाल करनी पड़ी। मेरी बीवी को डाक्टर के पास जाना पड़ा।
राजू	तब तो बात दूसरी है। अच्छा सुनो, आज सुरेन्द्र का पत्र मिला। तुम्हें इसे पढ़ना चाहिए - बड़ा मज़ाकिया आदमी है वह!
हसन	हाँ दे दो। मैं उसे बाद में पढ़ लूँगा। अभी तो मुझे घर जाना है।
राजू	तो तुम्हें चाय नहीं पीनी है? सामनेवाले ढाबे पर बढ़िया समोसे मिलते हैं!
हसन	इस बार तुम्हें चाय अकेले पीनी पड़ेगी। कल हम सब मिलकर खाना खाने चलेंगे।

Raju	Listen Hasan, what do you have to do today?
Hasan	Right now I have to write some urgent letters, then I have to fetch some things from the shops. You remember don't you, I always have to go to the shops on Saturday.
Raju	But you should have written those letters yesterday – you should do everything at the right time, otherwise you'll get into difficulties.
Hasan	Yes certainly, but yesterday my wife became unwell so I had to look after[1] the children. My wife had to go to the doctor.[2]
Raju	Then it's another matter. Anyway listen, I got a letter from Surendra today. You should read it – he's a very funny person.
Hasan	Yes, give it to me. I'll read it later. Right now I'll have to go home.

1 मुझे बच्चों की देखभाल करनी पड़ी: lit. '*I had to do the supervision of the children*'.
2 Note this use of the postposition के पास in the sense '(to go) *to* a person'.

Raju So aren't you going to have some tea? You can get very good samosas in the cafe opposite!

Hasan This time you'll have to have your tea by yourself. Tomorrow we'll all go and eat together.

55 'Should' and 'ought'

The most common way to express 'should' and 'ought' in Hindi is to use the infinitive followed by चाहिए, with the English subject in the oblique case with को. To express the negative, न or नहीं comes before the infinitive.

मुझको वहाँ जाना चाहिए।	*I should go there.*
मुझको वहाँ जाना चाहिए था।	*I should have gone there.*
तुमको यहाँ न रहना चाहिए।	*You should not stay here.*
तुमको यहाँ न रहना चाहिए था।	*You should not have stayed here.*

If the infinitive has a direct object without को, then the infinitive will agree in number and gender with the object. If the sentence is in the past, then the past tense verb (था, etc.) will also agree with the object. If the direct object is in the oblique with को, then the infinitive remains in the -ना form and the past tense verb remains as था.

हमको हिन्दी बोलनी चाहिए।	*We should speak Hindi.*
हमको हिन्दी बोलनी चाहिए थी।	*We should have spoken Hindi.*
उसको कपड़े धोने चाहिए।	*He should wash the clothes.*
उसको कपड़े धोने चाहिए थे।	*He should have washed the clothes.*
आपको ये पुस्तकें पढ़नी चाहिए।	*You should read these books.*
आपको ये पुस्तकें पढ़नी चाहिए थीं।	*You should have read these books.*
तुम्हें राम को न मारना चाहिए था!	*You shouldn't have beaten Ram!*
आपको इसी किताब को पढ़ना चाहिए था।	*You should have read* **this** *book.*

56 'Must' and 'have to'

'Must' and 'have to' use a similar construction to that just described. The difference is that, in place of चाहिए/चाहिए था the verbs होना *to be* and पड़ना literally *to fall* are used. पड़ना gives a relatively strong sense of compulsion; in the imperfective, it gives a habitual sense.

मुझे जाना है।	*I have to go.*
मुझे रोज़ जाना पड़ता है।	*I have to go every day.*

As in the चाहिए construction, the English subject takes the postposition को, the infinitive ending agrees with a direct object *not* followed by को, and the verb होना or पड़ना also agrees with the object:

उसको चिट्ठी लिखनी थी।	*He had to write a letter.*
मुझको कपड़े धोने पड़ते हैं।	*I (usually) have to wash clothes.*

Again as in the चाहिए construction, the infinitive and the होना or पड़ना verb remain in the invariable masculine singular form if the direct object is in the oblique with को:

मुझे इन कामों को करना है।	*I have to do these jobs.*

The होना construction may also be used to express intention rather than actual obligation:

तुम्हें चाय पीनी है?	*Are you going to drink tea? (Would you like to drink tea?)*
आज मुझे आराम करना है।	*Today I'm going to rest.*

Since 'must' and 'have to' may refer to situations yet to take place, future forms of the verb (होना, पड़ना) may be involved in this construction:

उसको चिट्ठी लिखनी होगी।	*He will have to write a letter.*
मुझको कपड़े धोने पड़ेंगे।	*I will have to wash clothes.*
मुझे जाना है।	*I have to go / I must go.*
उन्हें अँग्रेज़ी सीखनी थी।	*They had to learn English.*
हमें हर रोज़ सात बजे उठना होता है।	*We have to get up at seven o'clock every day.*
कल तुमको अपनी किताबें लानी होंगी।	*Tomorrow you will have to bring your books.*
उसे ढाई बजे की रेल पकड़नी पड़ी।	*He had to catch the 2.30 train.*
राधा को अपनी बहिन की साड़ी पहननी पड़ेगी।	*Radha will have to put on her sister's sari.*
कुछ लोगों को आठ बजे काम शुरू करना पड़ता है।	*Some people have to start work at eight o'clock.*
आज हमें मनोज की चाबियाँ ढूँढ़नी हैं।	*Today we have to look for Manoj's keys.*

Note that use of पड़ना in the perfective, as in उसे जाना पड़ा *He had to go*, may imply that the obligation was somehow unexpected or suddenly imposed. Compare the following:

घर लौटकर उसे तार देना था। *When he got home he had to send a telegram* (suggesting that this was the next item on his prearranged schedule).

घर लौटकर उसे तार देना पड़ा। *When he got home he had to send a telegram* (suggesting that he had found that some crisis had arisen unexpectedly).

57 The verb मिलना

In its primary sense, मिलना means 'to accrue'; it is commonly used in a construction to give the sense 'get', 'receive', etc. The English subject takes the postposition को, and the English object becomes the Hindi subject with which the verb agrees:

मुझे राम का तार मिला है। *I have received Ram's telegram.*

महीने में उसे चार सौ रुपये मिलते हैं। *He gets four hundred rupees a month.*

मेरा पत्र आपको कल मिलेगा। *You will get my letter tomorrow.*

The same construction also gives the sense 'is available', 'is found', 'can be had':

उस दुकान पर बढ़िया कपड़ा मिलता है। *Excellent cloth is obtainable in that shop.*

यहाँ अख़बार भी मिल सकते हैं। *Here you can get newspapers too.*

आजकल जंगलों में बाघ बहुत कम मिलते हैं। *These days tigers are found in the jungle very rarely.*

अगर पैसा मिल जाएगा तो मैं गाड़ी ख़रीद लूँगा। *If the money is available I'll buy a car.*

The same construction is also used to mean 'to meet' if the meeting referred to is accidental or unexpected:

कल शहर में मुझे सीता मिली। *I met Sita in town yesterday (by chance).*

If, however, the meeting is arranged or intended, then the English subject is the Hindi subject also, and the person met takes the postposition से (this usage has already occurred in such contexts as मैं उससे मिलने गया *I went to meet him*).

कल शहर में मैं सीता से मिला।	*I met Sita in town yesterday (by intention)*
मैं तुमसे कल सुबह मिलूँगा।	*I'll meet you tomorrow morning.*
वह मुझसे मिलना नहीं चाहती।	*She doesn't want to meet me.*
आपसे मिलकर मुझे बहुत ख़ुशी हुई।	*I'm very pleased to have met you.*

से is also used with मिलना-जुलना, lit, 'to meet', but often meaning 'to resemble':

रमेश अपने पिता से मिलता-जुलता है।	*Ramesh looks like his father.*

Finally, note the adverbial expression सब मिलकर *all together*:

हम सब मिलकर चलें।	*Let's all go together.*
हम सब को मिलकर शान्ति से रहना चाहिए।	*We should all live in peace together.*

Further examples:

वहाँ तो आपको शाकाहारी खाना ही मिलेगा।	*There, you'll get only vegetarian food.*
उस होटल में आपको कमरा ज़रूर मिल जाएगा।	*You'll certainly get a room in that hotel.*
एक महीने तक मुझे कोई पत्र नहीं मिला।	*I didn't get any letter for a month.*
रास्ते में हमें तुम्हारे रिश्तेदार मिले।	*On the way we came across your relatives.*
अगर फ़ुरसत हो तो आप उससे ज़रूर मिलें।	*Be sure to meet him if you're free.*
वर्मा जी अपने भाइयों से बहुत मिलते-जुलते हैं।	*Mr Varma looks very much like his brothers.*
क्या ये कपड़े तुझे मुफ़्त में मिले?	*Did you get these clothes for nothing?*
हम सब को मिलकर काम करना चाहिए।	*We should all work together.*
ऐसा मौक़ा आपको दोबारा नहीं मिलेगा।	*You won't get such an opportunity again.*

Dialogue 13B *Maya's new home, and her husband's job*

सरला कहिए माया जी, यह नया मकान आपको कैसा लगता है?

माया बहुत अच्छा लगता है। और सबसे अच्छी बात यह है कि दफ़्तर पहुँचने में केवल पंद्रह बीस मिनट लगते हैं।

सरला आप लोग कब से यहाँ रह रहे हैं? लगता है, आपने मकान को अच्छी तरह सजा लिया है।

माया जब से दिलीप ने डाकख़ाने में काम करना शुरू किया, तब से हम यहाँ रह रहे हैं।

सरला पर जब मैं पिछली बार आपसे मिली थी तब तो आपने कहा कि हमें नया मकान नहीं चाहिए।

माया यह सही है, मगर जैसे ही मैंने इस मुहल्ले को देखा वैसे ही मैंने महसूस किया कि मैं यहीं रहना चाहूँगी। न जाने क्यों, यहाँ मेरा दिल ख़ूब लगता है।

सरला तो दिलीप कितने बजे घर वापस आते हैं? दिन भर काम करके उन्हें भूख लगती होगी?

माया और क्या! जब भी दफ़्तर में ज़्यादा काम होता है तो उसे देर से छुट्टी मिलती है। जब तक बेचारे को इस से अच्छा पद न मिले, तब तक यही स्थिति रहेगी।

सरला मुझे तो ऐसा लगता है कि वे काफ़ी अच्छी तरक़्क़ी कर रहे हैं अपने काम में। उनके लिए तो डाकख़ाने का काम बायें हाथ का खेल होगा।

माया हाँ, कल सुबह जब दिलीप अपने मालिक से मिले तो मालिक ने कहा कि हम तुम्हारे काम से बहुत प्रसन्न हैं, अगले साल तुम्हें इज़ाफ़ा मिलना चाहिए।

Sarala Well Maya jī, how do you like this new house?

Maya I like it very much. And the best thing is that it only takes fifteen or twenty minutes to get to the office.

Sarala How long have you been living here? It seems you've decorated the house very well.

Maya We've been living here since Dilip started working at the post office.

Sarala But when I met you last time you said you didn't want a new house.

Maya That's true, but as soon as I saw this district I felt that I would like to live right here. I don't know why,[1] but I feel really at home here.

Sarala So what time does Dilip get home? He must get hungry after working all day?

Maya Of course![2] Whenever there's a lot of work at the office he gets off work late. Until the poor fellow gets a better position than this, the situation will remain the same.

Sarala It seems to me that he is making very good progress in his work. The post office work must be child's play for him.[3]

Maya Yes, yesterday morning when Dilip met his boss, the boss said he[4] was very pleased with his (Dilip's) work, and that he should get a rise next year.

1 न जाने: *God knows, Heaven knows,* i.e. *I've no idea.*

2 और क्या: *What else?,* i.e. *Of course.*

3 बायें हाथ का खेल: lit. *a game for the left hand,* i.e. something very easily accomplished.

4 Note that the boss refers to himself with the first person plural, हम.

58 The verb लगना

The primary meaning of लगना is 'to be applied (to), as in दीवारों पर कई तस्वीरें लगी थीं *Several pictures were fixed to the walls;* but it also occurs in a range of usages with the basic sense 'to strike one', in which the person concerned takes the postposition को.

भारत आपको कैसा लगता है?	*How do you like India?*
यह देश मुझे बहुत अच्छा लगता है।	*I like this country very much.*
उसे चोट लग गई।	*He got hurt.*
उसे डर लग रहा था।	*He was feeling frightened.*
उन्हें ठंड लग रही है।	*They are feeling cold.*
उन्हें गरमी लगेगी।	*They will feel hot.*
ऊपरवाले कमरे में आग लग गई थी।	*Fire had broken out in the upstairs room.*
मुझे प्यास लगी है।	*I am thirsty.*
हमें भूख लगी है।	*We are hungry.*
मुझे भूख लग रही है।	*I am getting hungry.*

In the same general sense, लगना and ऐसा लगना may mean 'to seem', 'to appear':

लगता है कि वह सब कुछ खा गया है।	*It seems that he has eaten everything up.*
ऐसा लगता है कि कोई नहीं आएगा।	*It seems that nobody will come.*

Similar to this usage is the sense 'to suit', 'to fit':

चाबी ताले में नहीं लगी।	*The key didn't fit the lock.*
उनको साड़ियाँ अच्छी नहीं लगतीं।	*Saris don't suit them.*
यह कोट आपको बहुत अच्छा लगता है।	*This coat suits you very well.*

लगना is also used in a construction expressing 'the time taken to do something'. The action performed is expressed by the infinitive with the postposition में, and the unit of time taken forms the subject of the verb लगना:

मुझे यहाँ आने में दस ही मिनट लगे।	*It took me just ten minutes to get here.*
इस काम को करने में कितने दिन लगेंगे?	*How many days will it take to do this work?*

इस पत्र को लिखने में मुझे एक घंटा लगा।	*It took me an hour to write this letter.*
दिल्ली पहुँचने में सात घंटे लगते हैं।	*It takes seven hours to reach Delhi.*

Further examples:

लगता है कि वह मज़ाक कर रही थी।	*It seems she was joking.*
बच्चों को ये मिठाइयाँ बहुत अच्छी लगती हैं।	*The children like these sweets a lot.*
कोट पहन लो, नहीं तो तुम्हें ठंड लग जाएगी।	*Put on your coat, otherwise you'll get cold.*
आधीरात को आग लग गई।	*Fire broke out at midnight.*
लगता है कि उसे प्यास लग रही है।	*It seems he is feeling thirsty.*
सब से मीठे आम उस छोटे पेड़ में लगते हैं।	*The sweetest mangoes grow on that little tree.*
दीवार पर जो नोटिस लगा है उस में क्या है?	*What is in the notice that is stuck on the wall?*
तुम्हें डर नहीं लगना चाहिए।	*You should not feel afraid.*
ऐसा लगता है कि उसके पास ज्यादा पैसा नहीं था।	*It seems he didn't have much money.*
आज का पाठ पूरा करने में तुम्हें कितना समय लगा?	*How long did it take you to finish today's lesson?*
आग लगने में देर नहीं लगी।	*It didn't take long for fire to break out.*

59 Relative-correlative constructions for time

Relative clause expressing time function in the same way as clauses with the relative pronoun जो and its correlative वह: the English sentence 'I will tell him when he comes' becomes in the Hindi order 'When he comes then I will tell him'. The relative adverb for this example is जब *at which time, when,* and its correlative is तब *at that time, then.*

The main relative-correlative adverbs expressing time are as follows:

Relative		**Correlative**	
जब	*at which time, when*	तब	*at that time, then*
जब से	*since which time, since when*	तब से	*since that time, since then*

जब तक	*as long as, until, by the time that*	तब तक	*until then, by then*
		तभी	*then*
जब भी	*whenever*	त्योंही	*at that moment, then*
ज्योंही	*as soon as*	वैसे ही	*at that moment, then*
जैसे ही	*as soon as*		

Examples:

जब से मैं लंदन लौटा हूँ तब से मेरी तबियत ख़राब रही है।	*Since I returned to London my health has been bad.*
जब तक मेरे पास पैसा रहेगा तब तक मैं इसी होटल में ठहरूँगा।	*As long as I have money I shall live in this very hotel.*
जब तक मैं पहुँचा तब तक वह जा चुकी थी।	*By the time I arrived, she had already gone.*
जब भी मैं बाहर जाता हूँ तभी पानी पड़ता है।	*Whenever I go out, it rains.*
ज्योंही उसने घंटी बजाई त्योंही बस चल दी।	*As soon as he rang the bell the bus started off.*
जैसे ही वह कमरे में आया वैसे ही बिजली बंद हो गई।	*The moment he came into the room the electricity went off.*

To express the sense 'until', Hindi uses जब तक followed by the negative particle न, and either the subjunctive, the future, or the perfective:

जब तक वह न आएगा, तब तक मैं यहीं रहूँगा।	*I'll stay right here until he comes* (lit. *'as long as he doesn't come...*)
जब तक वह न आया तब तक मैं यहीं रहा।	*I stayed right here until he came.*

तब may be replaced by तो, especially in a clause which expresses a *consequence* of the जब clause (rather than emphasising a particular point in time):

जब मैंने उसे यह ख़बर सुनाई तो वह रो दिया।	*When I related this news to him he began to cry.*

Further examples:

जब आपको जाना हो तब मुझे बुलाना।	*Call me when you have to go.*
जब से मैंने यह गाड़ी ख़रीदी है तब से वह यहाँ नहीं आया है।	*Since I bought this car he hasn't come here.*

जब तक पानी पड़ेगा तब तक मैं बाहर नहीं जाऊँगा।	*As long as it rains I shan't go out.*
जब तक तुम काम न करोगे तब तक तुम ग़रीब रहोगे।	*As long as you don't work you will remain poor.*
जब भी मैं कुछ कहता हूँ तभी वह हँस देता है।	*Whenever I say anything he starts laughing.*
ज्योंही मैंने काम ख़त्म किया त्योंही मालिक कमरे में आया।	*As soon as I finished work the boss came into the room.*
जैसे ही उसका पत्र मिलेगा वैसे ही मैं जवाब दूँगा।	*As soon as I get his letter I shall answer it.*
जब लड़के ने प्याला गिरा दिया तो माँ ग़ुस्से में आ गईं।	*When the child dropped the cup, mother became angry.*
जब तक तुम मुझे पैसा न दोगे तब तक मैं यहीं बैठा रहूँगा।	*I'll stay sitting here until you give me the money.*
तब तक न आओ जब तक मैं तुम्हें न बुलाऊँ।	*Don't come until I call you.*
तू तब तक रह सकता है जब तक दूसरे लोग न आएँ।	*You can stay until the others come.*

In the last example, the order of the relative and correlative clauses is reversed (as also happens in the जो...वह construction, para. **54**); note that the correlative (तब, etc.) must then follow the subject of its clause (here तू).

60 Indirect speech

In English, indirect or 'reported' speech follows the pattern 'He asked me how I was'. The same pattern also occurs in Hindi: उसने मुझसे पूछा कि मैं कैसा था. In an alternative construction, the verb ('asked') is followed by कि and then the *actual words* originally spoken: उसने मुझसे पूछा कि आप कैसे हैं.

The same construction is used with verbs of thinking, etc.: उसने सोचा कि मेरे जाने में कोई फ़ायदा नहीं होगा *He thought there was no point in his going* (lit. *He thought that, 'There is no point in my going'*). कि may sometimes be omitted from such a sentence. Notice that inverted commas are *not* used in the Hindi construction.

With indirect commands, it is usual to use the subjunctive in place of the imperative: मैंने उससे कहा कि वह घर जाए *I told him to go home.* Alternatively, the oblique infinitive with को may be used: मैंने उसे घर जाने को कहा। *I told him to go home.*

किसी ने मुझे बताया था कि सारी दुकानें बन्द हो चुकी हैं।	*Someone told me that all the shops had already shut.*
मैंने कहा कि मैं तो आज नहीं जा सकता।	*I said that I couldn't go today.*
शर्मा जी कह रहे थे कि वे भी वहाँ चलेंगे।	*Sharma jī was saying that he'd come there too.*
वह समझ गया कि अब तो कोई नहीं आएगा।	*He realised that nobody would come now.*
हम ने उसे चिट्ठी लिखने को कहा।	*We told him to write a letter.*
मैंने उससे कहा कि वह चुप रहे।	*I told him to keep quiet.*
माँ ने दूधवाले से कहा कि आज दूध नहीं चाहिए।	*Mother told the milkman that she didn't want any milk today.*

EXERCISE 13.1 Translate into English:

वाराणसी की रेल यात्रा

पिछले वर्ष मुझे वाराणसी जाने का मौका मिला। वाराणसी जाकर गंगा जी में स्नान करना हरेक हिंदू की अभिलाषा है। कहते हैं कि जो आदमी वहाँ गंगा जी के किनारे गुज़र जाता है उसे उसी क्षण मुक्ति मिल जाती है। इस दुनिया के झमेले से मुक्ति पाकर वह सीधे स्वर्ग को पहुँच जाता है। अभी तो मुझे मुक्ति पाने की कोई विशेष इच्छा तो नहीं है, उलटे दुनिया के झमेले में मेरा मन ख़ूब लग रहा है! पर मुझे ऐसा लगा कि भारतवर्ष को छोड़ने से पहले[1] मुझे दुनिया का सबसे पुराना नगर तो अवश्य देखना चाहिए। वाराणसी में तीन चार दिन बिताना बड़ा अच्छा लगेगा, यह सोचकर मैंने निश्चय कर लिया कि मैं कल ही वहाँ जाऊँगा। उसी वक़्त स्टेशन जाकर मैंने कल के लिए टिकट लिया।

गाड़ी के छूटने का समय निकट आ गया। गाड़ी पर चढ़कर मैंने अपना सामान सीट के नीचे रख लिया और आराम से बैठ गया। दिन के बारह बजे थे, धूप भी बड़ी तेज़ थी, और मुझे प्यास लग रही थी। मैंने सोचा, चाय पी लूँ। मुझे वह मीठी और तेज़ चाय बहुत पसंद है जो स्टेशन के चायवालों के पास मिलती है, सो मैंने खिड़की में से चायवाले को बुलाकर चाय ली। फेरीवाले को बुलाकर मैंने दो समोसे भी मँगवाए। जब तक मैंने ये समोसे खाए, तब तक काफ़ी लोग मेरे डिब्बे में घुस चुके थे। जिन लोगों को बैठने की जगह नहीं मिल सकी थी, उन्हें तो अपने सामान के ऊपर बैठना पड़ा। कुछ लोग तो फ़र्श पर भी बैठ गए थे, यहाँ तक कि डिब्बे के अंदर आना जाना[2] भी मुश्किल हो गया था। ख़ैर, ठीक पौन बजे सीटी बजी और गाड़ी चल दी।

कुछ समय बाद गाड़ी किसी छोटे स्टेशन पर आकर खड़ी हो गई। मुझे यह देखकर आश्चर्य हुआ कि स्टेशन के चारों तरफ़ हरियाली ही हरियाली[3] नज़र आ रही थी और थोड़ी ही दूर पर बहुत-सी गायें धूप में खड़ी थीं या इधर-उधर घूम रही थी। मुझे ऐसा लगा कि इस छोटी जगह को 'शहर' कहना ग़लत होगा परंतु जो बूढ़ा मुसाफ़िर मेरे सामने बैठा था उसने मुझे बताया कि यहाँ तो बहुत-से कारख़ाने हैं

1 से पहले = के पहले *before.*
2 आना जाना: *to come and go, move about.*
3 हरियाली ही हरियाली: *nothing but greenery.*

जिनमें तरह तरह की चीज़ें बनती हैं। उसने मुझसे यह भी कहा कि कुछ साल पहले तो मैं भी यहाँ काम करता था। जब मैंने उससे पूछा कि आप ऐसी शान्त जगह को छोड़कर क्यों चले गए तो उसने यह जवाब दिया कि मेरी नौकरी समाप्त हो गई थी, इसलिए मुझे अपना घर बेचना पड़ा।

वाराणसी पहुँचने में कितने घंटे लगे, कह नहीं सकता क्योंकि बीच में मुझे नींद आ गई। मैं कम से कम चार घंटे तक सोया हूँगा। जब तक हम वहाँ पहुँचे, तब तक सड़क की बत्तियाँ जल चुकी थीं। गाड़ी से उतरकर मैंने एक कुली कर लिया। वह मेरा सामान उठाकर भीड़ में दौड़ने लगा और आँखों से ओझल हो गया। परेशान होकर मैं भी उसके पीछे दौड़ा। जब मैं भीड़ से निकलकर सड़क पर पहुँचा तब मैंने कुली को वहाँ सड़क के किनारे खड़ा पाया। वह किसी साथी से बातें कर रहा था।

दूसरे क्षण एक टैक्सीवाले ने मेरे पास आकर कहा कि कहाँ जाना है साहब ? मैंने उसे बताया कि मुझे फ़लाने होटल जाना है, कितना लोगे ? उसने कहा कि हम मीटर के हिसाब से चलेंगे, आइए टैक्सी में बैठिए। जब तक मैं होटल पहुँचा तब तक मुझे थोड़ी भूख लगी थी। होटल में जाकर संयोग से मुझे एक दोस्त दिखाई दिया,[1] जिसने मुझे अपने साथ खाना खाने को बुलाया। जैसे ही[2] हम खाना खा चुके मैं ने उससे यह पूछा कि वाराणसी में मुझे कौनसी जगहें देखनी चाहिएँ। उसने यह जवाब दिया कि यहाँ की सारी मशहूर जगहों को देखने में तो कई हफ़्ते लगेंगे, पर आप को गंगा जी के घाट और तीन चार प्रमुख मंदिर तो अवश्य देखने चाहिए।

EXERCISE **13.2** Translate into Hindi:

Yesterday I went to the shop in which chairs and tables are made. I asked the proprietor when my chairs would be ready. He told me that the man who makes the chairs was ill, but as soon as he got well I would get the chairs. I said that in my opinion he should have given me the chairs last month. If he knew in the beginning how long it would take to complete the job, he should have told me. He didn't want me to go to some other shop, so he said nothing. But he knows that I won't give him the money until I have the chairs, so we both hope that the chair-maker will get better quickly! Until then, we shall have to sit on the floor. I actually like sitting on the floor, but when my parents come to visit us then it is difficult for them.

Vocabulary

अभिलाषा	*desire* (f.)
आँखों से ओझल होना	*to disappear from view*
आग	*fire* (f.)
आराम करना	*to rest*

1 दिखाई देना *to appear, to be visible* does not take ने: see para. **74.**

2 Note that the correlative वैसे ही is omitted from this sentence; the correlative clause begins मैं ने उससे...

इच्छा	*desire, wish* (f.)
इज़ाफ़ा	*increase, rise* (m.)
उलटे	*conversely*
ओझल	*out of sight*
किनारा	*bank, edge, border* (m.)
कुली करना	*to hire a porter*
के किनारे	*on/at the side of*
के चारों तरफ़	*all around*
क्षण	*moment* (m.)
खेल	*game* (m.)
गंगा	*the river Ganges* (f.)
गाय	*cow* (f.)
गिराना	*to drop* (tr.), *let fall*
गुज़रना	*to pass* (of time), (intr.); *to pass away*
घंटी	*bell* (f.)
घाट	*bathing place on a river,* etc. (m.)
घुसना	*to enter*
चिट्ठी	*letter, note* (f.)
चोट	*injury, hurt* (f.)
जंगल	*jungle, wilderness* (m.)
जब	*when*
जब तक	*as long as, until the time that*
जब भी	*whenever*
जब से	*since the time when*
जलना	*to burn* (intr.)
जैसे ही...वैसे ही	*as soon as*
ज्योंही...त्योंही	*as soon as*
झमेला	*mess, turmoil, botheration* (m.)
ठंड	*cold* (f.)
डर	*fear* (m.)
डाकख़ाना	*post office* (m.)
डाक्टर	*doctor* (m.)
तब	*then*
तरक़्क़ी	*progress, advancement* (f.)
तरक़्क़ी करना	*to progress, advance*
ताला	*lock* (m.)
तेज़	*sharp, acute, strong, quick*
दिखाई देना/पड़ना	*appear, be visible, come into sight*
दिन भर	*all day long*
दिल	*heart* (m.)
दिल लगना	*to feel content, feel at home*
की देखभाल करना	*to look after*

दोबारा	*again, a second time*
धूप	*sunshine* (f.)
न जाने	*God knows, who knows*
नज़र	*glance, sight* (f.)
नज़र आना	*to come into sight, be seen, appear*
निकट	*near*
निश्चय करना	*to decide, resolve*
नींद	*sleep* (f.)
नींद आना	*to feel sleepy, fall asleep*
नोटिस	*notice* (m.)
पद	*position, office* (m.)
पहनना	*to wear, put on*
प्यास	*thirst* (f.)
प्रमुख	*principal, chief, main*
प्रसन्न	*pleased, happy*
फ़लाना	*so-and-so, such-and-such*
फेरीवाला	*hawker* (m.)
बत्ती	*light, lamp* (f.)
बनना	*to become, be made*
बाघ	*tiger* (m.)
बीच में	*meanwhile, in the meantime*
बीवी	*wife* (f.)
बेचना	*to sell*
बेचारा	*poor, wretched, helpless; wretch, poor fellow* (m.)
बेशक	*of course, undoubtedly*
भर	*full, whole, complete* (suffix)
भागना	*to run, flee, escape*
भूख	*hunger* (f.)
मँगवाना	*to order, ask for, buy*
मज़ाक़	*joke* (m.)
मज़ाक़िया	*witty, funny, humorous*
मन	*mind, heart* (m.)
मन लगना	*to feel at home*
मशहूर	*famous*
महसूस करना	*to feel, experience*
मालिक	*boss, proprietor, master* (m.)
मिलना	*to be available*
मिलना-जुलना	*to meet, mix; to resemble* (with से)
मीटर	*meter* (m.)
मुक्ति	*liberation, salvation, deliverance* (f.)
मुफ़्त में	*free of charge*
मौक़ा	*opportunity, chance, occasion* (m.)

यहाँ तक कि	*to the point/extent that*
रास्ते में	*on the way, en route*
लगना	*to be applied; to seem* (para. 58)
वापस आना	*to come back, return*
शान्ति	*peace, tranquillity* (f.)
संभालना	*to take hold of, collect*
संयोग से	*by chance*
सजाना	*to decorate, arrange*
सनीचर	*Saturday* (m.)
सब मिलकर	*all together*
समाप्त होना	*to be ended, terminated*
सही	*correct, true, accurate*
सीटी	*whistle* (f.)
स्थिति	*situation* (f.)
स्नान करना	*to bathe* (esp. ritually)
स्वर्ग	*heaven* (m.)
हरियाली	*greenery, verdure* (f.)
हिसाब	*rate, account, calculation* (m.)

Unit Fourteen

Dialogue 14A *Learning languages*

श्याम पंडित जी, दिल्ली में कितनी भाषाएँ बोली जाती हैं?

पंडित जी वैसे दिल्ली की प्रमुख भाषा तो हिन्दी ही है, परंतु हिन्दी के अलावा उर्दू, पंजाबी और अँग्रेज़ी इत्यादि भी बोली जाती हैं।

श्याम मुझे बताया गया है कि आपको कई भाषाएँ अच्छी तरह आती हैं। आपको अँग्रज़ी भी आती होगी।

पंडित जी हाँ, आती तो है, पर जब मैं छोटा था तो पिताजी हमें अँग्रेज़ी पढ़ने नहीं देते थे। उन दिनों तो हमें अपनी मातृभाषा ही आती थी। जब मैं कालेज में दाखिल हुआ तो मैं थोड़ी अँग्रेज़ी सीखने लगा। कालेज़ में तो बहुत-से विषय पढ़ाए जाते थे।

श्याम आप को घर पर अँग्रज़ी क्यों नहीं बोलने दी जाती थी?

पंडित जी क्योंकि पिताजी को विदेशी भाषाओं से नफ़रत थी। कहते थे कि उन गोरों ने हमारे देश को बुरी तरह कुचला है, और जब तक हमें आज़ादी न दी जाए, तब तक हमें उनकी भाषा नहीं सीखनी चाहिए। पर तुम बताओ, तुमने अपनी शिक्षा कहाँ से पाई?

श्याम मैं लन्दन में पैदा हुआ था, और पहले तो वहीं स्कूल जाता था। पर जब मैं सोलह साल का हो गया तो मुझे अमेरिका भेजा गया था। वहाँ जाकर संस्कृत पढ़ने का इरादा था, पर वह तो इतनी कठिन भाषा है कि मुझसे सीखी नहीं गई। वहाँ हिन्दी बोलने का मौका मिला ही नहीं, इसलिए मैं अपनी मातृभाषा को भी भूलने लगा।

पंडित जी यहाँ रहकर तो तुम्हें हिन्दी ही बोलनी पड़ेगी और संस्कृत भी पढ़ जाओगे। जब तक तुम भगवद्गीता को न पढ़ने लगोगे, तब तक हम तुमको लन्दन वापस जाने नहीं देंगे!

Shyam Pandit jī, how many languages are spoken in Delhi?

Pandit jī Well, the principal language of Delhi is Hindi itself, but as well as Hindi, Urdu, Panjabi and English, etc. are also spoken.

Shyam I have been told that you know several languages well. You must know English too?

Pandit jī Yes, I do, but when I was young, Father used not to allow us to study English. In those days we knew only our mother-tongue. When I was admitted to college I began to learn a little English. In college, many subjects were taught.

Shyam Why weren't you allowed to speak English at home?

Pandit jī Because father hated foreign languages. He used to say that those white people have badly crushed our country, and we shouldn't learn their language until we are given freedom. But you tell me, where did you get your education?

Shyam I was born in London, and at first I went to school there. But when I turned sixteen I was sent to America. I intended to learn Sanskrit on going there, but that is such a difficult language that I couldn't learn it. I just didn't get the chance to speak Hindi there, so I even began to forget my mother tongue.

Pandit jī Living here though, you'll have to speak only Hindi, and you'll learn Sanskrit too. We won't let you go back to London until you begin to read the *Bhagavad Gita!*

61 The passive

In English, 'I sent' is active, and 'I was sent' is passive. In Hindi, the passive comprises the perfective participle followed by the verb जाना. There are two constructions used with the passive, both equally common. In the first, the passive verb (both parts– participle *and* जाना) agrees with the subject:

भारत में हिन्दी बोली जाती है।	*In India Hindi is spoken.*
यह साड़ी गुजरात में बनाई गई।	*This sari was made in Gujarat.*
यह काम आज शाम तक किया जाएगा।	*This work will be done by this evening.*
सारी तैयारियाँ कल तक की जाएँ।	*All the preparations should be done by tomorrow.*
फ्रांस में मेंढक खाये जाते हैं।	*Frogs are eaten in France.*
कहा जाता है कि अकबर अनपढ़ था।	*It is said that Akbar was illiterate.*
सारा पैसा ख़र्च किया जा चुका है।	*All the money has been spent already.*
बिजली बन्द कर दी गई थी।	*The electricity was cut off.*

In the second type of passive construction, the English subject takes the postposition को, and the verb is invariably in the masculine singular:

इन पुस्तकों को हवाई डाक से भेजा गया।	*These books were sent by air mail.*
चोरों को पकड़ा जाएगा।	*The thieves will be caught.*
सीता को ससुराल भेजा गया था।	*Sita was sent to her in-laws' house.*

हमें इसके बारे में बताया गया।	*We were told about this.*
इन किताबों को जलाया जाएगा।	*These books will be burned.*
इन तस्वीरों को डाक से भेजा जा सकता है।	*These pictures can be sent by post*

If it is necessary to indicate *by whom* the action was done, that person takes the postposition के द्वारा or द्वारा:

ताज महल शाहजहाँ के द्वारा बनाया गया था।	*The Taj Mahal was built by Shah Jahan.*
यह लेख मेरे द्वारा नहीं लिखा गया था।	*This article was not written by me.*
क्या सच्चे आदमी के द्वारा ऐसा झूठ बोला जाएगा?	*Would such a lie be spoken by an honest man?*

In the negative, the passive may express incapacity, inability or unwillingness to do something; this usage may even apply with intransitive verbs such as बैठना which one would not normally regard as having a passive: मुझसे नहीं बैठा गया *I couldn't sit down*. In this usage, the postposition से, and not (के) द्वारा, is invariably used. Notice that the perfective participle of जाना used in the passive is जाया and not the usual गया.

ऐसा खाना मुझसे नहीं खाया जाएगा।	*I can't eat such food.* (Lit. *Such food will not be eaten by me*).
मुझसे न रहा गया।	*I couldn't contain myself.*
उससे वहाँ नहीं जाया गया।	*He couldn't* (*bring himself to*) *go there.*
इतनी गरमी में किसी से नहीं सोया जाता।	*Nobody can sleep in such heat.*
उस आदमी का चेहरा मुझसे नहीं देखा जाता।	*I can't bear the sight of that man's face.*
मैंने ऐसी मार खाई थी कि मुझसे बैठा नहीं जाता।	*I'd taken such a beating that I couldn't sit down.*

It is often possible to use an active intransitive verb in place of a passive transitive: thus यहाँ अख़बार बिकते हैं *Newspapers are sold here* (using intransitive बिकना *to be sold* in an active construction) has the same sense as यहाँ अख़बार बेचे जाते हैं (using transitive बेचना in a passive construction). The passive tends, therefore, to be used less frequently in Hindi than in such languages as English which do not have such an extensive range of intransitive verbs. Further examples of active intransitive/passive transitive constructions are:

काम शुरू हुआ।	*Work began.* (intr. शुरू होना)
काम शुरू किया गया।	*Work was begun.* (tr. शुरू करना)
यहाँ साइकिलें बनती हैं।	*Bicycles are made here.* (intr. बनना)
यहाँ साइकिलें बनाई जाती हैं।	*Bicycles are made here.* (tr. बनाना)
कपड़े नदी में धुलते हैं।	*Clothes are washed in the river.* (intr. धुलना)
कपड़े नदी में धोए जाते हैं।	*Clothes are washed in the river.* (tr. धोना)

Finally, take care not to confuse the use of जाना in the passive construction (with a perfective participle) with the use of जाना as an auxiliary verb in a compound (with a verb stem):

वह खाना खाया गया।	*That food was eaten.* (subject वह खाना)
वह खाना खा गया।	*He ate up the food.* (subject वह)

62 The oblique infinitive with लगना *to begin to*

Following an oblique infinitive, लगना gives the sense 'to begin'; लगना is intransitive and does not take ने. वह गाने लगी *She began to sing.*

This construction with लगना is rarely used in the negative, and never in the imperative or in continuous tenses. With certain infinitives such as कहना the sense of 'beginning' may be quite weak, so that वह कहने लगा कि राम को दस रुपये चाहिए has the same sense as उसने कहा कि राम को दस रुपये चाहिए *He said that Ram needed ten rupees.*

पानी पड़ने लगा।	*It began to rain.*
दिन भर अकेले रहने से वह ऊबने लगा।	*Being alone all day he began to get bored.*
वह सोचने लगी कि अब तो कोई नहीं आएगा।	*She began to think that no one would come now.*
जब मेंह बहुत ज़ोर से पड़ने लगता है तो मुझे डर लगने लगता है।	*When it rains very heavily I begin to feel frightened.*
चीनी खाना खाने के दो ही घंटे बाद मुझे भूख लगने लगती है!	*Just two hours after eating Chinese food I begin to feel hungry!*

63 The oblique infinitive with देना *to allow to*

देना with the oblique infinitive means 'to allow to': मुझको वहाँ जाने दीजिए *Allow me to go there.* Since देना is transitive and requires the ने

construction, the perfective of देना must agree with an object (without को) of the infinitive; the infinitive itself remains unchanged in the oblique: उसने मुझको अपनी गाड़ी चलाने दी *He let me drive his car*. Examples:

बच्चों को बग़ीचे में खेलने दो।	*Allow the children to play in the garden.*
बिल्ली को दूध न पीने देना!	*Don't let the cat drink the milk!*
पहले तो गाड़ी आने दो, फिर स्टेशन जाना।	*First let the train come, then go to the station.*
बारिश होने दो!	*Let it rain (for all I care)!*
उसे अपने घर में काम करने दिया जाए।	*He should be allowed to work in his own house.*
पिता जी ने राम को मिठाइयाँ खाने दीं।	*Father let Ram eat the sweets.*

Notice also the expressions रहने दो *Let it be*, जाने दो *Let it pass; forget it.*

Dialogue 14B *Hindi as the national language*

श्याम पंडित जी, हिन्दी को राष्ट्रभाषा के रूप में क्यों अपनाया गया है?

पंडित जी इसका मुख्य कारण यह है कि जितने लोग हिन्दी बोलते हैं, उतने कोई दूसरी भाषा नहीं बोलते। और आजकल हिन्दी को पढ़ाने के लिए सैकड़ों किताबें लिखी जा रही हैं, ताकि दूसरी भाषाओं के बोलनेवाले इसे आसानी से सीख सकें।

श्याम मैंने सुना है कि दक्षिण भारत के लोग हिन्दी से नफ़रत करते हैं। क्या यह सच है?

पंडित जी हर कोई समझता है कि जितनी सुंदर मेरी अपनी भाषा है, उतनी सुंदर कोई दूसरी भाषा नहीं हो सकती। यह आश्चर्य की बात नहीं है कि दक्षिण के लोग अपनी ही भाषाएँ रखना चाहते हैं। पर हिन्दी से नफ़रत करने की इसमें कोई बात नहीं है।

श्याम भारत सरकार ऐसा क्यों चाहती है कि हिन्दी दक्षिण में भी पढ़ाई जाए?

पंडित जी क्योंकि भारत में एक ऐसी भाषा की आवश्यकता है जिसमें विभिन्न प्रदेशों के लोग आपस में बात कर सकें, ताकि देश में एकता हो। इसे 'संपर्क भाषा' कहा जाता है।

श्याम तो इस काम के लिए अँग्रेज़ी क्यों नहीं चुनी गई? बड़े शहरों में उतनी ही अँग्रेज़ी चलती है जितनी हिन्दी, ऐसा लगता है मुझे।

पंडित जी बड़े शहरों की बात दूसरी है। गाँवों में जाइए तो आप अँग्रेज़ी बोलनेवाले बहुत कम पाएँगे। और भारत तो गाँवों का ही देश है। उत्तर भारत के गाँवों में हिन्दी का कोई न कोई रूप बोला जाता है।

श्याम पर क्या यह सच नहीं कि उत्तर में भी करोड़ों ऐसे लोग हैं जिन्हें हिन्दी नहीं आती?

पंडित जी पश्चिम भारत के लोग गुजराती या मराठी बोलते हैं, जब कि पूर्व की ओर बंगला और उड़िया बोली जाती हैं। पर इन भाषाओं के बोलनेवाले भी थोड़ी-बहुत हिन्दी समझ लेते हैं।

Shyam Pandit jī, why has Hindi been adopted as the national language?

Pandit jī The main reason for this[1] is that more people speak Hindi than speak any other language. And these days hundreds of books for teaching Hindi are being written, so that the speakers of other languages may learn it easily.

Shyam I have heard that the people of South India detest Hindi. Is this true?

Pandit jī Everybody thinks that no other language can be as beautiful as his own[2]. It is not surprising that the people of the South want to keep their own languages. But it is not a matter of hating Hindi.

Shyam Why does the Indian Government want Hindi to be taught in the South as well?

Pandit jī Because there is a need in India for such a language in which the people of the various states can speak with one another, so that there may be unity in the country. This is called a 'link language'.

Shyam So why wasn't English chosen for this task? In the big cities as much English is used[3] as Hindi, so it seems to me.

Pandit jī The big cities are another matter. Go into the villages and you'll find the speakers of English are very few. And India is after all a country of villages. In the villages of Northern India, some or other form of Hindi is spoken.

Shyam But is it not true that even in the North there are tens of millions of people who don't know Hindi?

Pandit jī The people of Western India speak Gujarati or Marathi, while towards the East Bengali and Oriya are spoken. But even the speakers of these languages understand a certain amount of Hindi.

[1] इसका मुख्य कारण यह है: lit. *the main reason of this is...*

[2] मेरी अपनी: use of the possessive adjective अपना together with the personal pronoun gives emphasis: 'my own, my very own'. Compare यह मेरा अपना कैमरा है *This is my very own camera*; हमारा अपना मकान नहीं है *We don't have a house of our own.*

[3] This use of चलना gives the sense 'to be current'.

64 Relative-correlative constructions for quantity

The relative adjective for quantity is जितना *as much as, as many as;* this correlates with उतना *that much, that many*:

आपको जितना पैसा चाहिए उतना लीजिए।	*Take as much money as you need.*

जितना may be followed by भी, giving the sense 'however much/many'; उतना may be followed by emphatic ही, giving the sense 'just that much/many':

आपको जितना भी पैसा चाहिए उतना लीजिए।	*Take however much money you need.*
आपको जितना पैसा चाहिए उतना ही लीजिए।	*Take just the amount of money you need.*

As in other relative-correlative constructions, the order of the two clauses may be reversed:

उतना पैसा लीजिए जितना आपको चाहिए।	*Take as much money as you need.*
जितने लोग अँग्रेज़ी बोलते हैं उतने उर्दू नहीं बोलते।	*Not as many people speak Urdu as speak English.*
जितना खाना तैयार हो उतना लाओ।	*Bring as much food as happens to be ready.*
जितना अच्छा यह कपड़ा है उतना अच्छा वह नहीं था।	*That cloth wasn't as good as this.*
उनकी जितनी ज़मीन है उतनी ही हमारी भी है।	*We have just as much land as they.*
इस कुएँ में उतना पानी नहीं है जितना होना चाहिए।	*There isn't as much water in this well as there should be.*
तुम उतनी अच्छी हिन्दी बोलते हो जितनी वह।	*You speak as good Hindi as he.*

Notice in the last example that in Hindi, as in English, the full clause जितनी वह बोलता है *as he speaks* is not required.

The sense 'so much...that' is expressed by इतना (*this much, this many*)...कि:

मेरे पास इतना सामान था कि मुझे कुली को बुलाना पड़ा।	*I had so much luggage that I had to call a porter.*
तरकारी में इतना मसाला है कि यह मुझसे नहीं खाई जाएगी।	*There is so much spice in the vegetable curry that I can't eat it.*
वह इतनी नाराज़ हो गई कि उससे कुछ बोला नहीं गया।	*She became so angry that she couldn't say anything.*

65 Purpose clauses

The use of the infinitive to express purpose has already been introduced (para. **41**), as in मैं राम से मिलने आया हूँ *I have come to meet Ram.* More complex sentences expressing purpose require the use of clauses introduced by ताकि *so that, in order that* or जिससे कि *by which, whereby* and having the verb in the subjunctive.

मैंने दरवाज़ा बन्द कर लिया ताकि धुआँ कमरे में न आए।	*I closed the door so that the smoke wouldn't come into the room.*
मच्छरदानी लगाइए जिससे कि आप मच्छरों से बच सकें।	*Put up a mosquito net in order to escape the mosquitoes.*
हमने हिन्दी में बातें कीं, जिससे कि दूसरे लोग हमारी बातें न समझ सकें।	*We conversed in Hindi so that the others couldn't understand what we said.*
आपको साइकिल ख़रीदनी चाहिए ताकि आपको बस से न आना पड़े।	*You should buy a bicycle so that you don't have to come by bus.*
दुकानदार ने ताला लगाया जिससे कि चोरी न हो।	*The shopkeeper put on a lock to prevent theft.*
उसने दवा खाई जिससे कि बुख़ार उतरे।	*He took medicine to make the fever come down.*

66 Aggregatives

Aggregatives, such as दोनों *both, the two*, express a total or aggregate number of component parts forming a group. दोनों itself is irregular in construction, but other aggregatives are formed simply by adding -ओं to the number:

तीनों	*all three*
दसों	*all ten*

Note also the following usages:

दर्जनों	*dozens of*	(दर्जन (m.) *a dozen*)
सैकड़ों	*hundreds of*	(सैकड़ा (m.) *a hundred*)
हज़ारों	*thousands of*	(हज़ार (m.) *a thousand*)
करोड़ों	*crores of*	(करोड़ (m.) *a crore, ten million*)

तीनों पड़ोसी झगड़ा करते हैं।	*All three neighbours quarrel.*
हमें सातों दिन काम करना पड़ता है।	*We have to work all seven days.*

हमने दर्जनों बंदर पेड़ों में देखे थे।	*We saw dozens of monkeys in the trees.*
उसके करोड़ों रुपए खो गए।	*He lost crores of rupees.*

EXERCISE 14.1 Translate into English:

सड़क की दुर्घटना

एक दिन ऐसा हुआ कि मैं घर से डाकख़ाने की तरफ़ जा रहा था। मुझे कोई ख़ास काम तो नहीं था, ज़रा धूप खाने के विचार से घूमने गया था। नाश्ता करने के बाद इस तरह से थोड़ी देर घूमना बड़ा अच्छा लगता है। दिन काफ़ी सुंदर था, और ठंडी हवा से मालूम हुआ कि सरदी का मौसम आनेवाला है। सड़क के किनारे कुछ बच्चे खेल रहे थे। लगता है कि आजकल जितने बच्चे स्कूल जाते हैं, उतने ही दिन भर सड़कों के किनारे खेलते हैं या बाज़ारों में घूमते हैं! हाँ, मैं भी बचपन में ऐसा करता था और जब मौसम सुहावना होता था तो मुझसे भी अँधेरे कमरे में न बैठा जाता था। मगर उन दिनों तो हम बच्चे लोग खेतों में या बाग़ में खेलते थे, माँ-बाप हमें सड़क के पास कभी खेलने नहीं देते थे। आजकल के बच्चों को तो सड़कों पर भी खेलने छोड़ दिया जाता है, और हर साल हज़ारों बच्चों को चोट लग जाती है। ख़ैर, इस बात को छोड़िए, नहीं तो मुझसे अपनी कहानी पूरी नहीं की जाएगी।

ज्योंही मैं उन बच्चों के पास पहुँचा जो सड़क के किनारे खेल रहे थे त्योंही एक बड़ी काली गाड़ी डाकख़ाने के पास नज़र आई। वह गाड़ी तेज़ रफ़्तार से हमारी तरफ़ आ रही थी। उसे देखकर मैंने उसी क्षण बच्चों को चिल्लाकर कहा कि बचो, गाड़ी आ रही है! पर जितने ज़ोर से मैं चिल्लाया था, उससे भी ज़्यादा ज़ोर से बच्चे लोग शोर मचा रहे थे, सो मेरी चिल्लाहट उनसे सुनी नहीं गई। उनमें से किसी ने एक गेंद हवा में फेंक दी। सारे बच्चे उसे पकड़ने दौड़े, पर किसी तरह से वह उनके हाथों से छूटकर सड़क पर आ गई। गाड़ी तो अब तक बिलकुल पास आ गई थी, पर बच्चों को उसका कुछ भी पता नहीं था। तीन बच्चे लपककर सड़क की ओर बढ़े। उन्हें देखकर गाड़ीवाले ने गाड़ी को दूसरी ओर घुमाया जिससे कि बच्चों को टक्कर न लगे। पर तब तक क्या हुआ कि सामनेवाली गली में से एक साइकिल निकली और गाड़ी से टकरा गई। ड्राइवर ने ज़ोर से ब्रेक लगाया और गाड़ी रुक गई। हम सब दौड़कर पास पहुँचे। साइकिल तो बुरी तरह से कुचल गई थी, मगर न जाने कैसे सवारी बच गई।[1] उसका बाल बाँका न हुआ था! ड्राइवर की लापरवाही को देखकर मुझसे न रहा गया, और मैं उसे गालियाँ देने लगा। पुलिस को बुलाया गया। अब तक तो दर्जनों लोग इस तमाशे को देख रहे थे। पुलिस आकर ड्राइवर को थाने ले गई, और मैं घर की तरफ़ चल दिया। कुछ दिन बाद मैंने अख़बार में पढ़ा कि उसे जेल की सज़ा हो गई थी। मेरे ख़्याल से यह उचित ही था क्योंकि उस बदमाश को इतनी तेज़ रफ़्तार से गाड़ी नहीं चलानी चाहिए थी!

EXERCISE 14.2 Translate into Hindi:

Last year I was sent to India by my father, in order that I might study Hindi, which is my father's mother tongue. My two brothers

[1] Note that the noun सवारी *rider, passenger* retains its feminine gender even when referring to a male.

were not allowed to go with me, because they had to go to school in London. In London I had not had much chance to speak Hindi, but arriving in India I began to speak it quite easily. In the town I lived in there were as many Bengali speakers as Hindi speakers. I was living in college with three friends; we all said to our teacher that we should be taught some Bengali too. But he said, 'First let me teach you Hindi; after that I'll teach you as much Bengali as you want to learn'. When I began to meet Bengali speakers, I found that Bengali was not as easy as Hindi. I have been told that this is not true, but Bengali seems quite hard to me at least.

Vocabulary

अँधेरा	*dark; darkness* (m.)
अनपढ़	*illiterate*
अपनाना	*to adopt, make one's own*
अमेरिका	*America* (m.)
आज़ादी	*freedom, independence* (f.)
आपस में	*with one another, mutually*
इत्यादि	*etc., and so on*
इरादा	*intention* (m.)
उतना	*that much*
ऊबना	*to be bored*
एकता	*unity* (f.)
करोड़	*ten million* (m.)
कारण	*reason, cause* (m.)
कुचलना	*to crush, trample; to be crushed, trampled on*
(के) द्वारा	*by, by means of*
के रूप में	*in the form of, as*
ख़र्च करना	*to spend*
गली	*lane, alleyway* (f.)
गाली	*abuse, invective, insult* (f.)
गाली देना	*to abuse, insult*
गुजरात	*Gujarat* (m.)
गुजराती	*the Gujarati language* (f.)
गेंद	*ball* (f.)
गोरा	*fair; white person, European* (m.)
घुमाना	*to turn* (tr.)
चिल्लाना	*to cry out, shout loudly*
चिल्लाहट	*cry, call* (f.)
चीनी	*Chinese*
चुनना	*to choose, pick*

चेहरा	*face* (m.)
चोट लगना	*to get hurt*
जब कि	*while*
जलाना	*to burn* (tr.), *set alight*
जितना	*as much as, as many as*
जिससे कि	*by which, whereby*
जेल	*jail* (f.)
झूठ	*lie* (m.)
टकराना	*to collide* (with से)
टक्कर	*collision* (f.)
टक्कर लगना	*a collision to take place* (with से)
ताकि	*so that, in order that*
ताज महल	*the Taj Mahal* (m.)
थाना	*police station* (m.)
दक्षिण	*south* (m.)
दर्जन	*a dozen* (m.)
दाख़िल होना	*to be admitted, to enter*
दुर्घटना	*accident* (f.)
द्वारा	*by means of*
धुआँ	*smoke* (m.)
धुलना	*to be washed*
धूप खाना	*to bask in the sun, enjoy the sun*
नफ़रत	*hatred* (f.)
नफ़रत करना	*to hate* (with से)
नाराज़	*displeased, angry*
पश्चिम	*western; west* (m.)
पूर्व	*east* (m.)
पैदा होना	*to be born, produced* (पैदा inv.)
प्रदेश	*province, state* (m.)
फेंकना	*to throw*
फ्रांस	*France* (m.)
बंदर	*monkey* (m.)
बाँका	*crooked, bent*
बारिश	*rain* (f.)
बारिश होना	*to rain, rain to fall*
बाल	*hair* (m.)
बाल बाँका न होना	*to escape without hurt, remain unscathed*
बिकना	*to be sold*
बिल्ली	*cat* (f.)
ब्रेक	*brake* (m.)
भगवद्गीता	*Bhagavad Gita* (f.)
भारत सरकार	*the Indian Government* (f.)

मच्छर	*mosquito* (m.)
मच्छरदानी	*mosquito net* (f.)
मराठी	*the Marathi language* (f.)
मसाला	*spice* (m.)
मातृभाषा	*mother-tongue* (f.)
मार	*beating* (f.)
मार खाना	*to undergo a beating*
मुख्य	*main, principal, chief*
मेंढक	*frog* (m.)
मेंह	*rain* (m.)
मोड़ना	*to turn* (tr.)
रफ़्तार	*speed* (f.)
राष्ट्रभाषा	*national language* (f.)
रुकना	*to stop* (intr.)
रूप	*form; beauty* (m.)
लगाना	*to apply, attach*
लपकना	*to rush forward, pounce*
लापरवाही	*carelessness* (f.)
लेख	*article, paper* (m.)
वापस जाना	*to go back, return*
विभिन्न	*various*
विषय	*subject* (m.)
शिक्षा	*education* (f.)
शोर	*row, noise, rumpus* (m.)
शोर मचाना	*to create a rumpus*
संपर्क	*contact, connection, link* (m.)
संपर्क भाषा	*link language* (f.)
सच्चा	*true, honest*
सज़ा	*punishment* (f.)
सत्ताईस	*twenty-seven*
सवारी	*passenger, rider* (f.)
साइकिल	*bicycle* (f.)
सैकड़ा	*a hundred* (m.)
हज़ार	*a thousand* (m.)
हवाई डाक	*air mail* (f.)

Unit Fifteen

Dialogue 15A *A proposed trip to India*

अनीता बच्चों का क्या हाल है सरला? पहले तो वे रोज़ हमारे यहाँ आया करते थे, आजकल दिखाई नहीं देते। उनकी तबियत ठीक है न?

सरला मेहरबानी, बिलकुल ठीक है। रवि तो दिन-ब-दिन लंबा होता जा रहा है। किसी को विश्वास नहीं होगा कि वह सिर्फ़ साढ़े आठ साल का है।

अनीता तुम लोगों का हिन्दुस्तान कब जाने का विचार है? तुम इसी साल जाने की बात कर रही थीं न? प्रोग्राम अभी पक्का है कि नहीं?

सरला हाँ, अगले महीने जाएँगे। बच्चे मुझसे कहते रहते हैं कि अम्माँ, हमें हिन्दुस्तान जाना है। उनके चचेरे भाई के पत्र बराबर आते हैं, जिसके साथ वे तीन साल पहले भारत में खेला करते थे। जैसा मज़ा उन्हें वहाँ कबड्डी खेलने में आता था, वैसा मज़ा यहाँ के किसी भी खेल में नहीं आता। तुम भी जाने की सोच रही हो?

अनीता इस साल तो नहीं। पहले तो हम लोग हर साल भारत जाया करते थे, पर किराया महीने-के-महीने बढ़ता जा रहा है। अब इतना पैसा खर्च करना हमारे लिए असंभव हो गया है। तुम भारत जाकर कई महीने रहोगी न?

सरला जी तो यही चाहता है। जैसा वातावरण अपने देश में होता है, वैसा और कहाँ मिलेगा? वैसे मैं इंग्लैंड की रहनेवाली हूँ, पर मैं भारत को सच्चे अर्थों में अपना देश समझती हूँ।

अनीता यह बात! जैसे ही मैं भारत पहुँचती हूँ वैसे ही मुझे लगता है कि मैं यहीं की हूँ, और विदेश लौटने का मन नहीं होता!

सरला रुपया जोड़ती जाओ, तो दो तीन साल के अंदर तुम भी जा सकोगी। मैं दो साल से लगातार पैसे बचाती रही हूँ, तब कहीं जाकर अब बच्चों को लेकर भारत जा सकती हूँ।

Anita How are the children Sarala? Previously they used to come to our place every day, now they're not to be seen. They are well aren't they?

Sarala Thank you, they're quite all right. Ravi's getting taller every day; nobody would believe[1] that he's only eight and a half.

1 किसी को विश्वास नहीं होगा: note this use of future tense to give the sense '**would** believe'.

Anita When are you people thinking of going to India?[2] You were talking about going this year, weren't you? Is your programme fixed yet or[3] not?

Sarala Yes, we are going next month. The children keep saying to me, 'Mummy, we want to go to India'. They keep getting letters from their cousin,[4] with whom they used to play in India three years ago. They don't enjoy any game here in the way they enjoyed playing *kabaddi* there. Are you thinking of going too?[5]

Anita Not this year anyway. Previously we used to go to India every year, but the fare goes on increasing month by month. Now it has become impossible for us to spend so much money. When you go to India, you will stay several months, won't you?

Sarala That's what I really long for.[6] Where else can you find the atmosphere that there is in one's own country? I do live in England,[7] but I consider India my home in the true sense.

Anita That's it exactly! As soon as I arrive in India it seems to me that I belong there, and don't want to return abroad.[8]

Sarala Carry on saving up money, then you'll be able to go too within two or three years. I've gone on saving continuously for two years, only then[9] am I able to go to India with the children.

67 The imperfective participle with रहना and जाना

The imperfective participle followed by the verbs रहना or जाना gives the sense 'to keep on doing'. रहना emphasises the continuity of an action, while जाना emphasises progressiveness. Thus, in मौसम बदलता रहता है *The weather keeps on changing,* emphasis is put upon the state of continuous changeability, while in किराया बढ़ता जाता है *The rent keeps on rising,* emphasis is put upon a *series* of increases.

2 Both the काs in this sentence agree with the noun विचार. The literal sense is 'When is your idea **of** going to India?'.

3 Note the use of कि as meaning 'or'.

4 Lit. *Letters from their cousin keep coming.*

5 की agrees with the word बात, which is here understood without being actually stated: 'Are you also thinking of [the idea of] going?'

6 Lit. [*my*] *mind so wishes.*

7 वैसे at the beginning of this clause anticipates the 'but' introducing the next clause; it may be translated as 'although'.

8 Lit. *I am of this place, and I don't have a mind to return abroad.*

9 तब कहीं जाकर: a set phrase meaning 'only then'.

पानी पड़ता रहा।	*The rain kept on falling. (It kept raining.)*
तुम अपना काम धीरे धीरे करते रहो।	*Keep doing your work slowly.*
फ़िल्म और आगे देखते जाओ, सबसे अच्छा दृश्य अभी आनेवाला है।	*Go on watching the film, the best scene is just coming up.*
जब तक उसे सज़ा नहीं दी जाएगी तब तक वह चोरी करता रहेगा।	*As long as he is not punished he will keep stealing.*
बैरा चपातियाँ लाता गया और मैं खाता गया।	*The waiter went on bringing chapattis and I went on eating [them].*
चारों विद्यार्थी बड़े चाव से व्याकरण की पुस्तक पढ़ते गए।	*All four students went on reading the grammar book with great enthusiasm.*

68 The invariable masculine singular perfective with करना

The perfective in the invariable masculine singular -आ form followed by करना expresses habitual action: हर हफ़्ते मुझे एक पत्र लिखा करो *Write me a letter every week.* This construction does not take ने in the perfective tenses. The perfective form of जाना used in this construction is जाया, not the usual गया. Examples:

भोजन करके हम प्रायः समाचार सुना करते थे।	*After dining we usually used to listen to the news.*
उन दिनों हम लोग रोज़ मंदिर जाया करते थे।	*In those days we used to go to the temple every day.*
पिता जी अख़बारों को पत्र क्यों लिखा करते हैं?	*Why is father always writing letters to the newspapers?*
शराब पीने के बाद वह पड़ोसियों को गालियाँ दिया करता था।	*After drinking he used to swear at the neighbours.*
शाम को हम फ़िल्में देखा किये।	*We watched films in the evenings.*
पहले तो मैं ही यह काम किया करता था।	*Previously **I** used to do this work.*
हर हफ़्ते किसी न किसी मकान में चोरी हुआ करती है।	*Every week there is a theft in some house or other.*

69 Relative-correlatives of kind and manner

जैसा *of which kind* has as its correlative वैसा *of that kind* in both adverbial and adjectival expressions:

Adverbial

जैसा तुम चाहो वैसा करो।	*Do as you like.*
जैसा वह बोलता है वैसा ही वह करता है।	*He does what he says.*

Adjectival

जैसी किताबें आपको चाहिएँ वैसी यहीं मिलेंगी।	*Books of the kind you need will be (are) available here.*
जैसा बाप वैसा बेटा।	*Like father, like son.*
जैसा मौका आज मिला है वैसा दोबारा नहीं मिलेगा।	*An opportunity such as has arisen today won't come again.*
जैसा देश वैसा भेष।	*'As is the country, so the appearance'* (i.e. *'When in Rome, do as the Romans do'*).

Note that जिस तरह...उस तरह may be used in similar contexts; it is followed by का/की/के when used adjectivally, and (optionally) by से when used adverbially:

जिस तरह (से) लोग भूतों से डरते हैं उसी तरह वह मुझसे भी डरता है।	*He is afraid of me in the way that people are afraid of ghosts.*
जिस तरह के लोग यहाँ रहते हैं, उस तरह के लोग चोरी नहीं करते।	*The kind of people who live here don't steal.*

The expression जैसे ही...वैसे ही has the special sense 'as soon as', synonymous with ज्योंही...त्योंही, as has been seen in para. **59**:

जैसे ही हम बाहर गये वैसे ही बर्फ़ गिरने लगी।	*As soon as we went out, snow began to fall.*

Dialogue 15B *Setting up business in England*

शिव शंकर भाई, तुम कब से इंग्लैंड में रह रहे हो?

शंकर हम लोग लगभग चौदह पंद्रह साल से यहाँ हैं। हम कई साल युगांडा में थे, पर सन् १९७२ में हम जैसे हज़ारों हिन्दुस्तानियों को वहाँ से एक दम निकाल दिया गया था।

शिव	क्या तुम्हें अपनी गाड़ी वग़ैरह चीज़ों को छोड़ना पड़ा, या उन्हें बेचकर आए थे ?
शंकर	हमने अपने मकान और दोनों दुकानों को बेचना चाहा, पर हमें उन्हें बेचने से रोक दिया गया था। इंग्लैंड आकर हमें एक नए सिरे से अपनी ज़िन्दगी शुरू करनी पड़ी। सिवाय कुछ छोटी-मोटी चीज़ों के, हम ख़ाली-हाथ इस देश में आए, एक दम अनाथ जैसे।
शिव	मगर इन पंद्रह सालों में तो तुमने अच्छी तरक़्क़ी की है, न ? अब तो तुम अनाथ जैसे नहीं नज़र आते !
शंकर	भगवान की दया से मैं अपने धंधे में काफ़ी सफल रहा हूँ। शुरू में तो मेरे पास मुश्किल से ढाई सौ पौंड की पूंजी रही होगी। फिर भी, हमारी ज़िन्दगी उतनी अच्छी नहीं है जितनी युगांडा में थी। यहाँ रहकर मुझे अपनी गाड़ी खुद ही चलानी पड़ती है, जब कि वहाँ पर मुझ जैसे सफल व्यापारियों के दो तीन नौकर हुआ करते थे !
शिव	जैसा कि तुमने कहा, जब से तुम यहाँ पहले-पहल आए तब से तुम्हारा व्यापार अच्छी तरह बढ़ गया है। इसे देखकर कुछ लोग तो जलते होंगे मारे ईर्ष्या के ?
शंकर	हाँ, कुछ ऐसे लोग हैं जो मेरी सफलता बरदाश्त नहीं कर सकते, जैसे कि मैंने कोई बुरा काम किया हो। पर मैं तो परवाह नहीं करता कि वे क्या कहते हैं ! मैंने अपने आप को सफल बनाया है, बहुत मेहनत करने से।

Shiv	Shankar my friend, how long have you been living in England?
Shankar	We've been here for about fourteen or fifteen years. We were in Uganda for several years, but in 1972 thousands of Indians like us were suddenly expelled from there.
Shiv	Did you have to leave behind things like your car, or did you sell them before leaving?
Shankar	We tried[1] to sell our house and our two shops, but we were stopped from selling them. When we came to England, we had to begin our life again from the beginning. Apart from a few odd things, we came to this country empty-handed, just[2] like orphans!
Shiv	But you've come on well in these fifteen years, haven't you? You don't look like an orphan now!
Shankar	Through God's grace I've been[3] pretty successful in my business. In the beginning, I can barely have had two hundred and fifty pounds of capital. But even so, our life isn't as good as it was in Uganda. Living here, I have to drive my car myself, while there successful businessmen like me had two or three servants!

1 In the perfective, चाहना often has the sense 'to try to'.

2 Note that एक दम has two different senses: here it means 'completely, utterly', whereas in Shankar's first speech it meant 'suddenly'.

3 सफल रहा हूँ: notice how this use of रहना in the perfect tense gives the sense 'I have been'.

Shiv As you said, since you first came here your business has expanded well. Some people must burn with jealousy when they see this?

Shankar Yes, there are some such people who can't bear my success, as though I'd done something bad. But I don't care what they say! I've made **myself** successful, by doing a lot of hard work.

70 जैसा as postposition and adverb

जैसा is used as a postposition meaning 'like'. In the same way as the possessive particle का (para. **21**), it must agree adjectivally with a following noun or pronoun, while also requiring a preceding noun or pronoun to be in the oblique:

मुझ जैसे आदमी काम नहीं करते।	*People like me don't work.*
उसके हाथी जैसे कान हैं।	*He has ears like an elephant('s).*

जैसा (कि) occurs at the beginning of a clause, with the sense 'just as':

जैसा कि तुम्हें मालूम होगा, यहाँ शराब पीना मना है।	*As you will know, it is forbidden to drink alcohol here.*
जैसा कि मैंने सुना था, कई लोग शिकायत कर रहे थे।	*As I had heard, several people were complaining.*

जैसे (कि), normally followed by a subjunctive verb, means 'as if, as though':

वह मेरी तरफ़ देखता रहा जैसे कि उसने मेरा मतलब न समझा हो।	*He kept looking at me as though he hadn't understood my meaning.*
सारे लोग हँस रहे हैं जैसे कि किसी ने मज़ाक किया हो।	*Everybody is laughing, as if some-one had made a joke.*

The sense 'as though, as if' can also be expressed by मानो:

वह जल्दी से खाने लगी मानों दिन भर कुछ न खाया हो।	*She began to eat quickly, as if she hadn't eaten anything all day.*
वह मेरी तरफ़ बढ़ी मानों वह मुझे मारनेवाली हो।	*She came towards me as though she were about to hit me.*

71 The postposition से

Uses of the postposition से are summarised in the following examples:

from:	वह दिल्ली से आया।	*He came from Delhi.*
by:	वह बस से आया।	*He came by bus.*
with:	उसने लाठी से चोर को मारा।	*He beat the thief with a truncheon.*
for, because of:	वह ठंड से बीमार हो गया।	*He became ill because of the cold.*
than:	वह मुझसे बड़ा है।	*He is bigger than me.*

In adverbial expressions:

जल्दी से	*quickly*
ख़ुशी से	*happily*
आसानी से	*easily*
मुश्किल से	*with difficulty*

With verbs:

किसी से मिलना	*to meet someone*
किसी से कहना	*to say to someone*
किसी से बोलना/बात करना	*to speak with someone*
किसी से पूछना	*to ask someone*
किसी से डरना	*to fear someone*
किसी से प्रेम/प्यार करना	*to love someone*
किसी से लड़ना	*to fight someone*
किसी से शिकायत करना	*to complain to someone*

से also means 'since'. In sentences expressing a state of affairs which has existed since a given time, and which *still* exists, the present tense verb is used:

हम लोग कल से यहाँ हैं।	*We have been here since yesterday.*
वह कल से यह काम कर रहा है।	*He has been doing this job since yesterday.*
जब से वह विदेश से लौटा है तब से वह राजा की तरह रुपया ख़र्च कर रहा है।	*Since he came back from abroad he has been spending money like a king.*

Sometimes से in this usage will translate as 'for':

एक साल से कोई चिट्ठी नहीं आई।	*No letter came for a year.*

Notice also the postpositions से पहले and से बाहर alongside के पहले and के बाहर.

72 Inverted postpositions

Some compound postpositions, such as के बिना *without*, may appear in an inverted order in which the second component (बिना) precedes the word to which it relates: बिना पैसे के *without money*; बिना झिझक के *without hesitation*. The sense is not affected. Further postpositions which may be inverted are:

के अलावा	*apart from, in addition to*
के बग़ैर	*without*
के बजाय	*instead of*
के बदले	*in place of, in exchange for*
के मारे	*because of, on account of, through*
के सिवा/सिवाय	*except for, but for*

Examples:

बिना आपके यह काम नहीं किया जाएगा।	*This work cannot be done without you.*
मारे डर के वह बोल नहीं सका।	*He was so frightened he couldn't speak.*
बजाय बधाई के वह गालियाँ देने लगा।	*He began offering insults instead of congratulations.*
सिवाय फल के वह कुछ नहीं खाती।	*She eats nothing but fruit.*

73 Reflexive pronouns

आप, ख़ुद and the more formal स्वयं (pronounced **svayam**) all give the sense 'oneself', 'myself', etc., and may be followed by emphatic ही:

वह आप ही मकान को साफ़ करेगा।	*He will clean the house himself.*
मैं ख़ुद गाड़ी चलाता हूँ।	*I drive the car myself.*
यात्री अपना सामान रेलगाड़ी में स्वयं जमा करें।	*Passengers should deposit their luggage in the train themselves.*

In the oblique case, अपने and अपने आप are used:

अमृत अपने को बड़ा आदमी समझता था।	*Amrit used to consider himself a big shot.*
वह अपने में शिकायत करने का साहस नहीं पाता।	*He doesn't find in himself the courage to complain.*
तुम इस मामले में अपने आप को धोखा दे रहे हो।	*You are deceiving yourself in this matter.*

अपने आप as an adverb has the sense 'of its own accord, by itself':

गाड़ी अपने आप चलने लगी।	*The car began moving by itself.*
दरवाज़ा मानों अपने आप आहिस्ता खुल गया।	*The door slowly opened as though of its own accord.*

Note also the expression आपस में, which has already occurred, meaning 'amongst themselves / ourselves', etc.

लड़कों ने मिठाइयाँ आपस में बाँट लीं।	*The boys shared out the sweets amongst themselves.*
महिलाएँ आपस में बोल रही थीं।	*The ladies were speaking amongst themselves.*

EXERCISE 15.1 Translate into English:

चिड़ियाघर में

कुछ लोगों का विचार यह है कि जंगली जानवरों को पिंजरे में बन्द करना उचित नहीं है। बेचारे जानवरों को बड़ी तक़लीफ़ होती होगी, क्योंकि उन्हें आज़ादी से जंगल में घूमने नहीं दिया जाता। पर मेरे ख़्याल में तो ऐसा समझना ग़लत है। चिड़ियाघर में जो जानवर मैंने देखे हैं वे तो बड़े ख़ुश मालूम होते हैं, मानों उन्हें किसी भी बात की फ़िक्र न हो। आख़िर चिड़ियाघर में जो जानवर पाले जाते हैं उनमें से ज़्यादातर जंगल में पैदा नहीं हुए बल्कि वहीं चिड़ियाघर में ही पैदा हुए थे। इस लिए उन्हें यह बात नहीं मालूम कि किसी दूर देश में एक जंगल है जिसमें उन जैसे जानवर आज़ादी से घूम रहे हैं। जंगल में तो जानवर बड़ी आसानी से भूख से या बीमारी से मर सकते हैं, या तो ख़ुद ही दूसरे जानवरों के शिकार हो सकते हैं। परंतु चिड़ियाघर के जानवरों को रहने के लिए अच्छी जगह मिलती है और खाने को बढ़िया खाना मिलता है। छोटे से छोटा जानवर भी बिना डर के अपने पिंजरे के अंदर आराम की ज़िन्दगी बिता सकता है। हाँ, चिड़ियाघर में बाघ जैसे बड़े जानवरों को खुले मैदान में शिकार करने का मज़ा तो नहीं आता, और शायद यह भी सच हो कि पिंजरे की चिड़िया आसमान के सपने देखती रहती हो। पर जंगली जानवरों की बहुत-सी ऐसी जातियाँ हैं जो चिड़ियाघर के कारण ही आज तक बच सकी हैं। बाघ का ही नमूना लीजिए। कोई तीस चालीस वर्ष पहले तो भारत के जंगलों में बाघ इतने थे कि बाघ को देखना मामूली बात थी। शिकार होने के कारण अब तो इनकी संख्या बहुत ही कम हो गई है। इतने बाघ मारे गए हैं कि

आजकल के शिकारियों को बदले बन्दूक़ के, कैमरे से ही शिकार करने दिया जाता है। इस तरह जंगल में बाघ बहुत कम मिलते हैं और इस जाति को बचाने में चिड़ियाघर का योगदान बहुत महत्त्वपूर्ण रहा है।

EXERCISE 15.2 Translate into Hindi:

Ram is a successful businessman. As I said to my cousin yesterday, people like Ram can live very comfortably. They do not have to worry about the little difficulties of which poor people like me are always afraid. I keep on working day by day, but when I dream of becoming a wealthy businessman I know I am deceiving myself. Ram lives in a big house like a palace. To buy such a house is not possible for me. The rent of my house keeps going up, so how could I save money from my pay? Without capital it is impossible to start a new business, and I cannot call myself a businessman in the true sense. I have an ordinary shop, in which I have been working for five years. But I never complain about my life to anybody. I hope that some day I may become successful, so that I may not have to do such hard work every day.

Vocabulary

अनाथ	*orphan* (m.)
अर्थ	*meaning, sense* (m.)
असंभव	*impossible*
आख़िर	*after all, at last*
आसमान	*sky* (m.)
आहिस्ता	*slowly*
ईर्ष्या	*jealousy, envy* (f.)
उनतीस	*twenty-nine*
एक दम	*at once, suddenly; completely, utterly*
कबड्डी	*a children's game, a kind of tag* (f.)
कान	*ear* (m.)
कि	*or*
के बग़ैर	*without*
के बजाय	*instead of*
के बदले (में)	*in place of, in exchange for*
के मारे	*because of, on account of, through*
के सिवा (य)	*except for, but for*
कैमरा	*camera* (m.)
ख़ाली	*empty, vacant, free* (inv.)
ख़ाली-हाथ	*empty-handed*
ख़ुद	*oneself*

खुला	*open*
गिरना	*to fall, drop* (intr.)
चचेरा भाई	*cousin* (m.) (son of चाचा)
चपाती	*chapatti* (f.)
चाव	*fondness, enthusiasm, zeal* (m.)
चिड़िया	*bird* (f.)
चिड़ियाघर	*zoo* (m.)
छोटा-मोटा	*insignificant, trifling, minor*
जंगली	*wild*
जमा करना	*to deposit*
जलना	*to burn with jealousy, be jealous*
जाति	*species, caste, type* (f.)
जानवर	*animal* (m.)
जी	*mind, heart* (m.)
जी चाहना	*to desire*
जैसा	*like, similar to, such as*
जैसे (कि)	*as, as if*
जोड़ना	*to join, add, accumulate, save up*
झिझक	*hesitation* (f.)
डरना	*to fear, be afraid of*
दया	*pity, mercy, compassion* (f.)
दिन-ब-दिन	*day by day*
धंधा	*occupation, business, work* (m.)
धोखा	*deceit, trickery* (m.)
धोखा देना	*to deceive, dupe*
नमूना	*example, specimen, type* (m.)
परवाह	*concern, care, heed* (f.)
परवाह करना	*to care*
पहले-पहल	*for the first time*
पालना	*to rear, bring up*
पिंजरा	*cage* (m.)
पूंजी	*capital, investment* (f.)
प्रायः	*usually, often; almost, more or less*
प्रेम	*love* (m.)
प्रेम करना	*to love* (with से)
बन्दूक़	*gun* (f.)
बरदाश्त करना	*to tolerate, endure, stand*
बराबर	*constantly, continuously*
बल्कि	*but rather*
बैरा	*waiter, 'bearer'* (m.)
भगवान	*God* (m.)
भूत	*ghost* (m.)

भेष	*appearance, guise* (m.)
मज़ा	*pleasure, fun* (m.)
मज़ा आना	*to enjoy, have fun*
मतलब	*meaning; motive, self-interest* (m.)
मरना	*to die*
महत्त्वपूर्ण	*important*
महीने के महीने	*month by month*
मानों	*as though, as if*
मामूली	*ordinary, commonplace*
मुश्किल से	*with difficulty, barely*
मेहनत	*hard work, labour* (f.)
मैदान	*plain, field* (m.)
युगांडा	*Uganda* (m.)
योगदान	*contribution* (m.)
रोकना	*to stop* (tr.)
लगभग	*about, approximately*
लगातार	*continuously*
लाठी	*staff, stick, truncheon* (f.)
वातावरण	*atmosphere* (m.)
विश्वास	*belief, trust, confidence* (m.)
वैसा	*of that kind, like that*
व्याकरण	*grammar* (m.)
व्यापारी	*businessman* (m.)
शिकायत	*complaint, grievance* (f.)
(की) शिकायत करना	*to complain (about)* (with से)
शिकार	*to prey, victim* (m.)
शिकार करना	*to hunt*
शिकार होना	*to fall prey to*
शिकारी	*huntsman, hunter* (m.)
संख्या	*number* (f.)
सच्चे अर्थों में	*in a true sense*
सन्	*year, era* (m.)
सपना	*dream* (m.)
सपना देखना	*to dream, have a dream*
सफल	*successful*
सफलता	*success* (f.)
साहस	*courage* (m.)
सिरा	*end, extremity* (m.)
नए सिरे से	*from a new beginning*
स्वयं	*oneself*
हाथी	*elephant* (m.)

Unit Sixteen

Dialogue 16A *Problems with the car*

मोहनलाल राजिन्दर, आप कहाँ रहते हैं आजकल ? मैं आपकी तलाश कर रहा था। बहुत दिनों से हमारी मुलाक़ात नहीं हुई है। अभी क्या कर रहे हैं ?

राजिन्दर मैं ज़रा अपने भाई का इंतज़ार कर रहा था, पर वह आया नहीं। वह हमारी गाड़ी की मरम्मत कर रहा होगा।

मोहनलाल क्यों, गाड़ी फिर से ख़राब हो गई क्या ? मेरी समझ में नहीं आता कैसी गाड़ी है जिस पर आप लोगों ने इतना पैसा ख़र्च कर दिया है !

राजिन्दर हाँ, गाड़ी बेकार ही है ! पर बहुत ज़रूरी है कि उसे ठीक कर दिया जाए क्योंकि अगले हफ़्ते हमें अमृतसर जाना है। आपको याद है न कि हमारी चचेरी बहिन की शादी हो रही है।

मोहनलाल रेल से जाइए तो ज़्यादा सुविधा होगी। मैं तो हमेशा रेल से यात्रा करना पसंद करूँगा। याद रहे कि अमृतसर यहाँ से काफ़ी दूर है, कम से कम दस घंटे का रास्ता है।

राजिन्दर मैं तो यही कह रहा था, मगर पिताजी ट्रेन से जाने से इनकार करते हैं। उनका कहना है कि जब हमने इतनी महँगी गाड़ी ख़रीदी है तो इसका इस्तेमाल तो करना ही चाहिए !

मोहनलाल तो क्या आपकी माताजी भी शादी में जा रही हैं ? कल उनसे मुलाक़ात हुई थी तो उन्होंने शादी का ज़िक्र नहीं किया था।

राजिन्दर अभी ठीक नहीं मालूम। जब से नानी जी का देहान्त हो गया तब से माता जी की तबियत इतनी अच्छी नहीं रही है। हम उन्हें समझाने की कोशिश बहुत करते हैं, पर वे कहती हैं कि मैं घर बैठकर बच्चों की देखभाल करूँ तो अच्छा रहेगा। ऐसी स्थिति में तो हम उन्हें जाने पर मजबूर नहीं कर सकते।

Mohanlal Rajinder, where do you keep yourself these days?[1] I was looking for you. We haven't met for ages. What are you doing just now?

Rajinder I was just waiting for my brother, but he didn't come. He must be mending our car.

1 Notice this idiomatic meaning of the literal question, 'Where do you stay?'

Mohanlal	Why, has the car gone wrong again? I don't understand what kind of car it is that you have spent so much money on!
Rajinder	Yes, the car's absolutely useless. But it's very important that it be fixed, because next week we're going to Amritsar. You remember, don't you, that our cousin is getting married?
Mohanlal	It would be more convenient if you went by rail.[2] I would always prefer to travel by rail. Remember that Amritsar is pretty far from here, it is at least ten hours' journey.
Rajinder	I was saying the same thing, but father refuses to go by train. He says that when we have bought such an expensive car, we should at least use it!
Mohanlal	So is your monther going to[3] the wedding too? When I met her[4] yesterday, she didn't mention a wedding.
Rajinder	I'm not sure yet. Since grandmother died, mother hasn't been so well. We try hard to console her, but she says that it would be better if she stayed at home and looked after the children. Under these circumstances we can't force her to go.

74 Conjunct verbs

Conjunct verbs, already introduced briefly in paragraph **32**, are most commonly formed by adjectives or nouns in conjunction with करना:

With adjectives:

साफ़ करना	*to clean*
बन्द करना	*to close*
ठीक करना	*to correct, put in order, fix*
कम करना	*to reduce*
ख़त्म करना	*to finish*

With nouns:

शुरू करना	*to begin*
ख़र्च करना	*to spend*
पसंद करना	*to like, prefer, choose*
प्रेम करना	*to love* (with से)
रंग करना	*to colour, paint*

2 The Hindi construction uses an imperative rather than an 'if' clause: 'Go by rail and there will be more convenience'.

3 Notice this use of में, and note also मीटिंग में जाना *to go to a meeting*, etc.

4 कल उनसे मुलाक़ात हुई: this is really a 'जब' clause, with जब omitted.

Intransitive equivalents are usually formed with होना instead of करना: बन्द होना *to close;* ख़र्च होना *to be spent.*

राजू को अपनी साइकिल ठीक करनी है।	*Raju has to fix his bike.*
दुकानदार दाम को कम नहीं करेगा।	*The shopkeeper won't reduce the price.*
रात को दरवाज़ा कितने बजे बंद होता है?	*What time does the door close at night?*
मैंने सुबह को काम शुरू किया और शाम तक ख़त्म कर लिया।	*I began work in the morning and finished by evening.*
उन्होंने अपना सारा पैसा ख़र्च कर दिया।	*They spent all their money.*
मैं तो पुरानी फ़िल्में पसंद करता हूँ।	*As for me, I prefer old films.*
मैं तुझसे प्रेम करता हूँ।	*I love you.*

Notice also the following usages:

मजबूर करना *to compel, force* takes a preceding infinitive with पर or को:

मैंने उसे पैसा स्वीकार करने पर मजबूर किया।	*I forced him to accept the money.*
शायद सिपाही हमें भीतर जाने को मजबूर करे।	*The soldier might make us go in.*

इनकार करना *to refuse* takes a preceding infinitive with से:

वह अपनी ग़लती को ठीक करने से इनकार कर रही है।	*She is refusing to correct her mistake.*

There is a large category of verbal expressions similar to the conjunct verbs described above, but in which the noun component retains its function as a noun: thus in the sentence मैं उसकी मदद करता हूँ *I help him,* (lit. *I do his help*), the feminine noun मदद is possessed by the English object 'him' and therefore requires the possessive particle की.

Among the most common verbs formed in this way are the following:

का इंतज़ार करना	*to wait for*
का पीछा करना	*to follow, chase*
का प्रयोग करना	*to use*
का इस्तेमाल करना	*to use*
का/के दर्शन करना[1]	*to see, visit, have an audience with*

[1] Note that this is often used as a plural noun: hence के.

की प्रशंसा करना	*to praise*
की देखभाल करना	*to look after*
की पूजा करना	*to worship, revere*
की निंदा करना	*to blame, speak ill of*
की तलाश करना	*to search for*
की कोशिश करना	*to try* (with preceding oblique infinitive)

गाँव के लड़के बिल्ली की तलाश कर रहे थे।	*The village boys were looking for the cat.*
आपके दोस्त हमारा इंतज़ार नहीं करेंगे।	*Your friends won't wait for us.*
मैं कल तक काम ख़त्म करने की कोशिश करूँगा।	*I'll try to finish work by tomorrow.*
बच्चों की देखभाल कौन करता है?	*Who looks after the children?*
कोई आदमी हमारा पीछा कर रहा था।	*Some man was following us.*
उन्होंने आपकी बहुत प्रशंसा की।	*They praised you highly.*
आपको अपने पिताजी की निंदा नहीं करनी चाहिए।	*You shouldn't speak ill of your father.*

With some verbs the का/की may be dropped, giving a true conjunct verb of the type described above:

पुलिस के सिपाही चोरी का माल तलाश कर रहे थे।	*The police constables were searching for the stolen property.*

Notice also the following intransitive verbal expressions formed with होना:

का जन्म होना	*to be born*
की शादी होना	*to get married*
का विवाह होना	*to get married*
की मृत्यु होना	*to die*
का देहान्त होना	*to die*
की मुलाक़ात होना	*to meet*

जिस दिन रामू का जन्म हुआ उसी दिन उसके बाप की मृत्यु हुई।	*On the very day that Ramu was born, his father died.*
मेरी शादी सन् १९७२ में हुई।	*I became married in the year* 1972.

Other conjunct verbs not involving करना or होना include दिखाई देना *to be seen, be visible* and सुनाई देना *to be heard, be audible*. These verbs do *not* take the ने construction. Alternative forms are दिखाई पड़ना, सुनाई पड़नाः

हमारा मकान दूर से दिखाई देता है।	*Our house is visible from far away.*
अचानक सुशीला ही दिखाई पड़ी।	*Suddenly Sushila herself appeared.*
गली में एक पुरानी गाड़ी दिखाई दी।	*An old car came into view in the lane.*
मकान में भी रेल की आवाज़ सुनाई पड़ती है।	*Even in the house the sound of the train can be heard.*

75 Conjunct verbs with याद

Conjunct verbs are formed not only with करना and होना but also with a number of other infinitives. The widest range is found in constructions with the feminine noun याद *memory*:

याद होना	*to be remembered, become remembered, be recalled* or *learnt*
याद करना	*to memorise, learn by heart, think of*
याद आना	*to come to mind, recur*
याद रहना	*to remain remembered*
याद रखना	*to bear in mind, keep in the memory*

In all these constructions the noun and the verb are conjunct, and the verb agrees with the English subject. In a rather less common usage, याद retains its function as a noun on the pattern of की मदद करना, giving की याद करना.

फ़ोन करने के लिए धन्यवाद –आपने मुझे कैसे याद किया ?	*Thank you for phoning–what made you think of me?*
क्या तुम्हें उसका पता याद है ?	*Do you remember his address?*
मुझे कल का पाठ याद हो गया है।	*I have learnt yesterday's lesson.*
इस कविता को याद करो।	*Learn this poem by heart.*
मैं अभी आपको याद कर रहा था !	*I was just thinking of you!*
बच्चों को देखकर मुझे अपना ही बचपन याद आने लगा।	*Seeing the children I began to recall my own childhood.*
जब तक मैं जिऊँगा तब तक उसका चेहरा याद रहेगा।	*I shall remember his face as long as I live.*
याद रखो कि मैं तुमसे बड़ा हूँ।	*Remember that I am older than you.*
मैं पुराने मकान की याद कर रहा था।	*I was thinking of the old house.*

Dialogue 16B *Looking for a job*

मनोज क्या बात है रमेश ? तुम बड़े उदास लगते हो। ठीक-ठाक हो न ? सच सच बताओ !

रमेश भैया मैं तो बड़ी मुसीबत में फँस गया हूँ। मुझे अपनी नौकरी से निकाल दिया गया है। अब मेरे पास न काम है न धंधा। जहाँ तुम काम करते हो वहाँ नौकरी पाने की कोई आशा है क्या ?

मनोज अभी तो उम्मीद कम दीखती है यार ! तुम्हें वहाँ कोशिश करनी चाहिए जहाँ तुम जैसे लोगों की हमेशा ज़रूरत रहती है — कहने का मतलब किसी स्कूल या कालेज में।

रमेश मैंने सब कहीं कोशिश की है मगर कुछ हाथ नहीं आता। अब मुझे एक एक पैसे को बचाना पड़ता है। कहीं न कहीं नौकरी ढूँढ़नी है, चाहे किसी स्कूल में हो या किसी कारख़ाने में। मुझे डर इस बात का है कि कहीं मैं महीनों तक बेकार न रहूँ।

मनोज पहले तो तुम अख़बारों के लिए लेख लिखा करते थे न ?

रमेश अरे वह तो बहुत पहले की बात है। मैंने न जाने कितने साल से कोई लेख-वेख नहीं लिखा है। जिस गली में मैं रहता हूँ वहाँ इतनी भीड़-भाड़ और शोर-शराबा हुआ करता है कि वहाँ मुझसे काम नहीं किया जाता।

मनोज तो अपना मकान बेचकर कहीं और चले जाओ। जहाँ मैं रहता हूँ वहाँ शान्ति बहुत है, और तुम्हें वहाँ एक अच्छा मकान आसानी से मिल जाएगा।

रमेश मकान की बात तो अलग है। पहले नौकरी की समस्या हल की जाए, फिर मकान-वकान देखा जाएगा।

Manoj What's up, Ramesh? You look very gloomy. You're all right, aren't you? Tell me the truth now!

Ramesh Brother, I'm caught up in a real crisis. I've been thrown out of my job. Now I have neither any work nor any job to do! Is there any hope of finding a job where you work?

Manoj There's not much hope to be seen at the moment, my friend! You should try where people like you are always needed–I mean[1] in some school or college.

Ramesh I've tried everywhere but nothing comes to hand. Now I have to save each and every penny. I have to find a job somewhere or other, whether it's in a school or in a factory. What I'm afraid of[2] is that I might stay unemployed for months.

Manoj Previously you used to write articles for the papers didn't you?

1 कहने का मतलब: lit. *the meaning of what I say.*

2 मुझे डर इस बात का है कि: note the emphasis given by the word order, with डर preceding इस बात का. A more neutral word order would be मुझे इस बात का डर है कि *I'm afraid that....*

Ramesh Oh, that was a long time ago. I haven't written an article or anything for god knows how long. In the street I live in there's so much hustle and bustle and uproar that I can't write anything.

Manoj Then sell your house and go somewhere else. There's plenty of quiet where I live, and you will get a good house there easily.

Ramesh The house is a different matter. First the job problem should be solved[1], and then the house and all that will be seen to.

76 Relative-correlative adverbs of place

The relative-correlative adverbs of place are जहाँ...वहाँ *in which place... in that place*. These are used in the same way as the relative-correlative constructions described in paras. **54** and **59.** जहाँ कहीं gives the indefinite sense 'wherever'.

जहाँ मैं रहता हूँ वहाँ कोई हिन्दी नहीं बोलता।	*No one speaks Hindi where I live.*
हम वहाँ चलें जहाँ हमारी पहली मुलाक़ात हुई थी।	*Let's go to the place where we first met.*
जहाँ भयंकर गरमी पड़ती है वहाँ मैं नहीं रह सकता।	*I cannot live in a place where there's terrible heat.*
जहाँ भी तू जाए, वहाँ से मुझे पत्र लिखा करना।	*Wherever you may go, write me letters from there.*
जहाँ फूल है वहाँ काँटा भी होगा।	*Where there is a flower, there will be a thorn also.*

77 Other adverbs of place

In addition to यहाँ *here* and वहाँ *there* is the pair of adverbs इधर *hither, over here, towards/to this place* and उधर *thither, over there, towards/to that place*. The distinction between यहाँ/वहाँ and इधर/उधर is apparent in the following pair of sentences:

यहाँ बैठो।	*Sit here.* (**in** this place)
इधर आओ।	*Come over here.* (**towards** this place)

The interrogative adverb associated with इधर/उधर is किधर *whither towards/at which place?*; the relative adverb जिधर *towards/at the place which* is rarely used.

[1] हल की जाए: passive of हल करना *to solve.*

Note also the expressions कहीं नहीं *nowhere* कहीं भी *anywhere (at all)*; सब कहीं *everywhere;* कहीं और or और कहीं *somewhere else;* कहीं न कहीं *somewhere or other;* इधर-उधर *here and there, hither and thither.*

सब कहीं वही बात सुनी जाती है।	*The same thing is heard everywhere.*
तुम किधर जा रहे हो? गाँव की तरफ़।	*Where are you going? Towards the village.*
ऐसा कपड़ा कहीं भी मिल जाएगा।	*You can get cloth like this anywhere.*
उसने आपको कहीं न कहीं देखा होगा।	*He must have seen you somewhere or other.*
लोग घबराकर इधर-उधर दौड़ने लगे।	*People began running hither and thither in a panic.*

78 कहीं

कहीं means 'somewhere', 'somehow', 'somewhat'. It also occurs in a number of usages expressing contingency, doubt, apprehension, etc., where it has such senses as 'should it happen that...', 'could it be that...', 'under some circumstances...', 'somehow...', 'somewhat, rather':

कहीं मेरी पत्नी आ जाए तो क्या होगा?	*What will happen if my wife should turn up?*
अगर कहीं पैसा मिल जाए तो यह समस्या दूर हो जाएगी।	*If somehow we were to get the money, this problem would be solved.*
यदि कहीं मैं बीमार हो जाऊँ तो तुम्हें जाना पड़ेगा।	*If I should become ill, you will have to go.*
दूसरा मकान इससे कहीं अधिक महँगा है।	*The other house is rather more expensive than this.*

कहीं may introduce a rhetorical question:

कहीं आशा करने से ही मेरी तबियत ठीक हो जाएगी?	*Will I get better just by hoping?*

Followed by न and a subjunctive verb, कहीं has the sense 'lest', or 'let it not be the case that'; it commonly follows verbs of fearing:

ख़बरदार, कहीं तुझे भी चोट न लगे।	*Be careful, lest you get hurt too.*
कहीं आग न लग गई हो!	*I hope fire hasn't broken out!*
मैं डर रहा था कि कहीं वह चला न गया हो।	*I was afraid that he might have gone.*

79 Repetition of words

Repetition of individual words usually gives a sense of distribution, as in हरेक लड़के को एक एक रुपया देना *Give each boy one rupee.* Repetition of interrogative words follows the pattern of तुमने क्या क्या देखा? *What (different things) did you see?* Repetition of adverbs or adjectives stresses the thoroughness of an action or quality: साफ़ साफ़ कहो *Tell me plainly;* बहुत बहुत धन्यवाद *Thank you very much indeed;* गरम गरम चाय *piping hot tea;* नया नया मकान *brand new house.*

When referring to a plural noun, repetition of an adjective may underline the fact that all the components of a group share the same quality: दीवाली के त्यौहार में छोटी छोटी बत्तियाँ जलाई जाती हैं *Little lamps are lit in the Divali festival.* Sometimes the second occurrence of a word may be represented by the numeral '2', as a kind of shorthand (most commonly in handwritten contexts): साथ २ गाइए *Sing in unison.* Examples:

हर आदमी का अलग अलग कमरा होना चाहिए।	*Each man should have a separate room.*
भारत में आम कहाँ कहाँ उगते हैं?	*Where in India do mangoes grow?*
शादी में कौन कौन लोग गए थे?	*Which people attended the wedding?*
सारे लड़के अपनी अपनी किताबें पढ़ रहे थे।	*All the children were reading their own books.*
हमारे बच्चे अभी छोटे छोटे हैं।	*All our children are still young.*
रास्ते में जगह जगह पर ढाबे होते हैं।	*There are eating-places everywhere along the road.*
हम ठंडी ठंडी हवा का आनंद लेने लगे।	*We began to enjoy the cool cool breeze.*

80 या तो...या, न...न, चाहे...चाहे/या

Complementary clauses beginning in English 'either...or', 'neither...nor' begin in Hindi यह तो...या, न...न respectively. चाहे...चाहे has the senses 'either...or' and 'whether...or':

या तो राम से पूछो या सुधा से।	*Ask either Ram or Sudha.*
चाहे बुरा हो चाहे अच्छा, वह मेरा बेटा ही तो है।	*Be he bad or be he good, he is my son.*
चाहे आज जाइए या कल।	*Go either today or tomorrow.*
मैं न पंजाबी बोलता न गुजराती।	*I speak neither Panjabi nor Gujarati.*

81 'Echo-words' and word pairings

Some words can be coupled with 'echo-words' to broaden and generalise their sense: चाय-वाय *tea and so forth*, as in आप कुछ चाय-वाय लेंगे? *Will you take some tea or anything?*

भीड़	*crowd* (f.)	भीड़-भाड़	*commotion, hustle and bustle* (f.)
ठीक	*all right*	ठीक-ठाक	*all right, shipshape, fine*
पेंसिल	*pencil* (f.)	पेंसिल-वेंसिल	*pencil or anything to write with* (f.)
गप	*gossip* (f.)	गप-शप	*gossip, tittle-tattle, chit-chat* (f.)

In formations of this kind the second word is merely an echo of the first, and has no independent sense. In a second type, a similar generalising effect is achieved by the pairing of words of close or identical meaning (though the second member is often a word which seldom occurs in its own right):

नौकर चाकर	*servant* (m.) *servant, menial* (m.)	नौकर-चाकर	*servants and domestics* (m.)
मिलना जुलना	*to meet, resemble* *to meet, resemble*	मिलना-जुलना मिल-जुलकर	*to associate, mix, resemble* *together, jointly*
दुबला पतला	*thin, weak* *thin, slender*	दुबला पतला	*scrawny, 'lean and thin'*
जानना बूझना	*to know* *to understand*	जान-बूझकर	*deliberately, knowingly*

EXERCISE 16.1 Translate into English:

मैं इंग्लैंड के मौसम से तंग आ गया हूँ। मई का महीना है, फिर भी मैं देखता हूँ कि बाहर पानी ज़ोरों से पड़ रहा है। पानी से बचने के लिए लोग इधर-उधर दौड़ रहे हैं। सब कहीं काले और रंगीन छाते दिखाई दे रहे हैं; आकाश में काले-काले बादल हैं, और समय समय पर गरज की आवाज़ भी सुनाई देती है। सूरज कहीं दिखाई नहीं देता। अब मैं समझ गया हूँ कि भारत जैसे देशों में सूरज की पूजा क्यों की जाती है। इंग्लैंड में सूरज की पूजा शायद ही की जाए, क्योंकि उसके दर्शन करने का मौका बहुत ही कम मिलता है!

यहाँ के मौसम की एक ख़ासियत यह है कि वह बदलता रहता है। एक दिन आप ख़ूब मज़े से बग़ीचे में बैठकर धूप खा सकते हैं, तो दूसरे ही दिन इतनी ठंड लगेगी कि आपको गरम कपड़े पहनकर घर के भीतर ही रहना पड़ेगा। कहीं कोई खिड़की खोल दी जाए तो ऐसा लगेगा कि कमरे के अंदर ही बर्फ़ गिर रही है। शायद यही कारण है कि इस देश में मौसम इतना दिलचस्प[1] विषय समझा जाता है—कहीं मौसम का ज़िक्र किया जाए तो अँग्रेज़ लोग इसी बात पर दस पंद्रह मिनट तक बोलने को तैयार होंगे! सड़क पर या बाज़ार में, कहीं भी हो, जब दो लोग एक दूसरे से मिलते हैं तो 'नमस्कार' के साथ साथ मौसम के बारे में भी कुछ कहना न भूलेंगे। अजीब बात तो यह है कि मौसम चाहे सुहावना हो चाहे ख़राब, लोगों को उससे अकसर शिकायत ही होती है!

EXERCISE 16.2 Translate into Hindi:

Yesterday the weather was so bad that I had to stay inside the house. I tried to read a book of poetry, but I soon became bored with that. I began to look for a new book which a friend had given to me on my birthday. I remembered that I had seen it on the table two or three days ago, and my sister had mentioned it just yesterday. But now it wasn't to be seen anywhere. Suddenly a noise was heard outside. Then, opening the window, I saw that a big monkey was sitting on top of the car. It seemed he liked this weather! In his hands was the very book I was looking for. The subject of this book must have been very interesting to the monkey, because he remained sitting there with it for at least ten minutes. After that he got bored with the book, or perhaps he got fed up with the rain at last. He dropped the book on the ground, and ran off towards the neighbours' house.

Note

Separate vocabularies are not given for the remaining units of the course; all new words may be found in the Hindi–English Vocabulary at the back of the book.

Unit Seventeen

Dialogue 17A *Talking about Holi*

पुनीत बुआ जी, हमें बहुत ख़ुशी है कि आप हमारे यहाँ होली मनाने आई हैं। अगर आप नहीं आई होतीं तो हमारी होली की छुट्टियाँ कितनी फीकी लगतीं।

बुआ जी अगर मैं हर साल इस समय खाली होती तो मैं हमेशा तुम लोगों के साथ होली खेलती। सारे त्यौहारों में से होली का त्यौहार ही मुझे सबसे प्रिय लगता है।

पुनीत अगर मैं प्रधान मंत्री होता तो मैं ऐसा क़ानून बनाता कि होली जैसा कोई न कोई त्यौहार हर महीने में कम से कम तीन दफ़ा मनाया जाए।

बुआ जी शाबाश! अगर तुम आनेवाले चुनाव में उम्मीदवार बन गए तो मैं तुम्हें ज़रूर वोट दूँगी! पर ज़रा सोचो, इतने त्यौहार मनाने से देश की हालत बिगड़ जाएगी कि नहीं?

पुनीत बिगड़ तो जाएगी, इसमें कोई संदेह नहीं, पर जनता कितनी ख़ुश होगी! मेरे ख़्याल से तो जनता को ख़ुश करना ही सरकार का सबसे महत्त्वपूर्ण कर्त्तव्य है।

बुआ जी यह सच है कि यदि जनता ख़ुश नहीं रही तो वह सरकार को वोट देने से इनकार कर देगी। पर अगर लोग काम ही न करें तो जिएँगे कैसे? यह बताओ!

पुनीत हाँ, आप ठीक बात कह रही हैं। ख़ैर, साल में होली एक बार तो आती ही है, यही क्या कम है। बुआ जी, इस साल आप दीवाली भी मनाने आएँगी न?

बुआ जी हाँ बेटे। और अगर तुम्हें मौका मिले तो तुम लोगों को गरमी की छुट्टियों में मेरे यहाँ भी आना चाहिए। तुम तो कई सालों से नहीं आए हो और मैं वहाँ अकसर अकेलापन महसूस करती हूँ। तुम्हें अपनी बूढ़ी बुआ को न भूलना चाहिए!

Punit Auntie, we're very pleased that you've come to our place to celebrate Holi. If you hadn't come, our Holi holidays would have seemed so dull.[1]

Auntie If I were free every year at this time I would always play Holi with you. Of all the festivals it is the Holi Festival which is my favourite.

Punit If I were prime minister, I would make such a law that some festival or other like Holi be celebrated at least three times every month.

[1] Note the rhetorical use of कितनी; another example is found in Punit's third speech, जनता कितनी ख़ुश होगी *How happy the people would be!*

Auntie Bravo! If you become a candidate in the coming election I'll certainly vote for you! But just consider, wouldn't the condition of the country be ruined by celebrating so many festivals?

Punit Ruined it would be, no doubt about that, but how happy the people would be! In my opinion, making the people happy is the government's most important duty.

Auntie It is true the if the people aren't happy then they'll refuse to vote for the government. But if people don't even work then how will they live?[1] Tell me that.

Punit Yes, what you are saying is right. Anyway, Holi does come once a year, and that in itself is no mean thing.[2] Auntie, you will come to celebrate Diwali as well this year, won't you?

Auntie Yes, son. And if you get the chance, you should come to my place in the summer holidays. You haven't been for several years and I often feel lonely there. You shouldn't forget your old auntie!

82 Conditional sentences

In the conditional sentences introduced in para. **44,** the 'if' clause used either a subjunctive or a future verb. Another very common usage involves the perfective participle (आया, etc.) in the 'if' clause; here there is usually some presupposition of the 'possibility' referred to being fulfilled.

अगर राम आया तो क्या तुम भी मेरे साथ चलोगे?	*Supposing Ram came, would you come with me too?*
अगर कुछ गरम पानी बाक़ी रहा तो मैं उसे इस बाल्टी में डाल दूँगा।	*If there is any hot water left, I'll pour it into this bucket.*
अगर गाड़ी मिली तो हमें साइकिल की ज़रूरत नहीं होगी।	*If we've got the car we won't need the bicycle.*
यदि भगवान ने चाहा तो स्वामी जी किसी दिन फिर से यहाँ आएँगे।	*God willing, the swami will come here again some day.*

Remember that while the word अगर is frequently omitted, especially in speech, तो is usually present (even if, as in the example below, the remainder of the 'then' clause is left unsaid):

1 जिएँगे कैसे?: this word order, as opposed to the more neutral कैसे जिएँगे? puts emphasis on the verb: 'How will they **live** [let alone anything else]'.
2 यही क्या कम है?: a set expression with the sense 'even this much is not inconsiderable'.

आज के बाद हम कभी मिलेंगे क्या ? हाँ, भगवान ने चाहा तो।	*Will we ever meet again after today? Yes, if God wills.*

The sense 'If I were…', 'If she knew…' is expressed by the imperfective participle, used *without* है, etc. in both clauses. Because such expressions relate to conditions which cannot be fulfilled, they are referred to as 'impossible conditions':

आप की जगह मैं होता तो मैं कभी इनकार नहीं करता !	*If I were in your place I would never refuse!*
अगर मैं अमीर होता तो महल में रहता।	*If I were rich I'd live in a palace.*
अगर पिता जी ज़िंदा होते तो ऐसी कोई मुश्किल नहीं होती।	*If father were alive, there would be no such difficulty.*
मैं तुम्हारा नाम जानता तो क्यों पूछता ?	*If I knew your name, why would I ask?*
अगर वह आनेवाली होती तो अब तक हम उसकी गाड़ी की आवाज़ सुनते।	*If she were on her way we would have heard her car by now.*

These sentences may also refer to past contexts: 'Had I been in your place, I would never have refused', etc. If a *specifically* past sense is needed, the 'if' clause takes the perfective participle followed by होता; the second clause still takes the imperfective participle:

अगर साँप मकान की तरफ़ बढ़ा होता तो मैं उसे अवश्य गोली मारता।	*If the snake had moved towards the house, I would definitely have shot it.*
अगर तुम ठीक समय पर आई होतीं तो हम गाड़ी पकड़ते।	*If you had come on time we would have caught the train.*
अगर आप ने सब्ज़ी को ठीक से पकाया होता तो मेरे पेट में दर्द नहीं होता।	*If you had cooked the vegetables properly I wouldn't have stomach-ache.*
उसने मेरे भाई को भी नहीं बुलाया होता तो मैं बड़ी ख़ुशी से स्वीकार करता।	*If he hadn't asked my brother as well I would have accepted very happily.*

Finally, notice that both 'possible' and 'impossible' conditions can also be expressed with the continuous tense (taking the subjunctive and imperfective of होना respectively):

अगर ठंड लग रही हो तो खिड़की बन्द कर लो।	*Close the window if you're feeling cold.*
यदि गाड़ी तेज़ रफ़्तार से चल रही होती तो पेड़ से टकरा जाती।	*If the car had been travelling at speed it would have hit the tree.*

Dialogue 17B *Why Arun is late*

अरुण माफ़ करना पूरन जी, बड़ी देर से आया हूँ। कसूर मेरा नहीं है, मेरे भाई का है। वह मेरी कार की चाबियाँ खो बैठा था, इसलिए मुझे बस से आना पड़ा। बड़ा बेवकूफ़ है वह!

पूरन तुम उसे अपनी गाड़ी क्यों चलाने देते हो? अभी वह बहुत जवान है। कहीं आपके पिताजी को पता चल गया कि अमृत गाड़ी चला रहा है तो गुस्से से उबल पड़ेंगे।

अरुण पर क्या करूँ? हालाँकि मैंने अमृत से हज़ार बार चलाने को मना कर दिया है, फिर भी वह मेरी एक नहीं मानता। आज मैंने उससे कह दिया कि कहीं तुमने किसी को सड़क पर मार डाला तो तुम्हें जेल की हवा खानी होगी।

पूरन अरे राम राम कहो! ऐसी बातें मत किया करो यार। अमृत कितना ही नटखट क्यों न हो, फिर भी तुम्हारा ही तो भाई है!

अरुण पर मेरे उसे चेतावनी देने से कोई असर नहीं पड़ता। स्थिति कितनी ही गंभीर क्यों न हो, जब भी मैं कुछ कहता हूँ तो अमृत हँस पड़ता है। मैं कुछ समझ नहीं पाता, क्या किया जाए।

पूरन ख़ैर, इन बातों को छोड़ो। बताओ न, तुम क्या खाओगे? तुम्हें भूख लगी होगी?

अरुण जी हाँ, काफ़ी भूख लगी है, हालाँकि सुबह मैंने ख़ूब नाश्ता किया था। तुम ही पसंद करो, तुम क्या लोगे?

पूरन बैरे से पूछ लें, आज इन लोगों ने ताज़ा क्या बनाया है। सुना है, यहाँ का शाकाहारी खाना बहुत बढ़िया होता है।

Arun I'm sorry[1] Puran jī, I've come very late. It's not my fault, it's my brother's. He had lost the keys of my car so I had to come by bus. A great fool, he is!

Puran Why do you let him drive your car? He's still very young. If ever your father found out that Amrit was driving the car, he'd boil with anger.

Arun But what should I do? Although I've prohibited Amrit from driving a thousand times, he doesn't listen to a thing I say[2]. Today I told him that if he happened to kill someone on the road he'd have a taste of jail life![3]

1 Lit. *forgive me.*
2 मेरी agrees with बात, which is omitted in this idiomatic expression.
3 Lit. *would have to eat the air of the jail.*

Puran Oh, God forbid![4] Don't say such things, friend. However naughty Amrit may be, he is your brother after all.

Arun But my warning him has no effect. No matter how serious the situation may be, whenever I say something Amrit bursts out laughing. I can't understand at all what should be done.

Puran Well anyway, leave all that. Say won't you, what will you eat? You must be hungry?

Arun Yes, I am quite hungry, although in the morning I had a lot of breakfast. You choose, what will you have?

Puran Let's ask the waiter what they've made fresh today. I've heard the vegetarian food is very good here.

83 Concessive sentences

In the informal language, the most common expression for 'although...even so' is हालाँकि...फिर भी/तो भी/लेकिन. More formal contexts use यद्यपि for 'although', correlating with तथापि or with फिर भी, etc. for 'even so', etc. अगरचे...फिर भी is also found.

हालाँकि मैंने ख़ूब तलाश की, तो भी तुम्हारा बक्सा नहीं मिला।	*Although I searched very thoroughly (even so) I didn't find your box.*
यद्यपि वह खाना खा चुका है फिर भी उसे भूख लग रही है।	*Although he has already eaten (nevertheless) he is still hungry.*

यद्यपि/हालाँकि may be omitted, providing that फिर भी/तो भी is retained:

वह नहीं आएगी, फिर भी मैं उसे बुलाऊँगा।	*She won't come, even so I'll invite her.*

If the phrase order is reversed, फिर भी/तो भी is omitted and हालाँकि retained:

मैं उसे बुलाऊँगा, हालाँकि वह नहीं आएगी।	*I'll invite her, although she won't come.*
हालाँकि वह ग़रीब है, फिर भी वह किसी से कुछ नहीं माँगता।	*Although he is poor, he never asks anyone for anything.*

4 The expression राम राम, a repetition of the name of God, is used (*a*) as a greeting, and (*b*) as an expression of surprise. The sense of राम राम कहो is 'Say "Ram Ram"', i.e. 'repeat the name of God [to avert disaster].' It is commonly considered very inauspicious to speak of potential calamities such as deaths, etc.

यद्यपि तुम्हारी तबियत ख़राब है, फिर भी तुम्हें कुछ तो खाना चाहिए।	*Although you're unwell, you ought to eat something.*
अगरचे माल की क़ीमत बढ़ गई है तो भी हमें उसे ख़रीदना पड़ेगा।	*Even though the price of the goods has gone up, we'll have to buy them.*
मज़दूरों ने हड़ताल भी कर दी, तो भी मालिक पर कोई असर नहीं पड़ा।	*The workers even went on strike, but still it had no effect on the boss.*

Also used in concessive sentences is चाहे *no matter whether,* and चाहे जो *no matter what:*

चाहे जो भी हो, तुम्हें किराया चुकाना पड़ेगा।	*No matter what might happen, you will have to pay off the rent.*

चाहे is also used in a construction involving the set phrase क्यों न हो. This construction can also be used *without* चाहे.

चाहे वह कितना ही बड़ा आदमी क्यों न हो, फिर भी मैं उससे नहीं मिलूँगा।	*However important a man he may be, I shall not meet him.*
कैसा ही बदमाश क्यों न हो, फिर भी सारी दुनिया उसका आदर करती है।	*No matter what kind of rogue he may be, the whole world respects him.*
कितनी ही मुश्किल क्यों न हो, फिर भी समस्या का हल हो सकता है।	*No matter how difficult it may be, the problem can be solved.*

84 Further compound verbs

Para. **52** introduced the auxiliary verbs जाना, लेना and देना, which combine with verb stems to form single 'compound' verbs: आ जाना etc. This section introduces further auxiliary verbs which are used in the same way.

डालना indicates that an action is done violently, recklessly, vigorously or decisively:

जवान ने दरवाज़े को तोड़ डाला।	*The soldier broke down the door.*
एक ही दिन में उसने सात किताबें पढ़ डालीं।	*In a single day he consumed seven books.*
दवा पीने से ही तबियत ठीक होगी। पी डालो।	*Only if you drink the medicine will you get better. Drink it down.*
दंगे के दिन उसने तीन आदमियों को मार डाला।	*On the day of the riot he killed three men.*

बैठना suggests regret about an action, or suggests that an action was done foolishly, stubbornly, or against better advice:

ओहो! प्रदीप कैसी शरारत कर बैठा है?	*Oho, what kind of mischief has Pradip got up to?*
हालाँकि मैंने उसे चेतावनी दी थी, तो भी वह अपना सारा पैसा गँवा बैठा है।	*Although I warned him, he has gone and wasted all his money.*
जो भी मन में आएगा, वही कह बैठेगा।	*He will just say whatever comes to mind.*
उस दिन मैं सचमुच ग़लती कर बैठा।	*That day I really blundered.*

पड़ना add a sense of suddenness and / or change of state. Its literal sense 'to fall' is sometimes apparent, suggesting downward movement:

साँप को देखकर श्री कृष्ण नदी में कूद पड़े।	*Seeing the snake, Lord Krishna jumped into the river.*
ज्योंही गाड़ी रुकी त्योंही हम उतर पड़े।	*We got down as soon as the train stopped.*
अचानक ऐसा हुआ कि तीन अजनबी डिब्बे में घुस पड़े।	*Suddenly it happened that three strangers burst into the compartment.*
वह रो पड़ा मगर उसकी बहिन हँस पड़ी।	*He burst out crying, but his sister burst out laughing.*

उठना gives a sense similar to that of पड़ना, but its literal meaning 'to rise' is sometimes apparent in contexts suggesting upward motion or the inception of an action:

हड़ताल की ख़बर सुनकर पिता जी बिगड़ उठे।	*Hearing the news of the strike, Father lost his temper.*
जब रेडियो बजने लगा तो बूढ़े नाच उठे।	*When the radio began playing, the old men broke into a dance.*
एकाएक लकड़ियों का ढेर जल उठा।	*Suddenly the pile of sticks burst into flames.*
उसका हाल देखकर माँ घबरा उठीं।	*Seeing his condition, Mother got into a flap.*

पाना gives the sense of 'to manage, to be able to'; it is often almost identical in sense to सकना. It most frequently occurs in negative sentences, giving the sense 'not to manage to [despite trying/wanting/hoping to].' Note that पाना does *not* take the ने construction when used as a compound verb.

तुम यह काम पूरा क्यों नहीं कर पाए?	*Why were you not able to complete this work?*
उसकी गाड़ी रुक नहीं पाई।	*His car couldn't stop.*
कल तो मैं जा नहीं पाया।	*I wasn't able to go yesterday.*
इतना खाना कौन खा पाएगा?	*Who could manage to eat so much food?*

(पाना is also used with the oblique infinitive: मैं जाने न पाया *I couldn't go.*)

EXERCISE 17.1 Translate the following passage into English:

[This passage uses the more formal style of Hindi, characteristic of the written language. The passage concerns the fifteenth to sixteenth century Hindi poet Surdas, who wrote devotional poetry in praise of Lord Krishna, and tells of his legendary meeting with the Mughal emperor Akbar, who lived from 1542 to 1605.]

महात्मा सूरदास

यद्यपि हिन्दी के बहुत-से कवियों ने श्री कृष्ण का वर्णन किया है, तथापि ऐसा कोई दूसरा कवि नहीं है जिसकी तुलना सूरदास से की जा सके। सूरदास की रुचि सबसे अधिक कृष्ण के बचपन में थी। इस विषय पर उन्होंने ऐसे मधुर पद रचे जो प्रायः पांच सौ साल से हिन्दुस्तान की जनता में लोकप्रिय रहे हैं। हालाँकि सूरदास की ब्रज भाषा और आज की खड़ी बोली हिन्दी में काफ़ी अन्तर है, फिर भी सूर की कविताएँ आज भी गाई जाती हैं। ब्रज भाषा में एक विशेष मिठास है, जिसे सूर ने बाल कृष्ण का वर्णन करके और भी मीठा बना दिया। साहित्य के संदर्भ में ही नहीं बल्कि धर्म और संगीत के संदर्भ में भी सूरदास की कविता का एक विशेष महत्त्व है।

हालाँकि सूर के जीवन के बारे में कई जनश्रुतियाँ प्रचलित हैं, पर इन में कितनी सच्चाई है यह कहना कठिन है। कहा जाता है कि उनका जन्म सन् १४७८ में दिल्ली के पास एक ग़रीब ब्राह्मण परिवार में हुआ। जनश्रुति के अनुसार सूरदास जन्म से ही अंधे थे। आजकल भी अंधे आदमी अक्सर 'सूरदास' कहलाते हैं। यदि सूर अंधे नहीं हुए होते, तो उनके माता पिता उनकी देखभाल ठीक प्रकार से अवश्य करते। पर ऐसा नहीं हुआ, और जब उनकी आयु केवल छह वर्ष की थी तो वे अपने माता-पिता तथा तीन बड़े भाइयों को छोड़कर यमुना नदी के किनारे पर रहने लगे। यह सुनकर कि सूरदास नामक एक ब्राह्मण बालक है जो अत्यन्त सुन्दर पद रचता है और जो अपने इन पदों को मीठे स्वर से गाता है, दूर दूर से लोग दर्शन करने के लिए आने लगे। कई लोगों ने उन्हें गुरु के रूप में अपनाया और उनकी पूजा करना शुरु कर दिया[1]।

1 In some areas, notably Delhi, this clause would be rendered उनकी पूजा करनी शुरु कर दी.

सूरदास का यश सारे देश में फैल गया, यहाँ तक कि उनका नाम अकबर बादशाह के कानों तक पहुँचा। अकबर को संगीत का बड़ा शौक था, और धर्म के विषय में भी वे बड़े उदार थे। उन्होंने सोचा कि मैं भी एक बार इस अंधे गायक का गाना सुन लूँ। सूरदास को अकबर के दरबार में बुलाया गया। अकबर तो बादशाह थे ही – अगर उन्होंने किसी को अपने पास बुलाया तो जाने से कौन इनकार कर सकता था। जब सूर ने दरबार में प्रवेश किया तो अकबर ने कहा कि मेरा यश सभी लोग गाते हैं, तुम भी कुछ सुनाओ। तुमने मुझे प्रसन्न कर दिया तो मैं तुम्हें दो तीन गाँव और बहुत-सा धन दे दूँगा। यह सुनकर सूरदास बोल उठे कि आप कितने बड़े आदमी क्यों न हों, मैं तो भगवान का ही यश गाता हूँ। आपका यश तो मुझसे नहीं गाया जाएगा। पैसे से मेरा क्या मतलब ! फिर अकबर आग्रह कर बैठे तो सूर उबल पड़े और बादशाह से कहा कि जो[2] तुम मेरा कोई उपकार करना चाहते हो तो आज के बाद मुझे अपने पास कभी मत बुलाना, और मुझसे कभी मत मिलना !

EXERCISE **17.2** Translate into Hindi:

If I get the chance to go to India next year, I shall certainly go. I had so much work to do in the office this year that I didn't manage to go. If the fare weren't so expensive I would go every year, no matter how much work I might have! My parents complain that I don't go to see them. It is true that if I hadn't got married after coming to London I would have returned to India within six months; but although I haven't seen my family for several years I write letters to them every month, and I keep getting all their news too. When at first I told my father that I wanted to work in London he boiled up with rage, and when I sold off the Delhi house he burst out 'Oh, what have you **done**? My children are all fools!' Although he was pretty angry then, he is now happy that we have adopted this country for a few years.

2 जो here means 'if'.

Unit Eighteen

Dialogue 18A *Some family photographs and an invitation*

लक्ष्मी वे फ़ोटो किसके हैं, जो उधर मेज़ पर पड़े हुए हैं? *(अलका की ओर देखते हुए)* तुम्हारे होंगे?

अलका *(फ़ोटोओं को उठाते हुए)* हाँ, मेरे हैं। यह फ़ोटो देखो, इसमें मेरे चाचा जी हैं। वे अपने आगरे-वाले मकान के आगे खड़े हैं। उनका एक दूसरा मकान दिल्ली में भी है, जो कई महीनों से ख़ाली पड़ा हुआ है।

लक्ष्मी और ये महिला तुम्हारी चाची जी होंगी, जो दुपट्टा ओढ़े सीढ़ियों पर बैठी हुई हैं?

अलका नहीं जी, मेरी चाची जी तो लगभग पाँच छह साल हुए चल बसी थीं। यह तो सरला है, वह मेरी चचेरी बहिन लगती है। चश्मा पहने हुए यह आदमी मेरा चचेरा भाई है। वह तो काफ़ी अच्छा खाता-पीता व्यक्ति है, कांग्रेस में ख़ूब जाना-पहचाना है, और अपने को बहुत समझता भी है! और मकान की तरफ़ देखती हुई यह लड़की तो सरला की कोई सहेली है।

लक्ष्मी मुझे तो आगरे गए क़रीब दस बारह साल हो गए हैं। तुम्हारे चाचा जी को वहाँ रहते हुए कितने साल हुए हैं?

अलका उन्हें उस मकान में रहते हुए कोई पैंतीस छत्तीस वर्ष हुए होंगे। अगर तुम्हें फ़ुरसत मिले तो कलकत्ते से लौटते समय आगरे में एकाध दिन ठहरना। मैं भी रहूंगी उस समय। बिना ताज महल देखे तुम्हें घर वापस नहीं जाना चाहिए!

लक्ष्मी कितना अच्छा विचार है! दिल्ली में पड़े-पड़े हम लोग ऊब जाते हैं। *(क़लम निकालते हुए)* तुम अभी मुझे अपने चाचाजी का नंबर दे दो, मैं लिख लूँ।

अलका नंबर तो इस समय मुझे याद नहीं। शाम को घर पहुँचते ही मैं तुम्हें फ़ोन करके नंबर बता दूँगी। चाचाजी के किसी पत्र पर लिखा होगा।

Lakshmi Whose are those photographs which are lying on the table over there? *(Looking at Alka)* They must be your?

Alka *(Picking up the photographs)* Yes, they're mine. Look at this one, in this there is my uncle. He is standing in front of his

Agra[1] house. He also has another house in Delhi, which has been lying empty for several months.

Lakshmi And this lady will be your aunt, who is sitting on the steps wearing a scarf?

Alka No,[2] my aunt passed on about five or six years ago. This is Sarala, she is my cousin.[3] This man wearing glasses is my [male] cousin. He's a pretty well-to-do person, well known in Congress, and he thinks highly of himself too! And this girl looking towards the house is some friend of Sarala's.

Lakshmi It's ten or twelve years since I went to Agra. How long has your uncle been living there?

Alka He must have been living in that house for thirty-five or thirty-six years. If you're free, stay in Agra for a few days while returning from Calcutta. I'll be there too at that time. You shouldn't go home without seeing the Taj Mahal!

Lakshmi What a good idea! We get bored, stuck in Delhi all the time. *(Taking out a pen)* You give me your uncle's number now, let me write it down.

Alka I don't remember the number just now. As soon as I get home in the evening I'll ring you and tell you the number. It must be written on some letter of Uncle's.

85 Participial constructions

(*a*) A participle is a verbal adjective, and Hindi has two: the imperfective participle–करता *doing,* खाता *eating,* जाता *going,* टूटता *breaking;* and the perfective participle–किया *done*, खाया *eaten,* गया *gone,* टूटा *broken.* Participles are more often than not strengthened by the perfective forms हुआ, हुई, हुए. When used adjectivally, participles agree with the nouns they qualify: हँसता हुआ आदमी *a laughing man,* फटी हुई किताब *a torn book.*

उसने जला हुआ मकान देखा।	*He saw a burnt-down house.*
उसने जलता हुआ मकान देखा।	*He saw a burning house.*

1 Well-known place-names ending in -आ, such as आगरा, कलकत्ता, etc. usually inflect as regular masculine -आ nouns; but less well-known place-names usually do *not* inflect; and आगरा में (etc.) is also possible.
2 नहीं जी: a variant for जी नहीं, particularly common among Panjabi speakers.
3 वह मेरी चचेरी बहिन लगती है: note this use of the verb लगना – 'She is related to me as cousin', i.e. 'She is my cousin.'

बीते दिनों की यादें बहुत मीठी होती हैं।	*Memories of days past are very sweet.*
फ़र्श पर कुछ कपड़े पड़े हुए थे।	*There were some clothes lying on the floor.*
उधर बैठा हुआ आदमी कौन है?	*Who is the man sitting over there?*
हमने मरी हुई चिड़िया देखी।	*We saw a dead bird.*
उसने अपने कमाए हुए पैसे उड़ा दिए।	*He wasted the money he had earned.*
उन्होंने भागते हुए चोर को पकड़ा।	*They caught the fleeing thief.*
एक मुस्कराते हुए सज्जन कमरे में आए।	*A smiling gentleman came into the room.*
माँ ने रोती हुई लड़की को गोद में उठा लिया।	*Mother lifted the crying girl onto her lap.*
यह साड़ी रेशम की बनी हुई है।	*This sari is made of silk.*

(*b*) Participles are also used adverbially, in which case the invariable -ए form occurs: हमने लड़कियों को गीत गाते हुए सुना *We heard the girls singing songs*; वह मुस्कराते हुए चल रहा था *He was walking along smiling*.

In some contexts there is little or no difference between the adjectival and the adverbial usage: वह रेशमी साड़ी पहनी हुई थी *or* वह रेशमी साड़ी पहने हुए थी *She was wearing a silk sari.* Examples:

वह सड़क पर काम करते हुए नज़र आया।	*He appeared working on the road.*
औरतें ध्यान लगाए कथा सुन रही थीं।	*The women were listening attentively to the recitation.*
वहाँ लोग भीड़ लगाए खड़े थे।	*People were standing there in a crowd.*
हमने भूत को चलते-फिरते देखा।	*We saw the ghost wandering about.*
माँ अपना सामान पकड़े हुए खड़ी थीं।	*Mother was standing holding her luggage.*
कुछ बच्चे फटे-पुराने कपड़े पहने हुए थे।	*Some children were wearing old torn clothes.*
वह सलवार क़मीज़ पहने हुए थी।	*She was wearing salwar qamiz.*[1]
मैंने तुम्हें उसकी तारीफ़ करते सुना है।	*I have heard you praising him.*
मैं उसे अपना दोस्त समझे हुए था।	*I had considered him my friend.*

[1] Loose trousers and shirt worn by Panjabi women.

(*c*) Repetition of the participle, be it adjectival or adverbial, emphasises the continuity or repetitiveness of an action. The form हुआ/हुई/हुए is not used when the participle is repeated.

समुद्र के किनारे खेलते खेलते बच्चे थक गए।	*The children got tired playing on the seashore.*
इंतज़ार करते करते मुझे नींद आने लगी।	*Waiting and waiting, I began to feel sleepy.*
उन छोटे अक्षरों को पढ़ते पढ़ते मेरी आँखें दुखने लगीं।	*Through constantly reading those small characters, my eyes began to ache.*
ऐश करते करते वह आलसी हो जाएगा।	*He'll get lazy, always living in luxury.*
पन्ने पलटते पलटते उसे और भी गलतियाँ मिलीं।	*As he turned over the pages, he found even more mistakes.*
पैसा जोड़ते जोड़ते वह लखपति बन गया।	*Gradually accumulating money, he became a millionaire.*

(*d*) The perfective participles of transitive verbs often have a passive meaning when they are used adjectivally: गांधीजी का नाम दीवार पर लिखा था *Gandhi jī's name was written on the wall.* When such participles are required to have an active meaning, they must take the adverbial -ए form: वह हाथ में चाकू लिए खड़ा था *He was standing with (having taken) a knife in his hand.*

(*e*) Both imperfective and perfective participles can be used as nouns: मेरा कहा *the thing I said*; आपके पहुँचते *on your arriving.*

Notice also the following usage, involving a pairing of transitive and intransitive forms of the same verb: हमारे बचाए पैसा नहीं बचता *Money's not saved no matter how we try to save it* (Lit. despite our saving).

उसका कहा तुम्हें बुरा लगा होगा।	*What he said must have offended you.*
रवि के लंदन में रहते हम कुछ नहीं कर सकते।	*As long as Ravi's in London, we can't do anything.*
चालक के रोके भी कार रुक नहीं पाई।	*Though the driver tried to stop it, the car couldn't stop.*

(*f*) Inclusion of emphatic ही after the imperfective participle gives the sense 'immediately on doing'; the participle (*without* हुआ, etc.) is in the masculine oblique:

घर पहुँचते ही हम खाना खाएँगे।	*We'll eat as soon as we get home.*
दाम सुनते ही वह बिगड़ गया।	*As soon as he heard the price, he got angery.*
पानी के पड़ते ही हम अंदर चले जाएँ।	*Let's go inside as soon as it rains.*
आपके स्वीकार करते ही मैं दूसरों को बुलाऊँगा।	*As soon as you accept I'll invite the others.*

(*g*) The use of बिना before the invariable perfective participle in -ए gives the sense 'without doing':

बिना कुछ कहे वह बैठ गया।	*Without saying anything, he sat down.*
बिना चाय पिए वह काम में जुट गया।	*He set to work without drinking tea.*
बिना सोचे कुछ मत कर।	*Don't do anything without thinking.*
बिना कष्ट उठाए कुछ नहीं मिलेगा।	*You won't get anything without taking trouble.*

(*h*) A very common use of the imperfective participle is exemplified in the sentence लंदन में रहते हुए आपको कितने दिन हो गए हैं? *How long have you been living in London?* (lit. 'How many days have passed to you living in London?'). This use describes a state or action which is *still in force* at the time of speaking. Compare this with use of the *perfective* participle in the sentence: मुझे यहाँ आए हुए दस दिन हो गए हैं *It's ten days since I came here,* which relates the length of time which has elapsed *since* an event took place.

The participle हुए is also used adverbially as a synonym for पहले, as in दस दिन हुए *ten days ago.*

किताब को छपे हुए दो साल हो चुके थे।	*It was already two years since the book had been printed.*
उर्दू सीखते हुए हमें डेढ़ साल हो गया है।	*We've been learning Urdu for one and a half years.*
श्रुति को ससुराल गए कितने दिन हुए हैं?	*How long is it since Shruti went to her in-laws?*
अस्पताल में नौकरी करते हुए हमें दस साल हो गए हैं।	*We've been working in the hospital for ten years.*
सिगरेट पीना छोड़े हुए मुझे ढाई साल हो गए हैं।	*I gave up smoking two and a half years ago.*

(*i*) The imperfective participle is commonly used in expressing 'at the time when'; notice agreement with the feminine noun दफ़ा in the last example:

घर लौटते समय मैंने उसका पत्र पढ़ा।	*As I got home I read his letter.*
मरते वक़्त लोगों को अपना बचपन याद आता है।	*At the time of death people remember their childhood.*
आती दफ़ा अपना सामान यहाँ जमा करें।	*Would you deposit your things here as you arrive.*

Dialogue 18B *An introduction*

रमेश कपूर नमस्ते जी। मैं अपना परिचय कराऊँ? मैं रमेश कपूर हूँ। आपका शुभ नाम?

विमल शास्त्री मुझे विमल शास्त्री कहते हैं। मैं मंत्री जी के दफ़्तर में अधिकारी हूँ। बताइए, क्या आप भी मंत्री जी से मिलने आए हैं?

रमेश कपूर जी हाँ, मेरी बहिन को मंत्री जी की धर्मपत्नी से काम है। आपने सुना होगा कि उनके पिताजी का स्वर्गवास हो गया है।

विमल शास्त्री जी हाँ, समाचार सुनकर मुझे बहुत दुःख हुआ। वैसे बहुत दिनों से कुछ बीमार-से लग रहे थे बेचारे। वे मेरे स्वर्गीय चाचाजी के घनिष्ठ मित्र थे।

(कुछ समय बाद)

रमेश कपूर अच्छा जी आज्ञा दीजिएगा, मंत्री जी से मिलने का समय हो गया है। किसी दिन आप हमारे यहाँ अवश्य पधारिए। हमारी छोटी-सी झोंपड़ी है, फिर भी आपका हमेशा स्वागत है।

विमल शास्त्री आपका बहुत आभारी हूँ। आप भी कभी समय निकालकर हमारी कुटिया पवित्र करें! और हाँ, मंत्री जी के दर्शन करते समय हमारा भी प्रणाम कहिएगा।

Ramesh Kapoor Hello. May I introduce myself? I am Ramesh Kapoor. May I know your name?

Vimal Shastri I am called Vimal Shastri. I am an official in the minister's office. Tell me, have you come to see the minister too?

Ramesh Kapoor Yes, my sister has some business[1] with the minister's wife. You will have heard that her father has died.

Vimal Shastri Yes, I was very sorry to hear the news. Actually he had been looking rather unwell for a long time, poor fellow. He was a close friend of my late uncle's.

(*Some time later*)

[1] Not necessarily commercial business – just something to talk about, some reason for meeting.

Ramesh Kapoor Well, may I take my leave? It's time for me to meet the minister. Be sure to come to our place sometime. We have a humble little home[1] but you are always welcome.

Vimal Shastri I am very grateful to you. You too sometime find the time to honour our little house.[2] And yes–while meeting the minister please give him my[3] greetings too.

Dialogue 18C *Waiting to see the minister*

रहमान हुसैन आदाब अर्ज़, ख़ाँ साहब। तशरीफ़ लाइए। कैसा मिज़ाज है?

अब्दुल ख़ाँ दुआ है आपकी। आप सुनाइए, कैसे हैं?

रहमान हुसैन मेहरबानी है। ख़ाँ साहब, वर्मा जी से मिलिए। ये लखनऊ से हैं, इन्होंने अभी इसी सड़क पर एक अच्छा-सा मकान ख़रीद लिया है। वर्मा जी, ये ख़ाँ साहब हैं, मेरे बहुत पुराने दोस्त हैं।

रवि वर्मा बड़ी ख़ुशी हुई आपसे मिलकर। आइए, तशरीफ़ रखिए।

(थोड़ी देर बाद)

अब्दुल ख़ाँ अच्छा जनाब, अब मुझे इजाज़त दीजिए।

रहमान हुसैन ख़ाँ साहब, एक बात कहनी थी आपसे।

अब्दुल ख़ाँ फ़रमाइए जनाब!

रहमान हुसैन सलीम साहब जो हैं न, उन्हें मेहरबानी करके याद दिलाना कि मुझे उनसे मिलना है।

अब्दुल ख़ाँ बस, इतनी-सी बात है? ज़रूर कह देंगे उनसे। ख़ुदा हाफ़िज़।

रहमान हुसैन और रवि वर्मा *(एक साथ)* ख़ुदा हाफ़िज़ ख़ाँ साहब।

Rahman Husein Greetings, Khan Sahab. Please do come in. How are you?

Abdul Khan I am well, thank you. And you, how are you?

Rahman Husein Thank you, I'm fine. Khan Sahab, please meet Mr Varma. He is from Lucknow, he has just bought a pretty good house on this very road. Varma ji, this is Khan Sahab, he is a very old friend[4] of mine.

1 Lit. *a smallish hut*. A conventional expression of humility.
2 Lit. *take out the time to sanctify our cottage*.
3 हमारा: first person plural here stands for first person singular, the 'royal we'.
4 पुराना दोस्त can only mean 'a friend of long standing'; a friend of advanced years would be बूढ़ा दोस्त.

Ravi Varma Very pleased to meet you. Come, please have a seat.
(A little while later)
Abdul Khan Well sir,[1] may I take my leave now?
Rahman Husein Khan Sahab, there was one thing I wanted to say to you.
Abdul Khan Please go ahead, sir!
Rahman Husein You know Salim Sahab don't you,[2] kindly remind him that I have to meet him.
Abdul Is that all, such a small thing? Of course I will tell him.[3] Goodbye.
Rahman Husein and Ravi Varma *(together)* Goodbye Khan Sahab.

86 The particle -सा

-सा is a declinable particle which is suffixed to adjectives (and some other forms as described below), usually with a hyphen. (The forms बहुत-सा and थोड़ा-सा have already been introduced in para. **40**.) The effect of -सा is to moderate or 'dilute' the sense of the adjective to which it is attached: अच्छा-सा कमरा *a rather good room;* बड़ी-सी खिड़की *a biggish window;* पुराने-से चित्र *fairly old pictures.*

-सा may suffix perfective participles used adjectivally: फटे-से कपड़े *ragged clothes.* It may also suffix imperfective participles, commonly in expressions for 'to appear to be': कागज़ जलता-सा जान पड़ता था *The paper seemed to be burning*; उसके हाथ काँपते-से नज़र आते थे *His hands appeared to be trembling.*

Following a noun, -सा gives the sense 'like'. It requires preceding nouns and pronouns to be in the oblique case: बच्चों-सा स्वभाव *a child-like nature;* सूरज का-सा प्रकाश *light like that of the sun.*

Notice also the adjectival expression एक-सा *alike, uniform, similar.*

1 As explained below, जनाब does not have the same sense of deference as 'sir'; but there is no closer rendering.

2 जो हैं *who / which exists:* the purpose of this common conversational idiom is to establish the subject under discussion before getting down to details. Further examples are: वह घड़ी जो है, तुम्हें उसको बेचना पड़ेगा *Now about that watch, you'll have to sell it*; सलीम जो है न, वह तो बड़ा तेज़ लड़का है *You know Salim, don't you–he's a very bright boy.* In the present example, the verb is plural to agree with the honorific subject (Salim Sahab).

3 कह देंगे: another example of the 'royal we'.

तमाम विद्यार्थी एक-से नहीं होते।	*All students are not alike.*
आपकी कविता में एक शहद-सी मिठास है।	*There is a honey-like sweetness in your poetry.*
उसका चाँद-सा चेहरा कितना सुंदर लग रहा था!	*How lovely his moon-like face was looking!*
दिल्ली के आस-पास कश्मीर की-सी आब-हवा नहीं मिलेगी।	*You won't find a climate like Kashmir's around Delhi.*
एक लंबा-सा आदमी मंत्री जी से बातें कर रहा था।	*A tallish man was talking to the minister.*

87 Conversational etiquette

Hindi has a wide range of conventional phrases for expressing greetings, introductions, leave-takings and the other niceties of social intercourse. The characteristic conversational use of vocative words such as भाई, यार, etc. and of imperative verbs such as कहिए, सुनाइए, etc. has been demonstrated in the dialogues. This section introduces a further range of such conversational devices. The lists below include a number of expressions which may strictly be defined as Urdu rather than Hindi; of these, those which are mainly confined to Muslim speakers are marked with an asterisk.

सलाम अलैकुम*	*greetings, goodbye* (Lit. *peace be with you*)
सलाम	*greetings, goodbye* (Lit. *peace:* usually said by a तुम person to an आप person)
आदाब अर्ज़*	*greetings, salutation*
प्रणाम	*greetings, salutation*
सत श्री अकाल	*greetings, goodbye* (the Sikh greeting and leave-taking: lit. *Truth is the immortal Lord*)
तशरीफ़ लाइए।	*Please come, come in.* (Lit. *bring your noble presence*)
तशरीफ़ रखिए।	*Please have a seat, be seated*
तशरीफ़ ले जाइए।	*Please leave; please go (there)*
पधारिए।	*Please come, come in.*
विराजिए।	*Please have a seat, be seated.*

आपका शुभ नाम?	*May I know your name?* (शुभ *auspicious*)
आपका इस्म-ए शरीफ़?*	*May I know your name?* (इस्म-ए शरीफ़ *noble name*)
जनाब	*sir* (used respectfully between equals)
हुज़ूर	*sir* (used by a तुम person to an आप person)
फ़रमाइए।	*Please (be so good as to) speak out, give a command.*
किसी के दर्शन करना।	*to meet, have an audience with someone*
कल आपके दर्शन करूँगा। कल आपके दर्शन होंगे।	*I will [be fortunate enough to] meet you tomorrow.*
बहुत दिनों से आपके दर्शन नहीं हुए।	*I haven't [been lucky enough to have] seen you for a long time.*
किसी का मिज़ाज पूछना	*to ask after someone's health*
आपका मिज़ाज-ए शरीफ़? आपका मिज़ाज कैसा है?	*How are you? How do you do?*
आपकी दुआ है।	*I am well, thank you.* (Lit. *it is [through] your prayer [that I am well]*)
परिचय	*introduction, acquaintance* (m.)
मैं आपसे उसका परिचय कराऊँगा।	*I will introduce him to you.*
सारे मेहमानों ने अपना अपना परिचय दिया।	*All the guests introduced themselves.*
उससे मेरा परिचय नहीं है।	*I am not acquainted with him/do not know him.*
उनसे मेरा परिचय हुआ है।	*I have met him.*
मिलाना	*to cause to meet, bring about a meeting*
हमने मेहमानों को आपस में मिलाया।	*We introduced the guests to each other.*

It is customary to request 'permission' to go before getting up and leaving:

आज्ञा दीजिए। इजाज़त दीजिए।	*Please give me permission [to go]; May I go now?/I'll be going now if you don't mind.*
तुम्हें जाने की आज्ञा है।	*You have permission to leave.*
ख़ुदा हाफ़िज़।*	*Goodbye.*

A traditional reticence among women about referring to their husbands by name leads to the common use of honorific expressions for 'husband': श्रीमान जी, पतिदेव. Note also the honorific usage धर्मपत्नी (*true*) *wife*.

Since it is often considered inauspicious or distasteful to refer directly to death, euphemisms are often used:

गुज़र जाना	*to pass on, pass away*
चल बसना	*to pass over* (Lit. *to go off and reside elsewhere*)
प्रभु का प्यारा हो जाना	*to go to heaven* (Lit. *to become a beloved of the Lord*)
का स्वर्गवास होना	*to go to heaven* (Lit. *to have residence in heaven*)

Note also the adjective स्वर्गीय *deceased, the late*.

EXERCISE 18.1 Give answers in Hindi to the following questions:

१ आपको हिन्दी सीखते हुए कितने साल हुए हैं?
२ यह पाठ पढ़ते समय आप कैसे कमरे में बैठे हैं?
३ आपस में मिलते समय मुसलमान लोग क्या कहते हैं?
४ क्या इस पुस्तक में सारे पाठ एक-से हैं?
५ आपको सिनेमा देखे कितने दिन हुए हैं?

EXERCISE 18.2 Translate into English:

स्टेशन पहुँचते ही मुझे पता चला कि लखनऊ-वाली गाड़ी चल चुकी थी। मैंने निश्चय किया कि दूसरी गाड़ी का इंतज़ार करूँगा। दो घंटे की देर थी। टिकट-घर के सामने एक लंबी-सी क़तार लगी हुई थी, इसलिए अपना सामान उठाकर मैं प्लेटफ़ार्म के एक कोने में चला गया। वहाँ भी ख़ाली जगह पाना आसान न था, सब कहीं लोग बैठे हुए या खड़े हुए गाड़ी का इंतज़ार करते नज़र आए। आख़िर मुझे बैठने की जगह मिली, और मैं आस-पास का दृश्य देखने लगा। थोड़ी दूर पर एक चायवाला 'चाय, गरम चाय' चिल्ला रहा था, तो दूसरी ओर एक नमकीन बेचनेवाला इधर-उधर घूमते हुए अपना माल बेच रहा था। टिकट-घर के पास खड़ा हुआ एक फेरीवाला दोनों हाथों में लकड़ी के बने हुए खिलौने लिए एक लाल साडी पहने हए महिला से मोल भाव कर रहा था। इतनी चहल-पहल मैंने कभी नहीं देखी थी! समोसेवाला हालाँकि फटे पुराने कपड़े पहने हुए था, मगर समोसों का बाज़ार गरम था और

मैंने मन में सोचा कि अगर वह इस प्रकार दिन भर अपना माल बेचता रहेगा तो शाम तक वह एक मोटी-सी रक़म जोड़ लेगा। चारों तरफ़ नज़र दौड़ाते हुए मैंने देखा कि मेरी बग़ल में घिसे-पिटे चिथड़ों का एक मैला-सा ढेर पड़ा हुआ था, और दूसरी तरफ़ कुछ लोग भीड़ लगाए खड़े-खड़े हँसी मज़ाक कर रहे थे। उनकी बातों को सुनने से मालूम हुआ कि वे अभी कुछ ही मिनट हुए लखनऊ से आए थे, और उन्होंने यात्रा का मज़ा ख़ूब लिया था। सहसा मेरे उधर फिर देखने से पता चला कि जिसको मैं चिथड़ों का ढेर समझे हुए था वह कोई बूढ़ा-सा भिखारी था जो ज़मीन पर लेटे लेटे सो गया था। वह जँभाई लेते हुए उठ खड़ा हुआ, और साधु की तरह 'राम राम' जपते हुए इधर उधर टहलने लगा। तब मुझ जैसे गोरे को वहाँ प्लेटफ़ार्म पर बैठे हुए देखकर वह दौड़ते हुए आया और अपनी राम कहानी सुनाने लगा। उसकी चालाकी-भरी बातें सुनते सुनते पता ही नहीं चला था कि कब दो घंटे गुज़र गए। अचानक काला धुआँ उगलती हुई गाड़ी स्टेशन पर आकर रुक गई। गाड़ी के रुकते ही प्लेटफ़ार्म पर इंतज़ार करते लोगों में एक तूफ़ान-सा उठा। लाल कुरते पहने हुए कुली एक जगह से दूसरी जगह भागे जा रहे थे, और कुलियों के हाथों में अपना सामान थमाते हुए डिब्बे में जगह पाने की दौड़ में तमाम यात्री एक-से लगने लगे। सभी को अपने अपने काम से मतलब था। जब मैंने इतने लोगों को चढ़ते देखा तो मैं हैरान-सा हो गया, और बिना टिकट ख़रीदे मैं भी औरों की तरह गाड़ी की तरफ़ दौड़ा गया। आख़िर एक डिब्बे में मैं घुस ही पाया। सीट पाने का सवाल ही नहीं था, पर किसी तरह फ़र्श पर ही एक छोटी-सी जगह मिल गई, और मैं अपने सामान के ऊपर बैठ गया। मेरी रेल-यात्रा शुरू हो गई थी।

EXERCISE 18.3 Translate the following dialogue into Hindi:

Mr Varma Good morning Shankar jī! Please come in, do have a seat. I haven't seen you for a long time. How are you?

Mr Shankar Thank you for asking, I'm well. It's about three years since I have seen you. I'm very glad to see you again after such a long time.

Mr Varma I was told that you've taken a room in the Akbar Hotel. How many days have you been staying there?

Mr Shankar We've been staying there for four days. As soon as we arrived here from London we went straight there. It's quite a good hotel, we like it very much. Tell me, whose photograph is that lying on the table over there?

Mr Varma That is my son Raju. And that little boy wearing the bluish shirt is his cousin Ramesh. You must have seen them playing in the garden as you got out of the car.

Mr Shankar Yes, that's right. Well, may I go now? I'll come to see you again tomorrow on my way to the station.

Mr Varma Please do come. I will introduce you to some friends. Please give my greetings to your wife.

Appendix A Numbers, money and the calendar

Cardinal numbers

The cardinal numbers are here set out in a table showing (vertically) the progression of units and (horizontally) the progression of tens.

० शून्य				
१ एक	११ ग्यारह	२१ इक्कीस	३१ इकत्तीस	४१ इकतालीस
२ दो	१२ बारह	२२ बाईस	३२ बत्तीस	४२ बयालीस
३ तीन	१३ तेरह	२३ तेईस	३३ तैंतीस	४३ तैंतालीस
४ चार	१४ चौदह	२४ चौबीस	३४ चौंतीस	४४ चवालीस
५ पाँच	१५ पंद्रह	२५ पच्चीस	३५ पैंतीस	४५ पैंतालीस
६ छह, छै, छः	१६ सोलह	२६ छब्बीस	३६ छत्तीस	४६ छियालीस
७ सात	१७ सत्रह	२७ सत्ताईस	३७ सैंतीस	४७ सैंतालीस
८ आठ	१८ अठारह	२८ अट्ठाईस	३८ अड़तीस	४८ अड़तालीस
९ नौ	१९ उन्नीस	२९ उनतीस	३९ उनतालीस	४९ उनचास
१० दस	२० बीस	३० तीस	४० चालीस	५० पचास
५१ इक्यावन	६१ इकसठ	७१ इकहत्तर	८१ इक्यासी	९१ इक्यानवे
५२ बावन	६२ बासठ	७२ बहत्तर	८२ बयासी	९२ बानवे
५३ तिरपन	६३ तिरसठ	७३ तिहत्तर	८३ तिरासी	९३ तिरानवे
५४ चौवन	६४ चौंसठ	७४ चौहत्तर	८४ चौरासी	९४ चौरानवे
५५ पचपन	६५ पैंसठ	७५ पचहत्तर	८५ पचासी	९५ पचानवे
५६ छप्पन	६६ छियासठ	७६ छिहत्तर	८६ छियासी	९६ छियानवे
५७ सत्तावन	६७ सरसठ	७७ सतहत्तर	८७ सत्तासी	९७ सत्तानवे
५८ अट्ठावन	६८ अड़सठ	७८ अठहत्तर	८८ अट्ठासी	९८ अट्ठानवे
५९ उनसठ	६९ उनहत्तर	७९ उन्यासी	८९ नवासी	९९ निन्यानवे
६० साठ	७० सत्तर	८० अस्सी	९० नब्बे	१०० सौ

Above one hundred, the numbers proceed as in English, but with no conjunction 'and':

१८४ एक सौ चौरासी
२३६ दो सौ छत्तीस

Note the following terms:

हज़ार, सहस्र	*thousand* (m.)
लाख	*one hundred thousand, 'lac', 'lakh'* (m.)
करोड़	*ten million, 'crore'* (m.)
दस प्रतिशत	*ten per cent*

The splitting up of high numerals by commas reflects the three-tier system of हज़ार, लाख and करोड़ rather than the multiples of thousands used in English. For example, the number 29,230,637 will appear as:

२,९२,३०,६३७ दो करोड़ बानवे लाख तीस हज़ार छह सौ सैंतीस

The word एक is sometimes used after a cardinal number to express an indefinite or approximate number:

पचास एक	*about fifty*
दो एक	*about two, a couple*

Money

Decimal currency was introduced in India in 1957. There are 100 पैसे (or नए पैसे) to the रुपया. Sums of money are quoted according to the usual decimal system, preceded by the abbreviation रु. (= रुपया); this is rendered 'Rs.' in English, with 'Re.' for the singular. Thus रु. ४२.५० is Rs. 42.50.

Under the old currency, one रुपया was divided into 16 आने; one आना consisted of four पैसे; and one पैसा consisted of three पाइयाँ. Survivals of this system are common in colloquial Hindi usage.

आठ आने	*half a rupee, 50 paisā*
मेरे पास एक पाई भी नहीं।	*I haven't a farthing.*
यह बात सोलह आने ठीक है।	*This is 100% correct.*

Some further expressions are:

यह कितने का (की) है?	*How much is this?*
इसका क्या दाम है?	*What is the price of this?*
यह किताब दस रुपये की है।	*This book costs ten rupees.*
कितना पैसा हुआ?	*How much does that make?*
कुल मिलाकर बीस रुपये हुए।	*That makes twenty rupees altogether.*

भाव बढ़ गया है।	*The rate has increased.*
डेढ़ सौ रुपये में कितना कपड़ा मिलेगा ?	*How much cloth will I get for Rs. 150!*
कुछ तो रिआयत दीजिए, न ?	*Give some discount, won't you?*
हिसाब में अभी ५०० रुपये बाक़ी हैं।	*There are still Rs. 500 outstanding on the account.*
हिसाब चुक गया है।	*The account has been settled.*
हमें हिसाब को चुकाना है।	*We have to settle the account.*
यह सोने की अँगूठी आपको कितने में मिली ?	*How much did you get this gold ring for?*

The Hindu calendar

The Hindu calendar, which is still in use in religious and ceremonial contexts, is based on lunar months (but solar years). Each month is divided into two halves of 15 lunar days (called तिथि): the first half of the month begins with the full moon and is called शुक्ल पक्ष or सुदि (*bright* or *waxing half*); the second half begins with the new moon and is called कृष्ण पक्ष or बदी (*dark* or *waning half*). A leap month, called मलमास or अधिकमास, is added after every thirtieth month in order to compensate for the discrepancy between the lunar and solar calendars. The new year begins on the first day of the कृष्ण पक्ष of the month चैत.

The Hindi names of the lunar months, with their Sanskrit equivalents (which are also in current use in the religious calendar) are given below with their traditional pairings into six seasons. Note that the Hindu month names are all masculine; of the season names, वर्षा *rains* and शरद *autumn* are feminine and the rest are masculine.

Hindi	**Sanskrit**	**Season** (ऋतु (f.), काल (m.))	
चैत	चैत्र	बसंत *spring* (m.)	*March–April*
बेसाख	वैशाख		*April–May*
जेठ	ज्येष्ठ	ग्रीष्म *summer* (m.)	*May–June*
असाढ़	आषाढ़		*June–July*
सावन	श्रावण	वर्षा *rains* (f.)	*July–August*
भादों	भाद्रपद		*August–September*
आश्विन, क्वार	आश्विन	शरद *autumn* (f.)	*September–October*
कातिक	कार्तिक		*October–November*
अगहन	आग्रहायण	हेमंत *winter* (m.)	*November–December*

पूस	पौष		*December–January*
माघ	माघ	शिशिर *cool season* (m.)	*January–February*
फागुन	फाल्गुन		*February–March*

Remember that the nouns जाड़ा and सरदी (*cold*) are in common use for 'winter', and गरमी *heat for* 'summer'. They are usually used in the plural, (जाड़ों में *in the winter*), but remain in the singular when used in composition with other nouns (जाड़े की छुट्टियाँ *the winter holidays*).

The most commonly used of the various Indian dating systems is the विक्रमादित्य or विक्रम era, traditionally said to have been founded by the legendary king Vikramaditya in 57-58 BC. Since the year begins in the month चैत (March-April), the Vikram chronology does not tally exactly with the Christian calendar. To convert dates in the first nine and a half months of the Vikram year into the Christian calendar, subtract 57 years; for the remaining two and a half months, subtract 58. Vikram dates are usually identified by the Sanskrit word संवत् *year, era,* while dates according to the Christian calendar are preceded by the Arabic equivalent, सन् (or ईसवी सन् *Christian year*). Thus संवत् २०४५ = सन् १९८७/८८

Examples of dates expressed according to the Vikram calendar are:

माघ शुक्ल पक्ष १२ संवत् २००९	*12th day of the bright half of the month* माघ, *VS (Vikram Samvat) 2009 (= AD 1952)*
आश्विन बदी ३ संवत् १७६८	*3rd day of the dark half of the month* अश्विन, *VS 1768 (= AD 1711)*

Many Hindu festivals take their names from the Sanskrit ordinal numbers which refer to their date in the month: राम नवमी *Rama's 9th*, the birthday of Rama celebrated on the ninth day of the bright fortnight of चैत; जन्माष्टमी *the birth 8th [of Krishna]*: the eighth day of the dark fortnight of भादों.

Appendix B Terms of relationship

Family relationships are expressed much more precisely in Hindi than they are in English: there are different and specific names for the various kinds of uncles and aunts, for example, and their spouses. The most commonly encountered terms are given in the following family tree, in which relationships are shown based on a male subject (स्वयं *self*):

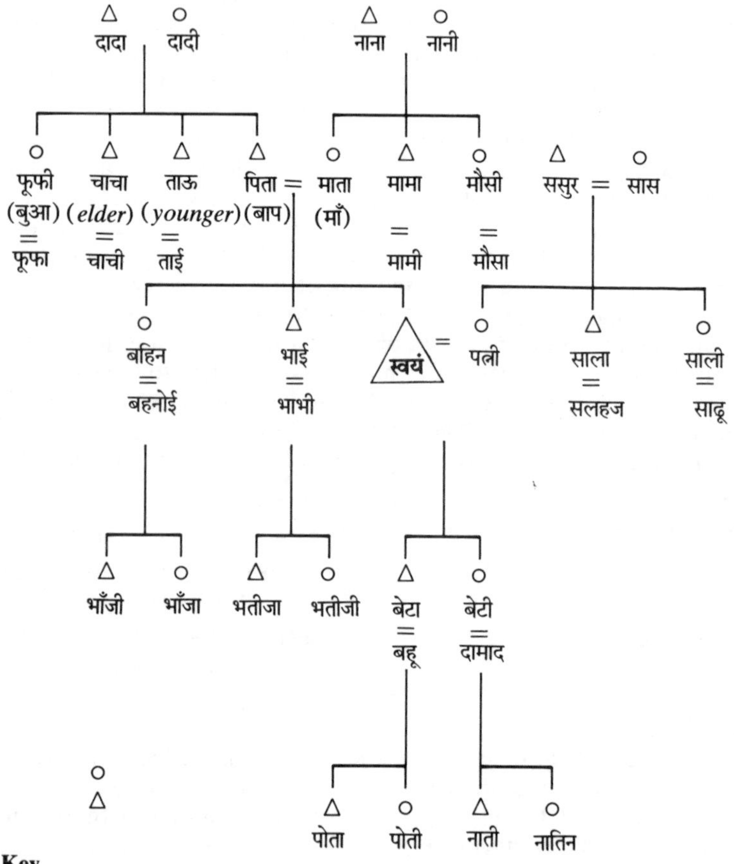

Key

○ *female*

△ *male*

= *link by marriage*

The same scheme applies with a female subject, except for the following relationships by marriage:

X's husband's elder brother:	जेठ (*married to* जेठानी)
X's husband's younger brother:	देवर (*married to* देवरानी)
X's husband's sister:	ननद (*married to* ननदोई)

The family tree given here does not exhaust all the possibilities. Amongst the regional and other variant usages encountered, the following should be noted:

पतोहू	for	बहू	*daughter-in-law*
जीजी, दीदी	for	बहिन	*sister*
काका	for	चाचा	*father's elder brother*
काकी	for	चाची	*wife of father's elder brother*
बाबा	for	दादा	*grandfather*

First cousins are called चचेरा भाई/चचेरी बहिन on the father's side, ममेरा भाई/ममेरी बहिन on the mother's side. These are distinguished from सगा भाई/सगी बहिन *real brother/sister* (and the terms 'cousin-brother', 'real brother', etc. are common in Indian English).

Urdu usage differs from Hindi in many respects. Note especially the following:

ख़ाविंद	for	पति	*husband*
बीवी/बीबी	for	पत्नी	*wife*
वालिद (साहब)	for	पिता (जी)	*father*
वालिदा (साहबा)	for	माता (जी)	*mother*
सुसर	for	ससुर	*father-in-law*

Lastly, note that great care must be taken with the use of the term साला *brother-in-law*, because this is very commonly used as a form of strong abuse in Hindi. (To refer to or address someone as साला is to imply that one has carnal knowledge of his sister.)

Appendix C Parts of the body, and health

These lists do not include words which have already occurred in the course.

1 Parts of the body

अँगूठा	*thumb* (m.)	कमर	*waist* (f.)
ओठ	*lip* (m.)	कोहनी	*elbow* (f.)

दाँत	*tooth* (m.)	नाखून	*nail* (m.)
नाक	*nose* (f.)	पाँव की उँगली	*toe* (f.)
ख़ून	*blood* (m.)	पीठ	*back* (f.)
गरदन	*neck* (f.)	पैर	*foot* (m.)
गला	*throat, neck* (m.)	फेफड़ा	*lung* (m.)
गाल	*cheek* (m.)	बाँह	*arm* (f.)
घुटना	*knee* (m.)	माथा	*forehead* (m.)
चमड़ी	*skin* (f.)	मुख	*mouth, face* (m.)
छाती	*chest* (f.)	शरीर	*body* (m.)
जीभ	*tongue* (f.)	हड्डी	*bone* (f.)
जोड़	*joint* (m.)		

2 Words relating to health and the body

इलाज	*treatment, cure, remedy* (m.)
उलटी	*vomiting* (f.)
उलटी करना	*to vomit*
कब्ज़	*constipation* (f.)
कमज़ोर	*weak*
कमज़ोरी	*weakness* (f.)
क़ै	*vomiting, nausea* (f.)
क़ै आना	*to feel nausea*
क़ै करना/होना	*to be sick, vomit*
गर्भ	*womb, pregnancy* (m.)
गर्भ होना	*to be pregnant*
खाँसी	*cough* (f.)
गला बैठना	*to have a hoarse voice*
टट्टी	*faeces, stool* (f.)
टट्टी करना	*to pass faeces*
तंदुरुस्त	*healthy, fit*
तंदुरुस्ती	*health* (f.)
दर्द करना	*to hurt*
दस्त	*diarrhoea* (m.)
दस्त आना	*to have diarrhoea*
नाक बहना	*to have a runny nose* (*the nose to run*)
पचाना	*to digest*
पट्टी	*bandage* (f.)
पट्टी बाँधना	*to apply a bandage*
पेशाब	*urine* (m.)
पेशाब करना	*to pass urine*
मरीज़	*patient* (m.) / (f.)
मूर्च्छा	*fainting* (f.)
रोग	*illness* (m.)
रोगी	*patient* (m.) / (f.)
सुई	*injection, needle* (f.)
सुई लगाना	*to give an injection*
सेहत	*health* (f.)

स्वस्थ	*healthy, fit*
स्वास्थ्य	*health* (m.)

मुझे दस्त आते हैं।	*I have got diarrhoea.*
मुझे दस्त लग गए हैं।	*I am suffering from diarrhoea.*
वह क़ै कर रहा है/उसे क़ै हो रही है।	*He is vomiting.*
मुझे सोमवार से सख़्त कब्ज़ है।	*I have had severe constipation since Monday.*
मेरी पत्नी को गर्भ है और उसे क़ै आ रही है।	*My wife is pregnant and is feeling nauseous.*
मुझे खाँसी (आती) है।	*I have a cough.*
उसका गोलियों और दवा से इलाज किया गया।	*He was treated with tablets and medicine.*
रवि का गला ख़राब है/बैठ गया है।	*Ravi has a sore throat / has gone hoarse.*
कल तक तुम्हारी हालत कुछ बेहतर हो जाएगी।	*Your condition will improve somewhat by tomorrow.*
आपको अस्पताल में इलाज कराना चाहिए।	*You should get treated in hospital.*
मेरे सिर में तेज़/हलका दर्द है।	*I have a bad / slight headache.*
मेरे जोड़ दुख रहे हैं।	*My joints are aching.*
वह तीन दिन तक बिस्तर से उठ नहीं पाई।	*She could not get up from her bed for three days.*
उबला पानी ही पीना—उसे १० मिनट तक उबाल लेना।	*Drink only boiled water: boil it for 10 minutes.*
गरमी के कारण उसे मूर्च्छा आ गई।	*He fainted because of the heat.*
पेशाब-घर/शौचालय किधर है?	*Where is the urinal / lavatory?*

Appendix D Letter-writing

As already seen (e.g. in Unit 10), informal letters begin simply प्रिय X, *Dear X,* and end आपका/की Y, *Yours Y*. This usage is appropriate throughout a wide range of contexts, with जी added to the name of the person addressed if necessary: प्रिय रमेश जी. Relationship terms may also be expressed here: प्रिय भाई विनोद, or simply भाई विनोद (even when addressing a close friend rather than an actual brother). Letters to older relatives, and to other people of relatively high status, are likely to replace प्रिय with a term such as पूज्य or आदरणीय *revered*: पूज्य पिता जी, etc.

A formal or official letter may begin प्रिय महोदय *Dear Sir*, or प्रिय महोदया *Dear Madam*, and may end भवदीय *Yours sincerely* (भवदीया for a female signatory). Again, greater formality can be expressed by replacing प्रिय with a more deferential adjective: माननीय महोदय *Respected Sir*, श्रद्धेय महोदय *Revered Sir* (still equivalent, however, to 'Dear Sir' in English usage). Alternatively, such a letter may begin श्रीमान् जी *Dear Sir*, श्रीमान् संपादक जी *Dear Editor*, etc. The expression सेवा में *in service [of], for the attention [of]* often precedes the name and address of the addressee at the head of an official or business letter.

The actual text of a relatively formal letter is likely to begin with a traditional greeting such as सादर नमस्कार *Respectful greeting*, सादर प्रणाम *Respectful salutation* or सप्रेम नमस्कार *Affectionate greeting*. Expressions of well-wishing may use similarly formal language: आशा है कि आप सपरिवार सानंद/सकुशल हैं *I hope you and your family are well*. A letter written in the formal style may close with a formula such as योग्य सेवाओं से सूचित करें *Kindly inform [me] of any fitting service.*

Some further expressions are:

बंधुवर	*Dear brother* (Lit. *kinsman*; not restricted to actual relatives)
प्रियवर	*Dearest, Very dear* (not necessarily indicating **romantic** love)
आपका कृपापत्र मिला।	*I received your kind letter.*
आपका ४ जून का पत्र मिला।	*I received your letter of 4th June.*
आपका पत्र पढ़कर बहुत ख़ुशी हुई/आनंद हुआ।	*I was very pleased to read your letter.*
सादर जय श्री कृष्ण!	*Respectful greeting*! (Lit. *victory to Lord Krishna*: many names of God are used in this way)
सेवा में निवेदन है कि...	*I humbly request that...*
प्रकाश की ओर से स्नेह।	*Prakash sends his love.*
शंकर की नमस्ते।	*Shankar sends his greetings.*
सब की नमस्ते।	*Greetings from everyone.*
रघु से मेरी नमस्ते कहना न भूलें।	*Don't forget to give my greetings to Raghu.*
चिरंजीव बच्चों को प्यार।	*Love to the 'long-lived' children.* (चिरंजीव, or its abbreviation चि॰ is a kind of blessing here)

आपका शुभाकांक्षी/हितैषी/हितू	*Your well-wisher*
दीवाली की शुभकामनाएँ।	*Best wishes for Diwali.*
पत्र का उत्तर शीघ्र दें तो आभारी रहूँगा।	*I would be grateful if you would reply promptly.*
शेष सब कुशल है।	*Everything else is all right.* (Used at close of letter)
पुनश्च	*P.S.* (postscript)
ह०(=हस्ताक्षर, usually used in plural)	*signature, signed*

Appendix E Intransitive, transitive and causative verbs

1 Some pairs of related verbs such as बनना/बनाना have already been encountered, in which the stem of the intransitive verb (बन-) is extended to from a transitive (बना-). A large numbers of verbs form pairs of this kind:

Intransitive		**Transitive**	
उठना	*to rise, get up*	उठाना	*to raise, lift up, pick up*
चलना	*to move*	चलाना	*to drive, run, manage*
जलना	*to burn*	जलाना	*to burn, set alight*
पहुँचना	*to arrive, reach*	पहुँचाना	*to make reach, deliver, convey*
बचना	*to escape, be saved*	बचाना	*to rescue, save*
समझना	*to understand, realise*	समझाना	*to explain, console*

2 In a second category of verbs, transitives are formed by the lengthening of the *non*-final syllable:

Intransitive		**Transitive**	
उतरना	*to get down, come down, alight*	उतारना	*to take down, take off (clothes)*
कटना	*to be cut*	काटना	*to cut*
छपना	*to be printed*	छापना	*to print*
निकलना	*to emerge, come/go out*	निकालना	*to take out, eject, dismiss*
बँटना	*to be distributed*	बाँटना	*to distribute*
मरना	*to die*	मारना	*to beat, kill*

3 In some verbs, the lengthening of the non-final stem syllable is accompanied by a shortening of the initial syllable: घूमना/घुमाना. In this process ए or ऐ becomes इ (बैठना/बिठाना) and ओ becomes उ (बोलना/बुलाना). A semi-vowel, usually ल, is added to a stem ending in a long vowel: रोना/रुलाना.

Intransitive		**Transitive**	
खेलना	*to play*	खिलाना[1]	*to make play*
घूमना	*to wander, stroll, tour*	घुमाना	*to revolve; to take round*
बैठना	*to sit*	बिठाना[2]	*to make sit, give a seat to*
रोना	*to cry*	रुलाना	*to make cry*
लेटना	*to lie down*	लिटाना[3]	*to make lie down*
सोना	*to sleep*	सुलाना	*to make/put to sleep*

4 Intransitive/transitive pairs are similarly encountered in verbs of the type खुलना/खोलना; in some pairs (such as छूटना/छोड़ना) the vowel change is accompanied by a change in consonant(s) also.

Intransitive		**Transitive**	
टूटना	*to be broken*	तोड़ना	*to break*
दिखना/दीखना	*to be seen, be visible*	देखना	*to see*
धुलना	*to be washed*	धोना	*to wash*
फटना	*to be torn, split*	फाड़ना	*to tear, split*
फिरना	*to turn, wander, undergo a change*	फेरना	*to turn, return, refund*
बिकना	*to be sold*	बेचना	*to sell*

5 Lengthening of the stem also occurs in the second of two related verbs where *both* are transitive, but where the two have different (though related) meanings: सीखना *to learn,* सिखाना *to teach.*

Transitive 1		**Transitive 2**	
खाना	*to eat*	खिलाना	*to give to eat, feed*
छोड़ना	*to leave, abandon*	छुड़ाना	*to get freed*

[1] Note that a verb खिलाना is also formed from खाना *to eat* (having the sense 'to give to eat, feed': see below); and खिलाना also exists as a transitive from खिलना *to blossom* (having the sense 'to make blossom').

[2] Also बैठाना.

[3] Also लेटाना.

देखना	*to see*	दिखाना	*to show*
देना	*to give*	दिलाना	*to cause to be given*
बोलना	*to speak*	बुलाना	*to call*
सुनना	*to listen, hear*	सुनाना	*to cause to hear, recite, relate*

Some groups of related verbs include all three of the types described above: an intransitive, plus two successive transitives.

टूटना	*to be broken*	तोड़ना	*to break*	तुड़ाना	*to have broken*
दिखना	*to be seen*	देखना	*to see*	दिखाना	*to show*

6 Verbs having a stem ending in -वा- are called 'causatives' because they express a sense of 'causing to be done'; the agent or 'doer' takes the postposition से. Thus बनवाना *to cause to be made, get made:* उसने मकान को अपने आप नहीं बनाया, मज़दूरों से बनवाया था *He didn't build the house himself, he had it built by labourers.*

Similarly:

करवाना	*to cause to be done, to have done*
तुड़वाना	*to cause to be broken, to have broken*
दिखवाना	*to cause to be shown, to have shown*
बिछवाना	*to cause to be spread, to have spread*
लिखवाना	*to cause to be written, to have written*
सिखवाना	*to cause to be taught, to have taught*
सिलवाना	*to cause to be sewn, to have sewn*

In the typical causative sentence, the purpose of the causative is not primarily to identify the agent of the action, but merely to demonstrate that some other agent was involved, i.e. that the action was not carried out by the subject himself: उसने अपने लिए नया मकान बनवाया *He had a new house built for himself.*

Appendix F The Hindi verb: summary of tenses and constructions

Imperfective	**Perfective**	**Continuous**
बोलता	**बोला**	**बोल रहा**
speaks	*spoke*	*speaking*
	वह बोला	
	he spoke **(47)**	

वह बोलता है	**वह बोला है**	**वह बोल रहा है**
he speaks **(23)**[1]	*he has spoken* **(47)**	*he is speaking* **(33)**
वह बोलता था	**वह बोला था**	**वह बोल रहा था**
he used to speak **(28)**	*he had spoken* **(47)**	*he was speaking* **(33)**
वह बोलता होगा	**वह बोला होगा**	**वह बोल रहा होगा**
he will/must speak **(38)**	*he will/must have spoken* **(38)**	*he will/must be speaking* **(38)**
वह बोलता हो	**वह बोला हो**	**वह बोल रहा हो**
he may speak, be speaking	*he may have spoken* **(47)**	*he may be speaking* **(42)**

वह बोलेगा	*he will speak* **(38)**
वह बोले	*he may speak* **(42)**
यह बोला जाता है	*it is spoken* **(61)**
वह बोलता जाता है	*he goes on speaking* **(67)**
वह बोलता रहता है	*he keeps speaking* **(67)**
वह बोला करता है	*he speaks* (habitually) **(68)**
उसे बोलना चाहिए	*he should speak* **(55)**
उसे बोलना है	*he has to speak* **(56)**
उसे बोलना पड़ता है	*he has to speak* (habitually) **(56)**
अगर वह बोले(गा)	*if he speaks* **(44)**
अगर वह बोला	*if he spoke, speaks* **(82)**
अगर वह बोलता	*if he spoke, had spoken* **(82)**
अगर वह बोला होता	*if he had spoken* **(82)**
अगर वह बोलता होता	*if he had been speaking*
वह बोल सकता है	*he can speak* **(51)**
वह बोल चुका है	*he has already spoken* **(51)**
वह बोलने लगता है	*he begins to speak* **(62)**
उसे बोलने दो	*let him speak* **(63)**
वह बोलना चाहता है	*he wants to speak* **(43)**
बोलकर	*having spoken* **(48)**
बोल, बोलो, बोलिए, बोलिएगा	*speak* (imperative) **(18)**

[1] Numbers in brackets refer to the relevant paragraphs in the course.

Key to Exercises

1.1

साफ़ क़मीज़ें sāf qamīzẽ	बड़े आदमी baṛe ādmī	हिन्दुस्तानी धोबी hindustānī dhobī
अँग्रेज़ लड़कियाँ ā̃grez laṛkiyā̃	माताएँ mātāẽ	हिन्दू राजा hindū rājā
सफ़ेद मेज़ें safed mezẽ	छोटी शक्तियाँ choṭī śaktiyā̃	छोटे लड़के choṭe laṛke
सफ़ेद कुरसियाँ safed kursiyā̃	गुजराती बहुएँ gujarātī bahuẽ	वे मकान ve makān
ये बड़े कमरे ye baṛe kamre	वे छोटी बेटियाँ ve choṭī beṭiyā̃	ये बुढ़ियाँ ye buṛhiyā̃

1.2 1 This room is large, those rooms are small. 2 Those tables are not small. 3 Is this girl little? 4 Those girls are Gujarati. 5 This is a small table. 6 These small tables are not clean, they are dirty. 7 Those men are Indian? 8 Those old women are Hindus. 9 These are big houses, but that is not large. 10 Is that house large? 11 The white shirts are not clean. 12 Are you not the washerman? 13 Are those people Pakistani? 14 There are only two tables here.

1.3

१	क्या वे लोग गुजराती हैं?	kyā ve log gujarātī haĩ?
२	वे सफ़ेद कुरसियाँ बड़ी नहीं, छोटी हैं।	ve safed kursiyā̃ baṛī nahī̃, choṭī haĩ.
३	तू छोटी लड़की है।	tū choṭī laṛkī hai.
४	ये साफ़ कमीज़ें हैं।	ye sāf qamīzẽ haĩ.
५	वे क़मीज़ें साफ़ नहीं हैं।	ve qamīzẽ sāf nahī̃ haĩ.
६	यह मेज़ बड़ी है, लेकिन वे मेज़ें छोटी हैं।	yah mez baṛī hai, lekin ve mezẽ choṭī haĩ.
७	क्या यह मकान बड़ा है? जी नहीं, लेकिन वे मकान बड़े हैं।	kyā yah makān baṛā hai? jī nahī̃, lekin ve makān baṛe haĩ.
८	नमस्ते। मैं अँग्रेज़ हूँ। क्या आप भारतीय हैं?	namaste. maĩ ā̃grez hū̃. kyā āp bhāratīy haĩ?

९	क्या वे चार आदमी राजा हैं?	kyā ve cār ādmī rājā haĩ?
१०	चाचा जी यहाँ हैं। वे हिन्दू नहीं हैं।	cācā jī yahā̃ haĩ. ve hindū nahī̃ haĩ.

2.1 1 These Hindi books are not very expensive. 2 We are all very happy. 3 You are fat, but sister is not fat. 4 (Friend), how are you? 5 Gopal and Mrs. Sharma are not here today. 6 Today the children too are ill. It's a pity. 7 Those shoes and sandals are very cheap. 8 Who is that tall boy? Is he a student? 9 Ravi and Uma are both well but mother is not well. 10 Are Ahmed Sahib and Mr. Varma both Muslims?

2.2

१	वे बूढ़े आदमी कौन हैं? क्या वे हिन्दुस्तानी हैं?	ve būṛhe ādmī kaun haĩ? kyā ve hindustānī haĩ?
२	जी नहीं, वे हिन्दुस्तानी नहीं, अँग्रेज़ हैं।	jī nahī̃, ve hindustānī nahī̃, ãgrez haĩ.
३	क्या वर्मा जी बड़े आदमी हैं? जी हाँ, वे बहुत बड़े आदमी हैं।	kyā Varmājī baṛe ādmī haĩ? jī hā̃, ve bahut baṛe ādmī haĩ.
४	पिताजी कैसे हैं? मेहरबानी है, वे अच्छे हैं।	pitājī kaise haĩ? meharbānī hai, ve acche haĩ.
५	राम और राधा दोनों बहुत लंबे हैं। हाँ, और राम मोटा भी है।	Rām aur Rādhā donõ bahut lambe haĩ. hā̃, aur Rām moṭā bhī hai.
६	वे क्या हैं? वे महँगे क़लम और पेंसिलें हैं।	ve kyā haĩ? ve mahãge qalam aur pensilẽ haĩ.
७	तुम बुरे बच्चे नहीं हो। तुम अच्छे बेटे हो।	tum bure bacce nahī̃ ho. tum acche beṭe ho.
८	वह कैसी मेज़ है? वह लंबी और काली है।	vah kaisī mez hai? vah lambī aur kālī hai.
९	वह बड़ी किताब कैसी है? वह बहुत अच्छी है।	vah baṛī kitāb kaisī hai? vah bahut acchī hai.
१०	क्या आप सब लोग हिन्दू हैं? जी नहीं, हम लोग हिन्दू हैं, लेकिन वे लोग मुसलमान हैं।	kyā āp sab log hindū haĩ? jī nahī̃, ham log hindū haĩ, lekin ve log musalmān haĩ.

3.1

बड़े कमरों में	साफ़ मेज़ों पर	मोटे आदमियों से
baṛe kamrõ mẽ	sāf mezõ par	moṭe ādmiyõ se
छोटे मकानों में	इस नए पलंग पर	नीली पेंसिल से
choṭe makāõ mẽ	is nae palang par	nīlī pensil se

हरी किताब में	लाल कुरसी पर	लंबी लड़कियों से
harī kitāb mẽ	lāl kursī par	lambī laṛkiyõ se
सस्ते होटल में	दूसरी खिड़कियों पर	उस क़लम से
saste hoṭal mẽ	dūsrī khiṛkiyõ par	us qalam se
पुरानी अलमारियों में	इन परदों पर	उन बसों से
purānī almāriyõ mẽ	in pardõ par	un basõ se

3.2 This is a new house. In this house there are seven rooms. From amongst these rooms one is a very large room, the other rooms are small. In the large room the walls are white and very clean. In one wall there are two windows and on them are green curtains. On one other wall there are three beautiful pictures. In the room there are three tables, one large and two small. There are also two cupboards and several chairs. On the large table there are a black pen and two pencils. In the small rooms too there are some tables and chairs, but up to now there are not curtains on the windows. Where are the new curtains? They are still here in this large cupboard.

3.3

१	उन पलंगों पर साफ़ चादरें और भारी कंबल हैं।	un palaṅgõ par sāf cādarẽ aur bhārī kambal haĩ.
२	इन बड़ी अलमारियों में कई पुरानी किताबें हैं।	in baṛī almāriyõ mẽ kaī purānī kitābẽ haĩ.
३	उन छोटे होटलों में सब कमरे सस्ते हैं।	un choṭe hoṭalõ mẽ sab kamre saste haĩ.
४	दूसरी दीवारों पर कई सुन्दर तस्वीरें हैं।	dūsrī dīvārõ par kaī sundar tasvīrẽ haĩ.
५	उस कमरे में खिड़कियों पर परदे नहीं हैं।	us kamre mẽ khiṛkiyõ par parde nahī̃ haĩ.
६	उस मेज़ पर कैसा पंखा है?	us mez par kaisā paṅkhā hai?
७	इस मकान में कितने लोग हैं?	is makān mẽ kitne log haĩ?
८	दिल्ली बंबई से सचमुच काफ़ी दूर है।	dillī bambaī se sacmuc kāfī dūr hai.
९	रसोईघर में कितनी कुरसियाँ हैं?	rasoīghar mẽ kitnī kursiyā̃ haĩ?
१०	लंबी मेज़ पर कुछ नए अख़बार और किताबें हैं।	lambī mez par kuch nae akhbār aur kitābẽ haĩ.

4.1 I like these new houses very much. On this street there are four new houses, and from amongst these this red house is the smallest. This red colour is very nice, and the children like it very much. Who does not like red? I do not know how many rooms there are in the other houses, but in this there are six. These are all pretty large. There is a beautiful garden too. The old house was much larger than this house, but I didn't like it because all the rooms in it were very small. How many people there are in the other new houses, this I don't know. In this house we are four people, and we are all very happy.

4.2 १ क्या आपको मालूम है कि पिताजी कल कहाँ थे? २ उसको अफ़सोस था कि मुझको ज़ुकाम और बुख़ार था। ३ हमको ख़ुशी है कि आपको लंदन पसंद है। ४ राम विनोद से लंबा है पर विमल सबसे लंबा है। ५ क्या नया मकान पुराने मकान से बड़ा है? जी हाँ, पर पुराना मकान ज़्यादा सुंदर था। ६ इन किताबों में से आपको कौनसी पसंद है? ७ किसको मालूम है कि बंबई कहाँ है? ८ बच्चों को नया बाग़ कम पसंद था। ९ क्या उनको मालूम था कि गाँव में दुकानें नहीं थीं? १० दिल्ली में ज़िन्दगी मुश्किल थी पर ज़्यादा दिलचस्प।

5.1

आना	आइए	आओ
करना	कीजिए	करो
कहना	कहिए	कहो
खाना	खाइए	खाओ
चलना	चलिए	चलो
जाना	जाइए	जाओ
देखना	देखिए	देखो
देना	दीजिए	दो
पढ़ना	पढ़िए	पढ़ो
पीना	पीजिए	पिओ
पूछना	पूछिए	पूछो
बताना	बताइए	बताओ
बुलाना	बुलाइए	बुलाओ
बैठना	बैठिए	बैठो
मारना	मारिए	मारो
लाना	लाइए	लाओ
लिखना	लिखिए	लिखो
लेना	लीजिए	लो
सुनना	सुनिए	सुनो

5.2 1 (Please) give this letter to Ram's brother. 2 Don't write in Sanjay's book. 3 Clean these rooms. 4 Don't go into the boys' room. 5 Tell me that man's name. 6 We are pleased that you are here. 7 Ram's keys are on that large table. 8 What is in the girl's pocket? 9 Please do not smoke. 10 Read this newspaper but don't show it to Mother.

5.3 १ उसे मत छुओ, उसे मुझे दो। २ विनोद को बुलाइए और विमल को भी लाइए। ३ ज़रा यहाँ बैठिए। ४ मुझको बताइए कि पिताजी कहाँ हैं। ५ देखो, यह प्याला साफ़ नहीं है, इसे लो और मुझे एक दूसरा दो। ६ मुझे मालूम नहीं कि अभी राम के कमरे में कौन है। ७ इस आदमी की क़मीज़ उस कुरसी पर है। ८ राम के पिताजी को जुकाम है। ९ पिताजी से नमस्ते कहिए। १० अरे बेटे वह दरवाज़ा बन्द कर!

6.1 This is my house. I live here with some of my friends. Opposite my house is my younger brother's house. My mother doesn't live with us now, she lives in another house. Her new house is much smaller than this house. Nowadays houses are very expensive, so more people live in small houses. My mother's health isn't good, so her neighbours cook and bring things from the shops for her. She only makes tea for herself. Sometimes my elder brother's letters come from London, and Mother asks me about England. Mother doesn't speak English, she only speaks Urdu and Hindi.

6.2 १ वे औरतें यहाँ नहीं रहतीं, मालूम होता है कि उनका मकान उधर है। २ उनका कमरा हमारे कमरे के नीचे है, रसोईघर के सामने। ३ वह अपने लिए किताब लाता है, लेकिन अपने दोस्त के लिए कुछ नहीं लाता। ४ हम हमेशा वहाँ लड़कियों के साथ जाते हैं, पर लड़के घर पर रहते हैं। ५ मुझे मालूम नहीं कि राजू क्या करता है, वह कहाँ रहता है? ६ मुझे खुशी है कि तुम भी स्कूल जाते हो। ७ हम अपने बारे में कुछ नहीं कहते। क्या वे हमारे बारे में कुछ कहते हैं? ८ वह अपने मकान में नहीं रहती, अपनी बहिन के मकान में रहती है। ९ कल हमारे यहाँ आइए, और अपने बच्चों को भी लाइए। १० क्या उसे मालूम नहीं कि हफ़्ते में सिर्फ़ सात दिन होते हैं?

7.1 *At the fruit shop.* 1 Come sir, which fruit do you want? 2 I want some mangoes – do you have some ripe mangoes? 3 Yes, of course. These mangoes are Bombay ones – look, they're both big and sweet! 4 Good, give [me] two kilos. Give [me] ten fresh oranges too. 5 Do you want anything else? Do you like apples? 6 Yes, I need some apples too. Which are the best? 7 These Kashmiri apples are very good, please take these. 8 All right. But look, that apple is unripe. Give me some other one.

7.2 1 Some people used to study Bengali and some people used to study Oriya. 2 Several ladies used to come here on Wednesday evenings. 3 Father used not to eat anything in the morning. 4 There was nobody in the room, but someone was standing in the garden. 5 Somebody's keys were lying on top of the table. 6 Don't say anything to anyone about this matter! 7 Does your brother know English? 8 I used to finish my work in the evening. 9 Nobody knew where the old temple was. 10 It seems that he always used to come by bus.

7.3 १ हम भारत में अपने पिताजी के साथ रहते थे। २ कोई न कोई बाज़ार से खाना लाता

था। ३ हमें कुछ पक्के संतरे चाहिए। ४ आपको कितनी भाषाएँ आती हैं? ५ वह अक्सर यहाँ गुरुवार की सुबह आती थी। ६ किसी को मालूम नहीं था कि वह कहाँ सोता था। ७ छुट्टियाँ अगस्त के तीसरे हफ़्ते में शुरू होती हैं। ८ मैं रात को दरवाज़ा बन्द करता था। ९ मुझे कोई सात नई किताबें चाहिएँ। १० हफ़्ते के पहले और पाँचवें दिनों के दो दो नाम हैं।

8.1 My name is Ganesh, and I live with my brother Mahesh in a small village. There is no big shop in the village, so every week we go to the town and buy some necessary things from the market. We don't have a car, and the town is quite far from the village, so we usually go to town by bus. I work in a big factory near the village, and my younger brother works there too. He has three children. They all go to school and this year they are studying Hindi. Yesterday Mahesh was saying that the children like the school very much, and they have several friends there. Last year they only went to school in the morning, and after school they used to play in the garden, but now they stay at school all day and they study very hard.

Today is Saturday. Nobody works on Saturday, and the children don't go to school, so we are all going to town. Some friends of ours are coming with us. They have a car, so today we're not going by bus. Sometimes the bus comes late; the driver has only one eye and he doesn't drive the bus well, so it's a good thing that our friends are bringing their car! It seems that they are quite well off. They have two houses–one here, opposite our house, and another in some good district of Bombay. They have their own factory too! Previously they used to live in Bombay but now they prefer village life. Their son used to work in the films in Bombay; now he writes children's stories for the newspapers. Next year he is going to London with his wife.

8.2 १ हम कल शाम को गाड़ी से शहर जा रहे हैं। २ पहले लन्दन में उसका एक बड़ा मकान था। ३ मेरे भाई के चार बच्चे हैं, और सबसे बड़ा बच्चा मेरे बेटे के साथ स्कूल जाता है। ४ पिछले महीने मैं उर्दू पढ़ रहा था पर इस महीने मैं हिंदी पढ़ रहा हूँ। ५ आपके मित्र किस समय आ रहे हैं? ६ ट्रेन धीरे धीरे चलती है और देर से पहुँचती है। ७ मैं कह रहा था कि मुझे यह खाना पसंद नहीं। ८ आप कितनी भाषाएँ अच्छी तरह से बोलते हैं? ९ मेरी बहिनें आम तौर पर बस से नहीं जातीं, ट्रेन से जाती हैं। १० मेरे सिर में दर्द है और मेरी माताजी को जुकाम है, इसलिए आज हम बाज़ार नहीं जा रहे हैं।

9.1 The day after tomorrow I am going to Delhi to learn Hindi. I shall stay there at least two months and I hope that after studying very hard I shall learn Hindi quite well. The sister of a friend of mine works in Delhi and it is with her that I shall stay. Her house is quite far from the college but the station is just nearby and so I shall go to college by train every day. It seems that a lot of students live in that district. They must go to college by train in the same way, and I shall go with them because Father says that it wouldn't be right for me to go alone. I don't agree with what he says, but I don't say anything because it would not be proper to speak like that in front of one's elders. My friend says that these days in India, especially in the big cities, the prices of things are very high and I'll need quite a lot of money.

The plane leaves here in the morning and will reach Delhi by night. My friend's sister will come to the airport to meet me. I don't know her so I don't know how I'll recognise her. Perhaps she will recognise me, because she's got an old picture of me. She has two boys, and they will be coming to the airport with her. The elder boy works in some factory. The younger boy is still at school, but on finishing his studies he will start to work in that same factory too. My sister says that they also have another house in some small village. They take a trip there on Sundays and in the school holidays, and I shall go with them too. This will be very good because I am very fond of village life and another thing is that the village people will only know Hindi so I will gain a lot by talking with them.

9.2 हम कल दिल्ली अपने दोस्तों से मिलने जाएँगे। हमारे पास गाड़ी नहीं है, इसलिए हम रेलगाड़ी से जाएँगे। शायद हमारे दोस्त हम से स्टेशन पर मिलने आएँगे, क्योंकि वे पास ही रहते हैं। उनसे मिलने के बाद हम किसी होटल में खाना खाने जाएँगे, और फिर तीसरे पहर हम उनके यहाँ जाएँगे। मुझे होटलों में खाना खाना पसंद नहीं, लेकिन बच्चों को बहुत पसंद है। हमारे दोस्तों के दो लड़के हैं, और हमारे बच्चे शाम तक उनके साथ बड़ी ख़ुशी से खेलेंगे। उनका मकान बहुत ही सुंदर है, और पास ही एक बहुत बड़ा बाग़ है। वह बहुत ही शान्त जगह है और बच्चों को वहाँ पर घूमना पसंद है। गरमियों में काफ़ी लोग वहाँ जाते हैं, पर जाड़ों में कोई नहीं जाता। कल हमें अपने कोटों की ज़रूरत नहीं होगी, क्योंकि कहते हैं कि पानी नहीं पड़ेगा। हमें आशा है कि उनका कहना ग़लत नहीं होगा!

10.1 Kanpur, 12th August 1987. Dear Sunil, I am very pleased that you are coming here to celebrate Diwali. If you're not in a hurry to return home then you should stay with us for at least ten days. At the moment we're pretty busy completing the preparations for Diwali. My elder brother Ravi won't be here on the day of Diwali, he's about to go to London for a few days. If it's possible for him he will phone us from London to wish us a happy Diwali. You may not know that negotiations about Ravi's marriage are going on. The bride's family is very wealthy–it will be a very good thing if the negotiations are confirmed. Actually Ravi has known the girl for several years, she's the sister of a friend of his. Grandmother says that in the olden days only the community elders used to choose the girl, and this practice still carries on in the villages; but town families do things rather differently. Ravi would be astonished if anyone were to say to him that the right of choosing a girl was up to the elders alone!

If possible, bring your family with you to celebrate Diwali. There's enough space in the house, and Mother says your coming won't be at all inconvenient for her. If you catch the Varanasi train from Delhi you'll get to Kanpur in just a few hours. If you phone me on reaching the station, I'll come straightaway to meet you. If the weather's good around Diwali we might go for a trip somewhere for a few days. The city isn't actually all that interesting, but many places in its vicinity are worth seeing. Well, I'll finish this letter. Give my greetings to your parents, and love to the children. Answer the letter soon! Yours, Ramesh.

10.2 १ अगर तुम ध्यान से नहीं पढ़ोगे, तो परीक्षा कैसे दोगे ? २ मैं चाहता हूँ कि वह यहाँ रहे, पर वह तो घर जाना चाहती है। ३ शायद वह इसके बारे में जानता हो। ४ संभव है कि वह फ़ोन करे, इसलिए आप अभी बाहर न जाएँ। ५ यदि मेरे पास समय होगा तो मैं इस पुस्तक को भी पढ़ूँगा। ६ असुविधा न हो तो हम सामनेवाले होटल में मिलें। ७ अगर आप देखें तो सारे अख़बारों में विज्ञापन पाएँगे। ८ आप उसे तुरंत फ़ोन करें, नहीं तो वह दूसरों के साथ बाज़ार जाए। ९ यदि आप चाहें तो आप शादीवाले मामले में मेरे माता-पिता की सलाह लें। १० मैं तो आज रात को नीचेवाले कमरे में रहूँगा।

11.1 15th December, 1987. Dear Rafiq, I hope you are all well. You have not written any letter since last year, and I too am writing this letter only after a vey long delay. Previously you used to know only Urdu, but Father told me that you will have learnt Hindi by now too, so I am writing this letter in Hindi.

Here the news is that I gave up my old job in July. Now, I have started to work in the office of a newspaper in the town. In the beginning I used only to prepare advertisements and so on, but last month I also began to write the news and from now on I shall do even more interesting work. The pay is not so good, but I think working here will be very advantageous for me. In my childhood days my grandfather always used to say, 'If you want to learn something about life when you grow up, you should go and work in some newspaper office.' Now I have found that what grandfather said has turned out completely right. Every week some or other special news comes. Actually, even ordinary news is special for some reader or other–if someone's marriage negotiations are going on, then he will like to read about marriage and wedding matters; for travellers, travel stories are interesting; and students will like to read some suggestions about the preparations for their exams. So the newspaper work is very interesting, and I am very happy working here.

The place here is very beautiful too. After doing a difficult job from half past eight in the morning until a quarter past six in the evening, I like to stroll in the garden. It's not so cold, even in the winter. If you're free in January you should come here with your family for three or four days. I'm sorry that in the coming holidays it won't be possible for me to meet you, because at that time I shall be working in the office. Write back soon! With best wishes, Your friend, Ashok.

11.2 प्रिय रवि, मुझे आशा है कि आप अच्छे हैं। आप छुट्टियों से घर लौटे होंगे, और अपनी नई नौकरी के लिए तैयारियाँ कर रहे होंगे। मैं यह पत्र मद्रास से लिख रहा हूँ। कुछ दिन दिल्ली में ठहकर मैं यहाँ कल रात को पहुँचा। पिताजी ने मुझे लन्दन से पत्र लिखा था, मुझे यह बताने के लिए कि हमारे कुछ दोस्त उस समय दिल्ली में होंगे। इसीलिए में दिल्ली होकर ही मद्रास आया। गाड़ी सुबह के छह

बजे पहुँची, और मैं होटल साढ़े छह तक पहुँचा। कुछ खाना खाने के बाद मैं बाहर शहर देखने गया, और मैंने देखा कि उस समय बहुत-से लोग काम पर जा रहे थे या ढाबों में खा पी[1] रहे थे। मैंने बच्चों के लिए कुछ चीज़ें ख़रीदीं, कुछ फ़ोटो खींचे और फिर बाज़ार में सैर करके होटल को लौटा। अब मैं क़रीब दो या ढाई बजे तक सोऊँगा, फिर एक दोस्त के यहाँ जाऊँगा क्योंकि उसने अभी फ़ोन करके मुझे खाने के लिए बुलाया है। कुछ दिनों के बाद मैं एक और पत्र लिखूँगा। आपका, राम.

[1]खा पी रहे थे - i.e. खा रहे थे और पी रहे थे।

12.1 *The guard's story*. You will be amazed to hear what a passenger did in my train yesterday. It was the Delhi train, which leaves Calcutta at half past seven in the evening and reaches Delhi in the morning. It is quite a long journey, but to travel by air has become so expensive that most people prefer to travel by train. Only people who have a lot of money, or whose company gives them travelling expenses, can travel by air. Anyway, yesterday as always the train was very crowded. Those people who had arrived early had already loaded their luggage, etc. onto the train and had sat down comfortably, and were watching the station scene. Those who had their families with them were seating them on seats or on boxes or even on the floor. Some travellers had even gone to sleep. Most people had brought food for themselves too. Those who had eaten had gone to sleep, or were getting ready to sleep.

At about seven o'clock I saw that one man whom I have seen perhaps two or three times on this same train got into a compartment and sat down. He must be one of those businessmen who go to Delhi or Bombay every month. But this time his family was with him too. At about midnight this man called me and said that a box of his which he had put on the rack had gone missing. Actually I always say to the passengers that when they go to sleep they should not leave their valuable things on the rack, but they are so careless that–just don't ask! Sometimes they even forget that they even have luggage with them–they get off the train and set off home very happily, or go off to drink tea, and all the luggage is left right there in the compartment. Anyway, the box this man had left on the rack had gone missing, so he'd become very upset. I was just talking to him when suddenly he discovered that the box he was looking for was lying right there in front of him! His son was sitting on top of the box. So I really realised what fools there are in this world. Only those like me who have worked on the railway can understand how difficult a guard's life is.

12.2 किसी ने मेरी घड़ी को ग़ायब कर दिया है। घड़ी तो इतनी क़ीमती नहीं थी, और मेरे पिताजी, जो अक्सर ऐसी बातों के बारे में बहुत सख़्त रहते हैं, यह कहते हैं कि मैं उसके बारे में फ़िक्र न करूँ। पर मैं चाहता हूँ कि जिसने उसे लिया, वह उसे अभी वापस कर दे। जो लोग यहाँ काम करते हैं, उनसे मैंने पूछ-ताछ कर ली है, पर वे कुछ भी नहीं जानते। आम तौर पर मैं घड़ी को अपने पास ही रखता हूँ, पर कल मैंने उसे मेज़ पर रख दिया था, यह सोचकर कि कुछ घंटों में उसको कुछ नहीं होगा। पर जिस छोटी मेज़ पर मैंने उसे रखा था, वह खिड़की के पास ही है। जिस किसी ने उसे ले लिया था उसने किसी चीज़

के ऊपर चढ़कर खिड़की को तोड़ दिया होगा। अब पुलिस को बुलाने में कोई फ़ायदा नहीं है, क्योंकि वह तो कुछ भी नहीं कर सकती।

13.1 *A train journey to Varanasi.* Last year I got the chance to go to Varanasi. It is the ambition of every Hindu to go to Varanasi and bathe in the Ganges. They say that he who passes away there on the banks of the Ganges attains salvation instantaneously. Gaining liberation from the turmoil of this world, he goes straight to heaven. Just now, I have no particular desire to obtain salvation, quite the reverse, I am very much enjoying myself in the turmoil of the world! But it struck me that before leaving India I should certainly see the oldest city in the world. Thinking that it would be very good to spend three or four days in Varanasi, I decided that I would go there the very next day. I went immediately to the station and bought a ticket for the next day.

The time for the train to leave came near. Climbing aboard the train, I put my luggage beneath the seat and sat down comfortably. It was twelve noon, and the sun was very hot, and I felt thirsty. I thought I'd have some tea. I very much like that sweet and strong tea which you can get from the tea-sellers at the station, so I called a tea-seller through the window and bought some. I also called the hawker and asked for two samosas. By the time I had eaten these samosas, quite a lot of people had already come into my compartment. People who hadn't been able to find a place to sit had to sit on top of their luggage. Some people even sat on the floor, so much so that even to come and go within the compartment had become quite difficult. Anyway, at exactly a quarter to one the whistle blew and the train set off.

Some time later the train came and stood at some little station. I was surprised to see that all around the station there was nothing but greenery to be seen, and just a little way off many cows were standing in the sun or roaming here and there. It seemed to me that to call this little place a 'town' would be wrong, but the elderly passenger sitting opposite me told me that there were many factories here in which all kinds of things were made. He also told me that he too used to work here some years ago. When I asked him why he had gone away and left such a peaceful place, he replied that his employment had come to an end and so he had had to sell his house.

I cannot say how long it took me to reach Varanasi, because I fell asleep in the meantime. I must have slept for at least four hours. By the time we arrived, the street lamps had already lit. I got out of the train and hired a porter. He picked up my luggage and began to run into the crowd, and disappeared from sight. Anxious, I ran after him. When I emerged from the crowd and reached the road, I found the porter standing there at the roadside. He was chatting with some friend.

The next moment a taxi-driver came up and said, 'Where do you want to go to, Sahib?' I told him that I had to go to such-and-such a hotel, how much would he take? He said he would go according to the meter, and asked me to get in and sit down. By the time I reached the hotel I was feeling a bit hungry. By chance, when I went into the hotel I happened to see a friend, who invited me to eat with him. As soon as we had finished eating I asked him what places I should see in Varanasi. He replied that it would take several weeks to see all the famous places there, but that I was certainly to see the ghats of the Ganges, and three or four principal temples.

13.2 कल मैं उस दुकान पर गया जिसमें कुरसियाँ और मेज़ें बनती हैं। मैंने मालिक से पूछा कि मेरी कुरसियाँ कब तैयार होंगी। उसने मुझसे कहा कि जो आदमी कुरसियाँ बनाता है, वह बीमार है, पर ज्योंही वह ठीक होगा त्योंही आपको कुरसियाँ मिल जाएँगी। मैंने कहा कि मेरे ख़्याल से तो उसको मुझे कुरसियाँ पिछले महीने दे देनी चाहिए थीं। अगर शुरू में ही उसे मालूम था कि यह काम पूरा करने में कितना समय लगेगा, तो उसे मुझे बता देना चाहिए था। वह यह तो नहीं चाहता था कि मैं किसी दूसरी दुकान पर जाऊँ, इसलिए वह कुछ नहीं बोला। पर वह जानता है कि जब तक मुझे कुरसियाँ नहीं मिलेंगी, तब तक मैं उसे पैसा नहीं दूँगा, इसलिए हम दोनों को आशा है कि कुरसी बनानेवाला जल्दी ही ठीक हो जाएगा ! तब तक तो हमें फ़र्श पर ही बैठना होगा। मुझे तो फ़र्श पर बैठना अच्छा लगता है, पर जब मेरे माता पिता हमसे मिलने आते हैं तो उनको मुश्किल होती है।

14.1 *A road accident.* One day it so happened that I was going from my house towards the post office. I had nothing in particular to do, I had just gone out for a walk with the idea of enjoying the sun a little. I am very fond of walking for a little while like this after breakfast. It was quite a nice day, and from the cool air I knew that the winter weather was on its way. Some children were playing at the side of the road. It seems that these days, just as many children play all day at the roadside, or wander in the bazaars, as go to school ! True, I used to do the same in my childhood, and when the weather was good I couldn't bear to sit in a dark room either. But in those days, we children played in the fields or in the garden, our parents never allowed us to play near the road. Today's children are left to play even on the roads, and every year thousands of children get hurt. Anyway, leave that, otherwise it will not be possible for me to complete my story.

As soon as I came close to the children who were playing at the roadside, a big black car came into view near the post office. The car was coming at speed towards us. When I saw it I straight away called out to the children to get out of the way, a car was coming. But the children were making a din even louder than my shouting, so my call went unheard. One of them threw a ball into the air. All the children ran to catch it, but somehow it got out of their hands and came onto the road. The car by this time had come really close, but the children were still not aware of it at all. Three children ran forwards towards the road. Seeing them, the car driver turned the car the other way so as not to hit the children. But what should happen at that moment but that a bicycle came out of a lane opposite and collided with the car. The driver braked hard and the car stopped. We all ran up. The bicycle had been badly crushed, but God knows how, the rider had escaped. Not a scratch! Having seen the driver's carelessness I couldn't contain myself, and I began hurling abuse at him. The police were called. By now, dozens of people were watching this spectacle. The police came and took the driver to the police station, and I set off home. Some days later I read in the paper that he had been given a jail sentence. In my view this was quite appropriate, because the villain should not have driven the car so fast!

14.2 पिछले साल मुझे पिताजी द्वारा भारत भेजा गया था ताकि मैं हिन्दी पढ़ूँ, जो पिताजी की मातृभाषा है। मेरे दोनों भाइयों को मेरे साथ नहीं जाने दिया गया, क्योंकि उन्हें तो लन्दन में ही स्कूल जाना था। लन्दन में तो मुझे हिन्दी बोलने का अधिक मौक़ा नहीं मिला था, पर भारत पहुँचकर मैं उसे काफ़ी आसानी से बोलने लगा। जिस शहर में मैं रहता था, वहाँ जितने हिन्दी बोलनेवाले लोग थे, उतने ही बंगला बोलनेवाले भी थे। मैं कालेज मैं तीन दोस्तों के साथ रहता था। हम चारों ने अपने अध्यापक से कहा कि हमें कुछ बंगला भी पढ़ाई जाए। पर उन्होंने कहा कि पहले मुझे तुम्हें हिन्दी पढ़ाने दो, उसके बाद तुम जितनी बंगला पढ़ना चाहोगे मैं उतनी तुम्हें पढ़ा दूँगा। जब मैं बंगला बोलनेवालों से मिलने लगा तो मैंने पाया कि बंगला इतनी आसान नहीं है जितनी हिन्दी। मुझे बताया गया है कि यह सच नहीं है, पर मुझे तो बंगला काफ़ी मुश्किल लगती है।

15.1 *In the zoo.* Some people are of the opinion that it is not right to shut up wild animals in cages. The poor animals must be very distressed, because they are not allowed to roam freely in the jungle. But in my opinion it is wrong to think like this. The animals I have seen in the zoo seem very content, as though they had nothing to worry about. After all, the animals which are reared in the zoo were mostly not born in the wild but rather were born there in the zoo itself. So they do not know that in some distant land there is a jungle in which animals like them are roaming freely. In the jungle, animals can very easily die through hunger or illness, or may themselves fall prey to other animals. But zoo animals get a good place to live, and very good food to eat. Even the very smallest animal can spend a life of ease in its own cage without fear. True, in the zoo big animals like the tiger do not get the fun of hunting in the open field, and it may also be true that the caged bird might be constantly dreaming of the open sky. But there are many species of wild animals which have been able to survive until today only because of the zoo. Take the example of the tiger itself. Some thirty or forty years ago there were so many tigers in the jungles of India that to see a tiger was an ordinary matter. Because of being hunted, their number has now become very small. So many tigers have been killed that today's hunters are allowed to hunt only with a camera, instead of a gun. In this way tigers are found very rarely in the jungle, and in saving this species the contribution of the zoo has been very important.

15.2 राम सफल व्यापारी है। जैसा कि मैंने कल अपने चचेरे भाई से कहा, राम जैसे लोग बहुत आराम से रह सकते हैं। जिन छोटी-मोटी मुश्किलों से मुझ जैसे ग़रीब लोग हमेशा डरते रहते हैं, उनके

बारे में उन्हें फ़िक्र नहीं करनी पड़ती। मैं तो दिन-ब-दिन काम करता रहता हूँ, पर मुझे मालूम है कि जब मैं अमीर व्यापारी बनने का सपना देखता हूँ तो मैं अपने को धोखा दे रहा हूँ। राम तो एक महल जैसे बड़े मकान में रहता है। मेरे लिए वैसा मकान ख़रीदना संभव नहीं है। मेरे मकान का किराया बढ़ता जाता है, तो मैं अपनी तनख़ाह में से पैसा कैसे बचाऊँ ? बिना पूंजी के, नया व्यापार शुरू करना असंभव है, और मैं अपने को सच्चे अर्थों में व्यापारी नहीं कह सकता। मेरी एक मामूली दुकान है जिस में मैं पाँच साल से काम कर रहा हूँ। पर मैं किसी से अपने जीवन के बारे में शिकायत कभी नहीं करता। मुझे आशा है कि किसी दिन मैं सफल हो जाऊँ, जिससे कि मुझे हर रोज़ इतनी मेहनत न करनी पड़े।

16.1 I am fed up with England's weather. It is the month of May; even so I see that outside it is raining heavily. People are running here and there in order to escape the rain. Everywhere black and coloured umbrellas are to be seen; in the sky there are dark black clouds, and from time to time the sound of thunder is heard. The sun is nowhere to be seen. Now I understand why the sun is worshipped in countries like India. The sun could scarcely be worshipped in England, because one rarely gets a chance to have a view of it!

A peculiarity of the weather here is that it keeps changing. One day you can sit very happily in the garden soaking up the sun, then the very next day it will be so cold that you will have to put on warm clothes and stay inside the house. If any window should be opened, it will seem as though snow were falling inside the room itself. Perhaps this is the reason why the weather is considered such an interesting subject in this country–if ever the weather is mentioned, the English will be ready to talk on this subject for ten or fifteen minutes! On the street or in the market, wherever it may be, when two people meet, then as well as greeting each other, they will not forget to say something about the weather too. The strange thing is that whether the weather is pleasant or bad, people usually have nothing but complaints about it.

16.2 कल मौसम इतना ख़राब था कि मुझे मकान के भीतर रहना पड़ा। मैंने एक कविता पढ़ने की कोशिश की, पर जल्दी ही उससे ऊब गया। मैं एक नई किताब की तलाश करने लगा, जिसे एक दोस्त ने मुझे मेरे जन्मदिन पर दिया था। मुझे याद थी कि मैंने उसे दो तीन दिन पहले मेज़ पर देखा था, और मेरी बहिन ने उसका ज़िक्र कल ही किया था। पर अब वह कहीं भी दिखाई नहीं दे रही थी। अचानक बाहर से कोई आवाज़ सुनाई पड़ी। फिर खिड़की को खोलकर मैंने देखा कि एक बड़ा बंदर गाड़ी के ऊपर बैठा था। ऐसा लगता था कि उसे यह मौसम पसंद था ! उसके हाथों में वही किताब थी, जिसकी मैं तलाश कर रहा था। किताब का विषय बंदर को बहुत दिलचस्प लगा होगा, क्योंकि वह वहाँ कम से कम दस मिनट तक उसे लेकर बैठा रहा। उसके बाद वह किताब से ऊब गया, या शायद वह आख़िर बारिश से ही तंग आ गया था। उसने किताब को ज़मीन पर गिरा दिया, और पड़ोसियों के मकान की तरफ़ भागने लगा।

17.1 *Mahatma Surdas*. Although many Hindi poets have described Lord Krishna, there is no other poet who could be compared with Surdas. Surdas' liking was mostly for the childhood of Krishna. On this subject he composed such sweet poems, which have remained popular among the people of India for nearly five hundred years. Although there is quite a difference between Surdas' Braj Bhāṣā and today's Khaṛī Bolī Hindi, Sur's poems are still sung today. Braj Bhāṣā has a special sweetness, which Sur made even sweeter by describing the child Krishna. Not only in the context of literature, but also in the context of religion and of music, Surdas' poetry has a particular importance.

Although many traditions about Sur's life are current, it is difficult to say how much truth there is in them. It is said that he was born in 1478 AD in a poor Brahmin family near Delhi. According to tradition, Surdas was blind from birth. Even today, blind people are often called 'Surdas'. If Surdas had not been blind, then his parents would certainly have looked after him properly. But it was not so, and when he was only six years old he left his parents and his three elder brothers and began to live on the bank of the Yamuna. Hearing that there was a Brahmin boy named Surdas who composed extremely beautiful poems, and who sang these poems of his in a sweet voice, people began to come from far away to have an audience. Some people accepted him as their guru and began to revere him.

Surdas' renown spread throughout the whole country, to the extent that his name reached the ears of the emperor Akbar. Akbar was very fond of music, and also in the subject of religion he was very liberal. He thought that he should hear this blind singer's singing one time. Surdas was summoned to Akbar's court. Akbar was the emperor, and if he summoned anyone to him who could refuse to go? When Surdas entered the court Akbar said, 'Everyone sings of my fame, you too recite something. If you please me I will give you two or three villages and much wealth.' Hearing this Surdas declared, 'No matter how great a man you may be, I sing only of the renown of God. I cannot sing of your renown. What concern do I have with money?' Then Akbar persisted, and Sur fumed in anger and said to the emperor, 'If you want to do something for me then never call me again after today, and never meet me!'

17.2 अगर मुझे अगले साल भारत जाने का मौक़ा मिला तो मैं ज़रूर जाऊँगा। इस साल तो दफ़्तर में इतना काम करना था कि मैं जा नहीं पाया। अगर किराया इतना महँगा नहीं होता तो मैं हर साल जाता, मेरे पास चाहे कितना ही काम क्यों न होता ! मेरे माता पिता इस बात की शिकायत करते हैं कि मैं उनसे मिलने नहीं जाता। यह तो सच है कि अगर लन्दन आने के बाद मैंने शादी न की होती तो मैं छह महीनों के अंदर भारत लौट जाता। पर हालाँकि मैं कई सालों से अपने परिवार से नहीं मिला हूँ, मैं उन्हें हर महीने पत्र लिखा करता हूँ, और मुझे उनके भी समाचार मिलते रहते हैं। जब पहले पहल मैंने पिता जी से कहा कि मैं लंदन में काम करना चाहता हूँ तो वे उबल पड़े, और जब मैंने दिल्ली-वाला मकान बेच दिया तो वे बोल उठे कि 'अरे, तुमने क्या कर डाला ? मेरे तो सारे बच्चे बेवक़ूफ़ हैं !' हालाँकि वे उस समय काफ़ी नाराज़ हुए, पर वे अब ख़ुश हैं कि हमने कुछ सालों के लिए इस देश को अपनाया है।

18.1 १ हिन्दी सीखते हुए मुझे एक साल हो गया है/दो साल हो गए हैं। २ यह पाठ पढ़ते समय मैं छोटे/बड़े/सुंदर कमरे में बैठा/बैठी हूँ। ३ आपस में मिलते समय मुसलमान लोग 'सलाम अलैकुम' या 'आदाब अर्ज़' कहते हैं। ४ जी नहीं, सब एक-से नहीं हैं, कुछ सरल हैं और कुछ कठिन हैं! ५ मुझे सिनेमा देखे क़रीब दस दिन/दो महीने हो गए हैं।

18.2 As soon as I reached the station I discovered that the Lucknow train had already left. I decided to wait for the next train. There was a wait of two hours. A long queue was formed in front of the ticket office, so picking up my luggage I went off to a corner of the platform. Even there it was not easy to find an empty space; everywhere were to be seen people sitting or standing, waiting for the train. Finally I got a place to sit down, and I began watching the scene round about me. At a little distance a tea-seller was calling out, 'Tea, hot tea!' and in the other direction a vendor of savoury snacks was wandering to and fro selling his wares. A hawker standing near the ticket office, with toys made of wood in both hands, was haggling with a woman wearing a red sari. I had never seen so much hustle and bustle! Although the samosa man was wearing tattered old clothes, the samosas were selling fast and I thought to myself that if he goes on selling his wares like this all day, then by night-time he will make a goodish sum. Looking all around, I saw that next to me was lying a dirtyish pile of worn-out rags, and on the other side some people were standing in a crowd laughing and joking. Listening to their conversation it was clear that they had come from Lucknow just a few minutes earlier, and had very much enjoyed the journey. Suddenly, looking again in that direction, I realised that the thing I had taken to be a pile of rags was some oldish beggar, who had fallen asleep lying on the ground. He stood up yawning, and began to wander up and down repeating the name 'Ram Ram!' like a sadhu. Then, seeing a white person such as me sitting on the platform, he came running up to me and began to relate his tale of woe. Listening to his crafty story, I just don't know when two hours passed by. Suddenly the train came into the station and stopped, belching out black smoke. Something like a typhoon broke out among the people waiting on the platform as soon as the train stopped. Porters wearing red shirts were running from one place to another, and all the passengers alike, handing their luggage over to the porters, became involved in a race to find room in a compartment. Everyone was concerned only for himself. I became perplexed to see so many people getting in and out of the train, but without buying a ticket I too, like the others, ran towards the train. Eventually I managed to get into a compartment. There was no question of finding a seat, but somehow I got a little space on the floor, and I sat down there on top of my luggage. My railway journey had begun.

18.3

वर्मा जी नमस्ते शंकर जी। आइए, तशरीफ़ रखिए। बहुत दिनों से आपके दर्शन नहीं हुए! कैसी तबियत है?

शंकर जी आपकी मेहरबानी है, अच्छी है। आपसे मिले हुए क़रीब तीन साल हो गए हैं। इतने दिनों के बाद आपसे मिलकर बहुत ख़ुशी हुई।

वर्मा जी मुझे बताया गया था कि आपने अकबर होटल में कमरा लिया है। वहाँ रहते हुए कितने दिन हो गए हैं?

शंकर जी वहाँ रहते हुए हमें चार दिन हुए हैं। लंदन से यहाँ पहुँचते ही हम सीधे वहाँ गए थे। अच्छा-सा होटल है, हमें बहुत पसंद है। बताइए, उधर मेज़ पर पड़ा हुआ वह किसका फ़ोटो है?

वर्मा जी वह मेरा लड़का है, राजू। और नीली-सी क़मीज़ पहने हुए वह छोटा लड़का उसका चचेरा भाई रमेश है। कार से उतरते समय आपने उन्हें बग़ीचे में खेलते हुए देखा होगा।

शंकर जी हाँ, ठीक है। अच्छा जी, आज्ञा दीजिए। कल स्टेशन जाते समय आपसे दोबारा मिलने आऊँगा।

वर्मा जी आप अवश्य आएँ। मैं अपने कुछ दोस्तों से आपका परिचय कराऊँगा। अपनी धर्मपत्नी से मेरी नमस्ते कहिए।

Hindi-English Vocabulary

(1) A number or letter following the transliteration of a word refers to the Unit or Appendix in which that word first appears.
(2) Verbs which take the ने **ne** construction in past perfective tenses are marked with a capital N, e.g. करना^{N} **karnā**; verbs with which the ने **ne** construction is sometimes required are marked with a small n, e.g. बदलना^{n} **badalnā**. (See para. **47**; and see paras **51, 52** and **84** for the circumstances in which the ने **ne** construction is not used with any verb.)
(3) Following the usual convention of dictionaries, most causative verbs are *not* listed here.

(4) Abbreviations are as follows:

abbr.	abbreviated
adj.	adjective
adv.	adverb
conj.	conjunction
emph.	emphatic
esp.	especially
excl.	exclamation
fam.	familiar
foll.	following
f.	feminine
intr.	intransitive verb
m.	masculine
m./f.	noun used as either masculine or feminine
interrog.	interrogative
intr.	intransitive verb
inv.	invariable adjective (in -आ **-ā**)
lit.	literally
pl.	plural
tr.	transitive verb
usu.	usually

अँगूठा	āgūṭhā	C	*thumb* (m.)
अँगूठी	āgūṭhī	A	*finger-ring* (f.)
अंगूर	aṅgūr	10	*grape* (m.)

अँग्रेज़ (अंग्रेज)	āgrez (aṅgrez)	1	*Englishman/-woman* (m.)/(f.)
अँग्रेज़ी (अंग्रेज़ी)	āgrezi (angrezi)	6	*the English language* (f.)
अंडा	aṇḍā	10	*egg* (m.)
अंत	ant	11	*end* (m.)
अंतर	antar	17	*difference* (m.)
अंदर	andar	8	*inside*
अंधा	andhā	17	*blind*
अँधेरा	ādherā	14	*dark; darkness* (m.)
अकेला	akelā	6	*alone*
अकेलापन	akelāpan	17	*loneliness* (m.)
अकेले	akele	9	*alone* (adv.)
अक्तूबर	aktūbar	8	*October* (m.)
अक्षर	akṣar	18	*letter of alphabet, character* (m.)
अक्सर	aksar	7	*often, usually*
अख़बार	akhbār	2	*newspaper* (m.)
अगर	agar	10	*if*
अगरचे	agarce	17	*although*
अगला	aglā	8	*next*
अगस्त	agast	7	*August* (m.)
अगहन	agahan	A	*the month Āgrahāyaṇ* (Nov.–Dec.) (m.)
अचानक	acānak	12	*suddenly*
अच्छा	acchā	1	*good*
अच्छी तरह (से)	acchī tarah (se)	8	*well*
अजनबी	ajnabī	17	*stranger* (m.)
अजीब	ajīb	16	*strange, peculiar*
अट्ठानवे	aṭṭhānve	A	*ninety-eight*
अट्ठावन	aṭṭhāvan	A	*fifty-eight*
अट्ठासी	aṭṭhāsī	A	*eighty-eight*
अठहत्तर	aṭhhattar	A	*seventy-eight*
अठाईस	aṭhāīs	A	*twenty-eight*
अठारह	aṭhārah	8	*eighteen*
अड़तालीस	aṛtālīs	A	*forty-eight*
अड़तीस	aṛtīs	A	*thirty-eight*
अड़सठ	aṛsaṭh	A	*sixty-eight*
अत्यन्त	atyant	17	*extremely*
अधिक	adhik	9	*much, more*
अधिक से अधिक	adhik se adhik	9	*at the most*
अधिकमास	adhikmās	A	*leap month* (m.)
अधिकार	adhikār	10	*right, authority* (m.)

अधिकारी	adhikārī	18	*official* (m.)
अध्यापक	adhyāpak	7	*teacher* (m.)
अनपढ़	anpaṛh	14	*illiterate*
अनाथ	anāth	15	*orphan* (m.)
अपना	apnā	6	*one's own*
अपनाना[N]	apnānā	14	*to adopt, make one's own*
अप्रैल	aprail	8	*April* (m.)
अफ़सोस	afsos	2	*regret, a pity* (m.)
अब	ab	5	*now*
अब की बार	ab kī bār	12	*this time*
अभिलाषा	abhilāṣā	13	*desire* (f.)
अभी	abhī	3	*right now*
अभी तक	abhī tak	3	*yet, up to now*
अमीर	amīr	8	*rich, wealthy*
अमृतसर	amṛtsar	16	*Amritsar* (m.)
अमेरिका	amerikā	14	*America* (m.)
अम्माँ	ammā̃	5	*Mother, Mummy* (f.)
अरे	are	4	*Oh! Hey! Come off it!*
अरज़ी	arzī	10	*application* (f.)
अरज़ी देना[N]	arzī denā	10	*to apply* (tr.)
अर्थ	arth	15	*meaning, sense; money* (m.)
अलग	alag	16	*separate, apart*
अलमारी	almārī	3	*cupboard, almirah* (f.)
अल्मोड़ा	almoṛā	9	*Almora* (m.)
अवकाश	avkāś	11	*leisure, leave, free time* (m.)
अवश्य	avaśy	10	*certainly*
असंभव	asambhav	15	*impossible*
असर	asar	17	*effect, influence* (m.)
असर पड़ना	asar paṛnā	17	*to effect* (with **par**)
असल में	asal mẽ	11	*in fact, actually*
असली	aslī	9	*real, genuine*
असाढ़	asāṛh	A	*the month Āṣāṛh* (June–July)
असुविधा	asuvidhā	10	*inconvenience* (f.)
अस्पताल	aspatāl	18	*hospital* (m.)
अस्सी	assī	A	*eighty*
अहमदाबाद	ahmadābād	5	*Ahmedabad* (m.)
आँख	ā̃kh	8	*eye* (f.)
आँखों से ओझल होना	ā̃khõ se ojhal honā	13	*to disappear from view*
आकाश	ākāś	12	*sky* (m.)

आख़िर	ākhir	7	*end* (m.); *after all, at last* (adv.)
आग	āg	13	*fire* (f.)
आगरा	āgrā	18	*Agra* (m.)
आगे	āge	8	*forward, ahead, hereafter*
आगे चलकर	āge calkar	11	*in future, from now on*
आग्रह करना[N]	āgrah karnā	17	*to insist*
आग्रहायण	āgrahāyaṇ	**A**	*name of a month* (Nov.–Dec.) (m.)
आज	āj	2	*today* (m.)
आजकल	ājkal	2	*nowadays*
आज़ादी	āzādī	14	*freedom, independence* (f.)
आज्ञा	ājñā	18	*order, permission* (f.)
आज्ञा देना[N]	ājñā denā	18	*to order, permit*
आठ	āṭh	3	*eight*
आठवाँ	āṭhvā̃	7	*eighth*
आठों पहर	aṭhõ pahar	11	*all day long, constantly*
आदमी	ādmī	1	*man* (m.)
आदर	ādar	17	*respect* (m.)
का आदर करना[N]	kā ādar karnā	17	*to respect*
आदरणीय	ādarṇīy	**D**	*respected, worthy of respect*
आदाब अर्ज़	ādāb arz	18	*greetings* (*m.*)
आध	ādh	**A**	*half*
आधा	ādhā	12	*half*
आधीरात	ādhīrāt	12	*midnight* (*f.*)
आनंद	ānand	16	*joy, pleasure* (m.)
का आनंद लेना[N]	kā ānand lenā	16	*to enjoy*
आना[1]	ānā	5	*to come*
आना[2]	ānā	**A**	*anna coin* (16th of a rupee in old currency)
आप	āp	1	*you* (formal/polite); *oneself*
आपस में	āpas mẽ	14	*with one another, mutually*
आब हवा	āb havā	18	*climate* (f.)
आभारी	ābhārī	18	*grateful, indebted*
आम[1]	ām	7	*mango* (m.)
आम[2]	ām	8	*general, usual; public*
आम तौर पर	ām taur par	8	*generally, usually*
आयु	āyu	17	*age* (f.)
आरंभ	ārambh	11	*beginning* (m.)
आरंभ करना[N]	ārambh karnā	11	*to commence, begin* (tr.)
आराम	ārām	3	*rest, comfort* (m.)

आराम करना[N]	ārām karnā	13	*to rest*
आराम-कुर्सी	ārām-kursī	3	*armchair* (f.)
आराम से	ārām se	12	*comfortably, easily*
आलसी	ālsī	18	*lazy, lethargic*
आवश्यक	āvaśyak	10	*necessary*
आवश्यकता	āvaśyaktā	9	*necessity, need* (f.)
आवाज़	āvāz	16	*sound, voice* (f.)
आशा	āśā	9	*hope* (f.)
आश्चर्य	āścary	10	*surprise* (m.)
किसी को आश्चर्य होना	kisī ko āścarya honā	10	(*someone*) *to be surprised*
आश्विन	āśvin	A	*name of a month* (Sept.–Oct.) (m.)
आषाढ़	āṣāṛh	A	*name of a month* (June–July) (m.)
आस-पास	ās-pās	18	*nearabout*
आसमान	āsmān	15	*sky* (m.)
आसान	āsān	4	*easy*
आसानी	āsānī	12	*ease* (f.)
आसानी से	āsānī se	12	*easily*
आहिस्ता	āhistā	15	*slowly*
इंग्लैंड	iṅglaiṇḍ	6	*England* (m.)
इंडिया	iṇḍiyā	6	*India* (m.)
इंतज़ार	intazār	16	*wait* (m.)/(f.)
का/की इंतज़ार करना[N]	kā/kī intazār karnā	16	*to wait for*
इक्तालीस	iktālīs	A	*forty-one*
इकत्तीस (इकतीस)	ikattīs (iktīs)	16	*thirty-one*
इकसठ	iksaṭh	A	*sixty-one*
इकहत्तर	ikhattar	A	*seventy-one*
इक्कीस	ikkīs	8	*twenty-one*
इक्यानवे	ikyānve	A	*ninety-one*
इक्यावन	ikyāvan	A	*fifty-one*
इक्यासी	ikyāsī	A	*eighty-one*
इच्छा	icchā	13	*wish* (*f.*)
इजाज़त	ijāzat	18	*permission* (f.)
इजाज़त देना[N]	ijāzat denā	18	*to permit*
इज़ाफ़ा	izāfā	13	*increase, rise* (*m.*)
इतना	itnā	10	*so much/many, this much/many*
इतवार	itvār	7	*Sunday* (*m.*)
इत्यादि	ityādi	14	*etc., and so on*

इधर	idhar	5	*here, over here*
इधर-उधर	idhar-udhar	16	*here and there, hither and thither*
इनकार	inkār	16	*refusal, denial* (m.)
इनकार करना^{N}	inkār karnā	16	*to refuse* (with **se**)
इमारत	imārat	9	*building* (f.)
इम्तहान	imtahān	11	*examination* (m.)
इरादा	irādā	14	*intention* (m.)
इलाक़ा	ilāqā	6	*area, district, locality* (m.)
इलाज	ilāj	C	*treatment, cure, remedy* (m.)
का इलाज करना^{N}	kā ilāj karnā	C	*to treat*
इश्तहार	iśtahār	11	*advertisement* (m.)
इसलिए	islie	6	*so, therefore, because of this*
इसी लिए	isī lie	9	*that's why, for this very reason*
इस्तेमाल	istemāl	16	*use* (m.)
का इस्तेमाल करना^{N}	kā istemāl karnā	16	*to use*
इस्म-ए शरीफ़	ism-e śarīf	18	'*good name*' (m.)
ईर्ष्या	īrṣyā	15	*jealousy, envy* (f.)
ईसवी सन्	īsvī san	A	*'Christian year', AD date*
उँगली	ũglī	12	*finger* (f.)
उगना	ugnā	16	*to grow* (intr.)
उगलना^{N}	ugalnā	18	*to disgorge, vomit out*
उचित	ucit	9	*fitting, proper, right*
उठना	uṭhnā	12	*to rise, get up*
उठाना^{N}	uṭhānā	18	*to lift up, pick up, raise, remove*
उड़ाना^{N}	uṛānā	18	*to squander*
उड़िया	uṛiyā	7	*the Oriya language (f.)*
उतना	utnā	14	*that much*
उतरना	utarnā	12	*to get down, descend, alight*
उतारना^{N}	utārnā	12	*to take down; to take off (clothes)*
उत्तर^1	uttar	11	*northern; north* (m.)
उत्तर^2	uttar	11	*reply, answer* (m.)
उदार	udār	17	*generous, liberal*
उदास	udās	16	*sad, gloomy*
उधर	udhar	5	*there, over there*
उनचास	uncās	A	*forty-nine*
उनतालीस	untālīs	A	*thirty-nine*

उनतीस	untīs	15	*twenty-nine*
उनसठ	unsaṭh	A	*fifty-nine*
उनहत्तर	unhattar	A	*sixty-nine*
उन्नीस	unnīs	8	*nineteen*
उन्यासी	unyāsī	A	*seventy-nine*
उपकार	upkār	17	*good, good deed, favour* (m.)
उपकार करना[N]	upkār karnā	17	*to do a favour*
उबलना	ubalnā	17	*to boil* (intr.); *to boil in anger*
उबालना[N]	ubālnā	C	*to boil* (tr.)
उम्मीद	ummīd	9	*hope* (f.)
उम्मीदवार	ummīdvār	17	*candidate* (m.)
उमर (उम्र)	umar, umr	8	*age, lifespan* (f.)
उर्दू	urdū	6	*Urdu* (f.)
उलटी	ulṭī	C	*vomiting* (f.)
उलटी करना[N]	ulṭī karnā	C	*to vomit*
उलटे	ulṭe	13	*conversely*
ऊँचा	ū̃cā	6	*high, tall* (not of people, trees: see **lambā**)
ऊपर	ūpar	8	*above, up*
ऊबना	ūbnā	14	*to be bored*
ऋतु	ṛtu	A	*season* (f.)
एअर इंडिया	ear iṇḍiyā	8	*Air India*
एक	ek	1	*one, a*
एक दम	ek dam	15	*at once, suddenly; completely, utterly*
एक साथ	ek sāth	18	*together*
एकता	ektā	14	*unity* (f.)
एकाएक	ekāek	17	*all of a sudden, suddenly*
एकाध	ekādh	10	*a few, one or two*
ऐश	aiś	18	*luxurious enjoyment, pleasure* (m.)
ऐसा	aisā	9	*of such a kind* (adj.); *thus, so* (adv.)
ऐसे	aise	9	*thus, so, in this way* (adv.)
ओझल	ojhal	13	*out of sight*
ओठ	oṭh	C	*lip* (m.)
ओढ़ना[N]	oṛhnā	10	*to cover, wrap, wear*

और	aur	1	*and; more*
और कुछ	aur kuch	7	*something else*
और कोई	aur koī	7	*someone else, some other*
औरत	aurat	2	*woman* (f.)
कंजूस	kañjūs	10	*miserly, mean*
कंपनी	kampanī	10	*firm, company* (f.)
कंबल	kambal	3	*blanket* (m.)
कई	kaī	3	*several*
कच्चा	kaccā	7	*unripe, raw, uncooked; crude, rough*
कटना	kaṭnā	12	*to be cut*
कठिन	kaṭhin	11	*difficult, hard*
कठिनाई	kaṭhināī	12	*difficulty* (f.)
क़तार	qatār	18	*line, row* (f.)
कथा	kathā	18	*(religious) narration* (f.)
कन्या	kanyā	10	*girl, daughter, virgin* (f.)
कपड़ा	kapṛā	4	*cloth; garment*
कब	kab	7	*when?*
कबड्डी	kabaḍḍī	15	*a children's game, kind of tag* (f.)
कब्ज़	kabz	C	*constipation* (f.)
कभी	kabhī	6	*sometime, ever*
कभी कभी	kabhī kabhī	6	*sometimes*
कभी नहीं	kabhī nahī̃	6	*never*
कम	kam	4	*little, less*
कम करना[N]	kam karnā	9	*to reduce*
कम से कम	kam se kam	9	*at least*
कमज़ोर	kamzor	C	*weak*
कमज़ोरी	kamzorī	C	*weakness* (f.)
कमर	kamar	C	*waist* (f.)
कमरा	kamrā	1	*room* (m.)
कमाना[N]	kamānā	18	*to earn*
क़मीज़	qamīz	1	*shirt* (f.)
करना[N]	karnā	5	*to do*
क़रीब	qarīb	8	*close, near* (adj.); *about, near, almost, nearly* (adv.)
करोड़	karoṛ	14	*a crore, ten million* (m.)
कर्त्तव्य	karttavy	17	*duty* (m.)
कल	kal	4	*yesterday; tomorrow* (m.)
कलकत्ता	kalkattā	7	*Calcutta* (m.)
क़लम	qalam	2	*pen* (m.)/(f.)
कवि	kavi	17	*poet* (m.)

कविता	kavitā	16	*poem, poetry* (f.)
कश्मीर	kaśmīr	9	*Kashmir* (m.)
कश्मीरी	kaśmīrī	6	*Kashmiri* (m.)/(f.)/(adj.)
कष्ट	kaṣṭ	10	*trouble* (m.)
कष्ट देना[N]	kaṣṭ denā	10	*to give trouble*
कसूर	kasūr	17	*fault, guilt* (m.)
कहना[N]	kahnā	5	*to say*
कहलाना	kahlānā	17	*to be called*
कहाँ	kahā̃	3	*where?*
कहानी	kahānī	8	*story* (f.)
कहीं	kahī̃	10	*somewhere; somewhat; lest*
कहीं और	kahī̃ aur	16	*somewhere else; somewhat more*
कहीं न कहीं	kahī̃ na kahī̃	16	*somewhere or other*
कहीं नहीं	kahī̃ nahī̃	16	*nowhere*
कहीं भी	kahī̃ bhī	16	*anywhere*
काँग्रेस	kā̃gres	18	*the Congress Party* (f.)
काँटा	kā̃ṭā	16	*thorn; fork* (m.)
काँपना	kā̃pnā	18	*to tremble, shiver*
काका	kākā	**B**	*father's elder brother* (m.)
काकी	kākī	**B**	*wife of father's elder brother* (f.)
काग़ज़	kāg̲az	7	*paper, piece of paper* (m.)
काटना[N]	kaṭnā	**E**	*to cut; to spend (time)*
कातिक	kātik	**Ạ**	*the month Kārtik* (Oct.–Nov.) (m.)
कान	kān	15	*ear* (m.)
कानपुर	kānpur	10	*Kanpur* (m.) (formerly *Cawnpore*)
क़ानून	qānūn	17	*law* (m.)
काफ़ी[1]	kāfī	3	*quite, quite a few, enough, very*
काफ़ी[2]	kāfī	6	*coffee* (f.)
काम	kām	4	*work* (m.)
कार	kār	17	*car* (f.)
कारख़ाना	kārk̲h̲ānā	8	*factory, workshop* (m.)
कारण	kāraṇ	14	*reason, cause* (m.)
कार्तिक	kārtik	**A**	*name of a month* (Oct.–Nov.) (m.)
काल	kāl	**A**	*time; season* (m.)
काला	kālā	2	*black*
कालेज	kālej	9	*college* (m.)
कि	ki	4	*that; or* (conj.)

कितना	kitnā	2	*how much/many?*
किताब	kitāb	2	*book* (f.)
किधर	kidhar	8	*which way?, where?*
किनारा	kinārā	13	*bank, edge, border* (m.)
किराया	kirāyā	3	*rent, fare* (m.)
किलो	kilo	7	*kilo(gram)* (m.)
किस तरह (से)	kis tarah (se)	8	*how?, in what manner?*
किस समय	kis samay	8	*at what time?*
की ओर	kī or	6	*towards*
की जगह	kī jagah	17	*in (the) place of*
की तरफ़	kī taraf	6	*towards*
की तरह	kī tarah	12	*like*
की बग़ल में	kī bagal mẽ	18	*next to, alongside*
क़ीमत	qīmat	17	*price, value* (f.)
क़ीमती	qīmatī	12	*costly, valuable*
कुआँ	kuā̃	6	*well* (m.)
कुचलना^{n}	kucalnā	14	*to crush, trample; to be crushed*
कुछ	kuch	3	*some*
कुछ और	kuch aur	5	*some more, something else*
कुछ न कुछ	kuch na kuch	7	*something or other*
कुछ नहीं	kuch nahī̃	7	*nothing*
कुटिया	kuṭiyā	18	*hut* (f.)
कुमारी	kumārī	2	*unmarried girl; Miss* (f.)
कुरता	kurtā	11	*kurta, loose-cut shirt* (m.)
कुरसी	kursī	1	*chair* (f.)
कुली	kulī	12	*porter* (m.)
कुली करना^{N}	kulī karnā	13	*to hire a porter*
कूदना	kūdnā	17	*to jump*
कृपया	kṛpayā	5	*please*
कृपा	kṛpā	11	*kindness* (f.);
कृपा करके	kṛpā karke	11	*kindly, please*
कृपापत्र	kṛpāpatr	D	'*kind letter*' (m.)
कृष्ण पक्ष	kṛṣṇ pakṣ	A	*dark, or waning, half of a lunar month* (m.)
के अंदर	ke andar	6	*inside, within*
के अनुसार	ke anusār	17	*according to*
के अलावा	ke alāvā	11	*besides, apart from, as well as*
के आगे	ke āge	6	*in front of, before*
के आस-पास	ke ās-pās	10	*around, in the vicinity of*
के ऊपर	ke ūpar	6	*on top of, on*

के कारण	ke kāraṇ	12	*because of*
के किनारे	ke kināre	13	*at/on the side of*
के चारों तरफ़	ke cārõ taraf	13	*all around*
(के) द्वारा	(ke) dvārā	14	*by, by means of*
के नीचे	ke nīce	6	*below, beneath*
के पहले	ke pahle	6	*before*
के पास	ke pās	6	*close, near to*
के पीछे	ke pīche	6	*behind*
के बग़ैर	ke bagair	15	*without*
के बजाय	ke bajāy	15	*instead of*
के बदले (में)	ke badle (mẽ)	15	*in place of, in exchange for*
के बाद	ke bād	6	*after*
के बारे में	ke bāre mẽ	6	*about, concerning*
के बाहर	ke bāhar	6	*outside*
के बिना	ke binā	11	*without*
के बीच में	ke bīc (mẽ)	10	*between, amidst, among*
के भीतर	ke bhītar	8	*inside, within*
के मारे	ke māre	15	*because of, on account of, through*
के यहाँ	ke yahā̃	6	*at the place of*
के योग्य	ke yogy	9	*worthy of, worth*
के रूप में	ke rūp mẽ	14	*in the form of, as*
के लायक़	ke lāyaq	9	*worthy of, worth*
के लिए	ke lie	6	*for*
के साथ	ke sāth	6	*with*
के सामने	ke sāmne	6	*opposite*
के सिवा(य)	ke sivā(y)	15	*except for, but for*
केला	kelā	10	*banana* (m.)
केवल	keval	11	*only*
क़ै	qai	C	*vomiting, nausea* (f.)
क़ै आना	qai ānā	C	*to feel sick*
क़ै करना[N]	qai karnā	C	*to be sick*
क़ै होना	qai honā	C	*to be sick*
कैमरा	kaimrā	15	*camera* (m.)
कैसा	kaisā	2	*of what kind?*
कैसे	kaise	7	*how?*
को	ko	3	*to* (etc.)
कोई	koī	7	*some, any; someone, anyone;* (with number) *about;*
कोई न कोई	koī na koī	7	*someone or other;*
कोई नहीं	koī nahī̃	7	*nobody*
कोट	koṭ	3	*coat* (m.)

कोना	konā	18	*corner* (m.)
कोशिश	kośiś	16	*try, attempt*
की कोशिश करना[N]	kī kośiś karnā	16	*to try* (*to*)
कोहनी	kohnī	C	*elbow* (f.)
कौन	kaun	2	*who?*
कौनसा	kaunsā	4	*which?*
क्या[1]	kyā	1	(interrog. word: makes a foll. statement into a question)
क्या[2]	kyā	2	*what?*
क्यों	kyõ	4	*why?*
क्योंकि	kyõki	4	*because*
क्लास	klās	9	*class* (f.)/(m.)
क्वार	kvār	A	*the month Āśvin* (Sept.–Oct.)
क्षण	kṣaṇ	13	*moment* (m.)
खड़ा होना	khaṛā honā	7	*to stand* (intr.)
खड़ी बोली	khaṛī bolī	17	*standard modern Hindi* (f.)
ख़त	khat	6	*letter (correspondence)* (m.)
ख़त्म करना[N]	khatm karnā	7	*to finish* (tr.)
ख़त्म होना	khatm honā	7	*to end* (intr.)
ख़बर	khabar	17	*news* (f.)
ख़बरदार	khabardār	16	*watchful; watch out!*
ख़राब	kharāb	2	*bad, faulty*
ख़रीदना[N]	kharīdnā	8	*to buy*
ख़र्च	kharc	12	*expenditure, expenses;* (m.)
ख़र्च करना[N]	kharc karnā	14	*to spend*
खाँसना[N]	khā̃snā	11	*to cough*
खाँसी	khā̃sī	C	*cough* (f.)
खाँसी आना	khā̃sī ānā	C	*to have a cough*
खाना[1]	khānā	5	*food* (m.)
खाना[2N]	khānā	5	*to eat*
खाता-पीता	khātā-pītā	18	*well-to-do, prosperous*
ख़ाली	khālī	15	*empty, vacant, free* (inv.)
ख़ाली-हाथ	khālī-hāth	15	*empty-handed*
ख़ाविंद	khāvind	B	*husband* (m.)
ख़ास	khās	7	*special*
ख़ास तौर पर	khās taur par	8	*specially, particularly*
ख़ासकर	khāskar	12	*specially*
ख़ासियत	khāsiyat	16	*special quality, characteristic* (f.)
खिड़की	khiṛkī	3	*window* (f.)

खिलाना[N]	khilānā	10	*to give to eat, feed; to make play; to cause to blossom*
खिलौना	khilaunā	18	*toy* (m.)
खींचना[N]	khī̃cnā	11	*to pull, drag, draw*
ख़ुद	khud	15	*oneself*
ख़ुदा हाफ़िज़	khudā hāfiz	18	*goodbye*
खुला	khulā	15	*open*
ख़ुश	khuś	2	*happy*
ख़ुशी	khuśī	4	*happiness, pleasure;* (f.)
ख़ुशी से	khuśī se	8	*happily, gladly*
ख़ून	khūn	C	*blood* (m.)
ख़ूब	khūb	11	*good, abundant* (adj.)*; very very well, very much* (adv.)
ख़ूबसूरत	khūbsūrat	11	*beautiful*
खेत	khet	4	*field, farming land* (m.)
खेद	khed	11	*regret* (m.)
खेल	khel	13	*game* (m.)
खेलना	khelnā	6	*to play*
ख़ैर	khair	12	*well, anyway* (interj.)
खोना[n]	khonā	12	*to lose; to be lost*
खोलना[N]	kholnā	11	*to open* (tr.)
ख़्याल	khyāl	9	*opinion, thought* (m.)
गंगा	gaṅgā	13	*the river Ganges* (f.)
गंदा	gandā	1	*dirty*
गंभीर	gambhīr	17	*deep, serious*
गँवाना[N]	gā̃vānā	17	*to lose, waste*
गणेश	gaṇeś	8	*Ganesh, elephant-headed god of wisdom, remover of obstacles* (m.)
गति-विधि(याँ)	gati-vidhi(yā̃)	10	*working(s), activities, behaviour* (f.)
गप	gap	16	*gossip* (f.)
गप-शप	gap-śap	16	*gossip, tittle-tattle, chit-chat* (f.)
गरज	garaj	16	*thunder, roar* (f.)
गरदन	gardan	C	*neck* (f.)
गरम	garam	5	*warm, hot*
गरमी	garmī	9	*heat* (f.)*; summer* (pl.)
गरमी पड़ना	garmī paṛnā	9	*to get hot* (of weather)
ग़रीब	garīb	9	*poor*
गर्भ	garbh	C	*womb* (m.)
गर्भ होना	garbh honā	C	*to be pregnant*

ग़लत	galat	9	*wrong, mistaken*
ग़लती	galtī	16	*mistake* (f.)
गला	galā	C	*throat, neck voice* (m.)
गला बैठना	galā baiṭhnā	C	*to have a hoarse voice*
गली	galī	14	*lane, alleyway* (f.)
गाँव	gā̃v	4	*village* (m.)
गाँववाला	gā̃vvālā	10	*villager* (m.)
गाड़ी	gāṛī	4	*car; train* (f.)
गाना[1]	gānā	9	*song* (m.)
गाना[2N]	gānā	9	*to sing*
गाय	gāy	13	*cow* (f.)
गायक	gāyak	17	*singer* (m.)
ग़ायब	gāyab	12	*disappeared, missing;*
ग़ायब करना[N]	gāyab karnā	12	*to make off with;*
ग़ायब होना	gāyab honā	12	*to disappear, go missing*
गार्ड	gārḍ	12	*railway guard* (m.)
गाल	gāl	C	*cheek* (m.)
गाली	gālī	14	*abuse, invective, insult* (f.)
गाली देना[N]	gālī denā	14	*to abuse, insult*
गिरना	girnā	15	*to fall, drop* (intr.)
गिराना[N]	girānā	13	*to drop, let fall* (tr.)
गीत	gīt	18	*song* (m.)
गुज़रना	guzarnā	13	*to pass (time)* (intr.) *to pass away*
गुजरात	gujarāt	14	*Gujarat* (m.)
गुजराती	gujarātī	1	*Gujarati* (m.)/(f.)/(adj.); *Gujarati language* (f.)
गुरु	guru	17	*teacher, spiritual guide* (m.)
गुरुवार	guruvār	7	*Thursday* (m.)
गुस्सा	gussā	9	*anger* (m.)
गुस्सा होना	gussā honā	9	*to get angry* (with **par**)
गेंद	gẽd	14	*ball* (f.)
गोद	god	18	*lap* (f.)
गोरा	gorā	14	*fair; white person,* *European* (m.)
गोली	golī	11	*tablet, pill; bullet* (f.)
गोली मारना[N]	golī mārnā	17	*to shoot*
गोश्त	gośt	6	*meat* (m.)
ग्यारह	gyārah	6	*eleven*
ग्रीष्म	grīṣm	A	*summer* (m.)
घंटा	ghaṇṭā	10	*hour* (m.)
घंटी	ghaṇṭī	13	*bell* (f.)

घड़ी	gharī	11	*watch, clock* (f.)
घनिष्ठ	ghaniṣṭh	18	*close, intimate*
घबड़ाना (-र-)	ghabṛānā (-r-)	10	*to worry, be nervous, panic*
घर	ghar	3	*house, home* (m.)
घर पर	ghar par	4	*at home*
घाट	ghāṭ	13	*bathing place on river,* etc. (m.)
घास	ghās	4	*grass* (f.)
घिसा-पिटा	ghisā-piṭā	18	*worn out*
घी	ghī	4	*clarified butter, ghee* (m.)
घुटना	ghuṭnā	C	*knee* (m.)
घुमाना[N]	ghumānā	14	*to make round; to revolve, turn*
घुसना	ghusnā	13	*to enter*
घूमना	ghūmnā	9	*to tour, visit, wander about, turn*
घोड़ा	ghoṛā	5	*horse* (m.)
चचेरा-भाई	cacerā bhāī	15	*cousin* (m.) (*son of* **cācā**)
चचेरी बहिन	cacerī bahin	16	*cousin* (f.) (*daughter of* **cācā**)
चढ़ना	caṛhnā	12	*to climb, rise, mount, board*
चपाती	capātī	15	*chappatti* (f.)
चप्पल	cappal	2	*sandal* (f.)
चमड़ी	camṛī	C	*skin* (f.)
चम्मच	cammac	5	*spoon* (m.)
चलना	calnā	5	*to move, go*
चल बसना	cal basnā	18	*to die*
चला आना	calā ānā	12	*to come along*
चला जाना	calā jānā	12	*to go along, set off, leave*
चलाना[N]	calānā	8	*to drive; to run, manage*
चवालीस	cavālīs	A	*forty-four*
चश्मा	caśmā	7	*glasses, spectacles* (m.)
चहल-पहल	cahal-pahal	18	*hustle and bustle* (f.)
चाँद	cā̃d	12	*moon* (m.)
चाकर	cākar	16	*servant, menial servant* (m.)
चाक़ू	cāqū	12	*knife* (m.)
चाचा	cācā	1	*paternal uncle* (m.)
चाची	cācī	18	*aunt* (f.) (*wife of* **cācā**)
चादर	cādar	3	*sheet* (f.)
चाबी	cābī	5	*key* (f.)
चाय	cāy	5	*tea* (f.)
चार	cār	1	*four*
चालक	cālak	18	*driver* (m.)

चालाकी	cālākī	18	*craftiness, cunning* (f.)
चालीस	cālīs	11	*forty*
चाव	cāv	15	*fondness, enthusiasm, zeal* (m
चावल	cāval	11	*rice* (m.)
चाहना[N]	cāhnā	10	*to wish, want*
चाहिए	cāhie	7	*wanted, needed*
चाहे ... चाहे/या	cāhe ... cāhe/yā	16	*whether ... or*
चिट्ठी	ciṭṭhī	13	*letter, note* (f.)
चिड़िया	ciṛiyā	15	*bird* (f.)
चिड़ियाघर	ciṛiyāghar	15	*zoo* (m.)
चिथड़ा	cithṛā	18	*rag* (m.)
चिरंजीव	ciranjīv	D	*blessed with long life*
चिल्लाना	cillānā	14	*to cry out, shout loudly*
चिल्लाहट	cillāhaṭ	14	*cry, call* (f.)
चीज़	cīz	4	*thing* (f.)
चीनी[1]	cīnī	5	*sugar* (f.)
चीनी[2]	cīnī	14	*Chinese* (adj.)/(m.)
चुकना	cuknā	12	*to be finished* (para. **51**); *to be settled, paid off*
चुकाना[N]	cukānā	17	*to pay a bill, settle a debt*
चुनना[N]	cunnā	14	*to choose, pick*
चुनाव	cunāv	17	*election, selection* (m.)
चुप	cup	10	*quiet, silent*
चुप रहना	cup rahnā	10	*to be quiet, stay quiet*
चेतावनी	cetāvanī	17	*warning* (f.)
चेतावनी देना[N]	cetāvanī denā	17	*to warn*
चेहरा	cehrā	14	*face* (m.)
चैत	cait	A	*the month Caitra* (March–April) (m.)
चैत्र	caitr	A	*name of a month* (March–April) (m.)
चोट	coṭ	13	*injury, blow, hurt* (f.)
चोट लगना	coṭ lagnā	14	*to get hurt*
चोर	cor	12	*thief* (m.)
चोरी	corī	12	*theft* (f.)
चौंतीस	caũtīs	17	*thirty-four*
चौंसठ	caũsaṭh	A	*sixty-four*
चौड़ा	cauṛā	6	*wide, broad*
चौथा	cauthā	7	*fourth*
चौदह	caudah	7	*fourteen*
चौबीस	caubīs	9	*twenty-four*
चौरानवे	caurānve	A	*ninety-four*

चौरासी	caurāsī	A	*eighty-four*
चौवन	cauvan	A	*fifty-four*
चौहत्तर	cauhattar	A	*seventy-four*
छः	chaḥ	A	*six*
छठा	chaṭhā	7	*sixth*
छत्तीस	chattīs	A	*thirty-six*
छपना	chapnā	18	*to be printed*
छप्पन	chappan	A	*fifty-six*
छब्बीस	chabbīs	11	*twenty-six*
छह	chah	3	*six*
छाता	chātā	16	*umbrella* (m.)
छाती	chātī	C	*chest* (f.)
छात्र	chātr	8	*pupil, student* (m.)
छापना^N	chāpnā	E	*to print*
छियानवे	chiyānve	A	*ninety-six*
छियालीस	chiyālīs	A	*forty-six*
छियासठ	chiyāsaṭh	A	*sixty-six*
छियासी	chiyāsī	A	*eighty-six*
छिहत्तर	chihattar	A	*seventy-six*
छींकना^N	chī̃knā	11	*to sneeze*
छुट्टी	chuṭṭī	7	*holiday, leave, release from work* (f.)
छुड़ाना^N	chuṛānā	E	*to get freed*
छूटना	chūṭnā	8	*to leave, be left*
छूना^N	chūnā	5	*to touch*
छै	chai	A	*six*
छोटा	choṭā	1	*small*
छोटा-मोटा	choṭā-moṭā	15	*insignificant, trifling, minor*
छोड़ना^N	choṛnā	11	*to leave, abandon, give up;*
को छोड़कर	ko choṛkar	11	*apart from*
जंगल	jaṅgal	13	*jungle, wilderness* (m.)
जंगली	jaṅgalī	15	*wild*
जँभाई	jā̃bhāī	18	*yawn, yawning* (f.)
जँभाई लेना^N	jā̃bhāī lenā	18	*to yawn*
जगह	jagah	9	*place* (f.)
जनता	jantā	17	*the public, the people* (f.)
जनवरी	janvarī	8	*January* (f.)
जनश्रुति	janśruti	17	*tradition, legend* (f.)
जनाब	janāb	18	*'sir'*
जन्म	janm	16	*birth* (m.)
का जन्म होना	kā janm honā	16	*to be born*

जन्मदिन	janamdin	11	*birthday* (m.)
जन्माष्टमी	janmāṣṭamī	A	*Krishna's birthday* (f.) (8th day of the dark half of *Bhādõ)*
जपना[N]	japnā	18	*to repeat* (the name of God, etc.)
जब	jab	13	*when*
जब कि	jab ki	14	*while*
जब तक	jab tak	13	*until*
जब भी	jab bhī	13	*whenever*
जब से	jab se	13	*since when*
ज़बान	zabān	11	*language, tongue* (f.)
जमा करना[N]	jamā karnā	15	*to deposit* (**jamā** inv.)
ज़माना	zamānā	7	*period, time* (m.)
ज़मीन	zamīn	10	*land, earth, ground* (f.)
जय	jay	10	*victory* (f.)
ज़रा	zarā	5	*just, a little*
ज़रूर	zarūr	4	*of course, certainly*
ज़रूरत	zarūrat	9	*need, necessity* (f.)
ज़रूरी	zarūrī	8	*important, necessary, urgent*
जर्मन	jarman	1	*German* (m.)/(f.)/(adj.)
जलना	jalnā	13	*to burn* (intr.), *be lit; to burn with jealousy, be jealous*
जलाना[N]	jalānā	14	*to burn* (tr.), *set alight*
जल्दी	jaldī	5	*quickly, early; hurry* (f.)
जल्दी से	jaldī se	8	*quickly*
जवान	javān	17	*young, youthful; young man, private/soldier* (m.)
जवाब	javāb	10	*answer* (m.)
जवाब देना[N]	javāb denā	10	*to answer*
जहाँ	jahā̃	16	*where, in which place*
जहाँ कहीं	jahā̃ kahī̃	16	*wherever*
जागना	jāgnā	E	*to be awake*
जाड़ा	jāṛā	9	*cold* (m.); *winter* (pl.)
जाति	jāti	15	*species, caste, type* (f.)
जान	jān	12	*life; dear one* (f.)
जानकारी	jānkārī	9	*knowledge, information* (f.)
जानना[N]	jānnā	7	*to know*
जान पड़ना	jān paṛnā	18	*to seem*
जान-बूझकर	jān-būjhkar	11	*deliberately*
जाना-पहचाना	jānā-pahcānā	18	*well-known, widely recognised*

जानवर	jānvar	15	*animal* (m.)
जाना	jānā	5	*to go*
ज़िंदगी	zindagī	4	*life* (f.)
ज़िंदा	zindā	17	*alive* (inv.)
ज़िक्र	zikr	16	*mention, reference* (m.)
का ज़िक्र करना[N]	kā zikr karnā	16	*to mention, refer to*
जितना	jitnā	14	*as much as, as many as*
जिधर	jidhar	16	*wherever, in which direction*
जिस से कि	jis se ki	14	*by which, whereby, so that*
जी	jī	15	*mind, heart* (m.)
जी चाहना[N]	jī cāhnā	15	*to desire*
जी नहीं	jī nahī̃	1	*no*
जी हाँ	jī hā̃	1	*yes*
जीजी	jījī	B	*sister* (f.)
जीतना[n]	jītnā	11	*to win*
जीना	jīnā	16	*to live, be alive*
जीभ	jībh	C	*tongue* (f.)
जीवन	jīvan	11	*life* (m.)
ज़ुकाम	zukām	4	*a cold, catarrh* (m.)
जुटना	juṭnā	18	*to be engaged in work*
जुलाई	julāī	7	*July* (f.)
जूता	jūtā	2	*shoe* (m.)
जून	jūn	8	*June* (m.)
जेठ[1]	jeṭh	A	*the month Jyeṣṭh* (May–June) (m.)
जेठ[2]	jeṭh	B	*husband's elder brother* (m.)
जेठानी	jeṭhānī	B	*wife of husband's elder brother* (f.)
जेब	jeb	5	*pocket* (f.)
जेल	jel	14	*jail* (f.)
जैसा	jaisā	15	*like, similar to, such as*
जैसे (कि)	jaise (ki)	15	*as, as if*
जैसे ही...वैसे ही	jaise hī... vaise hī	13	*as soon as... then*
जो	jo	12	*that which, which, who, the one which/who; if*
जो कुछ	jo kuch	12	*whatever*
जो कोई	jo koī	12	*whoever*
जो भी	jo bhī	12	*whoever, whatever*
जोड़	joṛ	C	*joint* (m.)
जोड़ना[N]	joṛnā	15	*to join, add, accumulate, save up*
ज़ोर	zor	8	*force, strength* (m.)
ज़ोर से	zor se	8	*forcefully, loudly*
ज़ोरों से	zorõ se	16	*forcefully, heavily*

ज़्यादा	zyādā	4	*more, much, too much*
ज़्यादा से ज़्यादा	zyādā se zyādā	9	*at the most*
ज्यादातर	zyādātar	12	*mostly; most*
ज्येष्ठ	jyeṣṭh	A	*name of a month* (May–June) (m.)
ज्योंही....त्योंही	jyõhī ... tyõhī	13	*as soon as...then*
झगड़ा	jhagṛā	10	*quarrel* (m.)
झमेला	jhamelā	13	*mess, botheration, turmoil* (m.)
झाड़ना[N]	jhāṛnā	11	*to sweep, dust*
झिझक	jhijhak	15	*hesitation* (f.)
झूठ	jhūṭh	14	*lie* (m.)
झोंपड़ी	jhõpṛī	18	*hut* (f.)
टँगना	ṭãgnā	11	*to hang, be suspended*
टकराना	ṭakrānā	14	*to collide* (with **se**)
टक्कर	ṭakkar	14	*collision*
टक्कर लगना	ṭakkar lagnā	14	*a collision to take place* (with **se**)
टट्टी	ṭaṭṭī	C	*faeces, stool* (f.)
टट्टी करना[N]	ṭaṭṭī karnā	C	*to pass faeces*
टलना	ṭalnā	E	*to be averted, postponed, put off*
टहलना	ṭahalnā	18	*to stroll, amble*
टाँग	ṭā̃g	12	*leg* (f.)
टालना[N]	ṭālnā	E	*to avert, postpone, put off, evade*
टिकट	ṭikaṭ	9	*ticket; stamp* (m.)
टिकटघर	ṭikaṭghar	18	*ticket office* (m.)
टूटना	ṭūṭnā	12	*to break* (intr.)
टैक्सी	ṭaiksī	10	*taxi* (f.)
ट्रेन	ṭren	7	*train* (f.)
ठंड	ṭhaṇḍ	13	*cold* (f.)
ठंडा	ṭhaṇḍā	9	*cold* (adj.)
ठहरना	ṭhaharnā	5	*to stop, stay, wait*
ठीक	ṭhīk	2	*all right, correct, fine, OK*
ठीक करना[N]	ṭhīk karnā	9	*to fix, put right*
ठीक-ठाक	ṭhīk-ṭhāk	16	*all right, fine, shipshape*
ठीक तरह (से)	ṭhīk tarah (se)	8	*properly*
ठीक समय (पर)	ṭhīk samay (par)	8	*punctually, at the right time*
ठीक से	ṭhīk se	8	*properly*
डर	ḍar	13	*fear* (m.)
डरना	ḍarnā	15	*to fear, be afraid of*
डाक	ḍāk	11	*post* (f.)
डाकख़ाना	ḍākkhānā	13	*post office* (m.)

डाकघर	ḍākghar	11	*post office* (m.)
डाक्टर	ḍākṭar	13	*doctor* (m.)
डालना[N]	ḍālnā	17	*to pour, put, cast*
डिब्बा	ḍibbā	12	*train compartment* (m.)
डूबना	ḍūbnā	12	*to sink, drown* (intr.)
डेढ़	ḍeṛh	11	*one and a half*
ड्राइवर	ḍrāivar	8	*driver* (m.)
ढाई	ḍhāī	11	*two and a half*
ढाबा	ḍhābā	11	*small cafe, food stall* (m.)
ढूँढ़ना[N]	ḍhū̃ṛhnā	8	*to look for, search, trace*
ढेर	ḍher	17	*heap, pile, mass* (m.)
तंग आना	taṅg ānā	16	*to be fed up with, tired of* (with **se**)
तंदुरुस्त	tandurust	C	*healthy, fit*
तंदुरुस्ती	tandurustī	C	*health* (f.)
तक	tak	3	*up to, as far as, until; even*
तक़लीफ़	taqlīf	8	*trouble* (f.)
तक़लीफ़ देना[N]	taqlīf denā	8	*to trouble, bother*
तथापि	tathāpi	17	*even then, still, yet*
तनख़्वाह	tankhāh	10	*pay, salary* (f.)
तब	tab	13	*then*
तबियत	tabiyat	5	*health, disposition* (f.)
तमाम	tamām	18	*whole, entire, all*
तमाशा	tamāśā	11	*show, spectacle*
तमिल	tamil	7	*the Tamil language* (f.)
तरकारी	tarkārī	11	*vegetable dish* (f.)
तरक़्क़ी	taraqqī	13	*progress, advancement* (f.)
तरक़्क़ी करना[N]	taraqqī karnā	13	*to progress, advance*
तरफ़	taraf	8	*direction, side* (f.)
तरह	tarah	8	*manner, kind;* (f.)
तरह तरह का	tarah tarah kā	12	*of various kinds*
तलाश	talāś	16	*search* (f.)
की तलाश करना[N]	kī talāś karnā	16	*to search for, look for*
तशरीफ़	taśrīf	18	(honorific: see foll.) (f.)
तशरीफ़ रखना[N]	taśrīf rakhnā	18	*to be seated*
तशरीफ़ लाना	taśrīf lānā	18	*to come, to grace a place with one's presence*
तस्वीर	tasvīr	3	*picture* (f.)
ताई	tāī	B	*wife of father's younger brother* (f.)
ताऊ	tāū	B	*father's younger brother* (m.)
ताकि	tāki	14	*so that, in order that*

ताज महल	tāj mahal	14	*the Taj Mahal* (m.)
ताज़ा	tāzā	6	*fresh*
तार	tār	9	*telegram, cable* (m.)
तार देना[N]	tār denā	9	*to send a telegram*
तारीख़	tārīkh	8	*date* (f.)
तारीफ़	tārīf	18	*praise* (f.)
की तारीफ़ करना[N]	kī tārīf karnā	18	*to praise*
ताला	tālā	13	*lock* (m.)
तिथि	tithi	A	*date; lunar day* (f.)
तिरपन	tirpan	A	*fifty-three*
तिरसठ	tirsaṭh	A	*sixty-three*
तिरानवे	tirānve	A	*ninety-three*
तिरासी	tirāsī	A	*eighty-three*
तिहत्तर	tihattar	A	*seventy-three*
तीन	tīn	2	*three*
तीस	tīs	6	*thirty*
तीसरा	tīsrā	7	*third*
तीसरे पहर	tīsre pahar	8	*in the afternoon*
तुड़ाना[N]	tuṛānā	E	*to (cause to) break*
तुम	tum	1	*you* (fam.)
तुम्हारा	tumhārā	6	*your, yours* (fam.)
तुरत (तुरंत)	turat (turant)	10	*immediately*
तुलना	tulnā	17	*comparison* (f.)
की तुलना करना[N]	kī tulnā karnā	17	*to compare*
तू	tū	1	*you* (intimate)
तूफ़ान	tūfān	18	*storm, typhoon* (m.)
तेईस	teīs	8	*twenty-three*
तेज़	tez	13	*sharp, acute, strong, quick*
तेरह	terah	7	*thirteen*
तेरा	terā	6	*your, yours* (intimate)
तैंतालीस	taĩtālīs	A	*forty-three*
तैंतीस	taĩtīs	17	*thirty-three*
तैयार	taiyār	5	*ready, prepared*
तैयार करना[N]	taiyār karnā	11	*to prepare*
तैयारी	taiyārī	10	*preparation* (f.)
तो	to	10	*then; so; at any rate*
तोड़ना[N]	toṛnā	12	*to break* (tr.)
तौर	taur	8	*manner* (m.)
त्यौहार	tyauhār	16	*festival, feast day*
थकना	thaknā	18	*to be tired*
थमाना[N]	thamānā	18	*to hand over*
था	thā	4	*was; were*

थाना	thānā	14	*police station* (m.)
थीं	thī̃	4	*were*
थी	thī	4	*was; were*
थूकना[N]	thūknā	11	*to spit*
थे	the	4	*were*
थैला	thailā	12	*bag* (m.)
थोड़ा	thoṛā	8	*little, few*
थोड़ा-बहुत	thoṛā-bahut	9	*a certain amount*
थोड़ा-सा	thoṛā-sā	9	*a few, a little* (adj.)
दंगा	daṅgā	17	*riot* (m.)
दक्षिण	dakṣiṇ	14	*south* (m.)
दफ़ा	dafā	17	*time, occasion* (m.)
दफ़्तर	daftar	6	*office* (m.)
दया	dayā	15	*pity, mercy, compassion* (f.)
दरबार	darbār	17	*royal court* (m.)
दरवाज़ा	darvāzā	3	*door* (m.)
दराज़	darāz	12	*drawer* (f.)
दर्जन	darjan	14	*a dozen* (m.)
दर्द	dard	8	*pain* (m.)
दर्द करना[N]	dard karnā	C	*to hurt* (intr.)
दर्शन	darśan	16	*sight, view* (m.)
का/के दर्शन करना[N]	kā/ke darśan karnā	16	*to see, have vision of/audience with*
दवा	davā	11	*medicine* (f.)
दवाख़ाना	davākhānā	11	*pharmacy, dispensary* (m.)
दस	das	4	*ten*
दस्त	dast	C	*diarrhoea* (m.)
दस्त आना/लगना	dast ānā/lagnā	C	*to have diarrhoea*
दाँत	dā̃t	C	*tooth* (m.)
दाख़िल होना	dākhil honā	14	*to be admitted; to enter*
दादा	dādā	7	*paternal grandfather* (m.)
दादा-दादी	dādā-dādī	7	*paternal grandparents* (m.)
दादी	dādī	7	*paternal grandmother* (f.)
दाम	dām	9	*price* (m.)
दामाद	dāmād	B	*daughter's husband* (f.)
दाल	dāl	9	*pulse, lentil* (f.)
दाहिना	dāhinā	8	*right* (of direction)
दिक़्क़त	diqqat	12	*difficulty, trouble* (f.)
दिखना	dikhnā	E	*to be visible, be seen*
दिखाई देना/पड़ना	dikhāī denā/paṛnā	13	*to appear, seem, come into sight*

दिखाना[N]	dikhānā	5	*to show*
दिन	din	4	*day* (m.)
दिन-ब-दिन	din-ba-din	15	*day by day*
दिन भर	din bhar	13	*all day long*
दिल	dil	13	*heart* (m.)
दिल लगना	dil lagnā	13	*to feel content, feel at home*
दिलचस्प	dilcasp	4	*interesting*
दिलाना[N]	dilānā	18	*to cause to be given*
दिल्ली	dillī	3	*Delhi* (f.)
दिसंबर	disambar	8	*December* (m.)
दीखना	dīkhnā	12	*to be seen, appear*
दीवार	dīvār	3	*wall* (f.)
दीवाली	dīvālī	10	*Diwali, festival of lamps* (f.)
दुआ	duā	18	*prayer, good wishes* (f.)
दुःख (दुख)	duḥkh (dukh)	18	*sorrow, distress, suffering* (m.)
दुकान	dukān	4	*shop* (f.)
दुकानदार	dukāndār	8	*shopkeeper* (m.)
दुखना	dukhnā	18	*to hurt, ache*
दुनिया	duniyā	12	*world* (f.)
दुपट्टा	dupaṭṭā	18	*scarf* (m.)
दुबला	dublā	16	*thin, weak*
दुबला-पतला	dublā-patlā	16	*scrawny, 'lean and thin'*
दुर्घटना	durghaṭnā	14	*accident* (f.)
दूध	dūdh	4	*milk* (m.)
दूर	dūr	3	*far, distant; distance* (f.)
दूसरा	dūsrā	3	*second, other*
दृश्य	dṛśy	12	*scene* (m.)
देखना[N]	dekhnā	5	*to see, look*
देखभाल	dekhbhāl	13	*care, supervision* (f.)
की देखभाल करना[N]	kī dekhbhāl karnā	13	*to look after, care for*
देना[N]	denā	5	*to give*
देर	der	8	*delay, lateness, period of time* (f.)
देर से	der se	8	*late*
देर होना	der honā	8	*to get late*
देवर	devar	**B**	*husband's younger brother*
देवरानी	devrānī	**B**	*wife of husband's elder brother* (f.)
देश	deś	7	*country, region* (m.)

देहान्त	dehānt	16	*death, demise* (m.)
का देहान्त होना	kā dehānt honā	16	*to die*
दो	do	1	*two*
दोनों	donõ	1	*both, the two*
दोपहर	dopahar	11	*midday, noon*
दोबारा	dobārā	13	*again, a second time*
दोस्त	dost	6	*friend* (m.)
दौड़	daur̥	18	*race* (f.)
दौड़ना	daur̥nā	11	*to run*
द्वारा	dvārā	14	*by, by means of*
धंधा	dhandhā	15	*occupation, business, work* (m.)
धन	dhan	17	*wealth* (m.)
धन्यवाद	dhanyavād	2	*thanks; thank you* (m.)
धर्म	dharm	17	*faith, religion, righteous duty* (m.)
धर्मपत्नी	dharmpatnī	18	*wife* (f.)
धीरे-धीरे	dhīre-dhīre	8	*slowly, gradually*
धुआँ	dhuā̃	14	*smoke* (m.)
धुलना	dhulnā	14	*to be washed*
धूप	dhūp	13	*sunshine* (f.)
धूप खाना^N	dhūp khānā	14	*to bask in the sun, enjoy the sun*
धोखा	dhokhā	15	*deceit, trickery* (m.)
धोखा देना^N	dhokhā denā	15	*to deceive, dupe*
धोना^N	dhonā	10	*to wash* (clothes, etc.)
धोबी	dhobī	1	*washerman* (m.)
ध्यान	dhyān	8	*attention* (m.)
ध्यान से	dhyān se	8	*attentively*
नंबर	nambar	10	*number* (m.)
न	na	4	*not*
न जाने	na jāne	13	*God knows, who knows*
न...न	na...na	16	*neither...nor*
नगर	nagar	11	*city, town* (m.)
नज़र	nazar	13	*glance, sight* (f.)
नज़र आना	nazar ānā	13	*to come into sight, be seen, appear*
नज़र दौड़ाना^N	nazar daur̥ānā	18	*to look around*
नटखट	naṭkhaṭ	17	*naughty, mischievous*
ननद	nanad	**B**	*husband's sister* (f.)
ननदोई	nandoī	**B**	*husband of husband's sister*

नफ़रत	nafrat	14	*hate, dislike* (f.)
नफ़रत करना[N]	nafrat karnā	14	*to hate* (with **se**)
नब्बे	nabbe	**A**	*ninety*
नमक	namak	9	*salt* (m.)
नमकीन	namkīn	18	*salty; savoury snacks* (m.)
नमस्कार	namaskār	2	*greetings, goodbye* (m.)
नमस्ते	namaste	1	*greetings, goodbye* (f.)
नमूना	namūnā	15	*example, specimen, type* (m.)
नया	nayā	3	*new*
नल	nal	8	*pipe, tap* (m.)
नवंबर	navambar	8	*November* (m.)
नवासी	navāsī	**A**	*eighty-nine*
नहाना	nahānā	10	*to bathe, wash oneself*
नहीं	nahī̃	1	*no, not*
नहीं तो	nahī̃ to	10	*otherwise*
नाक	nāk	**C**	*nose* (f.)
नाक बहना	nāk bahnā	**C**	*have a runny nose* (the *nose to run*)
नाखून	nākhūn	**C**	*nail* (m.) (of finger, toe)
नाचना	nācnā	17	*to dance*
नातिन	nātin	**B**	*daughter's daughter* (f.)
नाती	nātī	**B**	*daughter's son* (m.)
नाना	nānā	9	*maternal grandfather* (f.)
नाना-नानी	nānā-nānī	9	*maternal grandparents* (m.)
नानी	nānī	9	*maternal grandmother* (f.)
नाम	nām	5	*name; renown* (m.)
नामक	nāmak	17	*named* (suffixes name, e.g. **rām nāmak ādmī** *a man named Ram*)
नाराज़	nārāz	14	*displeased, angry*
नाश्ता	nāśtā	12	*breakfast* (m.)
नाश्ता करना[N]	nāśtā karnā	12	*to have breakfast*
निंदा	nindā	16	*blame, speaking ill of, condemnation* (f.)
की निंदा करना[N]	kī nindā karnā	16	*to blame, speak ill of, condemn*
निकट	nikaṭ	13	*near*
निकलना	nikalnā	11	*to emerge, come/go out*
निकालना[N]	nikālnā	12	*to take out, extract, turn out, bring out*
निन्यानवे	ninyānve	**A**	*ninety-nine*

निवेदन	nivedan	D	*request, submission* (m.)
निश्चय करना[N]	niścay karnā	13	*to decide, resolve*
नींद	nī̃d	13	*sleep* (f.);
नींद आना	nī̃d ānā	13	*to feel sleepy, fall asleep*
नीचे	nīce	8	*under, below, beneath*
नीला	nīlā	2	*blue*
नोटिस	noṭis	13	*notice* (m.)
नौ	nau	2	*nine*
नौकर	naukar	8	*servant* (m.)
नौकर-चाकर	naukar-cākar	16	*servants and domestics* (m.)
नौकरी	naukarī	8	*service, job* (f.)
नौकरी करना[N]	naukarī karnā	8	*to serve, do a job*
पंखा	paṅkhā	3	*fan* (m.)
पंजाबी	pañjābī	1	***Panjabi; the Panjabi language*** (f.)
पंडित	paṇḍit	9	***learned man, pandit*** (m.)
पंद्रह	pandrah	8	*fifteen*
पकड़ना[N]	pakaṛnā	10	*to catch, grab, hold*
पकाना[N]	pakānā	17	*to cook* (tr.)
पक्का	pakkā	7	*ripe, cooked, well-made*
पगड़ी	pagṛī	10	***turban*** (f.)
पचपन	pacpan	A	*fifty-five*
पचहत्तर	pachattar	A	*seventy-five*
पचानवे	pacānve	A	*ninety-five*
पचाना[N]	pacānā	C	*to digest*
पचास	pacās	A	*fifty*
पचासी	pacāsī	A	*eighty-five*
पच्चीस	paccīs	11	*twenty-five*
पट्टी	paṭṭī	C	*bandage* (f.)
पट्टी बाँधना[N]	paṭṭī bā̃dhnā	C	*to apply a bandage*
पड़ना	paṛnā	9	*to fall, lie*
पड़ा	paṛā	7	*lying*
पड़ोसी	paṛosī	6	*neighbour* (m.)
पढ़ना[n]	paṛhnā	5	*to read, study*
पढ़ाई	paṛhāī	9	*study, studies* (f.)
पढ़ाना[N]	paṛhānā	6	*to teach*
पता	patā	12	*address* (m.)
पता चलना	patā calnā	11	*to become aware of, learn of*
पति	pati	11	*husband*
पतिदेव	patidev	18	*husband* (m.)

पतला	patlā	16	*thin, slender*
पतोहू	patohū	B	*son's wife* (f.)
पत्नी	patnī	8	*wife* (f.)
पत्र	patr	5	*letter, paper* (m.)
पद[1]	pad	13	*position, office* (m.)
पद[2]	pad	17	*lyric poem, hymn* (m.)
पधारना	padhārnā	18	*to grace (a place by coming or arriving); to depart*
पन्ना	pannā	18	*page* (m.)
पर[1]	par	3	*on; at* (etc.)
पर से	par se	12	*from on*
पर[2]	par	4	*but*
परंतु	parantu	11	*but*
परदा	pardā	3	*curtain; purdah* (m.)
परवाह	parvāh	15	*concern, care, heed* (f.)
परवाह करना[N]	parvāh karnā	15	*to care*
परसों	parsõ	7	*the day before yesterday; the day after tomorrow*
परिचय	paricay	18	*introduction, acquaintance* (m.)
परिचय कराना[N]	paricay karānā	18	*to introduce*
परिवार	parivār	7	*family* (m.)
परीक्षा	parīkṣā	10	*examination* (f.)
परीक्षा देना[N]	parīkṣā denā	10	*to sit an examination*
परेशान	pareśān	10	*worried, anxious*
पलंग	palaṅg	3	*bed* (m.)
पलटना[n]	palaṭnā	18	*to turn over, turn back*
पवित्र	pavitr	18	*pure, sacred, holy*
पवित्र करना[N]	pavitr karnā	18	*to impart sanctity (to a place by visiting it)*
पश्चिम	paścim	14	*western; west* (m.)
पसंद	pasand	4	*pleasing, favourite; liking* (f.)
पसंद करना[N]	pasand karnā	10	*to choose, prefer, like*
पहचानना[N]	pahcānnā	9	*to recognise, identify*
पहनना[N]	pahannā	13	*to wear, put on*
पहर	pahar	8	*8th part of a day, 3-hour period* (m.)
पहला	pahlā	7	*first*
पहले	pahle	8	*previously, ago, (at) first*
पहले-पहल	pahle-pahal	15	*for the first time*
पहाड़	pahāṛ	6	*mountain, hill* (m.)

पहुँचना	pahũcnā	7	*to reach, arrive at*
पहुँचाना[N]	pahũcānā	8	*to convey, cause to reach, deliver*
पाँच	pā̃c	3	*five*
पाँचवाँ	pā̃cvā̃	7	*fifth*
पाँव	pā̃v	8	*foot, leg* (m.)
पाँव की उँगली	pā̃v kī ũglī	C	*toe* (f.)
पाई	pāī	A	*'pie'* (f.) (one third of an old **paisā**)
पाकिस्तानी	pākistānī	1	*Pakistani* (m.)/(f.)/(adj.)
पागल	pāgal	11	*mad, crazy; madman* (m.)
पाठ	pāṭh	12	*lesson; reading* (m.)
पाना[N]	pānā	10	*to find, obtain*
पानी	pānī	5	*water* (m.)
पानी पड़ना	pānī paṛnā	9	*to rain*
पालना[N]	pālnā	15	*to rear, bring up*
पास	pās	8	*nearby*
पिंजरा	pĩjrā	15	*cage* (m.)
पिछला	pichlā	8	*previous, last*
पिता	pitā	1	*father*
पिलाना[N]	pilānā	E	*to give to drink*
पीछा	pīchā	16	*rear part; pursuit* (m.)
का पीछा करना[N]	kā pīchā karnā	16	*to follow, chase, pursue*
पीछे	pīche	8	*behind, after*
पीठ	pīṭh	C	*back* (f.)
पीना[N]	pīnā	5	*to drink, smoke*
पीला	pīlā	4	*yellow*
पुकारना[N]	pukārnā	12	*to call, call out*
पुनश्च	punaśc	D	*PS, postscript*
पुराना	purānā	3	*old* (not of people)
पुलिस	pulis	12	*police* (f.)
पुस्तक	pustak	7	*book* (f.)
पूँजी	pũjī	15	*capital, investment* (f.)
पूछना[N]	pūchnā	5	*to ask*
पूछ-ताछ	pūch-tāch	12	*inquiry, investigation* (f.)
पूछ-ताछ करना[N]	pūch-tāch karnā	12	*to enquire, make enquiries* (with **se**)
पूजा	pūjā	16	*worship, adoration* (f.)
की पूजा करना[N]	kī pūjā karnā	16	*to worship, adore*
पूज्य	pūjy	D	*revered*
पूरा	pūrā	10	*full, complete, whole*
पूरा करना[N]	pūrā karnā	10	*to complete*

पूरा होना	pūrā honā	10	*to be complete*
पूर्व	pūrv	14	*east* (m.)
पूस	pūs	A	*the month Paus* (Dec.–Jan.) (m.)
पेंसिल	pensil	2	*pencil* (f.)
पेट	peṭ	17	*stomach* (m.)
पेड़	peṛ	4	*tree* (m.)
पेशाब	peśāb	C	*urine* (m.)
पेशाब करना[N]	peśāb karnā	C	*to urinate*
पेशाब-घर	peśāb-ghar	C	*toilet, urinal* (m.)
पैंतालीस	paĩtālīs	A	*forty-five*
पैंतीस	paĩtīs	A	*thirty-five*
पैंसठ	paĩsaṭh	A	*sixty-five*
पैकेट	paikeṭ	12	*packet* (m.)
पैदल	paidal	10	*on foot*
पैदा होना	paidā honā	14	*to be born/produced* (**paidā** inv.)
पैर	pair	C	*foot* (m.)
पैसा	paisā	6	*money; one 100th of a rupee* (m.)
पोता	potā	B	*son's son* (m.)
पोती	potī	B	*son's daughter* (f.)
पौधा	paudhā	4	*plant* (m.)
पौन	paun	11	*three-quarters*
पौना	paunā	11	*three-quarters*
पौने	paune	11	*a quarter to, less a quarter*
पौष	pauṣ	A	*name of a month* (Dec.–Jan.) (m.)
प्यार	pyār	10	*love* (m.)
प्यार करना[N]	pyār karnā	10	*to love* (with **se**)
प्यारा	pyārā	18	*dear, beloved; dear one, beloved* (m.)
प्याला	pyālā	5	*cup* (m.)
प्यास	pyās	13	*thirst* (f.)
प्रकार	prakār	17	*variety, kind; manner, way* (m.)
प्रकाश	prakāś	18	*light* (m.)
प्रचलित	pracalit	17	*current*
प्रणाम	praṇām	18	*respectful greeting* (m.)
प्रतिशत	pratiśat	A	*per cent*
प्रदेश	pradeś	14	*province, state* (m.)
प्रधान मंत्री	pradhān mantrī	17	*prime minister* (m.)

प्रभु	prabhu	18	*lord;* (m.)
प्रभु का प्यारा होना	prabhu kā pyārā hona	18	*to go to heaven*
प्रमुख	pramukh	13	*principal, chief, main*
प्रयोग	prayog	16	*use* (m.)
का प्रयोग करना[N]	kā prayog karnā	16	*to use*
प्रवेश करना[N]	praveś karnā	17	*to enter*
प्रशंसा	praśansā	16	*praise* (f.)
की प्रशंसा करना[N]	kī praśansā karnā	16	*to praise*
प्रसन्न	prasann	13	*pleased, happy*
प्रायः	prāyaḥ	15	*usually, often, almost*
प्रिय	priy	10	*dear, favourite*
प्रियवर	priyvar	D	*dearest*
प्रेम	prem	15	*love* (m.)
प्रेम करना[N]	prem karnā	15	*to love* (with **se**)
प्रोग्राम	progrām	10	*programme* (m.)
प्लेटफ़ार्म	pleṭfārm	18	*platform* (m.)
फँसना	phā̃snā	16	*to be ensnared, involved, caught up*
फटना	phaṭnā	18	*to be torn, split*
फ़रमाना[N]	farmānā	18	*to (be so graceful as to) speak out, make a command or request*
फ़रवरी	farvarī	8	*February* (f.)
फ़र्श	farś	12	*floor* (m.)
फल	phal	4	*fruit* (m.)
फ़लाना	falānā	13	*so-and-so, such-and-such*
फागुन	phāgun	A	*the month Phālgun* (Feb.–March) (m.)
फाड़ना	phāṛnā	E	*to tear, split, cleave* (tr.)
फ़ायदा	fāydā	9	*advantage, profit, gain* (m.)
फाल्गुन	phālgun	A	*name of a month* (Feb.-March) (m.)
फ़िक्र	fikr	12	*anxiety, worry, concern* (f.)
फ़िक्र करना[N]	fikr karnā	12	*to worry, be anxious*
फिर	phir	7	*then, again*
फिर भी	phir bhī	17	*even so*
फिरना	phirnā	18	*to turn, return, wander*
फ़िल्म	film	8	*film* (f.)
फीका	phīkā	17	*tasteless, dull; unsweetened*

फ़ुरसत	fursat	10	*leisure, spare time, free time* (f.)
फूफा	phūphā	**B**	*husband of father's younger sister* (m.)
फूफी	phūphī	**B**	*father's younger sister* (f.)
फूल	phūl	4	*flower* (m.)
फेंकना[N]	phẽknā	14	*to throw*
फेफड़ा	phephṛā	**C**	*lung* (m.)
फेरना[N]	phernā	**E**	*to turn, return* (intr.)
फेरीवाला	pherīvālā	13	*hawker* (m.)
फैलना	phailnā	12	*to spread* (intr.)
फ़ोटो	foṭo	11	*photograph* (m.)
फ़ोटो खींचना	foṭo khĩcnā	11	*to take a photograph*
फ़ोन करना	fon karnā	9	*to telephone*
फ्रांस	frāns	14	*France* (m.)
फ्रांसीसी	frānsīsī	11	*French* (adj.); *the French language* (f.)
बंगला	baṅglā	7	*the Bengali language* (f.)
बँटना	bãṭnā	**E**	*to be distributed, shared, divided*
बंद	band	5	*closed*
बंद करना[N]	band karnā	7	*to close* (intr.)
बंद होना	band honā	5	*to close* (tr.)
बंदर	bandar	14	*monkey* (m.)
बंदूक़	bandūq	15	*gun* (m.)
बँधना	bãdhnā	**E**	*to be tied, fastened*
बंधु	bandhu	**B**	*kinsman, brother* (m.)
बंधुवर	bandhuvar	**D**	*kinsman* (m.) ·
बंबई	bambaī	3	*Bombay* (f.)
बक्सा	baksā	12	*box* (m.)
बग़ल	bagal	18	*side, flank, armpit* (f.)
बचना	bacnā	12	*to be saved, escape, survive*
बचपन	bacpan	11	*childhood* (m.)
बचाना[N]	bacānā	12	*to save, rescue*
बच्चा	baccā	2	*child* (m.)
बजना	bajnā	11	*to resound, ring, chime*
बजाना[N]	bajānā	9	*to play (musical instrument)*
बड़ा	baṛā	1	*big*
बड़े-बूढ़े	baṛe-būṛhe	10	*elders* (m.pl.)
बढ़ना	baṛhnā	11	*to increase, advance* (intr.)
से बढ़कर	se baṛhkar	11	*better than, superior to*

बढ़िया	baṛhiyā	5	*fine, excellent, of good quality* (inv.)
बतानाᴺ	batānā	5	*to tell*
बत्ती	battī	13	*light, lamp* (f.)
बत्तीस	battīs	16	*thirty-two*
बदमाश	badmāś	12	*rogue, villain* (m.)
बदलनाⁿ	badalnā	8	*to change*
बदी	badī	A	*the waning half of a lunar month* (f.)
बधाई	badhāī	15	*congratulations, felicitations* (f.)
बनना	bannā	13	*to become, be made*
बनानाᴺ	banānā	6	*to make*
बयालीस	bayālīs	A	*forty-two*
बयासी	bayāsī	A	*eighty-two*
बरदाश्त करनाᴺ	bardāśt karnā	15	*to tolerate, endure, stand*
बराबर	barābar	15	*constantly, continuously*
बराम्दा	barāmdā	6	*verandah* (m.)
बर्फ़	barf	6	*snow, ice* (f.)
बल्कि	balki	15	*but rather*
बस[1]	bas	2	*that's all*
बस[2]	bas	3	*bus* (f.)
बसंत	basant	A	*spring (season)* (m.)
बसना	basnā	18	*to settle, inhabit; to be situated*
बहत्तर	bahattar	A	*seventy-two*
बहनोई	bahnoī	B	*sister's husband* (m.)
बहिन (बहन)	bahin (bahan)	2	*sister* (f.)
बहुत	bahut	2	*very; much, many*
बहुत-सा	bahut-sā	9	*much, quite a lot*
बहू	bahū	1	*daughter-in-law; wife* (f.)
बाँका	bā̃kā	14	*crooked, bent*
बाँटनाᴺ	bā̃ṭnā	12	*to distribute, share out*
बाँह	bā̃h	C	*arm* (f.)
बाईस	bāīs	8	*twenty-two*
बाक़ी	bāqī	11	*remaining, left over* (inv.); *remainder, arrears* (f.)
बग़ीचा	bagīcā	4	*(small) garden* (m.)
बाग़	bāg	4	*garden* (m.)
बाघ	bāgh	13	*tiger* (m.)
बाज़ार	bāzār	7	*bazaar, shopping area, market* (m.)

बाज़ार गरम होना	bāzār garm honā	18	*to be doing brisk business*
बाज़ी	bāzī	11	*turn (in game), play, bet*
बाढ़	bāṛh	12	*flood* (f.)
बात	bāt	4	*thing, matter, idea, thing said*
बात करना[N]	bāt karnā	7	*to talk, converse* (with, **se**);
बातें होना	bātẽ honā	8	*a conversation to take place;*
बातचीत	bātcīt	10	*conversation, dialogue, negotiations* (f.)
बाद	bād	8	*later*
बाद में	bād mẽ	10	*afterwards, later*
बादल	bādal	16	*cloud* (m.)
बादशाह	bādśāh	17	*emperor* (m.)
बानवे	bānve	**A**	*ninety-two*
बाप	bāp	**B**	*father* (m.)
बाबा	bābā	**B**	*grandfather* (m.)
बायाँ	bāyā̃	8	*left (direction)* (inflects like **pā̃cvā̃**)
बार	bār	11	*time, occasion* (f.)
बारह	bārah	6	*twelve*
बारिश	bāriś	14	*rain* (f.)
बारिश होना	bāriś honā	14	*to rain (rain to fall)*
बाल[1]	bāl	14	*hair* (m.)
बाल बाँका न होना	bāl bā̃kā na honā	14	*to escape unhurt, remain unscathed*
बाल[2]	bāl	17	*child* (m.)
बाल-बच्चे	bāl-bacce	10	*children, family* (m. pl.)
बालक	bālak	17	*child* (m.)
बालटी	bālṭī	17	*bucket* (f.)
बावन	bāvan	**A**	*fifty-two*
बासठ	bāsaṭh	**A**	*sixty-two*
बाहर	bāhar	7	*outside*
बिकना	biknā	14	*to be sold*
बिगड़ना	bigaṛnā	17	*to be spoiled, go wrong; to lose temper*
बिजली	bijlī	10	*electricity, lightning* (f.)
बिठाना[N]	biṭhānā	12	*to make sit*
बिताना[N]	bitānā	9	*to spend, pass (time)*
बिरादरी	birādarī	10	*community, fraternity* (f.)
बिलकुल	bilkul	9	*absolutely*
बिल्ली	billī	14	*cat* (f.)
बिस्तर	bistar	**C**	*bedding, bed* (m.)

बीच	bīc	10	*middle* (m.)
बीच में	bīc mẽ	13	*meanwhile, in the meantime*
बीड़ी	bīṛī	12	*small cigarette rolled in leaf* (f.)
बीतना	bītnā	18	*to pass, be spent (of time)*
बीमार	bīmār	2	*ill*
बीमारी	bīmārī	12	*illness* (f.)
बीवी	bīvī	13	*wife* (f.)
बीस	bīs	7	*twenty*
बुआ	buā	17	*aunt (father's sister)* (f.)
बुख़ार	bukhār	4	*temperature, fever* (m.)
बुज़ुर्ग	buzurg	2	*elderly*
बुढ़िया	buṛhiyā	1	*old woman* (f.)
बुद्धू	buddhū	12	*foolish; fool* (m.)
बुध	budh	10	*Wednesday* (m.)
बुधवार	budhvār	7	*Wednesday* (m.)
बुरा	burā	2	*bad*
का बुरा मानना^N	kā burā mānnā	9	*to take amiss, take offence* (at)
बुरी तरह (से)	burī tarah (se)	12	*badly*
बुलाना^N	bulānā	5	*to call, invite*
बूझना^N	būjhnā	11	*to understand* (*in* **jān-būjhkar**)
बूढ़ा	būṛhā	2	*old (of people)*
बृहस्पति	bṛhaspati	10	*Thursday* (m.)
बृहस्पतिवार	bṛhaspativār	7	*Thursday* (m.)
बेकार	bekār	16	*useless; out of work, unemployed*
बेचना^N	becnā	13	*to sell*
बेचारा	becārā	13	*poor, wretched, helpless*
बेटा	beṭā	2	*son* (m.)
बेटी	beṭī	1	*daughter, girl* (f.)
बेवक़ूफ़	bevaqūf	17	*foolish; fool* (m.)
बेशक	beśak	13	*of course*
बेहतर	behtar	C	*better*
बैंक	baiṅk	17	*bank* (m.)
बैठना	baiṭhnā	5	*to sit*
बैठा	baiṭhā	9	*sitting, seated*
बैठाना^N	baiṭhānā	E	*to make sit*
बैरा	bairā	15	*waiter, 'bearer'* (m.)
बैसाख	baisākh	A	*the month Vaiśākh* (April–May) (m.)

बोतल	botal	12	*bottle* (f.)
बोलना^{n}	bolnā	5	*to speak, say*
ब्योरा	byorā	12	*details, particulars* (m.)
ब्रज भाषा	braj bhāṣā	17	*Braj bhāṣā (a Hindi dialect)* (f.)
ब्राह्मण	brāhmaṇ	17	*Brahmin (priestly caste)* (m.)
ब्रेक	brek	14	*brake* (m.)
भई	bhaī	10	*eh, well, etc.* (excl.)
भगवद्गीता	bhagvadgītā	14	*Bhagavad Gita* (f.)
भगवान	bhagvān	15	*God* (m.)
भतीजा	bhatījā	B	*brother's son* (m.)
भतीजी	bhatījī	B	*brother's daughter* (f.)
भयंकर	bhayaṅkar	16	*terrible, fearful*
-भर	-bhar	13	*full, whole, complete* (suffix)
भरना^{n}	bharnā	11	*to fill; to be filled*
भवदीय(-ा)	bhavdīy(ā)	D	*yours sincerely, yours faithfully*
भाँजा	bhā̃jā	B	*sister's son* (m.)
भाँजी	bhā̃jī	B	*sister's daughter* (f.)
भाई	bhāī	2	*brother* (m.)
भाग	bhāg	12	*part, portion* (m.)
भागना	bhāgnā	13	*to run, flee, escape*
भादों	bhādõ	A	*the month Bhādrapad* (Aug.–Sept.) (m.)
भाद्रपद	bhādrapad	A	*name of a month* (Aug.–Sept.) (m.)
भाभी	bhābhī	B	*brother's wife* (f.)
भारत	bhārat	6	*India* (m.);
भारत सरकार	bharat sarkār	14	*the Indian Government* (f.)
भारतवर्ष	bhāratvarṣ	6	*India* (m.)
भारतीय	bhāratīy	1	*Indian* (m.)/(f.)/(adj.)
भारी	bhārī	3	*heavy*
भाव	bhāv	A	*rate, price* (m.)
भाषा	bhāṣā	7	*language* (f.)
भिखारी	bhikhārī	18	*beggar* (m.)
भिन्न	bhinn	10	*different*
भी	bhī	2	*also, too; even*
भी ... भी	bhī ... bhī	6	*both ... and*
भीड़	bhīṛ	8	*crowd* (f.)
भीड़-भाड़	bhīṛ-bhāṛ	16	*hustle and bustle* (f.)
भीतर	bhītar	8	*inside, within*

भूख	bhūkh	13	*hunger* (f.)
भूत	bhūt	15	*ghost* (m.)
भूलना	bhūlnā	10	*to forget*
भूलकर भी	bhūlkar bhī	11	*even by mistake*
भेंट	bhẽṭ	11	*gift; meeting* (f.)
भेजना[N]	bhejnā	9	*to send*
भेष	bheṣ	15	*appearance, guise* (m.)
भैया	bhaiyā	12	*brother* (m.)
भोजन	bhojan	10	*food* (m.)
भोजन करना[N]	bhojan karnā	10	*to eat, dine*
मंगल	maṅgal	10	*Tuesday* (m.)
मंगलवार	maṅgalvār	7	*Tuesday* (m.)
मँगवाना[N]	mãgvānā	13	*to order, ask for, buy*
मंत्री	mantrī	18	*minister* (m.)
मंदिर	mandir	7	*temple* (m.)
मई	maī	8	*May* (f.)
मकान	makān	1	*house* (m.)
मक्खन	makkhan	4	*butter* (m.)
मगर	magar	12	*but*
मच्छर	macchar	14	*mosquito* (m.)
मच्छरदानी	macchardānī	14	*mosquito net* (f.)
मज़दूर	mazdūr	17	*labourer* (m.)
मजबूर	majbūr	16	*helpless, compelled*
मजबूर करना[N]	majbūr karnā	16	*to compel* (with **par**)
मज़ा	mazā	15	*pleasure, fun* (m.)
मज़ा आना	mazā ānā	15	*to enjoy, have fun*
मज़ा लेना[N]	mazā lenā	18	*to enjoy*
मज़ाक़	mazāq	13	*joke* (m.)
मज़ाक़िया	mazāqiyā	13	*witty, funny, humorous*
मत	mat	5	*do not* (with imperative)
मतलब	matlab	15	*meaning; motive, self-interest* (m.)
मदद	madad	16	*help* (f.)
की मदद करना[N]	kī madad karnā	16	*to help*
मद्रास	madrās	10	*Madras* (m.)
मधुर	madhur	17	*sweet, melodious*
मन	man	13	*mind, heart* (m.)
मन लगना	man lagnā	13	*to feel at home*
मना	manā	9	*forbidden, prohibited* (inv.)
मना करना[N]	manā karnā	17	*to forbid, prohibit*
मनाना[N]	manānā	9	*to celebrate* (festival, holiday)

ममेरा भाई	mamerā bhāī	**B**	*maternal cousin* (m.)
ममेरी बहिन	mamerī bahin	**B**	*maternal cousin* (f.)
मरज़ी	marzī	10	*wish, preference* (f.)
मरना	marnā	15	*to die*
मरम्मत	marammat	16	*repair* (f.)
की मरम्मत करना[N]	kī marammat karnā	16	*to repair, mend; to beat up* (slang)
मराठी	marāṭhī	14	*the Marathi language* (f.)
मरीज़	marīz	**C**	*patient* (m.)/(f.)
मलमास	malmās	**A**	*leap month* (m.)
मशहूर	maśhūr	13	*famous*
मसाला	masālā	14	*spice* (m.)
महँगा	mahā̃gā	2	*expensive*
महत्त्व	mahattv	17	*importance* (m.)
महत्त्वपूर्ण	mahattvpūrṇ	15	*important*
महल	mahal	11	*palace* (m.)
महसूस करना[N]	mahsūs karnā	13	*to feel, experience*
महात्मा	mahātmā	17	*saintly; saint* (m.) (lit. *great soul*)
महिला	mahilā	2	*lady* (f.)
महीना	mahīnā	6	*month* (m.)
महीने के महीने	mahīne ke mahīne	15	*month by month*
महोदय	mahoday	**D**	*sir*
महोदया	mahodayā	**D**	*madam*
माँ	mā̃	9	*mother* (f.)
माँ-बाप	mā̃-bāp	8	*parents* (m.)
माँग	mā̃g	10	*demand* (f.)
माँगना[N]	mā̃gnā	10	*to demand, ask for*
माँस	mā̃s	9	*meat* (m.)
माघ	māgh	**A**	*name of a month* (Jan.–Feb.) (m.)
माता	mātā	1	*mother* (f.)
माता-पिता	mātā-pitā	2	*parents* (m.)
मातृभाषा	mātṛbhāṣā	14	*mother tongue* (f.)
माथा	māthā	**C**	*forehead* (m.)
मानना[N]	manna	9	*to accept, agree, believe*
माननीय	mānanīy	**D**	*revered, respected*
मानों	mānõ	15	*as though, as if*
माफ़ करना[N]	māf karnā	12	*to pardon, forgive*
मामला	māmlā	10	*matter, affair* (m.)
मामा	māmā	**B**	*maternal uncle* (m.)
मामी	māmī	**B**	*wife of maternal uncle* (f.)

मामूली	māmūlī	15	*ordinary, commonplace*
मार	mār	14	*beating* (f.)
मार खाना[N]	mār khānā	14	*to undergo a beating*
मारना[N]	mārnā	5	*to beat, hit, kill*
मार्च	mārc	8	*March* (m.)
माल	māl	16	*goods, produce, stuff, property* (m.)
मालिक	mālik	13	*boss, proprietor, master* (m.)
मालूम	mālūm	4	*known*
मास	mās	11	*month* (m.)
मिज़ाज	mizāj	18	*mood, temperament* (m.)
मिठाई	miṭhāī	10	*sweet, sweetmeat* (f.)
मिठास	miṭhās	17	*sweetness* (f.)
मित्र	mitr	8	*friend* (m.)
मिनट	minaṭ	8	*minute* (m.)
मिलनसार	milansār	6	*friendly, sociable*
मिलना	milnā	9	*to meet* (with **se**); *to be available*
मिलना-जुलना	milnā-julnā	13	*to associate, mix, resemble* (with **se**)
मिलाना[N]	milānā	18	*to bring together, unite, mix*
मीटर	mīṭar	13	*meter* (m.)
मीठा	mīṭhā	5	*sweet*
मील	mīl	A	*mile* (f.)
मुँह	mũh	11	*face, mouth* (m.)
मुक़ाबिला करना[N]	muqābilā karnā	20	*to compete, compare* (with **se**); *to confront*
मुक्ति	mukti	13	*liberation, salvation* (f.)
मुख	mukh	C	*mouth, face*
मुख्य	mukhy	14	*main, principal, chief*
मुड़ना	muṛnā	8	*to turn* (intr.)
मुफ़्त में	muft mẽ	13	*free of charge*
मुबारक	mubārak	10	*blessed*
मुमकिन	mumkin	11	*possible*
मुलाक़ात	mulāqāt	16	*meeting, acquaintance* (f.)
की मुलाक़ात होना	kī mulāqāt honā	16	*to meet* (with **se**)
मुश्किल	muśkil	4	*difficult; difficulty* (f.)
मुश्किल से	muśkil se	15	*with difficulty, barely*
मुसलमान	musalmān	2	*Muslim* (m.)/(f.)/(adj.)
मुसाफ़िर	musāfir	7	*traveller* (m.)
मुसीबत	musībat	16	*difficulty, calamity* (f.)
मुस्कराना[n]	muskarānā	11	*to smile*

मुहल्ला	muhallā	8	*locality, area of town* (m.)
मूँगफली	mū̃gphalī	11	*peanut* (f.)
मूर्च्छा	mūrcchā	C	*fainting* (f.)
मूर्ति	mūrti	8	*idol, image, statue* (f.)
मृत्यु	mṛtyu	16	*death* (f.)
की मृत्यु होना	kī mṛtyu honā	16	*to die*
में	mẽ	3	*in*
में से	mẽ se	3	*from amongst, out of*
मेंढक	mẽḍhak	14	*frog* (m.)
मेंह	mẽh	14	*rain* (m.)
मेज़	mez	1	*table* (f.)
मेरा	merā	6	*my, mine*
मेला	melā	11	*fair* (m.)
मेहनत	mehnat	15	*hard work, labour* (f.)
मेहमान	mehmān	6	*guest* (m.)
मेहरबानी	meharbānī	2	*kindness* (f.)
मैं	maĩ	1	*I*
मैदान	maidān	15	*plain, field* (m.)
मैला	mailā	18	*dirty*
मोटा	moṭā	2	*fat, coarse*
मोड़	moṛ	8	*bend, turning, fold* (m.)
मोड़ना[N]	moṛnā	14	*to turn* (tr.)
मोल-भाव करना[N]	mol-bhāv karnā	18	*to bargain, haggle*
मौक़ा	mauqā	13	*opportunity, chance, occasion* (m.)
मौसम	mausam	2	*weather* (m.)
मौसा	mausā	B	*husband of maternal aunt* (m.)
मौसी	mausī	B	*maternal aunt* (f.)
यदि	yadi	10	*if*
यद्यपि	yadyapi	17	*although*
यमुना	yamunā	17	*the river Yamuna (Jumna)* (f.)
यश	yaś	17	*fame, reputation* (m.)
यह	yah	1	*this, he, she, it*
यहाँ	yahā̃	1	*here*
यहाँ तक कि	yahā̃ tak ki	13	*to the point / extent that*
यहीं	yahī̃	9	*right here, in this very place*
या	yā	7	*or*
या तो ... या	yā to ... yā	16	*either ... or*
यात्रा	yātrā	11	*journey, travel* (f.)
यात्रा करना[N]	yātrā karnā	16	*to travel*

यात्री	yātrī	11	*traveller* (m.)
याद	yād	10	*memory, recollection* (f.)
याद आना	yād ānā	16	*to come to mind, recur to the memory*
याद करना[N]	yād karnā	16	*to memorise, learn by heart*
याद दिलाना[N]	yād dilānā	18	*to remind*
याद रखना[N]	yād rakhnā	16	*to bear in mind*
याद रहना	yād rahnā	16	*to remain remembered*
याद होना	yād honā	16	*to be remembered, recalled*
यार	yār	9	*friend, mate* (m.)
युगांडा	yugāṇḍā	15	*Uganda* (m.)
युवक	yuvak	12	*youth, young man* (m.)
ये	ye	1	*these, they; he, she* (honorific)
योगदान	yogdān	15	*contribution* (m.)
योग्य	yogy	9	*capable, worth, suitable, worthy*
रंग	raṅg	4	*colour* (m.)
रंग करना[N]	raṅg karnā	16	*to colour*
रंगीन	raṅgīn	16	*coloured*
रक़म	raqam	18	*sum, amount* (f.)
रखना[N]	rakhnā	9	*to put, place, keep, hold*
रचना[N]	racnā	17	*to compose, create*
रफ़्तार	raftār	14	*speed* (f.)
रविवार	ravivār	7	*Sunday* (m.)
रसोईघर	rasoīghar	3	*kitchen* (m.)
रहना	rahnā	6	*to stay, remain, reside, live*
रहनेवाला	rahnevālā	10	*inhabitant* (m.)
राजधानी	rājdhānī	9	*capital city* (f.)
राजा	rājā	1	*king, rajah* (m.)
रात	rāt	3	*night* (f.)
राम कहानी	rām kahānī	18	*tale of woe* (f.)
राम नवमी	rām navamī	A	*Rām's birthday* (f.) *(9th day of the bright half of Caitr)*
राम राम	rām rām!	17	*Greetings!*
राम राम कहना[N]	rām rām kahnā	17	*to say 'Ram Ram', to take the name of god*
राष्ट्रभाषा	rāṣṭrabhāṣā	14	*national language* (f.)
रास्ता	rāstā	8	*road, way, route* (m.)
रास्ते में	rāste mẽ	13	*on the way, en route*
रिआयत	riāyat	A	*concession, discount* (f.)
रिक्शा	rikśā	12	*rickshaw* (m.)

रिवाज	rivāj	10	*practice, custom, usage* (m.)
रिश्तेदार	riśtedār	9	*relative* (m.)
रुकना	ruknā	14	*to stop* (intr.)
रुचि	ruci	17	*interest, liking, taste* (f.)
रुपया	rupayā	3	*rupee; money* (m.)
रुलाना	rulānā	E	*to make cry*
रूप	rūp	14	*form, beauty* (m.)
रेडियो	reḍiyo	11	*radio* (m.)
रेलगाड़ी	relgāṛī	7	*train* (f.)
रेलवे	relve	12	*railway* (f.)
रेशम	reśam	18	*silk* (m.)
रेशमी	reśmī	18	*silken*
रैक	raik	12	*rack* (m.)
रोकना^{N}	roknā	15	*to stop* (tr.)
रोग	rog	C	*illness* (m.)
रोगी	rogī	C	*patient* (m.)
रोज़	roz	9	*daily, every day; day* (m.)
रोना	ronā	9	*to cry, weep*
रोना-धोना	ronā-dhonā	9	*to weep and wail*
लंबा	lambā	2	*tall* (of people, trees)
लंबा-चौड़ा	lambā-cauṛā	12	*huge, vast, 'great big'*
लकड़ी	lakṛī	17	*wood; stick* (f.)
लखनऊ	lakhnaū	11	*Lucknow* (m.) (capital of UP)
लखपति	lakhpati	18	*wealthy person, 'millionaire'* (m.)
लगना	lagnā	13	*to be applied; to seem* (para. **58**); *to begin to* (para. **62**)
लगभग	lagbhag	15	*about, approximately*
लगातार	lagātār	15	*continuously*
लगाना^{N}	lagānā	14	*to apply, attach*
लड़का	laṛkā	1	*boy* (m.)
लड़की	laṛkī	1	*girl* (f.)
लड़ना	laṛnā	9	*to fight*
लन्दन	landan	3	*London* (m.)
लपकना	lapaknā	14	*to rush forward, pounce*
लस्सी	lassī	11	*lassi (a yoghourt drink* (f.)
लाख	lākh	A	100,000, *lac, lakh* (m.)
लाठी	lāṭhī	15	*staff, stick, truncheon* (f.)
लादना^{N}	lādnā	12	*to load*

लाना	lānā	5	*to bring*
लापरवाह	lāparvāh	12	*careless*
लापरवाही	lāparvāhī	14	*carelessness* (f.)
लाभ	lābh	11	*profit, advantage* (m.)
लायक़	lāyaq	9	*capable, worth, suitable, worthy*
लाल	lāl	2	*red*
लिखना[N]	likhnā	5	*to write*
लिटाना[N]	liṭānā	E	*to make lie down*
लेकिन	lekin	1	*but*
लेख	lekh	14	*article, paper* (m.)
लेटना	leṭnā	18	*to lie down*
लेटाना[N]	leṭānā	E	*to make lie down*
लेना	lenā	5	*to take*
लोकप्रिय	lokpriy	17	*popular*
लोग	log	1	*people*
लौटना	lauṭnā	9	*to return* (intr.)
वक़्त	vaqt	11	*time* (m.)
वग़ैरह	vagairah	11	*etc., and so on*
वर्णन	varṇan	17	*description* (m.)
का वर्णन करना[N]	kā varṇan karnā	17	*to describe*
वर्ष	varṣ	11	*year* (m.)
वह	vah	1	*that, he, she, it*
वहाँ	vahā̃	1	*there*
वहीं	vahī̃	9	*right there, in that very place*
वाक्य	vāky	12	*sentence* (m.)
वातावरण	vātāvaraṇ	15	*atmosphere* (m.)
वापस आना	vāpas ānā	13	*to come back, return*
वापस करना[N]	vāpas karnā	12	*to give back, return*
वापस जाना	vāpas jānā	14	*to go back, return*
वाराणसी	vārāṇasī	10	*Varanasi, Benares* (f.)
-वाला	-vālā	10	(see para. **46**)
वालिद	vālid	B	*father* (m.)
वालिदा	vālidā	B	*mother* (f.)
विक्रम	vikram	A	*Vikramaditya* (m.)
विक्रमादित्य	vikramādity	A	*name of king from whose reign the Hindu calendar begins* (m.)
विचार	vicār	11	*thought, idea, opinion* (m.)
विज्ञापन	vijñāpan	10	*advertisement* (m.)
विदेश	videś	10	*foreign country* (m.)

विदेशी	videśī	10	*foreigner* (m.); *foreign* (adj.)
विद्यार्थी	vidyārthī	2	*student* (m.)
विभिन्न	vibhinn	14	*various*
विराजना	virājnā	18	*to grace* (*a place with one's presence*), *to be seated*
विवाह	vivāh	11	*wedding, marriage* (m.)
का विवाह होना	kā vivāh honā	16	*to marry*
विशेष	viśeṣ	11	*special, particular*
विश्वास	viśvās	15	*belief, trust, confidence*
विषय	viṣay	14	*subject*
वे	ve	1	*those, they; he, she* (honorific)
वेतन	vetan	11	*wage, salary, pay* (m.)
वैशाख	vaiśākh	A	*name of a month* (April–May) (m.)
वैसा	vaisā	15	*of that kind, like that*
वैसे	vaise	10	*actually*
वोट	voṭ	17	*vote* (m.)
वोट देना[N]	voṭ denā	17	*to vote, give a vote*
व्यक्ति	vyakti	12	*person, individual* (m.)
व्यस्त	vyast	10	*busy*
व्याकरण	vyākaraṇ	15	*grammar* (m.)
व्यापार	vyāpār	10	*trade* (m.)
व्यापार करना[N]	vyāpār karnā	10	*to trade*
व्यापारी	vyāpārī	15	*businessman* (m.)
शक्ति	śakti	1	*power* (f.)
शनिवार	śanivār	7	*Saturday* (m.)
शब्द	śabd	12	*word* (m.)
शरद	śarad	A	*autumn* (f.)
शराब	śarāb	6	*alcoholic drink* (f.)
शरारत	śarārat	17	*mischief* (f.)
शरीर	śarīr	C	*body* (m.)
शहद	śahad	18	*honey* (m.)
शहर	śahar	4	*town, city* (m.)
शाकाहारी	śākāhārī	9	*vegetarian* (m.)/(adj.)
शादी	śādī	10	*marriage, wedding* (f.)
की शादी होना	kī śādī honā	16	*to marry*
शान्त	śānt	9	*peaceful, quiet*
शान्ति	śānti	13	*peace, tranquillity* (f.)
शाबाश	śābāś	7	*well done! bravo!*
शाम	śām	7	*evening, dusk* (f.)

शायद	śāyad	9	*perhaps*
शायद ही	śāyad hī	16	*scarcely, hardly*
शिकायत	śikāyat	15	*complaint, grievance* (f.)
की शिकायत करना[N]	kī śikāyat karnā	15	*to complain* (with **se**)
शिकार	śikār	15	*prey, victim* (m.)
शिकार करना[N]	śikār karnā	15	*to hunt*
शिकार होना	śikār honā	15	*to fall prey to*
शिकारी	śikārī	15	*huntsman, hunter* (m.)
शिक्षा	śikṣā	14	*education* (f.)
शिशिर	śiśir	**A**	*cool season* (m.)
शिष्य	śiṣy	12	*disciple* (m.)
शीघ्र	śīghr	**D**	*promptly*
शुक्र	śukr	10	*Friday* (m.)
शुक्रवार	śukravār	7	*Friday* (m.)
शुक्रिया	śukriyā	2	*thanks; thank you* (m.)
शुक्ल पक्ष	śukl pakṣ	**A**	*moonlit half of lunar month* (m.)
शुभ	śubh	18	*auspicious, good*
शुभकामनाएँ	śubhkāmnāẽ	11	*good wishes* (f.pl.)
शुभाकांक्षी	śubhākā̃kṣī	**D**	*well-wishing; well-wisher* (m.)
शुरू करना[N]	śurū karnā	7	*to begin* (tr.)
शुरू होना	śurū honā	7	*to begin* (intr.)
शून्य	śūny	**A**	*zero, blank* (m.)
शेष	śeṣ	**D**	*remainder; remaining* (m.)/(adj.)
शोर	śor	14	*row, noise, rumpus* (m.)
शोर मचाना[N]	śor macānā	14	*to create a rumpus*
शोर-शराबा	śor-śarābā	16	*noise and tumult* (m.)
शौक़	śauq	17	*fondness; hobby* (m.)
शौचालय	śaucālay	**C**	*toilet, latrine* (m.)
श्रद्धेय	śraddhey	**D**	*revered*
श्रावण	śrāvaṇ	**A**	*name of a month* (m.) (July–Aug.)
श्री	śrī	2	*Mr; lord*
श्रीनगर	śrīnagar	9	*Srinagar*
श्रीमती	śrīmatī	2	*Mrs* (abbr. as 'Smt.')
श्रीमान	śrīmān	18	(honorific title) (m.)
संख्या	saṅkhyā	15	*number* (f.)
संगीत	saṅgīt	9	*music* (m.)
संतरा	santarā	7	*orange* (m.)

संदर्भ	sandarbh	17	*context* (m.)
संदेह	sandeh	17	*doubt, suspicion, apprehension* (m.)
संपर्क	sampark	14	*contact, connection, link* (m.)
संपर्क भाषा	sampark bhāṣā	14	*link language* (f.)
संपादक	sampādak	D	*editor* (m.)
संभव	sambhav	10	*possible, probable*
सँभालना[N]	sābhālnā	13	*to take hold of, collect*
संयोग से	sanyog se	13	*by chance*
संवत्	samvat	A	*year, era* (m.)
संस्कृत	sanskṛt	6	*Sanskrit* (f.)
सकना	saknā	12	*to be able to* (para. **51**)
सकुशल	sakuśal	D	*well*
सख़्त	sak͟ht	12	*hard, severe, harsh, strict*
सगा	sagā	B	*'real' (brother etc.)*
सच	sac	5	*true; truth* (m.)
सचमुच	sacmuc	3	*really, truly*
सचाई	sacāī	17	*truth, fact* (f.)
सच्चा	saccā	14	*true, honest*
सच्चे अर्थों में	sacce arthõ mẽ	15	*in a true sense, truly*
सज़ा	sazā	14	*punishment* (f.)
सजाना[N]	sajānā	13	*to decorate, arrange*
सज्जन	sajjan	18	*gentleman* (m.)
सड़क	saṛak	4	*road* (f.)
सत श्री अकाल	sat śrī akāl	18	*greeting (used by and to Sikhs)*
सतहत्तर	sathattar	A	*seventy-seven*
सत्तर	sattar	A	*seventy*
सत्ताईस	sattāīs	14	*twenty-seven*
सत्तानवे	sattānve	A	*ninety-seven*
सत्तावन	sattāvan	A	*fifty-seven*
सत्तासी	sattāsī	A	*eighty-seven*
सत्रह	satrah	8	*seventeen*
सन	san	15	*year, era* (as **san 1947** *the year 1947 [AD]*)
सनीचर	sanīcar	13	*Saturday* (m.)
सपना	sapnā	15	*dream* (m.)
सपना देखना[N]	sapnā dekhnā	15	*to dream, have a dream*
सपरिवार	saparivār	D	*with one's family*
सप्ताह	saptāh	11	*week* (m.)
सप्रेम	saprem	D	*affectionate, affectionately*

सफ़र	safar	7	*journey, travel* (m.)
सफ़र ख़र्च	safar kharc	12	*travelling expenses* (m.)
सफल	saphal	15	*successful*
सफलता	saphaltā	15	*success* (f.)
सफ़ेद	safed	1	*white*
सब	sab	2	*all*
सब कहीं	sab kahī̃	16	*everywhere*
सब कुछ	sab kuch	9	*everything*
सब मिलकर	sab milkar	13	*all together*
सब्ज़ी	sabzī	4	*vegetable* (f.)
सभी	sabhī	4	*all* (emph.)
समझ	samajh	12	*understanding* (f.)
समझ में आना	samajh mẽ ānā	12	*to understand*
समझना[n]	samajhnā	7	*to understand, think, consider*
समझाना[N]	samjhānā	16	*to explain, persuade, console*
समय	samay	8	*time* (m.)
समय निकालना[N]	samay nikālnā	18	*to find time*
समस्या	samasyā	16	*problem* (f.)
समाचार	samācār	11	*news* (m.)
समाचार पत्र	samācār patr	10	*newspaper* (m.)
समाप्त	samāpt	10	*finished, concluded*
समाप्त करना[N]	samāpt karnā	10	*to finish, conclude*
समाप्त होना	samāpt honā	13	*to be finished, terminated*
समुद्र	samudr	18	*sea, ocean* (m.)
समोसा	samosā	11	*samosa* (m.) *(fried triangular pie)*
सरकार	sarkār	10	*government* (f.)
सरकारी	sarkārī	10	*governmental*
सरदार	sardār	12	(lit. *chief; used as title of respect for Sikh men)*
सरदी	sardī	9	*cold; winter* (f.) (pl.)
सरल	saral	4	*simple, easy*
सरसठ	sarsaṭh	A	*sixty-seven*
सलवार क़मीज़	salvār qamīz	18	*loose trousers and shirt worn by Panjabi women* (f).
सलहज	salhaj	B	*wife of wife's brother* (f.)
सलाम	salām	18	*greeting, salutation* (m.)
सलाम अलैकुम	salām alaikum	18	*greeting, salutation*
सलाह	salāh	10	*advice* (f.)
सलाह लेना[N]	salāh lenā	10	*to take advice*

सवा	savā	11	*one and a quarter*
सवारी	savārī	14	*passenger, rider*
सवेरा	saverā	8	*morning* (m.)
सवेरे	savere	8	*early in the morning*
ससुर	sasur	**B**	*father-in-law*
ससुराल	sasurāl	12	*father-in-law's house*
सस्ता	sastā	2	*cheap*
सहसा	sahsā	18	*suddenly*
सहस्र	sahasr	**A**	*a thousand* (m.)
सही	sahī	13	*correct, true, accurate*
सहेली	sahelī	9	*(girl's) female friend* (f.)
साँप	sā̃p	17	*snake* (m.)
साँस	sā̃s	**C**	*breath, breathing* (f.)
साँस फूलना	sā̃s phūlnā	**C**	*to be out of breath, pant*
-सा	-sā	18	*like, -ish*
साइकिल	sāikil	14	*bicycle* (f.)
साठ	sāṭh	**A**	*sixty*
साड़ी	sāṛī	10	*sari* (f.)
साढ़ू	sāṛhū	**B**	*husband of wife's sister*
साढ़े	sāṛhe	11	*plus a half; half past (the hour)*
सात	sāt	2	*seven*
सातवाँ	sātvā̃	7	*seventh*
साथ-साथ	sāth-sāth	8	*together, along with*
साथी	sāthī	10	*companion, friend* (m.)
सादर	sādar	**D**	*respectful*
साधारण	sādhāraṇ	11	*ordinary*
साधु	sādhu	7	*Hindu holy man* (m.)
सानंद	sānand	**D**	*happy, happily*
साफ़	sāf	1	*clean*
साफ़ करना[N]	sāf karnā	5	*to clean*
साबुन	sābun	11	*soap* (m.)
सामने	sāmne	8	*opposite, facing*
सामान	sāmān	3	*furniture, luggage, goods* (m.)
सारा	sārā	6	*entire, whole, all*
साल	sāl	7	*year* (m.)
साला	sālā	**B**	*wife's brother* (m.); *(also term of abuse)*
साली	sālī	**B**	*wife's sister* (f.)
सावन	sāvan	**A**	*the month Srāvaṇ* (m.) (July–Aug.)

सास	sās	B	*mother-in-law* (f.)
साहब	sāhab	2	*sir; master* (m.)
साहस	sāhas	15	*courage* (m.)
साहित्य	sāhity	17	*literature* (m.)
सिख	sikh	7	*Sikh* (m.)/(f.)/(adj.)
सिखाना[N]	sikhānā	E	*to teach*
सिगरेट	sigreṭ	5	*cigarette* (f.)
सितंबर	sitambar	7	*September* (m.)
सितार	sitār	9	*sitar* (f.)
सिनेमा	sinemā	6	*cinema* (m.)
सिनेमा देखना[N]	sinemā dekhnā	8	*to see a film*
सिपाही	sipāhī	16	*private soldier, constable* (m.)
सिर	sir	7	*head* (m.)
सिरा	sirā	15	*end, extremity* (m.)
नए सिरे से	nae sire se	15	*from a new beginning*
सिर्फ़	sirf	1	*only*
सीखना[N]	sīkhnā	8	*to learn*
सीट	sīṭ	12	*seat* (f.)
सीटी	sīṭī	13	*whistle* (f.)
सीढ़ी	sīṛhī	10	*step, stair* (f.)
सीधा	sīdhā	8	*straight, straightforward*
सीधे	sīdhe	8	*straight*
सुंदर	sundar	3	*beautiful, nice*
सुई	suī	C	*injection; needle* (f.)
सुई लगाना[N]	suī lagānā	C	*to have an injection*
सुझाव	sujhāv	11	*suggestion* (m.)
सुदि	sudi	A	*waxing half of a lunar month* (f.)
सुनना[N]	sunnā	5	*to listen, hear*
सुनाई देना/पड़ना	sunāī denā/paṛnā	16	*to be heard, be audible*
सुनाना[N]	sunānā	7	*to tell, cause to hear, relate, recite*
सुबह	subah	7	*morning* (f.)
सुरक्षित	surakṣit	12	*safe, secure*
सुलाना[N]	sulānā	E	*to make sleep, lull to sleep*
सुविधा	suvidhā	16	*convenience* (f.)
सुसर	susar	B	*father-in-law* (m.)
सुहावना	suhāvnā	11	*pleasant, lovely*
सूचित करना[N]	sūcit karnā	D	*to inform*
सूती	sūtī	11	*made of cotton*
सूरज	sūraj	12	*sun* (m.)

से	se	3	*from* (etc.)
सेब	seb	6	*apple* (m.)
सेवा	sevā	17	*service* (f.)
सेहत	sehat	C	*health* (f.)
सैंतालीस	saĩtālīs	A	*forty-seven*
सैंतीस	saĩtīs	A	*thirty-seven*
सैकड़ा	saikṛā	14	*a hundred* (m.)
सैर	sair	10	*walk, trip* (f.)
सैर करना[N]	sair karnā	10	*to take a walk, go for a trip*
सो	so	8	*so*
सोचना[N]	socnā	11	*to think*
सोना[N]	sonā	7	*to sleep*
सोमवार	somvār	3	*Monday*
सोलह	solah	8	*sixteen*
सौ	sau	3	*a hundred* (m.)
स्कूल	skūl	5	*school* (m.)
स्टेशन	sṭeśan	6	*station* (m.)
स्थिति	sthiti	13	*situation* (f.)
स्नान करना[N]	snān karnā	13	*to bathe* (esp. *ritually*)
स्नेह	sneh	D	*love* (m.)
स्वभाव	svabhāv	18	*nature, temperament* (m.)
स्वयं	svayam	15	*oneself*
स्वर	svar	17	*voice, tone, musical note* (m.)
स्वर्ग	svarg	13	*heaven* (m.)
स्वर्गवास	svargvās	18	*death, 'residence in heaven'* (m.)
स्वर्गीय	svargīy	18	*the late, deceased*
स्वस्थ	svasth	C	*healthy, fit*
स्वागत	svāgat	18	*welcome* (m.)
स्वामी	svāmī	17	*master, owner, husband; title of respect for religious figures* (m.)
स्वास्थ्य	svāsthy	C	*health* (m.)
स्वीकार	svīkār	16	*accepted, granted; acceptance* (m.)
स्वीकार करना[N]	svīkār karnā	16	*to accept*
हँसना	hãsnā	9	*to laugh*
हँसी	hãsī	18	*laughter* (f.)
हँसी-मज़ाक़ करना[N]	hãsī-mazāq karnā	18	*to laugh and joke*
हज़ार	hazar	14	*a thousand* (m.)
हड़ताल	haṛtāl	17	*strike* (f.)
हड़ताल करना[N]	haṛtāl karnā	17	*to strike, come out on strike*
हड्डी	haḍḍī	C	*bone* (f.)
हफ़्ता	haftā	6	*week* (m.)

हम	ham	1	*we*
हमारा	hamārā	6	*our, ours*
हमेशा	hameśā	6	*always*
हर	har	3	*every, each*
हर कोई	har koī	9	*everyone*
हरा	harā	3	*green*
हरियाली	hariyālī	13	*greenery, verdure* (f.)
हरेक	harek	12	*every, each*
हल	hal	16	*solution* (m.)
हल करना[N]	hal karnā	16	*to solve*
हलका	halkā	4	*light (of weight, colour, etc.)*
हलो	halo	2	*hello*
हवा	havā	9	*air, wind, breeze* (f.)
हवाई अड्डा	havāī aḍḍā	9	*airport* (m.)
हवाई जहाज़	havāī jahāz	9	*aeroplane* (m.)
हवाई डाक	havāī ḍāk	14	*air mail* (f.)
हस्ताक्षर	hastākṣar	**D**	*signature* (m.); *'signed'*
हाँक	hā̃k	18	*calling aloud* (f.)
हाँकना[N]	hā̃knā	18	*to call aloud, urge on*
हाथ	hāth	6	*hand* (m.)
हाथ आना	hāth ānā	16	*to come to hand*
हाथी	hāthī	15	*elephant* (m.)
हारना[n]	hārnā	11	*to be defeated, lose*
हाल	hāl	2	*condition, state* (m.)
हालत	hālat	17	*condition, state* (f.)
हालाँकि	hālā̃ki	17	*although*
हितू	hitū	**D**	*well-wishing; well-wisher* (m.)
हितैषी	hitaiṣī	**D**	*well-wishing; well-wisher* (m.)
हिन्दी	hindī	2	*Hindi* (f.)
हिन्दुस्तानी	hindustānī	1	*Indian* (m.)/(f.)/(adj.)
हिन्दू	hindū	1	*Hindu* (m.)/(f.)/(adj.)
हिसाब	hisāb	13	*rate, account, calculation* (m.)
हिस्सा	hissā	12	*part, portion* (m.)
ही	hī	9	(emph. particle) *only* (etc.)
हुज़ूर	huzūr	18	*'your honour', 'sir'*
हूँ	hū̃	1	*am*
हेमंत	hemant	**A**	*winter* (m.)
हैं	haĩ	1	*are*
है	hai	1	*is; are* (with **tū**)
हैरान	hairān	18	*perplexed*
हो	ho	1	*are* (with **tum**)
होटल	hoṭal	3	*hotel, cafe* (m.)

होना	honā	5	*to be, become*
(से) होकर	(se) hokar	11	*via*
होली	holī	17	*Holi (a springtime 'festival of colours')*
होली खेलना	holī khelnā	17	*to celebrate Holi (by throwing coloured water, etc.)*

Index

References after the entry are to the numbered paragraph of the course, or to one of the Appendixes. Hindi words, in their transliterated form, are incorporated into the English alphabetical order. (The Vocabulary list cites the first occurrence of every word in the course, and may be used as a further index.)

address, forms of, **8**, **87**
adjectives, **4**; interrogative, **6**; in oblique case, **12**; + **-sā**, **86**; suffixed **-vālā** **46**
adverbs: **jaisā**, **70**; **kahī̃**, **78**; of place, **77**; relative-correlative, **76**; sentence order, **37**; with **-kar**, **-ke**, **48**; with **ko**, **35**
agreement: of adjectives, **4**, **7**, **9**; of verb and subject, **24**
'although', **83**
apnā, **26**

cāhe, **80**, **83**
cāhie, **30**; with infinitive, **55**
cāhnā, **43**
calendar, **36**, **App. A**
causative verbs, **App. E**
commands: *see* imperatives
comparisons, **14**
compound verbs, **52**, **84**
compulsion, **55**, **56**
concessive sentences, **83**
conditional sentences, **44**, **82**
conjunct verbs, **32**, **74**; with **yād**, **75**
conjunctive **-kar**, **-ke**, **48**
continuous tenses, **33**; future, **38**
conversation, **8**, **87**,
cuknā, **51**

dates, **30**, **36**, **App. A**
denā (as 'to allow'), **63**

'echo-words', **81**
emphatics: **hī**, **39**; **to**, **45**

future, **38**

gender: of adjectives, **4**; of nouns, **3**

genitive: *see* possessives
greetings, **87**

'to have', **34**
health, **App. C**
hī, **39**
honorific plurals, **1**, **9**

imperatives, **18**, **42**
imperfective: future, **38**; participial constructions, **85**; participle + **rahnā**, **jānā**, **67**; past, **28**; present, **23**
indirect speech, **60**
infinitive, **17**; as imperative **18**; in compulsion expressions **55**, **56**; oblique + **denā**, **63**; oblique + **lagnā**, **62**; oblique + **-vālā** **46**; as verbal noun, **41**
intensive verbs: *see* compound verbs
interrogatives, **2**, **6**
intransitive verbs *see* transitive verbs

jaisā, **70**
jo, **54**

kā, **21**
kahī̃, **78**
-kar, **-ke**, **48**
ko, **16**, **19**, **22**, **30**, **34**, **56**
koī, **29**
kuch, **29**
kyā: as interrogative pronoun, **6**; as question marker, **2**

lagnā, **58**; + oblique infinitive, **62**
letter-writing, **App. D**

milnā, **57**
money, **App. A**
'must', **56**

na ... na, **80**
nouns, **3**; oblique, **11**
numbers: aggregative, **66**; cardinal, **App. A**; ordinal, **31**; in telling the time, **49**

object + **ko**, **19**
oblique case, **12**

participial constructions, **85**
parts of the body, **App. C**
passive, **61**
past tenses: 'to be', **13**; continuous, **33**; imperfective, **28**; perfective, **47**
perfectives: in conditional sentences, **82**; participial constructions, **85**; participle + **karnā**, **68**; past, **47**

possessives: adjective **apnā**, **26**; participle **kā**, **21**; in conjunct verbs, **74**; pronouns, **25**; 'to have', **34**
postpositions: after nouns, **11**; after pronouns, **15**; compound, **27**; in adverbial expressions, **35**; inverted, **72**; **jaisā**, **70**; **se**, **71**; simple, **10**
present tenses: continuous, **33**; imperfective, **23**; 'to be', **1**
presumption, **38**
pronouns: interrogative, **6**; **koī**, **kuch**, **29**; oblique +**ko**, **22**; personal, **1**; possessive, **25**; +postpositions, **15**; reflexive, **73**;
purpose expressions: with oblique infinitive, **41**; with subjunctive, **65**

quantity, **40**
questions: *see* interrogatives

rahnā: as 'to be', **91**; with imperfective participle, **67**
relationship terms, **App. B**
relative-correlatives: of manner (**jaisā**), **69**; pronoun **jo**, **54**; of place (**jahā̃**), **76**; of quantity (**jitnā**), **64**; of time (**jab**), **59**
repetition of words, **79**; participles, **85**
reported speech: *see* indirect speech

-sā, **86**
saknā, **51**
se, **71**
'should', **55**
subjunctive, **42**; in conditional sentences, **44**; in purpose clauses, **65**

time, **30**, **49**, **59**
to, **44**; **45**
transitive and intransitive verbs, **47**, **61**, **App. E**

-vālā, **46**
verb stem, **17**, **App. E**
verbal noun, **41**
verbs in combination, **53**
vocabulary registers, **50**
vocative case, **20**

'was' and 'were', **13**
word order, **5**, **37**, **54**, **64**

yā to...yā, **80**
yād, **75**

३०५